Africa Now

Africa Now is an exciting new series, published by Zed Books
in association with the internationally respected Nordic Africa
Institute. Featuring high-quality, cutting-edge research from
leading academics, the series addresses the big issues confronting
Africa today. Accessible but in-depth, and wide-ranging in its
scope, Africa Now engages with the critical political, economic,
sociological and development debates affecting the continent,
shedding new light on pressing concerns.

Nordic Africa Institute

The Nordic Africa Institute (Nordiska Afrikainstitutet) is a centre
for research, documentation and information on modern Africa.
Based in Uppsala, Sweden, the Institute is dedicated to providing
timely, critical and alternative research and analysis of Africa and
to cooperating with African researchers. As a hub and a meeting
place for a growing field of research and analysis, the Institute
strives to put knowledge of African issues within reach for scholars,
policy-makers, politicians, the media, students and the general
public. The Institute is financed jointly by the Nordic countries
(Denmark, Finland, Iceland, Norway and Sweden).

www.nai.uu.se

Forthcoming titles

Ilda Lindell (ed.), *Africa's Informal Workers*
Iman Hashim and Dorte Thorsen, *Child Migration in Africa*

About the editors

Fantu Cheru is the Research Director at the Nordic Africa Institute in Uppsala, Sweden and Emeritus Professor of International Development at the School of International Service, American University in Washington, DC. Previously, he was a member of UN Secretary-General Kofi Annan's Panel on Mobilizing International Support for the New Partnership for African Development (NEPAD) as well a Convener of the Global Economic Agenda Track of the Helsinki Process on Globalization and Democracy. Cheru also served as the UN's Special Rapporteur on Foreign Debt and Structural Adjustment for the UN Commission for Human Rights in Geneva from 1998–2001. Dr Cheru's previous publications include: *African Renaissance: Roadmaps to the Challenges of Globalization* (2002); *The Millennium Development Goals: Mobilizing Resources to Tackle World Poverty* (2005); *Ethiopia: Options for Rural Development* (1990); *The Silent Revolution in Africa: Debt, Development and Democracy* (1989). His articles have appeared in *Third World Quarterly*, *World Development*, *Review of African Political Economy*, *International Affairs* and *Review of International Political Economy*, among others. Cheru also serves on the editorial board of a number of international journals.

Cyril Obi is a Senior Researcher, and Leader, Research Cluster on Conflict, Displacement and Transformation at the Nordic Africa Institute, Uppsala, Sweden. He has been on leave since 2005 from the Nigerian Institute of International Affairs (NIIA), Lagos, where he is an Associate Research Professor. In 2004, Dr Obi became the second Claude Ake Professor at the University of Uppsala. He had earlier received international recognition/awards: Council for the Development of Social Science Research in Africa (CODESRIA) Governance Institute fellow in 1993; fellow of the Salzburg Seminar in 1994; SSRC-MacArthur Foundation visiting fellow in 1996; visiting fellow to the African Studies Centre (ASC), Leiden in 1998; and visiting post-doctoral fellow to St Anthony's College Oxford in 2000. In 2001, he was a fellow of the 21st Century Trust, Conference on 'Rethinking Security for the 21st Century', also held at Oxford. He is a contributing editor to the *Review of African Political Economy*, and is on the editorial board of the *African Journal of International Affairs*, the *African Security Review* and the *Review of Leadership in Africa*. Dr Obi has been a guest editor to journals such as *African and Asian Studies*, and *African Journal of International Affairs*.

The rise of China and India in Africa

Challenges, opportunities and critical
interventions

edited by Fantu Cheru and Cyril Obi

Nordiska Afrikainstitutet
The Nordic Africa Institute

Zed Books
LONDON | NEW YORK

The Rise of China and India in Africa: Challenges, opportunities and critical interventions was first published in association with the Nordic Africa Institute, PO Box 1703, SE-751 47 Uppsala, Sweden in 2010 by Zed Books Ltd, 7 Cynthia Street, London N1 9JF, UK and Room 400, 175 Fifth Avenue, New York, NY 10010, USA

www.zedbooks.co.uk
www.nai.uu.se

Set in OurType Arnhem, Monotype Gill Sans Heavy by Ewan Smith, London
Index: ed.emery@thefreeuniversity.net
Cover designed by Rogue Four Design
Printed and bound in Great Britain by the MPG Books Group

Distributed in the USA exclusively by Palgrave Macmillan, a division of St Martin's Press, LLC, 175 Fifth Avenue, New York, NY 10010, USA

A catalogue record for this book is available from the British Library
Library of Congress Cataloging in Publication Data available

ISBN 978 1 84813 436 2 hb
ISBN 978 1 84813 437 9 pb
ISBN 978 1 84813 439 3 eb

Contents

Tables and figures

Acronyms and abbreviations

ACCZ   Association of Chinese Companies in Zambia
ACP   African-Caribbean-Pacific
AGOA   African Growth and Opportunity Act
ARPTC   Post and Telecommunications Regulatory Authority (DRC)
AU   African Union
BGRIMM   Beijing General Research Institute of Mining and Metallurgy
BITs   bilateral investment treaties
BOC   Bank of China
BRIC   Brazil, Russia, India and China
CAADP   Comprehensive African Agriculture Development Programme
CCT   Congo China Telecom
CEO   chief executive officer
CFA   Central African franc
CIBS   China, India, Brazil, South Africa Dialogue
CIF   China International Fund Limited
CII   Confederation of Indian Industries
CNOOC   China National Offshore Oil Corporation
CNPC   China National Petroleum Corporation
COMESA   Common Market for Eastern and Southern Africa
CPA   Comprehensive Peace Agreement (Sudan)
CSAs   country-specific advantages
CSIH   Sonangol International Holding
CSRC   China Securities Regulatory Commission
DAC   Development Assistance Committee
DRC   Democratic Republic of Congo
EAC   East Africa Community
ECOWAS   Economic Community of West African States
ELISA   Ethiopian Leather Industries Association
EMMNC   emerging market multinational corporation
EPA   Economic Partnership Agreement
EXIM   Export-Import
FDI   foreign direct investment
FG   'flying geese' (theorum)
FNLA   Frente Nacional para Libertação de Angola
FOCAC   Forum on China–Africa Cooperation

FSAs	firm-specific advantages
GDP	gross domestic product
GNPOC	Greater Nile Petroleum Operating Company Limited (Sudan)
GOI	Government of India
GRN	Gabinete de Reconstrução Nacional (Angola)
HIPC	heavily indebted poor countries
IBSA	India, Brazil, South Africa
ICBC	Industrial and Commercial Bank of China
ICC	International Criminal Court
ICT	information and communications technology
IFI	international financial institution
IMF	International Monetary Fund
IOC	Indian Oil Corporation Limited
IR	international relations
ITEC	Indian Technical and Economic Cooperation Programme
JCI	Joint Commission International
LOC	lines of credit
MFEZ	Multi-Facility Economic Zones
MNC	multinational corporation
MoU	memorandum of understanding
MPLA	Movimento Popular da Libertação de Angola
MUZ	Mineworkers Union of Zambia
NAM	Non-Aligned Movement
NAMA	Non-Agricultural Market Access
NEPAD	New Partnership for Africa's Development
NFC	Non-Ferrous Company (Zambia)
NGO	non-governmental organization
NNPC	Nigerian National Petroleum Corporation
NUMAW	National Union of Miners and Allied Workers (Zambia)
OAU	Organization of African Unity
OCPT	Office of Post and Telecommunications (DRC)
ODA	official development assistance
OECD	Organisation for Economic Co-operation and Development
OFDI	outward foreign direct investment
OIL	Oil India Limited
OMEL	ONGC Mittal Energy Limited
ONGC	Oil and Natural Gas Corporation (India)
OPEC	Organization of the Petroleum Exporting Countries
OSEC	officially supported exported credits
OVL	ONGC Videsh Limited
PPP	public–private partnership

PSO	peace support operation
PV	photovoltaic
RCAI	revealed comparative advantage index
REC	Regional Economic Community
RMBY	renminbi
RPT	Rally of the Togolese People
SADC	Southern African Development Community
SCAAP	Special Commonwealth African Assistance Programme
SINOPEC	China Petroleum and Chemical Corporation
SME	small and medium enterprise
SOE	state-owned enterprise
SOOE	state-owned oil enterprise
SPLM	Sudan People's Liberation Movement
SRC	Spearman's rank correlation
SSA	sub-Saharan Africa
SSI	Sonangol Sinopec International
TRIMs	Trade-Related Investment Measures
UNCTAD	United Nations Conference on Trade and Development
UNECA	United Nations Economic Commission for Africa
UNITA	União Nacional para Libertação de Angola
UNSC	United Nations Security Council
WB	World Bank
WNB	Wax Nana Benz
WTO	World Trade Organization
ZCCM	Zambia Consolidated Copper Mines
ZCCZ	Zambia–China Economic and Trade Cooperation Zone
ZCMT	Zambia–China Mulungushi Textiles
ZDA	Zambia Development Agency
ZIC	Zambian Investment Centre
ZTE	Zhong Xing Telecommunications Company

Foreword

China and India, aptly referred to as 'new' actors, are two giant economies and emerging powers that, in reality, are not very new to the African continent. But in recent years their presence has grown immensely.

China and India's renewed engagement with Africa has come at a time when the business climate has improved across Africa and interest in Africa as a market has grown. The value of EU trade with Africa has reached approximately US$200 billion per year. As regards Swedish interests in the continent, our total exports to Africa have increased by more than 200 per cent since 1998. Compared with China's trade with Africa, however, this is still rather modest. China has overtaken Britain as Africa's third-largest business partner, and is fast catching up with France. This provides for new opportunities and new thoughts on development.

Sweden's Africa Policy, launched in March 2008, sets out a clear vision that economic growth is a prerequisite for sustainable development and the fight against poverty; and that the core of government business is the will of the people it represents and its democratic legitimacy. Free trade, nationally and globally, is hence essential. Conditioning loans or agreements are not in line with what constitutes a healthy competitive business climate. As the economic engagement between China, India and Africa deepens, efforts must be made to ensure that environmental, economic and social issues are equally in focus to ensure sustainable development.

Concerns over human rights, democracy and environmental transparency have become pressing, particularly in the wake of China's ascendancy. In this regard, I believe there is a value in forging a partnership between China, India and the Nordic countries in order to draw upon the experiences of our human-centred development cooperation with the African continent. It is the firm belief of the Swedish government that human rights are not separate from economic development and can never be compromised.

In addition, economic growth must not undermine environmental sustainability. Today, Africa, China and India face the challenge of learning from our costly mistakes and leapfrogging directly to energy-efficient and environmentally friendly solutions. As what I believe to be a trusted and open partner, Sweden will encourage China and India to adopt policies towards Africa informed by key international norms and practices of environmental sustainability, respect for human rights and democracy. It is important that we jointly ensure the sustainability of the economic development and investment that Africa is increasingly experiencing. In the multilateral arena the EU, the AU and the UN provide important cooperation fora.

Finally, I commend the Nordic Africa Institute and the editors of and contributors to this important book for embarking on very timely research and a policy dialogue on the evolving relationship between the African continent and the emerging giants. China and India are important players in the global arena and Sweden is committed to supporting research and knowledge production on these two emerging donor countries. The knowledge generated by this research programme will help policy-makers in Sweden and the other Nordic countries to a better understanding of the policies of China and India towards Africa, and to enhance policy coordination and harmonization on African development between the Nordic countries on the one hand and between India, China and the Nordic countries on the other.

Gunilla Carlsson
Swedish Minister for Development Cooperation
Ministry for Foreign Affairs

Introduction – Africa in the twenty-first century: strategic and development challenges

Fantu Cheru and Cyril Obi

Africa's strategic options and developmental challenges are being redefined by the complex transformations in twenty-first-century international relations. The present 'moment' in international affairs suggests another opportunity to change the continent's marginal place in global political and economic power, and to shift from a post-cold-war US-led unipolar to a multipolar global order – in which the emerging powers of the global South will be key players. In this emerging order, China, India, Brazil and South Africa are poised to play a greater role, particularly in the face of the retreat of the Washington Consensus and its rather poor record in Africa, in providing some support and an enabling international environment for the continent to chart its own alternative developmental course.

There is no doubt that China and India have become Africa's most important economic partners, and their growing footprint on the continent is transforming Africa's international relations in a dramatic way. The West no longer enjoys a monopoly of influence over Africa's future development. These two emerging Asian economic powerhouses actively court African countries through aid, expanded trade, and investment in strategic sectors of African economies to leverage international politics, gain access to growing markets and acquire much-needed raw materials from the continent. China's new role as a major investor and development partner in Africa has in particular attracted much attention in the region and elsewhere, not least among the Western countries that have been dominant in Africa since colonial times. Besides China and India, other emerging economies, such as Brazil, South Korea, Malaysia and Vietnam, have become increasingly active in many African countries, a clear indication that North–South relations are being superseded by the South–East and emerging Africa–Gulf–Asia triangular relations, with profound implications for Africa's development. This is the first good news for Africa since the end of the bipolar political order and the recent demise of the theology of market fundamentalism.

From an African perspective, the emergence of China and India as potential important development partners has come at a time when Africans themselves are engaged in a major soul-searching exercise to find out what went wrong with Africa's development in the past half-century. The search for an alternative 'transformative development model' has led many in Africa to take a closer look at the instructive lessons from the Asian giants. China's and India's historical experience as former colonies and their spectacular development experience since the mid-1970s have raised hopes among African nations that they too can one day break away from the shackles of poverty, underdevelopment and aid dependency. Of particular note is the rekindling of interest within Africa in the role of the developmental states and the importance of experimenting with 'heterodox' economic policies in order to navigate successfully the cold currents of economic globalization, as China and India have both done successfully. There is a widespread belief among African policy-makers and some African scholars that China and India, with increased economic interest in Africa, can provide strategic options and a policy space that African countries have been compelled to surrender since the 1980s in the process of implementing donor-mandated punitive structural adjustment programmes. The evidence marshalled by the contributors to this volume, however, questions whether the ascendancy of the two Asian giants in Africa can really open up the 'policy space' that African countries badly need to experiment with alternative development strategies. China's and India's growing engagement in Africa can become a positive force only when African states are prepared to negotiate with the two Asian giants from a stronger and more informed platform. In the absence of deliberate and proactive African action, the outcome of China and India's involvement in Africa could turn out to be 'neocolonialism by invitation'.

China and India as preferred partners

China and India, as developing countries, have made great progress in transforming their backward economies and have been able to reduce absolute poverty dramatically (particularly in the case of China) in a relatively short twenty-five years under the guidance of a strong, development-oriented activist state. This is in sharp contrast to the experience of African countries, which, from the early 1980s, implemented deflationary 'structural adjustment' reform programmes under the watchful eyes of the World Bank and the International Monetary Fund (IMF). These policies, which assigned a minimal role to the state, helped to accentuate the scale of human deprivation while simultaneously crippling the productive sectors of African economies.

Today, Chinese and Indian companies are investing heavily in the much-neglected infrastructure sector of many African countries, from the construction of dams to major transport and telecommunications projects, which are critical for raising productivity and reducing poverty. These badly needed strategic investments have helped many African countries to register impressive growth rates for the first time in many decades. The Chinese and Indians are filling this critical infrastructure gap and they are doing it cheaply, less bureaucratically and

2

in a shorter time frame. The positive growth rates have been further fuelled by China's and India's demand for African resources to feed the appetites of their respective growing economies. Indeed, China has emerged as Africa's second-largest trading partner (after the USA), and is currently the biggest lender to, and investor in, infrastructural development on the continent.

Besides investments in strategic sectors of African economies, equally important is the example of China and India's own development experience to African countries. Indeed, there is a lot that African countries can learn from the Chinese, Indian and Vietnamese economic reform programmes of the past thirty years without having to import them in their entirety. What has been central to the economic success of these Asian countries is the role played by the state in guiding the market, and the willingness of the state to intervene and experiment with 'heterodox' policies to revive the economy, compete in global markets and reduce poverty in the process, while moving in a free market direction. Heavy investment in infrastructure, education, research and development (as opposed to the deflationary and austerity measures demanded by the Bretton Woods institutions) was complemented by adjustable policies designed to enhance the competitiveness of local producers through technological retooling and the retraining of workers, and subsequently deregulating the market accordingly.

It is important to note, however, that the strategies that China and India employ to extend their influence in Africa are not identical. While Chinese investment in Africa has been dominated by large state-owned enterprises (SOEs), investment from India is largely private sector driven. In this regard, Chinese investment has been more aggressive, with SOEs enjoying both political and financial support to undercut other competitors in the African market, including Indian private sector investors. A good illustration of this (see Vines and Campos in this volume) is the failed 2004 bid for oil exploitation in Angola by India's state-owned Oil and Natural Gas Corporation (ONGC). Although Shell, former licence partner of British Petroleum (BP), has agreed to sell its stake to ONGC, the Chinese, in their first involvement in the Angolan oil industry, have sidelined ONGC by offering double what it has offered. The Chinese state, therefore, uses its political and financial means to create conditions for globalization that favour China. Indian private sector operators, on the other hand, are struggling to catch up with China but lack the financial and political backing from the state that Chinese state-owned enterprises enjoy.

The Indian government recognizes the challenge posed by China as it tries to deepen its economic involvement in Africa. While a number of initiatives have been undertaken by the Indian Ministry of External Affairs to support Indian private sector operators as they attempt to expand their operations in Africa, such as the Focus Africa Programme and the India–Africa Partnership Project, launched under the auspices of the Export-Import Bank of India and the Confederation of Indian Industries (CII), these are minuscule in comparison with the high level of political and financial support (including subsidies to gain market penetration) that Chinese SOEs receive from their government (see Naidu, Modi, Sinha and Bhattacharya, this volume). The many initiatives the Indian government announced at the April 2008 India–Africa Summit are the first step towards establishing an enduring economic and political relationship with the continent of Africa. While China dominates the African market for now, in the long run India will have the comparative advantage: its strong diaspora community on the ground in Africa, its proximity to the continent, its first-class educational system and its enduring democratic tradition will all make it more competitive than China (see Modi, this volume).

Though this is not explicit, the Chinese and Indians are warmly welcomed in Africa for reasons other than those of economics and finance. There has been a titanic shift in attitudes towards the Western world on the part of a growing proportion of Africans. Disenchantment with the poor track record of Western development cooperation over fifty years, the double standards that Western governments practise in their relations with African states, the tendency to give aid with one hand and to retrieve it with the other, through unfair trade practices and debt structures, have generated a lot of debate among Africans over the past decade, and a rallying point for pursuing an alternative and independent African development agenda. In contrast, China portrays Africa in a positive light, as an equal partner rather than a recipient (see chapters by He and Liu, this volume). In contrast to the standard Western doom-and-gloom analysis of the African condition, China and India hold the view that Africa is a dynamic continent on the threshold of a development take-off, with unlimited business opportunities that would serve Chinese, Indian and African interests. Therefore, when China does pronounce on development cooperation, it avoids the language of aid and development assistance and instead prefers the language of solidarity, mutually beneficial economic cooperation, 'common prosperity' and shared 'developing country' status. Granted, there is more to the rhetoric than the eye can see, but this is music to the ears of the majority of African leaders and elites, who are weary of Western paternalism.

The overall impact of China's and India's engagement in Africa has been positive in the short term, partly as a result of higher returns from commodity exports fuelled by excessive demands from both countries. Yet little systematic research exists on the actual impact of China's and India's growing involvement on Africa's economic transformation. This book examines the opportunities and challenges posed by the increasing presence of China and India in Africa. It contains case studies from a select group of African countries, at the level of particular value chains (such as energy, agriculture, manufacturing and telecommunications), in order to trace the real impact of China and India on Africa's economic development. We conclude with an examination of possible critical

4

interventions that African governments must undertake at the national and sub-regional levels in order to negotiate with China and India from a stronger and much more informed platform.

Exit the Washington Consensus! Enter the Southern Consensus!

Of course, China and India are not newcomers to Africa. Both countries have had long political and economic relations dating back several decades. What is new has been the determination of both countries since the end of the cold war to spell out a clear Africa strategy centred on 'win-win equal partnership, mutual respect and benefits', to enhance their global status as great powers in their own right. Thus, in January 2006, the government of China issued an 'Africa Policy Paper', in which it put forward its proposals for cooperation with Africa in various fields in the coming years and declared its commitment to a new strategic partnership with Africa in the long term, on the basis of five principles of peaceful coexistence (including respect for African countries' independent choice of development path; mutual benefit and reciprocity; inter-action based on equality; and consultation and cooperation in global affairs). Important events, such as the China–Africa Forum, aim to further boost China's cooperation with Africa. While securing energy resources may be important for China's increasing engagement with Africa, China is also strengthening trade, investment and aid ties through various bilateral and multilateral forums, such as the Asia–Africa Summit, the Forum on China–Africa Cooperation (FOCAC) and the China–Africa Business Council. In addition, China has, in the context of its global activism, played an increasing role in peacekeeping missions on the continent. This is part of a wider effort to create a paradigm of globalization that favours China. Finally, China's engagement with Africa is also motivated by the need to gain African support for its one-China policy.

India is also moving fast to consolidate its growing presence in Africa. The April 2008 India–Africa Forum held in Delhi, though modest by comparison with the Forum on China–Africa Cooperation of November 2006, demonstrates India's commitment to securing its own footprint in Africa as it competes with China and with developed countries to secure energy and other raw material resources to fuel its growing economy (see chapters by Sinha, Modi, Naidu and Bhattacharya, this volume). It is also a culmination of India's cooperation with a 'renascent' Africa, through initiatives such as the Focus Africa Programme, launched in 2001, the Techno-Economic Movement for Cooperation with nine African countries and India (TEAM 9), launched in 2003 (Beri 2008; Sinha, this volume), and training and technical assistance to African countries provided through the Indian Technical and Economic Cooperation (ITEC) programme (see chapters by Naidu and Bhattacharya, this volume).

Moreover, the Indian diaspora has a significant presence across the African continent and has been assimilated into the culture and socio-economic milieu of many African countries. This reinforces the strong social and cultural bonds between Africa and India. Finally, though not explicit, India's growing relationship with Africa is also motivated by the need to secure African diplomatic support in New Delhi's quest to gain a permanent seat at the UN Security Council (see chapters by Bhattacharya and Naidu on historical and cultural premises, this volume).

Needless to say, there is a growing concern in Africa that the increasing engagement of the Asian giants, in their search for energy and minerals, could, if not managed properly, turn out to be just as bad as the 'scramble for resources' that led to the colonization of the continent during the second half of the nineteenth century. Additional risks explored by contributors to this volume include: increasing 'securitization' of African international relations (see chapters by Sinha and Obi); weak governance standards and misallocation of receipts from high raw-material prices (see chapters on Sudan, Nigeria and Angola); a weakening of the still-low local standards and regulations on environment and labour (see chapters on Zambia by Mutesa and Kragelund, Aning on Sudan, and Obi on Nigeria); the destruction of local economies unable to compete with China and India's hyper-competitive manufacturing sectors (see chapter by Axelsson and Sylvanus on women traders' response to the entry of Chinese wax prints to Togo and Ghana); and finally, political support to African regimes that are not open to democratic governance (see Vines and Campos on Angola, Obi on Nigeria and Aning on Sudan). Unless China and India immediately address these critical concerns expressed by Africans, the red carpet that has been rolled out to welcome them will quickly be rolled back up and taken away, and the stigma of China and India as 'new colonialists' will take decades to erase.

Scope of the book

This book provides incisive coverage of a number of issues and is organized in six parts. The chapters strive to avoid replicating existing studies on China–Africa and India–Africa relations. Rather, attention is directed towards a critical perspective that defines the priorities of an African response that can transform the opportunity provided by the deepening presence of China and India on the continent into concrete poverty-reduction and people-rooted African development.

This volume situates China's and India's engagement in Africa in the context of the shift in the balance of power in the world economy, from the West to the East, with the ascendancy of China and India as major economic powerhouses. This trend has provoked much discussion in policy and scholarly circles in Africa, Europe and the USA. But underlying the existing analysis are three strands of thought which can be summarized as China as 'development partner', China as 'economic competitor' and China as 'colonizer' (Alden 2007: 5). In reality, however, China–Africa relations are complex; they involve both benefits and risks. The extent to which both China and India can exert influence in Africa and elsewhere is largely dependent on their own position (and vulnerability) in the world economy, and this is demonstrated in both governments' response to the recent global financial crisis. Also of note are Western perceptions of the implications of the growing Chinese and Indian influence in Africa, and the policy directions that key Western governments take in seeking to prevent Africa's slipping out of their influence (National Intelligence Council 2004).

Despite the rhetorical statements of 'friendship' and 'solidarity' that are implicit in the official Africa policy documents of both China and India, competition over African resources and markets, and the quest for influence and support, are the principal motivation for both countries in their engagement with African nations. For China, the big prize is strong African support for its one-China policy with respect to Taiwan; for India, the big prize is going to be overwhelming African support in its quest for a permanent seat on the UN Security Council (Schaffer and Mitra 2005: 14). Also relevant are issues of strategic and energy security, as well as maritime security – with both China and India keen to pursue their interests in oil and gas – and the safety of commerce along the international shipping lanes off the coast of Africa. This is shown by the increasing projection of military power by both countries in Africa in response to a similar projection by the United States and Russia. Moreover, the record, particularly of Chinese enterprises, on wages, occupational health and safety standards, and corporate social responsibility, and the impact of Chinese products on local industry and livelihoods are beginning to affect Sino-African relations negatively (see chapters by Mutesa on Zambia, and Axelsson and Sylvanus on Ghana and Togo).

The book also examines the explosive rise of China and India and their impact on the emergence of a new architecture of international relations whereby the conventional North–South polarity is being replaced by a South–South–East relationship. This accordingly will have a long-term implication for Africa, namely the demise of the centuries-old domination of the USA and western Europe over the continent (Martin 2008: 349). The continent's increasing importance as a source of energy supplies and raw materials has led to the growing economic and military involvement of China, India and other emerging industrial powers, including Russia. In response, the USA has dramatically increased its military presence to protect what it has defined as its strategic national interest in Africa. This has ignited what has come to be known as the 'new scramble for Africa' and is transforming the security architecture of the continent.

A number of chapters in the book examine China's and India's investment strategy in several African countries, in terms of type, location and rationale. Focusing on specific sectors – manufacturing, agriculture, energy – the contributors document empirically the developmental impact of this investment. The analysis points out many areas of tensions, as well as potential areas of mutual benefit. Based on the empirical evidence, contributors to the volume warn of the dangers of generalization and call for more detailed research both on individual countries and at the level of particular value chains in order to trace the real impact of China and India on Africa's development (see chapters by Alemayehu and Atnafu, Vines and Campos, Draper et al. and Modi). We therefore caution the research and policy community in Africa and in the West to avoid being sucked into a 'Chinese- and Indian-bashing' campaign, which could only limit the ability of the scholarly community to do more empirical research on what has become a sensitive subject.

China's and India's ascendancy has shattered the dominant paradigm of the Washington Consensus of open markets and a minimal role for the state in national development. Back in the political discourse in Africa now is the role of the developmental state, the need for 'policy space' and the importance of experimenting and finding unorthodox solutions to Africa's development crisis. The final section of the book examines alternative formulations and conditions under which African countries must engage with the emerging giants as well as the rest of the West. It is recommended that growth and structural change be achieved through 'strategic integration' rather than through a rapid across-the-board opening up of African economies (see chapter by Cheru and Calais). This should be decided on the basis of how the policy supports the national interest of African countries in terms of promoting economic growth and structural change.

An important aspect of 'strategic integration' is regional integration. Such policies should support international competitiveness by promoting regional production chains and nurture the development of regional markets in order to reduce demand-side constraints on growth. The urgency of instituting counter-hegemonic policies has become self-evident in the light of the dramatic collapse of the dominant ideology of neoliberal globalization since the financial crisis that started in late 2008. Although this crisis has affected virtually every country in the world, China and India have not been affected on the same scale as the developed countries, which have championed for so long the ideology of an unrestricted market and minimal government intervention. These same developed countries are now forced to intervene in the market, a policy choice that they denied developing countries for so long.

The most successful 'developing' countries over the past two decades – those that have registered impressive growth and reduced poverty – have been those that marched to their own drummers, and danced to their own music. These are India, China and Brazil – hardly poster children of neoliberalism. Not only have they fared better in dealing with the current financial crisis, but they are the only countries that are likely to register some credible level of growth, while developed countries remain in a slump. Yet, while the example of these countries is appealing, there is a need for realism on the part of African countries so as to correctly read the trends in the evolving global order and not merely exchange one set of asymmetrical relations (those with the West) for another (new relations with the East). Just as China and India are increasing their investments in Africa, African states, entrepreneurs and private sector actors also need to raise African investments in China far above the currently limited levels (Cheng and Shi 2009: 107). The key will be to have a visionary African leadership with a clear and coordinated strategy at the continental level to engage the emerging giants from a stronger and well-informed platform in order to contribute to Africa's development in the twenty-first century.

PART ONE

The big picture: China and India as emerging giants

1 | China, India and (South) Africa: what international relations in the second decade of the twenty-first century?

Timothy M. Shaw

African international relations are in flux as a result of the impact of the 'emerging economies' of Brazil, Russia, India and China (BRIC) on the continent's few 'developmental' economies and many 'fragile states'. North–South relations are being superseded by South–East (Martin 2008), even Africa–East, alliances, with profound implications for the Group of Eight (G8) and the Group of 20 (G20) relations (Beeson and Bell 2009; Cooper and Antkiewicz 2008; Masters 2008). Thus the 'new' 'African' international relations (Cornelissen et al. 2010) may no longer be just non-state/informal/illegal cross-border relations but also formal economic, strategic and other relations, with China and India in particular.

The post-Washington (Beijing or Delhi) Consensus may present state and non-state Africans with policy options they had hardly anticipated. And the range of contemporary issues stretches from energy and mineral demand to the price of drugs, the proliferation of small arms and competition over access to land and water. South Africa is pivotal in these emerging equations as it holds an important position within IBSA (the India, Brazil, South Africa Dialogue) and other emerging economic formations, such as BRIC and the Next Eleven (N-11).[1] This chapter seeks to go beyond the burgeoning but somewhat generic debate about China and India (Denoon 2007) and to identify specific states, sectors, companies and civil societies central to the intercontinental relationship(s). It tries to identify who the catalysts and drivers are in the emerging intercontinental relationship, and assess their implications for Africa's development. Might the second decade of the twenty-first century finally herald Africa's belated renaissance?

China–India and Africa: the historical context

Halfway through the first decade of the new century, and after years of neglect, scholarly research on the growing role of China and India in Africa has been put centre stage in the relatively short time frame of five years (Goldstein et al. 2006; Alden 2007; Mills 2008). In retrospect, it is clear that China never really left Africa (Taylor 2006), but its own 'economic' transitions are arguably more dramatic than the set of political and economic liberalizations that have taken place in Africa over the past twenty-five years. China once again aspires to being a great power globally as well as regionally (Fenby 2008). The 'cold war' era when China built the Tazara Railway and provided support for some liberation movements is but a quarter-century away (Brautigam 1998). Then, Chinese support was a function of ideology; now its interest is motivated by geo-economics, especially in terms of resources.

En passant, unlike much established Sino-African literature, all sides of the governance 'triangle', local to global – state, corporate and civil society – matter more in the current context even if China's own economic relationship is led by state-owned enterprises (SOEs). By contrast, in the case of the two democratic countries – Brazil and India – and their relationship with Africa, the focus on corporate–state relations over the last two decades is the primary explanation for their respective successes as 'developmental states' (Pedersen 2008).

This chapter has four overlapping, interrelated themes. First, it seeks to go beyond uncritical descriptions of Africa–China economic exchanges, which overlook myriad differences and ignore human development/rights/security dimensions (Carey et al. 2007; Le Pere 2006; Lee et al. 2007; Mohan and Power 2008). The analysis offers second- or third-wave reconsideration/revisionism: beyond 'bilateral' macro analysis, which states, sectors, companies and communities are involved or ignored, positively or negatively? Is there an imminent revolution in North–South and South–East relations (Campbell 2008; Martin 2008; Shaw et al. 2007)?

Second, 'China' may constitute a challenge to the burgeoning debate about whether 'African' international relations (IR) are different (Cornelissen et al. 2009) because they are less interstate and formal than elsewhere; that is, cross-border relations on the continent have been largely non-state and informal, sometimes illegal (Dunn and Shaw 2001). By contrast, expanding economic relations with China at the turn of the century are largely state led and formal, especially on the Chinese side. So aside from description and analysis of the 'bilateral' relationship, in terms of comparative theory and explanation, I reflect on whether there are 'two' Africas or African IRs: the established, traditional, informal and the recent, novel, exclusive formal exchange with China.

Third, in terms of differences among and within (Cooper et al. 2007) BRIC (Armijo 2007), this chapter seeks in part to juxtapose literatures/discourses on African IR with those on BRIC, especially China, given its existential centrality and its state-centrism involving exclusion of non-state organizations. As Brazil and India (Broadman 2007) are both established, democratic federations with significant non-state corporate (Pedersen 2008) and civil society sectors, should one expect their relations with the continent to be different from those of undemocratic state-driven political economies like those of China and Russia?

Fourth, as indicated in the final section and based on the previous trio of concerns, this chapter may contribute unanticipated insights into IR (Alden

2007; Kitissou 2007; Mepham and Wild 2006), international political economy/ IPE (Le Pere and Shelton 2007; Mohan and Power 2008), development studies (Breslin 2007; Lee et al. 2007), regionalisms (Cai 2008; Denoon 2007) and business studies (Enderwick 2007) globally, which go beyond the debates at the start of the new century.

Africa and China: convergent or divergent national and regional interests?

The current context is one of global growth and shocks, especially shrinking demand and supply and increased prices for energy, minerals and food. The present historical conjuncture is not just the US-specific sub-prime crisis. Rather, the world economy is being buoyed by BRIC. In turn BRIC, especially China and India, presents more choices for African states, local entrepreneurs and civil societies, symbolized by the notion of a post-Washington 'Beijing Consensus' (Ramo 2004). As Martin has rightly observed:

> The explosive rise of China and India as leaders of the 'Global South' has been widely noted. What few have paused to consider, however, is the long-term implication for Africa, namely the demise of centuries-long dominion of the USA and Europe over the continent. Indeed, the prospect is even more radical in my view: the replacement of the North–South polarity by an East–South relationship. (Martin 2008: 349)

China accounted for 40 per cent of the growth of global demand for oil in the last four years of the middle of the decade as its own exports came to a halt. By 2003, it had already become the biggest consumer of oil after the USA. Chinese oil and gas companies now compete with those from the USA and the EU in West Africa (Campbell 2008; Klare and Volman 2006). There are already some eight hundred Chinese SOEs in Africa, many with interlocking directorships with the Chinese Communist Party, including China National Petroleum Corporation (CNPC) and China National Offshore Oil Corporation (CNOOC) (BCG 2006; Goldstein 2007: 35). In the space of a few years, China has become Africa's second-largest trading partner after the USA, ahead of France and Britain, with annual flows of some US$50 billion. By 2010 these may exceed US$100 billion per annum (Liang 2008; Mepham and Wild 2006; Sautman 2006; Sidiropolous 2006; Taylor 2006).

The tone of orthodox analysis and projection surrounding BRIC, especially China–India, is largely uncritical and triumphalist (Goldstein 2007; van Agtmael 2007; www2.goldmansachs.com). It is important, however, to balance economic, financial and technological performance and promise with recognition of environmental costs and social tensions, as several contributors in this volume have done successfully (see chapters in this volume by Obi, Axelsson and Sylvanus).

Africa and BRIC: from emerging economies to private capital and civil society

In the first decade of the new century, national development on the continent may be attributed to two, possibly antagonistic, factors: oil and mineral exports (for example, Botswana, Equatorial Guinea and Angola) or good governance (for example, Mozambique, Rwanda and Uganda) (Humphrey and Messner 2006; Kaplinsky and Messner 2008; Tull 2006; Vines 2007). Growing competition between Asian rather than European states over dominance on the continent has been symbolized by a series of African summits. Symbolic of its increasing presence, China organized a continent-wide gathering in Beijing in 2006, followed by the historic May 2007 annual meeting of the African Development Bank in Shanghai. Not to be overshadowed, as part of BRIC and IBSA, India organized its first selective African Summit with the Africa Union (AU) in New Delhi in April 2008 (Sidiropolous and Vines 2007). Japan, the only G8 member in Asia, also organized the Fourth Tokyo International Conference on African Development (TICAD V) in May 2008 in Yokohama (www.ticad.net).

China takes over 60 per cent of Sudan's oil exports of over 500,000 barrels per day – now 10 per cent of China's oil imports – and some 35 per cent of the flow from Angola. It owns 40 per cent of the Sudanese oil sector and one of its SOEs built a 1,600-kilometre oil pipeline to the coast in less than twelve months. Sudan's oil industry is located primarily in the disaffected south, and is therefore inseparable from conflict. When Canada's oil firm Talisman withdrew in 2002/03, all the owners of Greater Nile Petroleum Operating Company were state oil corporations – Chinese, Indian and Malaysian as well as Sudanese – operating with minimal accountability or transparency. China's energy demand has transformed sleepy tropical islands like Equatorial Guinea and São Tomé into centres of production, accumulation and corruption, even transnational coup attempts (Frynas 2004; Frynas and Paulo 2007; Klare and Volman 2006; Shaxson 2007; Taylor 2007; Zweig and Jianhai 2005).

Chinese official development assistance (ODA) is especially welcomed as it is free from familiar, ubiquitous Western donor conditionalities. Thus it gives African regimes alternatives to OECD terms advanced in the so-called Washington Consensus. This is especially so given the bilateral competition between China and the USA for African resources (Campbell 2008; Xu 2008). Such choice or space has led to the notion in a post-Washington Consensus era of a Beijing Consensus, characterized by more South–South content and empathy (Campbell 2008; Le Pere and Shelton 2007; Martin 2008; Vines and Sidiropolous 2008).

The growing engagement of Asia (China in particular) in Africa has raised a lot of questions. As African social movements and activists have pointed out, the downside of the new Asian–African relationship is that China has proved no friend of social movements in Africa or Asia, supporting repressive regimes from the Sudan to Equatorial Guinea to Zimbabwe (Martin 2008: 351). China has been willing to export arms in exchange for imports of raw materials. Unlike India, it is not a central player in the Kimberley Process, which seeks to outlaw the trading of guns for informal, alluvial diamonds. There is a parallel with the notorious 'conflict diamonds', which were traded for weapons for non-state agencies (Frynas 2004; Shaxson 2007).

By contrast, India's trade and investment connections with the continent may be rather limited compared to those of China, but there is one area in which India has an advantage: Indian diasporas in Africa. These are not uncontroversial (as in Idi Amin's expulsion of one of these in Uganda in the early 1970s), and for decades the Indian state ignored them. But at the century's turn, as India liberalized its economy, it came to welcome investment from established communities and remittances from recent migrant workers to the Gulf, among other places. The role of returning post-war Indian diasporas with business and engineering degrees is central to India's rise. And the networks of Indian non-governmental organizations (NGOs) and multinational companies are crucial to its expansion, from Global Organization for People of Indian Origin (GOPIO) to private companies such as Reliance, Tata and Wipro (BCG 2006; Goldstein 2007; Goldstein et al. 2006; van Agtmael 2007).

Traditionally, Indian communities could be found where the British Empire or Raj had sent them, mainly to anglophone East and southern Africa. By contrast, contemporary informal Chinese migration is to high-growth countries, such as Nigeria, South Africa, Sudan and Zimbabwe (Sautman 2006: 28). There are also possibilities of collaboration within BRIC when mutual interests can be advanced (Cooper et al. 2007), as in the case of joint ventures in oil production in southern Sudan. Thus Arcelor Mittal, the world's largest steel producer, has had talks with Angang, China's second-largest steel company, about a strategic alliance.

Which countries, companies, sectors and civil society groups gain or lose in Africa, China or India? For example, Angola is now the biggest single oil supplier to China; Industrial and Commercial Bank of China (ICBC), the world's largest, bought 20 per cent of Standard Bank of South Africa for US$5.56 billion, and in mid-2008 its president, Yang Kaisheng, became deputy chair of Standard Bank Group in South Africa; China Development Bank (CDB) bought a major stake in United Bank for Africa (UBA) in Nigeria; and China Investment Corporation, a sovereign wealth fund (SWF), has US$90 billion to invest overseas. Chinese mining companies in Zambia are not uncontroversial, however, and SWFs are increasingly controversial, as well as ubiquitous in the global economy (www.swfinstitute.org), especially when they are connected to distinctive states, whether Islamic (such as Dubai or Kuwait) or state socialist (such as China or Russia).

Africa and BRIC: compatible or competitive?

Africa's relationships with BRIC are quite heterogeneous and divergent. Historically, as an aspect of the nationalist and liberation movements, its links were closest with Russia and China. The continent's spurt in the first half of the first decade of the new millennium led *The Economist* (2008b) to revise its end-of-century negative analysis.

After four decades of political and economic stagnation that kept most people in poverty and gloom, the continent's forty-eight sub-Saharan countries have been growing for the past five years at a perky overall rate of 5 per cent or so ... Once described by this newspaper, perhaps with undue harshness, as 'the hopeless continent', it could yet confound its legion of gloomsters and show that its oft-heralded renaissance is not just another false dawn prompted by the passing windfall of booming commodity prices, but the start of something solid and sustainable.

Now the continent's economic exchanges are most extensive with the two largest, fastest-growing economies: China and India (Sidiropolous and Vines 2007). But those with the former are limited to interstate economic relations, whereas those with the latter involve non-state actors such as civil societies and private capital. Notwithstanding the mixed legacy of earlier Indian diasporas in eastern and southern Africa, relations among democracies in the anglophone world are more comprehensive than those between Africa and China.

Thus, aside from multilateral links within the Commonwealth – for example, through the Commonwealth Foundation, Commonwealth Parliamentary Association or Association of Commonwealth Universities (Shaw 2008) – Indian multi-national corporations (MNCs) like Tata are increasingly active, especially in Commonwealth markets like Ghana, Mozambique, Nigeria, South Africa and Uganda (Goldstein 2007; Goldstein et al. 2006). India assumed the chair of the Kimberley Process (KP) for 2008, reflective of the esteem of its civil society and corporate regime as some million Indians are employed in the diamond sector nationally. And its diaspora is not unimportant in diamond centres such as Antwerp. China is a less central member of the Kimberley Process, being most interested in the range of mineral imports from alluvial diamond producers such as Angola and Congo. Any weaknesses or gaps in the KP concern Brazil and West Africa rather than southern Africa. China has also refused to sign the Extractive Industries Transparency Initiative (EITI) (www.eitransparency.org).

Thus, Sino-African connections are rather 'shallow' or limited, as few have extra-state dimensions: for example, there is little migration from China to Africa or vice versa, and there are few remittances (compared, for example, with African diasporas in the EU, the USA and Canada). Some officially sanctioned or advanced migration via educational and health cadres plus contracts for infrastructural development is secured by Chinese SOEs which bring Chinese labour to execute on time and on budget. Aside from inexpensive textiles and manufactures, most exports are construction services in infrastructure. But Chinese exports are likely to go upmarket, symbolized by Lenovo, Haier and several automobile and light truck companies (Goldstein 2007).

South Africa within CIBS (China, India, Brazil, South Africa Dialogue) and IBSA: dominator or facilitator of Africa's interest?

Are South Africa's losses at home, in sectors like clothing, shoes and textiles, balanced by opportunities in sub-Saharan Africa (SSA) to supply Chinese demand in energy and mining industries, where its companies are increasingly well established and active (Shaw et al. 2007)? Can the Republic of South Africa be the link or the hub between SSA and East Asia? Can South Africa exploit Free Trade Agreement (FTAs) with the USA through the African Growth and Opportunity Act (AGOA) and with the European Union through the Economic Partnership Agreement (EPA) to its own advantage, as in, say, exports of textile and manufactures, as well as certain brands of car, to both China and India?

South Africa may have an imbalance in its more orthodox bilateral trade with China but its markets for goods and services in the rest of the continent are in part a function of Chinese demand for Africa's energy and mineral products. Hence South African brands and franchises in services (for example, Dstv, MTN, Stanbic) and logistics (for example, South African Airways, Shoprite). Thus South African Brewery's fifty-five breweries in China and ICBC's investment in Standard Bank with its eighteen-country network of branches on the continent may be contrasted with the more traditional bilateral imbalance. As Martin has argued, 'South Africa and China are not thus simply competing producers of light and medium industrial products: they are rooted in very different production networks directed at different buyers and consumer markets' (Martin 2008: 353).

By contrast, India's economic engagement with the continent is still quite minimal: 3 per cent versus 10 per cent of total trade. But South Africa's role in it is more important proportionally than with China – 68 per cent of SSA exports – which may explain or advance IBSA. Arcelor Mittal is South Africa's biggest steel producer and Tata is active in South Africa as well as in other Commonwealth states – Ghana, Mozambique, Nigeria, Uganda and Zambia – including a major ferro-chrome project at Richards Bay, freeze-dried coffee production for export in Uganda, imports of Tata Indica and Indigo into South Africa and Taj upmarket hotels in South Africa's three urban areas, plus Pamodzi in Lusaka (www.tataafrica.com).

South African MNCs are particularly ubiquitous in anglophone eastern and southern Africa, with myriad brands, franchises, service providers, supply chains and so on. Some have reached beyond the continent, notably those listed on the London Stock Exchange as well as the Johannesburg Stock Exchange: for example, Anglo American, de Beers and Old Mutual, plus the most global of them all, SABMiller; with the largest brand in China – Snow – along with fifteen others, plus ten in Russia and several in India (Goldstein 2007).

Are CIBS and IBSA (a formally constituted tripartite intergovernmental organization) compatible or competitive, as the former is largely statist, while the latter consists of exclusively democratic states (Le Pere and Shelton 2007)? And what are the implications, if any, for G8 and G20 relations both before and during the current global financial crisis (Beeson and Bell 2009; Cooper and Antkiewicz 2008; Masters 2008)? Unlike China, India can exert soft power in its external relations, given its resilient civil society as well as its strong private sector, including an increasingly global cultural sector, symbolized by Bollywood, which has a global presence (Shaw et al. 2008). It can therefore more readily engage in promising contemporary mixed-actor 'networks' rather than just the traditional and limited as well as exclusive 'club' diplomacy of states (Heine 2006).

Africa, China and IR from 'Africa': lessons from the continent?

Finally, by way of conclusion and projection, what if any lessons are there from Africa for international non-state and informal/illegal relations (Cornelissen et al. 2010; Dunn and Shaw 2001) given that the escalating relationship between China and Africa is largely interstate and formal (Alden 2007)? What framework to explain such dichotomies (Mohan and Power 2008)? BRIC challenges analysis, policy and practice in several overlapping fields: for example, comparative and international politics; development and environmental, gender and global, migration and security studies; and new regionalisms (Shaw et al. 2008). I end with two challenging citations from this burgeoning discourse:

> Five 'images' of China are set to shape the relationship with Africa: first its image as the new face of globalization; second its role in African development success; third as a mirror for the West; fourth as a pariah partner; and finally as a responsible stakeholder. (Alden 2007: 128)

> In the long run, as Africans transform their societies, the task will be to ensure that the relations between Africa and China do not repeat centuries of under-development and exploitation. (Campbell 2008: 104)

The shifting terrain of global economic power from Euroamerica to Asia with the exponential rise of China and India, and new trilateral formations such as BRIC and IBSA, presents challenges and opportunities to the African continent. While multipolarity may imply more room for individual African countries to manoeuvre, this will depend on the ability of African countries to articulate a long-term development vision that would enable the continent to break free of the Western-led (or G8-dominated) diktat. The rise of BRIC in itself does not produce the desired 'policy space'. National efforts in 'strategic integration' into world markets, complemented by strategic tactical alliance with BRIC, the G20 and other multilateral initiatives, are likely to create the necessary policy space for African countries to manoeuvre and to chart their own path of development.

2 | South–South strategic bases for Africa to engage China

Dot Keet

There is a growing body of academic and journalistic publications on the dominant features and the directions of the economic growth of present-day China
and its current and future economic and political role in the world. At both
the general and the specifically African-focused levels, the analyses (or specula-
tions) tend to focus mainly on the 'threat' posed by China's rapid processes of
industrialization and its growing trade and investment expansion throughout
the world. In most of the literature emanating from institutes and analysts
viewing China from the developed countries of the North, and in the strategic
assessments by their governments, there is also a pervasive concern – mostly
implicit but sometimes explicit – as to how the seemingly inexorable rise of
China to superpower status will affect the current global economic system and
international power regime, and the specific interests and continued role of the
currently dominant economies and countries, above all those of the EU, the
USA and Japan (Bernstein and Munro 1998; Thompson 2005).

What is somewhat less frank – but of fundamental significance to strategy
analysts within Africa – is the apprehension of the major powers at having,
henceforth, to face up to a new and very powerful competitor in accessing and
exploiting Africa's rich and strategically important resources. Despite the heavy
historic and continuing predominance of European companies in all sectors
and in all African countries, they are already foreseeing having to face up to
growing Chinese competition in the extractive sectors in Africa. They also foresee
being increasingly displaced by Chinese companies, not merely in the area of
cheap consumer goods, but even in the capital equipment supply sector, and
in major construction and other public projects across the continent (Gill et
al. 2006; CFR 2007).

What is also notable is the frank hypocrisy of the governments of the older
industrialized economies and their related think tanks, as well as independent
research centres and mainstream media suddenly converted to belated and
highly tendentious criticisms of Chinese 'colonialist' and 'imperialist' designs
on Africa. This constitutes a veritable chorus of concern, deploring the damaging economic and environmental effects in Africa from Chinese exploitation
of Africa's resources; and decrying the negative effects of the various forms of

Chinese official financial aid and economic support – and thus deliberate or de facto political backing – of highly questionable regimes in various African countries.

Notwithstanding the highly selective and self-serving analyses of China-in-Africa emanating from Northern research institutions and think tanks, the challenge facing African strategic policy analysts is to make independent and objective assessments of both the challenges as well as the opportunities presented by China's current interest(s) and future role in Africa (Brooks and Shin 2006). But such critical African responses to the motivations, perceptions and concepts informing Western governmental and non-governmental analyses also cannot divert independent African analysts from applying the same level of intellectual rigour to analysis of official Chinese declarations or rhetoric. This requires maintaining a clear analytical distinction between declarations of intent and 'principles', on the one hand, and actual practice and changing forces on the ground in China, and Beijing's subtly changing policies, on the other (Large 2008b).

Current African governmental engagements with China

At the outset, there is the long-standing strategic defensive aim of a united Africa combining and improving its bargaining power to obtain more favour-able terms and developmental returns from the operations of international investors anywhere on the continent. On the other hand, there is the more radical proactive vision of a united, more self-reliant and self-sustaining Africa better able to deal with external pressures and the challenges of an extremely difficult 'globalized' economy. This vision remains strong on paper but not in practice.

On the collective side, African government representatives have, in recent years, met with their Chinese counterparts in major gatherings, detailed elsewhere in this volume. Such high-level meetings have produced resounding joint declarations on the principles informing China–Africa relations, as well as multifaceted plans of engagement between Africa and China on such issues as reform of the global financial institutions. Nonetheless, in practice, and where the impact is most direct, African governments have, as always, been acting individually, signing separate agreements with the Chinese government and awarding major resource exploitation and/or exploration contracts to Chinese companies.

The information available on the rapidly expanding China–Africa interactions indicates that many African governments have signed bilateral agreements with the government in Beijing. These include some thirty 'framework agreements' on soft loans from China to African governments, most linked to a variety of projects on the ground. There have also reportedly been some twenty-eight bilateral trade and investment agreements signed by African governments with China, including guarantees for the protection of Chinese investment (Berger 2008).

There have also been more than forty 'cultural agreements' signed between China and African countries, providing for scientific and technical cooperation, the offer of high-level education and training for tens of thousands of African students in China, the supply of Chinese health and other technical personnel within Africa, and much else.

The terms of such agreements and their actual effects on the ground have to be the subject of rigorous examination because it is, of course, the implementation of these agreements which will go a long way towards demonstrating the practical nature and impacts of Chinese operations in Africa and relations with Africa. This would provide some indicators for the appropriate positioning, or would direct the repositioning, of African governments with regard to engagements with China. This is particularly important in light of the fact that bilateral investment treaties (BITs), similar to the Trade-Related Investment Measures (TRIMs) of the World Trade Organization (WTO), represent an interference with the sovereignty of host governments, essentially contracting the policy space for developing countries (Wade 2003). Thus, the promise of transfer of technology to Africa by Chinese FDI (foreign direct investment) and building export capacity may therefore not materialize.

In the final analysis, regardless of Beijing's long-term strategy in Africa, the onus is on African governments themselves to come together and agree on their common needs and aims. They could present a united front based on joint strategic approaches that concretize the declarations of principle and the avowals of good intentions by China, and which could go farther, to pose qualitatively different terms and modalities for these relations. These would need to be located within clearly articulated strategic perspectives for Africa on what China is or could be, and what Africa needs.

Alternative strategic perspectives for Africa

The ways in which African governments and independent analysts of the role of China in Africa should assess and could approach the strategic options facing the continent have to be located within a number of widely differing perceptions of the character of China, and interpretations of the aims and the implications of China's role in Africa, in the South and in the world. These different interpretations suggest differing tactical and strategic approaches as to the most effective, necessary or unavoidable ways for Africa to engage with China.

Countering 'Chinese imperialism' in Africa? The first approach depicts a broad equivalence between the old imperialism/imperialists of Europe and the USA, on the one hand, and China as a new emerging imperialist power (Melber 2007). In this scenario, both the old established colonialists and neocolonialists and the new putative 'mercantilist predator' have to be treated with appropriate circumspection (Le Pere 2006). All Africa's external engagements have to be based on the need to prevent a new generation or wave of exploiters of Africa's resources operating to the advantage of economic and political interests outside the continent.

Whatever the analytical merits of the 'imperialist' depiction of China, this scenario poses the same political challenges as arise from Africa's long-standing subordinate insertion into and exploitation in the global economy. The demands that would have to be made by African governments with regard to China's role, today or in the future, are the same as those made of Western investors in Africa during the 'development era' of the 1960s and 1970s. The common demand, at that time, from development analysts and practitioners was that foreign investors from the West should be required to include some significant undertakings that would increase the 'gains' or improve the effects of such investment in the host countries, and minimize or reduce the costs or negative effects (G. Kay 1975; Frank 1967; Amin 1976; Haggard 1990). Such strategies were often combined with domestic support to 'infant industries' and other external trade strategies and national tariff policies. Examples of pre-agreed investment conditions employed during this period can be found in Box 2.1 above.

During the 1980s, changes in the international balance of power, the triumph of the neoliberal 'market' paradigm in the North and then globally, and the Third World debt crises and consequent imposition in most African countries of IMF/World Bank (WB) structural adjustment programmes combined to dismiss, displace and actively dismantle the programmes and instruments of the development paradigm. Two decades later, however, in the context of the theoretical and empirical discrediting of the neoliberal 'free market' paradigm, and regardless of what neoliberal theorists and institutions dominated by Northern governments continue to argue, the fundamental question to be put to Beijing – given the claim by China to be operating according to principles different to those of the West – is whether the Chinese authorities would be prepared to instruct and require all Chinese trade operations and investment projects in Africa to abide by the above development terms.

Confronted informally with such views, Chinese officials reportedly reply that they are not opposed to discussing such proposals, but that African governments do not pose them.[1] Thus, the responsibility for putting such alternatives on the table rests with African governments. This in turn depends on their will and capacity, united within their regional economic communities or within the African Union as a whole, to formulate, negotiate and monitor such developmental terms and requirements to Chinese operations within Africa. Such a joint African approach is also essential in order to strengthen and protect all African countries, strong or weak, and to ensure a wider engagement by China, rather than one restricted to those African countries endowed with attractive resources. Such a united position could also prevent African countries being played off against one another, as is so evident in the manoeuvres they face from foreign investors within current competing African 'foreign investment promotion' and privatization programmes.

With the application of such basic 'developmental' terms, African governments and their countries could avoid exchanging one set of long-standing Northern neocolonial 'partners' for a new set of questionable Southern/Chinese 'partners'. If Beijing were to agree to negotiate and implement such developmental terms in its operations in Africa, this would go some way towards answering the question of whether China is simply a 'neocolonialist', a 'new imperialist' in Africa, or a 'developmental partner'. Such developmental terms and conditions for foreign investors would, conversely, also be very appropriate for Beijing, itself, to set for foreign companies operating within China.

Building on 'common experiences' and/or 'joint ventures'? A related approach is to locate China within the long history of Western colonial domination and exploitation that was experienced throughout Africa, Asia and the Pacific, Latin America and the Caribbean. This 'common experience' of China and Africa, and the other countries of the South, has long been a recurrent theme in official Chinese foreign policy pronouncements from the earliest days of the visit of Zhou Enlai to Africa, in the 1960s, to the most recent tour of Africa by Chinese President Hu Jintao in 2007 (People's Republic of China 2006).

In this perspective, the position to be adopted by Africa in relation to China today would emphasize and draw on that shared historical experience, including the economic, political and military support extended by the People's Republic of China to Africa in the anti-colonial and national liberation struggles during the decades of the 1960s and 1970s and into the 1980s. Emphasis on this shared experience and 'historic friendship' avowed by both Beijing and African governments would be pursued on the African side with a view to eliciting equivalent sympathy – although in different forms and levels of support – from the Chinese authorities today.

One major impediment in this scenario arises from indications that economic and political players in today's China – both within the Chinese government and ruling party, and in semi-independent entrepreneurial entities – are withdrawing from such an 'outdated ideological approach'. Emerging trends in Chinese governmental and business circles are reportedly shifting in favour of straight 'commercial' relations and other similarly 'practical' forms of economic support to Africa in the form of Chinese investment and construction projects, and so forth (Shelton 2007). The major question for African governments is how – or whether – their appeals to the 'political principles' officially espoused by the Chinese government will weigh henceforth both in Beijing's and in their own strategic approaches.

The counter-perspective to such state-led approaches is that African political-cum-economic interest groups will come to rely increasingly on quasi- (but increasingly) independent private sector Chinese enterprises engaged in 'joint ventures' with African companies. Such Africa–China or China–Africa joint ventures are beginning to feature more strongly in China's official approach to Africa. The engagement of African economic players with Chinese business partners could, however, reproduce earlier colonial patterns where local economic and political actors are co-opted. In this scenario, African entities partnering their much more powerful Chinese counterparts would come to constitute classic 'collaborationist' forces or 'comprador' agencies in the service of external interests and forces. Such a comprador relationship is illustrated in the 'investment' of some US$5 billion by the ICBC (the Industrial and Commercial Bank of China) through its acquisition of a 20 per cent stake in Standard Bank, South Africa. None of this 'investment', however, will actually enter South Africa, as it is intended for the South African-based bank to 'facilitate' Chinese operations in the rest of the African continent.

From the perspective of the role of African governments, there are two further corollaries to this type of proposed business relationship. These arise from the inherent dynamics within capitalist and even state-capitalist operations. On the one hand, if these joint enterprises are set up under the aegis of Africa–Chinese governmental agreements, the former may find themselves having to take responsibility for dealing with any labour problems or industrial and community disputes that may arise within or in relation to such operations.[2] Similarly, the Chinese authorities and Chinese businesses may find themselves in the unaccustomed position of facing labour disputes in circumstances where their own domestic methods and means cannot be applied; or, in the case of countries such as South Africa, Zambia, Nigeria or Senegal, where organized labour would prove very much more difficult to deal with than the tamed trade unions and 'disciplined' (or submissive) industrial workforces in China. How will African governments 'cooperate' with Chinese enterprises in their countries in relation to their own labour unions – and working people and communities – in such situations?

Furthermore, in contradistinction to the anticipated positive effects of Chinese companies in promoting the growth of African 'partner' companies, a very different effect could result from large, efficient and highly competitive Chinese companies undermining, sidelining and even displacing African companies. With the advantage of the efficiencies of scale, and various other economic, political and social/cultural advantages, Chinese enterprises will be able to oust their African competitors. This is already evident, for example, in the displacement by Chinese construction companies of major South African equivalents in public projects elsewhere on the continent, and even within South Africa. If this is evident with a relatively strong semi-industrialized economy such as South Africa, what can be expected in less developed economies elsewhere in Africa? The implantation of Chinese companies in Africa could, in fact, function to prevent or pre-empt the emergence of such indigenous companies elsewhere in Africa, where IMF/WB trade and investment liberalization prescriptions have long impeded new domestic companies from emerging or have actively undermined those that once existed. In this scenario, African countries will not be able to industrialize and diversify their economies, and Africa will be further entrenched in its traditional role as supplier of raw materials to other economies; in this latest phase to China.

This threat is made even more potent in view of the considerable direct financial, economic and political support provided to Chinese enterprises by Chinese national – and provincial – authorities. Apparently independent Chinese enterprises are assisted by Beijing in their operations abroad through political accords with African governments and forms of 'tied' financial agreements and soft loans attached to specific projects within Africa. This, of course, resembles the established 'aid' practices of governments of the older developed countries. As such it would require equivalent counter-responses from African governments. Advised and encouraged by independent analysts in Africa (and even by some critical independent non-governmental agencies in Europe) African governments would have to query any such tendencies in Beijing's approach to Africa, and challenge the terms of tied aid and investment agreements with Beijing that promote the operations and interests of Chinese companies (H. Abbas 2007). Therefore, African researchers have to apply to China the same rigorous critical scrutiny as has been applied to international companies and aid agencies from the more developed countries with respect to Chinese 'soft loans', aid and trade, as to whether these have been beneficial to Africa or not.

Relying on cooperation from China as a developing country? Another somewhat different approach is to see China itself as being still a developing country – not only in the context of historical experience but in the present-day situation of vast sectors of the Chinese population facing similar levels of poverty and marginalization as the majority of the population of Africa. Consequently, in strategic policy and planning terms, China faces similar challenges to those facing Africa in the growing urban–rural divide, gross social and geographical income disparities, extreme social and environmental stresses and other manifestations of imbalanced and distorted development and underdevelopment.

China has traditionally presented itself as a developing country and even as the leader of the developing world (especially during the Sino-Soviet dispute during the late 1960s and early 1970s). The continuing 'developing country' character of China today, or specific dimensions of China's economy and society, suggests on the one hand that the means and methods employed in Chinese operations in Africa are more likely to provide appropriate models and more instructive experiences in the conditions of underdevelopment, lack of basic infrastructures and other current technical incapacities in Africa. The Chinese are also viewed by some admiring governments and businesses, and even NGO analysts in Africa, as being highly efficient in delivering rapid results through their projects in Africa, and being prepared to go to geographical areas and sectors in Africa where most Western investors are not prepared to take business (or personal) 'risks'.

Even assuming the best of intentions on the part of China, however, and/or even if Chinese companies were to be persuaded to adopt exemplary labour, environmental and other standards for their operations in Africa, there remains a built-in and objective inequality in the 'cooperative relations' between China and African countries. Genuine win-win cooperation will not be achieved through relations based upon highly uneven levels of development and very different capacities to benefit from such interactions and cooperation – unless deliberate efforts are made by African countries to compensate for and counter such very different situations and capacities. Without consciously countervailing policies and compensatory provisions, the pronounced objective inequality will result in China making by far the greater gains.

Thus, in this short- to middle-term perspective, and on the basis of pragmatic calculations, African governments would have to move as rapidly as possible to obtain maximum benefits, while they can, from the Chinese government's current interest(s) in the continent, above all in its energy resources. Conversely, strategically far-sighted African governments should take due measures to ensure that they don't create a built-in dependence within their own plans and programmes on such current but not guaranteed long-term Chinese interest in the continent.

Engaging China through developing-country alliances? There is yet another – broader and international – approach for Africa's relations with China. This is located within key multilateral institutions and through the engagements of African and other developing countries in various alliances that include China. This is where China's self-identification as a developing country provides an important basis for other developing countries to engage, collectively, with Beijing. This has long been expressed in the G77 + China grouping of some 132 developing countries within the framework of the UN, dating back to the 1970s (Narlikar 2006). Their coordinated interventions are particularly evident and formally registered in joint declarations in ECOSOC (the Economic and Social Council of the General Assembly) and in key UN social and economic agencies.

The interventions of the G77 + China group in meetings of specialized UN agencies such as the United Nations Conference on Trade and Development (UNCTAD) and the UN Development Programme (UNDP), however, also often reflect the differing situations and divergent strategic approaches within the large number and wide range of developing countries participating (some only intermittently) in this 'common platform' of the developing countries. Despite this, the G77 + China succeeded, for example, in producing a comprehensive joint proposal on technology transfer for the UN Framework Convention on Climate Change (UNFCCC) in 2008. Thus, the G77 + China alliance exhibits both the countervailing collective potential of developing countries in relation to the dominant countries and the complexities inherent in reaching common positions within such an economically and politically diverse group of countries (Morphet 2004). This is further complicated insofar as China enjoys the privilege of its permanent seat and veto power in the UN Security Council: a power which could be, but is not necessarily, wielded in the service of other developing countries' collective positions.

There are, however, also more recent and very effective forms of developing country coordination and intervention in global institutions. This is most notable in the WTO, where China is engaged with other developing countries in the creation of focused tactical alliances and targeted engagements to reach joint positions in relation to major global issues and the major powers (Keet 2006). Over the years, Beijing representatives in the WTO have begun to criticize the 'unfair' terms required of China. The gradually more critical stand adopted by Beijing in the WTO has undoubtedly arisen in part from China's experience of the negative aspects of these terms, and growing perceptions of the national policy-restricting implications of WTO rules and regulations, and the blatant evasions and inconsistencies in the implementation of such rules by more powerful countries, above all the USA.

Thus, it is in large measure within the WTO that China has been exposed most directly to the active and collective resistance of other developing countries to the offensive geo-economic agendas of the USA and the EU. This resistance takes the form of innovative and highly skilful tactical alliance-building within various groupings of developing countries, and between such groupings, around their common interests on specific issues and their coordinated negotiating positions against their most powerful and aggressive adversaries. The best known of these developing-country groups is the Group of Twenty (G20), focusing on the distortions in global agricultural trade caused by the policies and actions of the highly industrialized countries. The G20 is led by Brazil, as its official spokesperson, but includes some key African countries, such as South Africa, and other major developing countries, such as India and China (Narlikar 2006; Narlikar and Wilkinson 2004).

The G33 group in the WTO unites some forty-six predominantly agricultural developing countries, including more than a dozen from Africa. The G33 acts as the lead group for the developing countries in the WTO context, promoting key demands for the protection of their food security and the production and livelihood needs of the millions of peasant and small-scale family farmers who constitute the majority of the populations in these countries. This group is formally led by Indonesia, but includes India and China (Bernal et al. 2004). The insistence of the G33 on their needs and their rights was probably the most important factor in the impasse and breakdown in the Doha Round in the WTO during 2008. This, in turn, was largely because the G33 managed to keep 'in check' the more narrowly focused, self-serving and potentially accommodating governments in the G20, most notably Brazil.[3]

The Non-Agricultural Market Access (NAMA 11), made up of semi-industrialized and industrializing developing countries, and led largely by South Africa, with Argentina and Venezuela, is concerned to resist the majors' demands for advanced and 'bound' (fixed) industrial tariff reductions by developing countries through the so-called Non-Agricultural Market Access (NAMA) agreement. India and Brazil are active participants in the NAMA negotiations, in which China is also becoming more vocal (Alves 2007; Keet 2006).

These 'issue-based' alliances are thus characterized by overlapping memberships, and undoubtedly entail backstage tactical coordinations. In this way, they are, together, creating significant shifts in the balance of power within the WTO. This, however, is not solely on account of the participation of major countries of the South in these groupings. The weaker and lesser developed WTO member states also come together periodically as the G90. This includes the African-Caribbean-Pacific (ACP) group, the formal UN grouping of LDCs (Least Developed Countries), mainly from Africa but also Asia and led by Bangladesh, and the group of SIVSs (Small, Island and Vulnerable States), led mainly by Mauritius; as well as other more ad hoc groups (Bernal et al. 2004; Patel 2003). The weaker, more vulnerable countries are together able to insert their specific needs – such as for Special and Differential Treatment (SDT in WTO jargon)

– into the composite developing-country platform. And they ensure, through their persistent collective interventions, that these are upheld and pursued by the larger and stronger developing countries in the formal engagements in all WTO negotiations.

In this way, the WTO negotiating alliances also provide significant opportunities with regard to Africa's more specific engagements with China. As members of the various distinctive but overlapping tactical alliances, African representatives are able to engage, separately and together, with their Chinese counterparts in detailed technical analyses, negotiation planning and political strategizing on how to promote their shared needs and to outflank the agendas of the more developed countries. They are, in the process, reaching common positions on what policies are necessary and justified for developing countries to demand of the more developed. A major question is how African governments can carry such shared understandings and agreed developmental proposals into their own policy and political engagements with China on the ground in Africa.

Furthermore, 'significant emerging countries', such as Brazil, China, India, Mexico and South Africa, are being co-opted into the global 'big boys' club. The G8 is reportedly due to be expanded into the putative G13 with the incorporation of Brazil, India, South Africa, China and Mexico. Thus, the challenge for the rest of the developing countries – and for African countries – is how to translate or transfer into their own bilateral and combined relations with China – and India and Brazil – the understandings and mutual commitments forged in their joint engagements against the major powers in the WTO and the UN, or other multilateral forums, and how to sustain and strengthen these. Conversely, how will African and other developing countries continue to engage with and influence the 'powers of the South' in the event that they are drawn into the inner circles of global powers and global power?

Playing on rivalries and tensions in a multipolar global order? The broadest and more long-term alternative perspective focuses on China's own economic and political trajectory into the future. This approach sees the inevitability of big-power political and economic interests, and related modes and modalities, playing an increasing role in China's external engagements and relations. In this perspective – whatever the political commitments and 'principles' that may currently inform China's stance and role in Africa – these could become less and less operational. Such principles as 'mutual benefit' and 'cooperation' could be eroded – directly or indirectly, explicitly or de facto – by the more hard-headed, and hard-hearted, realpolitik of a major power.

This scenario must, once again, alert African governments to the danger of creating a built-in dependence on such an international 'partner'. The lessons from Africa's post-colonial relations with Europe are highly instructive in this regard. Where Europe formerly supplied trade 'preferences', and earnest affirmations of 'partnership' between Europe and African, Caribbean and Pacific countries, through the Lomé Convention (which effectively served to sustain their commodity supply role and to reinforce the heavy trade orientation of these countries towards Europe), today it is shrugging off such 'outdated' 'partnership' relations in favour of 'reciprocal free trade' relations and other liberalization requirements located within the EU's many bilateral free trade agreements (FTAs) and in the misnamed Economic Partnership Agreements (EPAs) with the ACP countries (Stocchetti 2007).

Within this scenario Africa would also be confronted with the perspective that the growing power and ambitions of China will bring it into ever more direct and growing rivalry not only with the EU but with the current but weakening global hegemon, the USA; an opportunity opens up for gains to be made by Africa in such latter-day forms of 'inter-imperialist rivalries' if African governments have the strategic vision and political skills to take tactical advantage of these. Even if China does not rise to the status of global superpower, however – as the current superpower(s) fear – the very existence of new major emerging countries and economies, such as China, India and Brazil, provides African and other developing countries with an unprecedented range of options and alternatives to their established relations with – and dependencies on – the older developed countries. The mere fact of having many more choices in their external relations provides the governments of developing countries with some significant new or renewed leverage. This would include, for example, the deployment of explicit well-timed political warnings in the context of difficult external relations and negotiations, such as the denouncing of the EU's arm-twisting of African governments and extreme demands upon African countries in the context of the EPA negotiations conducted by President Wade of Senegal at the Africa–Europe Summit in Lisbon, in December 2007.

Similar public references have been made by South African government leaders to the fact that Brussels must bear in mind that Africa can now have recourse to alternative trade and investment partners. Such a deliberate intention and strategic aim is, in fact, a major reason why the South African government and some other African governments have rejected the EU's attempt to impose Most Favoured Nation (MFN) terms through the proposed EPAs. Such MFN terms would oblige African and other developing-country governments to confer on the EU the same preferential trade and investment terms as they might agree with other developing countries, such as China and India. Whereas – contrary to their past orientation towards and dependence upon the EU (and the USA) – many such governments in Africa and elsewhere are now aiming for the diversification of their trade and investment and other economic and technological relations. These can now be pursued through South–South relations, providing many possibilities and flexibilities within these more varied options.

It is of great potential advantage to Africa that the emergence of China – and India and Brazil – and thus the changing global economic system and power regime will end the 'simple' bipolar world of the cold war era. It will also end the attempted 'mono-polar' system of power that the USA has since been trying to impose on the rest of the world. There will henceforth be a much more complex multipolar system of economic and political power(s) that will provide many tactical opportunities and strategic alternatives for African and other weaker countries.

This, of course, requires that African governments understand the vital importance of uniting and formulating joint strategies in order to maximize their weight in counterbalancing or 'playing off' the various powers and in order to prevent themselves from being divided and played off against one another in such a much more complex emerging global scenario. The capacity – and the political will – of African governments to evaluate and act together on any of the above scenarios is the greatest challenge facing Africa.

3 | India's African relations: in the shadow of China?

Sanusha Naidu[1]

This chapter explores India's growing African footprint and the reasons behind it, particularly the extent to which Africa features in India's global ambitions. This is being shaped by the present discourse around whether India's footprint on the continent is being driven by the 'China factor' in Africa. As much as the official policy doctrine in Delhi and Beijing refutes such claims and argues that their respective engagements in Africa are driven by independent factors aligned to national interests, it is hard to ignore the similarities that underpin their Africa strategies. These can be found in their demand for resource security, trade and investment opportunities, forging of strategic partnerships, and the spirit of the Bandung Conference, African–Asian solidarity and South–South cooperation.

At the outset, it must be made clear that India is not a newcomer to Africa. On the contrary, India and Africa enjoy a long-standing historical relationship. Contacts and trade between the two sides have been noted as extending beyond British colonialism. Following independence, India saw its role in the international system as championing the struggles of anti-colonialism and anti-racism. Like China, India played a critical role in the Bandung Conference of 1955 which led to the emergence of the Non-Aligned Movement and used the occasion to promote and strengthen Asian–African solidarity.

But it was during the cold war that relations embraced deepening political solidarity. Africa was to have a significant role in Prime Minister Nehru's vision of creating a just international order. With India pushing for the independence of African states from colonial domination, India and Africa seemed likely to become strategic allies in the cold war, aided by the assumption that the large Indian diaspora would be a significant factor. Yet India's role on the African continent remained marginal. India's engagement with Africa was also motivated by the cold war polemics and the border dispute with China in 1962. Confronted with Africa's mixed reaction to the conflict, New Delhi was forced to realize that it 'did not have the strong ally it had hoped for in Africa and therefore actively worked towards countering Chinese penetration in Africa' (Serpa 1994: 187).

This led to the launch of Indian Technical and Economic Cooperation (ITEC). ITEC emerged as a result of a meeting in 1963 convened by the Indian government's heads of its trade missions from Africa and West Africa to examine ways to improve economic and technical cooperation with the continent. ITEC remains to this day an integral component of India's Development Initiative, delivering development assistance to Africa and elsewhere.

While China suffered from its own cold war polemic with Moscow vis-à-vis Africa, India's stance appeared to be more muted, which led to selective engagements with the continent during the 1970s and 1980s. In principle, however, India's international stance was geared towards promoting greater South–South cooperation and a greater voice for itself. But with the end of the cold war, India's foreign policy also had to be revisited and shaped to take into account the new impulses in the global arena.

Post-cold war relations: a rediscovery

For much of the cold war India's own regional and domestic pressures made it inward looking. With economic liberalization in the 1990s, however, India's policy-makers realized the importance of a foreign policy that resonated with its economic ambitions. Opening up to overseas investment also meant strengthening external relations that could help to realize its political and economic potential.

Like China's, India's post-cold-war foreign policy has been aligned with the principles of non-alignment and South–South cooperation. Reacting against the unilateral character of the post-cold-war international order, India has pushed for a multilateral world order. And, just as in the past, relations with Africa and the South are now based on shared mutual interests in fighting against the inequities of the global order. This time these are directed against underdevelopment and poverty as a result of an unbalanced global economic system, but are also aimed at the economic and developmental concerns of 'finding export markets, and attracting foreign capital and technological know-how' (S. K. Singh 2007b: 10).

Using the historical platform as a way to consolidate contemporary relations with Africa, India's current foreign policy relations with the continent are about reinventing and rejuvenating the old relationship. While China can make the claim that it has never enslaved or colonized Africa, India can also premise its relationship with the continent on the same moral high ground. According to official documentation, India's contemporary Africa policy is aligned with a confluence of interests relating to justice in the global order, aimed at increasing the leverage and influence of their respective global positions and promoting a new international order.

Broadening economic horizons: the quest for energy security

J. Peter Pham argues that the unprecedented concern with China's deepening involvement across the continent has enabled India's growing interest in Africa to go unnoticed. According to Pham, India's Africa strategy is based on the 'quest for resources, business opportunities, diplomatic initiatives and strategic partnerships', which is seen in the emerging trade, investments and developmental assistance relations that Delhi is crafting with African countries (Pham 2007).

Oil and gas are India's overriding preoccupation in achieving energy security. With only 0.4 per cent of the world's proven oil reserves and no significant oil discoveries since the 1970s, India's oil needs have to be sourced externally. Future projections are that by 2030 India will become the world's third-largest consumer of energy, ahead of Japan and Russia (Madan 2006). Presently India imports about 75 per cent of the oil it needs, and its dependence is projected to rise to over 90 per cent by 2020.

To achieve a sustained growth rate of 8 per cent until 2031/32 India's primary energy supply must be three to four times its 2003/04 levels, while its electricity capacity must increase by five to six times (Sharma and Mahajan 2007). With Delhi currently relying on the Middle East for most of its oil needs, and given the volatility of the region and the dominance of the USA therein, 'it is understandable that India would seek an alternative supply of energy in the burgeoning African sector' (Pham 2007) through 'an integrated set of policies to balance foreign policy, economic, environmental, and social issues with the rising demand for energy' (Madan 2006). As a result the Indian government has embarked on a policy of energy diplomacy. And to this end, India's energy footprint in Africa is becoming increasingly apparent.

The Indian state-owned Oil and Natural Gas Corporation (ONGC) has in recent years managed to secure exploration contracts and other related energy projects in the continent through its international division, ONGC Videsh (OVL) (see Table 3.1).

In 2005 OVL entered into a joint venture with LN Mittal Steel (now Arcelor Mittal), the world's largest steel multinational corporation, to form ONGC Mittal Energy Ltd (OMEL). OMEL entered into a US$6 billion infrastructure deal with Nigeria in exchange for two offshore acreages and oil exploration rights. Other OVL activities in Africa include:

- a 23.5 per cent interest in Côte d'Ivoire's offshore block CI-112;
- a 49 per cent participating interest in two onshore oil exploration blocks in Libya;
- a concession agreement to explore for oil in Egypt's North Ramadan Block;
- identified oil and gas properties in Gabon with potential investments of over US$500 million.

At the same time, ONGC is also on the hunt to acquire or buy equity stakes in foreign oil companies' projects in Africa and elsewhere. Given that it is India's principal energy company and that India is seeking long-term energy security, ONGC has embarked upon a massive overseas drive. Since 2003 the state-owned

TABLE 3.1 ONGC investments in Africa

Country	Indian company	Type of investment	Size of investment
Nigeria	Oil and Natural Gas Corporation (ONGC)	Oil pipeline	Not stated (25% stake in the in the Greater Nile Petroleum Operating Company (GNPOC) project
Sudan	ONGC	Oil production	Not stated (24% share in Block 5A & 24% share in Block 5B)
Sudan	ONGC	Oil refinery	US$1.2 billion
Sudan	ONGC	Multi-product export pipeline	US$200 million
Sudan	ONGC	Oil pipeline (part of the Greater Nile Petro- leum Operating Co.)	US$750 million

Source: Various newspaper articles

enterprise (SOE) has invested 'as much as US$3 billion in overseas exploration and energy projects' (Ganguly 2007: 2). But this has proved difficult with the likes of Chinese SOEs such as CNOOC, Sinopec and CNPC standing in its shadow and having state backing to sweeten most of the deals, with large concessional lending to upgrade and rehabilitate infrastructure. The aborted 2003/04 deal with Royal Dutch Shell to acquire 50 per cent of their equity in one of Angola's offshore oil blocks for US$600 million is a case in point where the Chinese were able to outbid the Indians with their state-backed US$2–3 billion oil deal (Sethuraman 2005).

But not all the blame should be apportioned to China's economic realism. A large part of the problem is also to be found in the bureaucratic nature of the Indian state when it comes to expediting and signing off on investments. In 2005/06 the Indian cabinet rejected a US$2 billion oil exploration bid that the ONGC had made for one of Nigeria's offshore blocks as being too risky. A successful bid for the block, which was subsequently part of the Akpo block, was rumoured to have been made by the Chinese – although, given the uncertainty regarding the nature of the contracts awarded by President Obasanjo before leaving office, it is not clear whether or not the Chinese contract is under review. Both examples reflect the fact that if ONGC is to become a significant actor in Africa's energy sector there needs to be more state backing from New Delhi. Otherwise bureaucratic inertia will hamper the ability of SOEs like ONGC to prevail over the Chinese and other actors, in Africa and elsewhere.

Having said this, it will be interesting to monitor whether the national elec-tions in India in 2009 will lead to greater economic liberalization for domestic policy and foreign economic engagements. The ruling coalition, the United Progressive Alliance, which originally included the two communist parties of India, has not been an easy berth for the dominant partner, the Congress Party, in furthering its economic liberalization programme. Following the controversial civilian nuclear deal, the Communist Party of India and the Communist Party of India (Marxist) have subsequently withdrawn from the alliance because of their ideological objections to it. Their strong ideological leanings and political strategies have made India's privatization of large-scale state-owned enterprises difficult to implement. This is something that will need to be evaluated if the Indian government wants to ensure that it is able to access the energy it needs to meet domestic demand and, more so, if ONGC is to strengthen its presence in international markets.

Nevertheless, India's diversification of energy sources shows that the government is moving towards creating an energy panel that will deliberate on ways of tapping into and consolidating India's oil interests in African countries that are becoming important suppliers (Dutta 2007). This was demonstrated in June 2007 when Indian foreign minister Anand Sharma led a delegation to Angola. During the meeting both sides expressed an interest in signing accords in the areas of oil, geology and mining, agriculture, health, education and tourism. Regarding oil prospects, India saw great possibilities in Angola as a supplier, and there was also talk of New Delhi engaging in the construction of an oil refinery.

TABLE 3.2 Other oil companies in Africa

Country	Indian company	Type of investment	Size of investment
Côte d'Ivoire	Unknown (various companies acting as a consortium)	Oil prospecting	US$1 billion
Nigeria	National Thermal Power Corporation (NTPC)	Liquefied natural gas (LNG)	US$1.7 billion
Nigeria	Indian Oil Corporation (IOC)	Oil refinery	US$3.5 billion
Nigeria	IOC	LNG plant and oil refinery	US$2–4 billion (proposed)
Sudan	Videocon Group	Oil prospecting	US$100 million (76% stake)

Source: Various newspaper articles

The impression is that Indian oil companies are playing catch-up with their Chinese counterparts and, like the Chinese, following a strategy of overseas equity acquisitions to reduce dependence on major oil companies from the developed countries as well as limit exposure to price volatility on the open market.

While the official Indian view tends to downplay the fact that it is competing with China for oil acreage in Africa and elsewhere, Delhi has recently lost important oil contracts to China.[2] To this end the Indian administration is seen as 'moving to put in place an energy panel on the lines of the cabinet committee on security to see how it can counter Beijing's policy of using financial and military aid to secure oilfields in Latin America and Africa' (Dutta 2007).

Trade and investment

Even though it may appear that 'India is sleepwalking in Africa', especially in terms of its trade partnerships, and that its trade with Africa is still a fraction of China's, the signs are that Delhi is awakening to the reality that Africa is a strategic partner/market and a priority in its global commercial expansion. India–Africa trade jumped from US$967 million in 1991 to approximately US$25 billion in 2007.

Table 3.3 shows that Indian exports to the continent increased from US$393.3 million in 1990/91 to over US$10 billion in 2006/07. During the same period Indian imports from Africa increased from US$573 million to over US$14 billion. The increase in Indian exports to Africa and Indian imports from Africa is significant. Africa's share of India's total exports rose from 2.2 per cent in 1990/91 to 8.1 per cent in 2006/07, while the concomitant rise in the continent's share of India's total imports almost doubled from 2.4 per cent to 7.7 per cent during the same period. According to Ahmed, in five years, 'India's exports to Africa grew by 120 per cent, compared to 76 per cent export growth with the world' (Ahmed 2006).

TABLE 3.3 India's trade with Africa (US$ million)

	1990/91	2003/04	2004/05	2005/06	2006/07*
Exports	393.6	3,861.7	5,578.4	7,013.6	10,255.7
Imports	573.4	3,202.1	4,006.4	4,878.8	14,722.8
Total trade	967.0	7,063.8	9,584.8	11,892.4	24,978.5

Note: * Imports for 2006/07 include oil receipts
Source: Directorate General of Commercial Intelligence & Statistics (DGCIS), Ministry of Commerce and Industry (MOCI), quoted in Export-Import Bank of India, Quarterly Publication (vol. XXII, issue 1, March 2008)

Indian exports to Africa consist mainly of manufactured items (49 per cent), chemical products (11 per cent) and machinery and transport equipment (10 per cent). In terms of the main export partners, South Africa features prominently, with exports totalling more than US$2 billion for the period 2006/07 and accounting for 22 per cent of total exports to Africa. This was followed by Kenya with US$1.3 billion, Nigeria at US$901 million, Egypt at US$739 million and Mauritius with US$539 million (Ahmed 2006).

On the other hand, Indian imports from Africa are mainly primary goods, with oil accounting for the largest share, followed by gold and other mineral commodities. For the period 2006/07 Nigeria was India's dominant import partner, accounting for US$7 billion or 47.6 per cent of total imports from Africa. This was followed by South Africa at US$2.4 billion, Egypt at US$1.7 billion, Algeria at US$749 million and Morocco at US$491 million.

Political and economic drivers

India's trade relationship with Africa is being promoted through various political and economic initiatives. While in the 1990s, when still undergoing its economic reform process, the Indian government was 'closing down missions in Africa as an economic measure, today it has twenty-five embassies or high commissions on the continent with four others scheduled to open over the next few years' (Pham 2007). The Indian Ministry of External Affairs has scaled up its diplomatic initiatives by creating three joint secretaries to manage the three regional divisions covering the continent, complemented by the Confederation of Indian Industries (CII) and the Export-Import (EXIM) Bank of India.

India–Africa Partnership Project Through the EXIM Bank, the Indian government has also stepped up its trade and investment relations with the continent as well as boosting its products in the African market. In November 2005 the EXIM Bank, together with the CII, organized a Conclave on India–Africa Partnership Project entitled 'Expanding Horizons', aimed at deepening economic ties with the continent. Approximately 160 delegates came from thirty-two African countries, and over seventy projects, estimated at more than US$5 billion, were discussed. This was followed by another meeting, which took place in October 2006, where over 300 African participants and 375 Indian business people attended and discussed over 300 projects worth US$17 billion. Among the 350-member African delegation visiting the 2006 Conclave meeting, 'Togo topped the list of investment seekers requesting US$4.6 billion', followed by 'South Africa's US$4 billion request, Ghana's US$3.7 billion, and Nigeria's US$2.6 billion (Baldauf 2006). In 2007 the Conclave Partnership Project was extended to three regional meetings that took place in Côte d'Ivoire, Mozambique and Uganda – countries chosen as important gateways into their respective regions.

From 19 to 21 March 2008, another Conclave was hosted in Delhi, drawing around five hundred delegates, including government officials from over twenty African countries. The meeting discussed over 130 projects to the value of over US$10 billion. A number of deals were signed in areas of mutual interest, including a memorandum of understanding between the Ethiopian Leather Industries Association (ELISA) and the CII to export high-quality Ethiopian leather to India. India's EXIM Bank also extended a US$30 million credit line to the African Export-Import Bank (Afreximbank) to finance India's exports to the latter's members. This meeting set the platform for India's first African summit, hosted from 8 to 9 April 2008 in the Indian capital.

Focus Africa programme The Focus Africa programme was launched as part of the EXIM Bank 2002–07 strategy. Through this programme the Indian government provides financial assistance to various trade promotion organizations, export promotion councils and umbrella trade associations in the form of Market Development Assistance. So far the total operative lines of credit extended to sub-Saharan Africa by the EXIM Bank amount to over US$550 million, targeting regional blocs like the Economic Community of West African States (ECOWAS) and the Common Market for Eastern and Southern Africa (COMESA). 'In May 2006 EIBI [EXIM Bank of India] extended US$250 million lines of credit to the ECOWAS Bank for Investment and Development, to finance Indian exports to ECOWAS member states.'[3]

The Indian government has also embarked on a set of initiatives to enhance its economic and political cooperation with Africa. These include:

- a US$200 million line of credit to NEPAD (the New Partnership for Africa's Development) under the India–Africa Fund designed to promote African economic integration;
- a US$500 million line of credit for the Techno-Economic Approach for Africa–India movement (Team 9), which is an initiative with eight francophone countries;[4]
- a US$1 billion investment in a joint venture with the African Union to build a Pan-African e-Network to provide telemedicine and tele-education through integrated satellite, fibre and wireless connectivity.[5]

The footprint of Indian companies Indian companies are also beginning to make significant strides in terms of Africa's non-oil resources. In Zambia Vendanta Resources has a US$750 million copper-mining investment; in Liberia and Nigeria Arcelor Mittal has a US$900 million management project for iron ore reserves and a US$30 million steel refinery respectively (the latter with an 80 per cent stake in the Nigeria-based Delta Steel Company).

The Tata Group has the most extensive presence in the continent. Operating in Ghana, Mozambique, Malawi, Namibia, South Africa, Tanzania and Uganda, the group claims to employ over seven hundred people in Africa. According to the group's profile, its activities range from infrastructure development, energy and hospitality services to financial, communication and automotive outputs. Some recent investments made by the company include: the US$800 million renovation of the Taj Pamodji Hotel in Lusaka; a vehicle assembly plant at

Box 3.1 The India–Africa Summit of April 2008: commitments made by India

- Increasing financial credits from about US$2 billion over the previous five years to US$5.4 billion over a similar period.

- Investing US$500 million in development projects across the continent over the next five years.

- Establishing an India–Africa peace corps aimed at development, especially in the area of public health.

- Allowing duty-free imports and preferential market access for primary and finished products, including cotton, cocoa, aluminium ores, copper ores, cashew nuts, cane sugar, clothing, fish fillets and gem diamonds from thirty-four least developed countries in Africa.

- Doubling trade from US$25 billion to US$50 billion by 2011.

- Increasing the number of scholarships and technical training programmes for African students and technocrats.

- Promoting the development of small- and medium-scale enterprises to help effect industrialization in African countries.

- Sharing experiences and capacity-building on policy and regulatory frameworks in the financial sector, including the microfinance sector.

- Supporting Africa's regional integration programme through the provision of financial support on mutually agreed integration projects carried out by the AU and the regional communities.

- Enhancing information and communications technology (ICT), science and technology, research and development, and trade through technical assistance and capacity-building programmes.

Source: 'Delhi Declaration on India–Africa Summit', 8–9 April 2008

Ndola in Zambia; a US$108 million high-carbon ferrochrome plant at Richards Bay in KwaZulu Natal, South Africa; and the construction of a US$12 million instant-coffee processing plant in Uganda.

Indian companies have also begun to invest in Africa's infrastructure as a way of cementing their commercial and commodity presence in the continent. For example, Rites and Ircon, the two large state-owned infrastructure and engineering companies, have been making inroads in Africa's rail and road development sector through projects and concessions for several years:

> Rites has refurbished and leased locomotives in Sudan and Tanzania, whilst supplying technical assistance to rail authorities in Kenya and Mozambique. Rites is also involved in design and construction of roads in Uganda and Ethiopia and

TABLE 3.4 Presence of Tata in Africa 1991–2006

Country	Year of entry	Sectors
Ghana	1998	Automotive, marketing steel products, mining
Malawi		Tata Zambia regional office
Mozambique	1991	Automotive marketing, mining
Senegal		Tata Zambia regional office
South Africa	1994	Automobiles, steel, chemicals, mining products, power, information technology (IT) and related services
Tanzania	1994	Commercial vehicles, industrial chemicals, textiles, food and beverages, pharmaceuticals
Uganda	1994	Vehicle sales and after-sales, healthcare products
Zambia	1977	Automobiles, food products, textiles, hospitality, engineering and general trading.
Zimbabwe	1989	Vehicle sales and after-sales
Kenya	2006	Automotive
Nigeria	2006	Automotive

Source: Compiled by Arno Negpen, Research Analyst, Centre for Chinese Studies, Stellenbosch University

is presently managing a railway concession in Tanzania. Ircon has constructed railways in Algeria and (currently) in Mozambique, and has also been active in the rail sectors in Sudan, Nigeria and Zambia. (Bonnet 2005)

Indian companies are also queuing up to take advantage of Africa's significant investments in power transmission projects. Companies like Kalapataru Power Transmission Ltd already have a presence in Zambia, and Kalapataru is also expecting to acquire a major contract worth US$35 million in Algeria. According to the company's director, Africa is an area for rich pickings: 'All these countries are rich in resources such as oil, gas and metals. Therefore when global prices of the resources increase, these countries make more money. Their investment in infrastructure projects has also increased exponentially ...' (Wadke 2007). KEC International Ltd is another transmission company that has a presence in Algeria, Tunisia, Libya, Kenya, Zambia, Nigeria, Ethiopia and Ghana.

The presence of Indian companies in Africa is surely going to increase in the future. Between 2002 and 2005 Indian firms topped the list of greenfield FDI (foreign direct investment) projects in Africa at forty-eight compared to thirty-two from China (UNCTAD 2007a). This indication, underpinned by the increasing global presence of Indian firms, signals that India is becoming a significant player in the African market. With India being one of the twenty-four non-African members of the African Development Bank, this growth is also

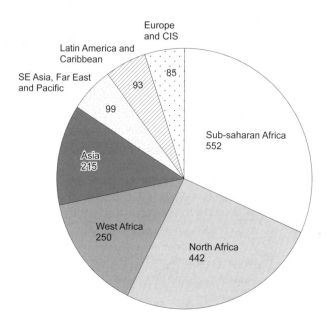

FIGURE 3.1 India's active lines of credit as of March 2006 (US$ million)
Source: Export-Import Bank of India, Annual Report, 2005/06

being propelled by the recent green light given to Indian firms to bid for US$4.6 billion set aside by the bank for infrastructural development projects.

Concessional finance is another factor boosting India's corporate presence in Africa. As of March 2006, India's total active lines of credit were valued at US$1,739 billion. Of this US$552 million was directed to the sub-Saharan African region, which constituted 32 per cent, followed by North Africa to the value of US$442 million, or 25 per cent of Delhi's global share (Figure 3.1). India had fifty-two operational lines of credit totalling US$2 billion in more than thirty African countries in March 2008 (Eximius: Export Advantage 2008). This will surely assist in doubling India's trade with Africa over the next five years.

Development assistance

Apart from the business investments, India has become a significant development partner to the continent. India's assistance to Africa plays to the strengths of its competitive advantage in areas such as infrastructure, pharmaceuticals, health, IT and automotive industries. For the period 1999–2005, the Ministry of External Affairs' aid to Africa was US$12 billion, which constituted only 3 per cent of Indian's total aid budget. The grant component is expected to increase to US$5.4 billion between 2007 and 2012. The Indian Technical and Economic Cooperation (ITEC) programme as well as the Special Commonwealth African Assistance Programme (SCAAP) develop capacity through training, study tours, project assistance and expertise to a select number of African countries. ITEC has provided more than US$1 billion worth of technical assistance and training of personnel. Moreover, in 2005 India became the first Asian country to become a full member of the African Capacity Building Foundation (ACBF), and pledged US$1 million towards the foundation's sustainable development and poverty alleviation capacity-building initiative.

Since independence India has been a significant contributor to the UN's global peacekeeping missions. Dating back to the UN's first mission in the Congo in 1960, India has retained its reputation of deploying 'forces' to all UN peacekeeping operations in Africa. According to Singh, India is currently the third-largest contributor of peacekeepers to the continent and sent the largest contingent of troops (3,500) to the mission to the Democratic Republic of Congo (DRC).[6] The 1,400-strong Indian military contingent constitutes the largest contribution to the UN mission in Ethiopia and Eritrea. In total more than 9,300 Indian peacekeepers are deployed in UN peacekeeping missions on the continent (S. K. Singh 2007a: 76).

Apart from providing peacekeepers India has also supplied the peacekeeping missions with helicopters and medical and communication equipment. 'India's participation in [UN Peacekeeping Operations, UNPKO] in Africa demonstrates its geo-strategic interests in [the] stability and well-being of the newly independent states of Africa' (ibid.: 79). Also, owing to China's increasing participation in UN peacekeeping in Africa, motivated by the desire to promote itself as a significant global player, and as well as China being a 'competitor in trade and energy in Africa', India keeps up its commitment and contribution. India's historical ties with Africa as well as its contributions to UNPKO give India a chance to promote itself as an emerging significant political and economic actor committed to peace and stability in the international arena (ibid.: 82).

In addition, given India's comparative advantage in the pharmaceutical sector, industry stakeholders and companies are looking towards the continent as an important sphere for collaborative exchanges. Considering the continent's battle with the HIV/AIDS pandemic and other infectious diseases, including malaria, linkages with Indian pharmaceutical companies will be critical in finding a vaccine and other medical breakthroughs in combating such illnesses.

In China's shadow?

Disaggregating India's Africa policy remains a complex exercise given that the relationship has been masked by the China factor. While India's Africa policy seems to mirror much of what China's Africa policy is, the nuances of its political and economic engagements suggest that there may be certain departures in its policy application. Chris Alden argues that China's contemporary relations with Africa are driven by four factors: resource security; the need for new markets and investment opportunities; symbolic diplomacy, development assistance and cooperation; and forging strategic partnerships (Alden 2005). It would appear that

India's strategy is not that different. And like the Chinese, India is aware that it needs to acquire key energy and commodity assets if it is to lessen its dependence and limit the risk on the open market. Therefore plying African governments with concessional loans and other economic incentives tied to its development assistance not only provides market traction for Indian exports but also enables India to gain leverage through what has been identified as a critical weakness in the continent – infrastructure investments. And India is rather open about the rationale that underpins its development assistance.

Unlike the West, and China to a lesser extent, which tend to shy away from the fact 'that their development co-operation might be a geo-strategic bargaining tool, the Indian Government explicitly emphasises that the goal of its development work is to further Indian interests abroad and to promote its own economic situation' (Jobelius 2007). The 2008 India–Africa Summit provides the platform for institutionalizing the engagement while the Conclave meetings formalize the economic diplomacy of this footprint.

While some may argue that this signifies India riding China's tail in Africa, Delhi would like to break out of Beijing's shadow by highlighting that it seeks to manage its engagement with Africa differently. This was illustrated at the 2008 India–Africa Summit where India's development-centric approach won praise from the African participants, with African delegates emphasizing that India should be a stakeholder and not a shareholder in the continent's development. At the same time India's business linkages are aimed more at horizontal trajectories with regional trade blocs like COMESA, the Southern African Development Community (SADC) and ECOWAS (Chaturyedi and Mohanty 2007). This reflects more alignment with continental regional trade processes as opposed to China's bilateral trade focus.

In addition Delhi has taken an aggressive stance regarding the successful resolution of the World Trade Organization (WTO) Doha Development Round. Pushing for more equity in trade and market access, notwithstanding some dismantling of agricultural subsidies in the North and the sensitivities of Non-Agricultural Market Access (NAMA), highlights the fact that India is flexing its muscles on critical issues affecting Africa and the South more generally. The Indian government has also voiced its frustrations over the exclusivity of the G8 and is now contemplating initiating a similar grouping to boost the strength of the South.

This is further supplemented by the India, Brazil, South Africa (IBSA) trilateral group, which demonstrates commitment to promoting a South–South trading market. Not only does IBSA augment the economic strength of its partners but it also opens a broader market for African producers to penetrate, given that the combined IBSA market represents a consumer base of over one billion people. To this end, India has also expressed a commitment to enabling more African products to enter its market duty free. This signals a leadership role for

India in promoting South–South cooperation through the G20 and alignment to the G90 of least developed countries. The recent hosting of the International Conference on 'India–Africa Cooperation in Industry, Trade and Investment' by the United Nations Industrial Development Organization in collaboration with the Indian government reflects New Delhi's seriousness in expanding this relationship beyond mercantilism. Indeed, some believe that India's experience in the development of the small and medium enterprise (SME) sector, as well as promotion of the private sector, could offer important lessons to Africa.

Emboldened by its democratic tradition, India's behaviour in the continent is less confrontational than that of China. This, indeed, enables India to take the moral high ground when it comes to advocating good governance and pushing the democratic agenda in Africa, and bodes well for Delhi in its relations with the West. Moreover, with India being increasingly seen as a strategic partner in Asia by the USA, this could lead to positive outcomes for it in its African relations, particularly African support for its candidature for a permanent seat on the reformed UN Security Council.

Notwithstanding the above, India's current African engagement should be viewed in relation to the neoliberal nature of the contemporary global economic system. Since the end of the cold war markets have become more liberalized, increasingly interdependent and much more fluid. With the ascendancy of the neoliberal philosophy more countries are reorienting their macroeconomic policies to reflect this orthodoxy. In this context it could be argued that India's rise and its increasing search for and presence in overseas markets dovetails with the neoliberal character of the global economy, and that Delhi's behaviour is a response to what has become an accepted norm of the current international system, namely embedded capitalism underpinned by realpolitik.

Given this state of affairs it is difficult to presume that India will not behave according to its national interests, which will, at times, be in direct or indirect competition with those of China and other actors in Africa. There are several areas where this is felt across the continent. The most obvious one is resource security. At the same time India will want to protect its economic interests and advance its comparative advantage in sectors where it does have a competitive edge over Beijing and other traditional and emerging powers. This is already evident in Africa's telecommunication sector. The launch of the Pan-African e-Network reflects the first step towards strengthening the ICT partnership before losing out to the Chinese, designed perhaps to enable India's telecom giants to become industry-shapers in the continent. But such manoeuvrings also open up spaces for strategic competition between Chinese and Indian corporations as they move towards consolidating their presence in African economies. The recent Reliance Communication bid for South Africa's mobile telephone network points to this, since it was rumoured a few years ago that China Mobile was attempting to make a similar offer to buy out the company.

The Indian Ocean Rim (IOR) best illustrates how India perceives China in its near neighbourhood. Whereas India's engagement with the continental hinterland reflects more of a subtle approach and the softer issues that Delhi considers as its comparative advantage, such as capacity-building in training, education, SME development and human resources, there is a more hard-line geostrategic focus when it comes to the IOR simply because it represents a strategic political and economic neighbourhood from which Delhi is able to penetrate African economies through the East African region. The region is also significant because of India's 2004 Maritime Doctrine, which enables it to conduct naval and security exercises in the region with its Indian Ocean partners. In short the IOR is an important commercial shipping lane for Indian exports to and imports from Africa.

Considering the IOR as its backyard, New Delhi has become increasingly aware of China's penetration of this region through its engagements with Mauritius, where it intends to set up its trade Special Economic Zone to gain access to COMESA, as well as competing with China in the Seychelles. As such, 'Chinese and Pakistani efforts in the African Indian Ocean Rim are closely monitored by India and concerns about Chinese expansionism have resulted in India looking to deepen its defense and commercial engagement with the Seychelles, Madagascar, Mauritius and Mozambique' (Vines and Orutimeka 2008: 12).

Even though China seems to have a greater share of and leverage in the African market than India does, India's future role in the continent should not be dismissed. Unlike China's global image, India's is not overshadowed or marred by negative reporting. Where China has to battle with criticism levelled against its policy of non-interference and respect for sovereignty when it comes to its commercial interests in terms of human right issues and relations with less than democratic governments in the continent (particularly Sudan), such denigration is less muted in the Indian context. This is despite the fact that India's national oil company, ONGC, is part of the Greater Nile Oil Project consortium, together with China National Petroleum Corporation (CNPC) and Malaysia's PETRONAS in Sudan.

Conclusions

While much of current scholarship has been preoccupied with China's deepening presence in Africa and the threat this poses to Western interests in the continent, the debates have failed to recognize that India is also becoming an important partner to African countries. For the moment India is seen as a junior or negligible player in Africa, but Delhi's role in the Great Game should not be treated lightly just because of its muted presence and the fact that it shares the same democratic traditions as Western powers. Like most emerging Great Powers, India is on the hunt to satisfy its resource needs, which are vital to its industrialization and modernization. Attempts to contain the 'China Challenge' overlook the fact that a new competition in Africa is being set in motion between China and India on the one hand and, more significantly, between emerging Asian rivals on the other hand, as other Asian countries enter the fray. And India is going to be a harder partner to contain, considering that Delhi represents what the West would like China to be.

Therefore, an effective partnership between Delhi and Africa will ultimately depend on how African governments structure their relations with India and how much of this is channelled through the multilateral process of the African Union and NEPAD. This means candid and robust discussions on what Africa's developmental needs are, how industrial relations should be conducted, greater implementation of investment codes of conduct and a regulatory environment, more skills-oriented programmes to improve the technical expertise of the local labour force, more transparency for Africa's public about the deals that are being negotiated, and fewer debt-risky loans. If Africa fails to recognize that the current mantra of the world today is 'the business of business is business', then it will definitely reinforce its image of being a beggar.

PART TWO

China and India's relations with Africa: a historical perspective

4 | China's development cooperation with Africa: historical and cultural perspectives

Liu Haifang

Although interest in China–Africa relations has grown in recent years, little research exists on the objectives of Chinese diplomacy towards Africa and the particular role assigned to development cooperation, including cultural diplomacy, as an instrument of foreign policy (DfID 2008). This chapter seeks to stimulate research on the aims and objectives of Chinese development co-operation with Africa, using historical and cultural perspectives, and to further demonstrate how the underlying assumptions and practice of Chinese foreign policy towards Africa have changed over the years.

Throughout the cold war period, China tried to distinguish its aid and political cooperation with Africa and the rest of the developing world from that practised by the Soviet Union and the dominant Western countries. Accordingly, the aim of Chinese development cooperation was to provide diplomatic and technical support to oppressed people in the South who were struggling against common ills, such as imperialism, and for the common goals of overcoming poverty and underdevelopment (G. T. Yu 1988b: 850). The language of solidarity and mutual respect was strongly underscored in official communiqués and documents.

The second aim of China's foreign policy towards Africa in the early 1960s was very much motivated by its need to secure international recognition as the sole legitimate government with respect to Taiwan, which Beijing regarded as an inseparable province of China (Hughes 2006). This was particularly important in light of the fact that Taiwan was making major inroads in securing the support and recognition of many newly independent African countries in exchange for substantial economic aid and investment (Taylor 2002a; Rawnsley 2000). As a result of its successful outreach to newly independent African countries, Taiwan had already secured the support of nineteen African countries by 1963, as opposed to thirteen for China, and the majority of these countries voted in favour of 'Chinese representation' of Taiwan at the General Assembly (Payne and Veney 2001; Wei Liang-Tsai (1982). Thus, from 1964 onwards, China vigorously attempted to lure African countries away from Taiwan, using aid and political support, in order to secure African support at the United Nations, and so as to counter Soviet and American expansionism in Africa.[1] But as China embraced the ideology of globalization and economic reform from the 1980s onwards, its foreign policy became more and more guided by economic rather than ideological factors, although the rhetoric of solidarity, non-interference and win-win partnership still prevails.

Cultural cooperation: to make friends first

With regard to all Asian, African and Latin American countries, the external cultural policy of the Chinese government was 'to make friends first, then to reinforce understanding, and finally to establish official relations naturally' (People's Republic of China 1990: 406).[2] At the 1955 Afro-Asian Bandung Conference, Zhou Enlai pointed out that African and Asian countries needed to develop economic and cultural cooperation with each other in order to overcome the historical legacies of imperialism and colonialism (Enfan 1997). His call for cultural cooperation was written into the final communiqué of the Bandung Conference. These cultural exchange initiatives prepared the way for the establishment of formal relations between China and an increasing number of newly independent African countries in subsequent decades (Miu Kaijin 2006: 70).

Most forms of cultural initiatives taken by China since the 1950s remain, while new forms have emerged to complement the new foreign policy goals of economic exchange between China and Africa (Liu 2006). The Chinese government currently allots 5–6 million Chinese yuan (CNY) every year for cultural diplomacy initiatives with African countries.[3] This sum is normally divided into two parts: the first is for people-to-people exchange (including cultural officials, performing troupes, academic exchanges, artists and performers), the second (approximately 1–1.5 million CNY) is used for cultural facilities or purchase of materials and equipment, such as books, DVD players and stereo systems.

While some Western scholars have described China's cultural diplomacy as a 'charm offensive' (Kurlantzick 2007), Chinese scholars seem to prefer to identify it as 'soft power' with a strong traditional cultural background (X. Yu 2007). In this context, the goal of Chinese development cooperation is not explained in terms of the conventional notion of 'poverty reduction', but of promoting China as a friend of developing countries through subtle mobilization of cultural norms and expressions that privilege solidarity and friendship over narrow economic interests (FOCAC 2003). It is therefore important to examine the shifting trajectories of Chinese foreign policy towards Africa through a Chinese cultural prism.

The evolution of Sino-African development cooperation, 1955–79

Although China is being identified as an 'emerging donor' in the current discourse about its growing global role, China has never left Africa (McCormick 2008; DfID 2008). In fact, China started its aid to Africa at more or less the same time that Western aid programmes started in the early 1950s. To be precise, China's aid to Africa and other developing countries started after the Bandung Conference of 1955. The Five Guiding Principles of Chinese aid, set out by

Premier Zhou Enlai during the India–China bilateral negotiations, were to be the mantra that guided relations with Africa.[4] These principles include:

- mutual respect for sovereignty and territorial integrity;
- mutual non-aggression;
- non-interference in each other's internal affairs;
- equality and mutual benefits;
- peaceful coexistence.

These principles have stood the test of time and very much underpin current Chinese foreign and aid policy towards African countries. China not only supported African liberation movements but also provided a great deal of economic assistance on a grant basis despite the fact that China itself was a struggling developing country with few resources (Xie Yixian 1998). Between 1973 and 1979, for example, aid to Africa amounted to 6.92 per cent of China's GDP annually, and forty-four African countries had signed economic and technical cooperation protocols with China (Shi Lin 1989). Despite increasing allocation of aid to Africa during this period, China avoided the term 'aid' in its cooperation with Africa; instead Chinese officials prefer to use the language of solidarity and friendship – a situation quite different from the often paternalistic Western aid language of poverty reduction and democratization.

The original Five Guiding Principles were later replaced by China's 'Eight Principles of Economic and Technical Aid', which Premier Zhou Enlai announced on 15 January 1964 during his visit to fourteen African countries. The additional guiding principles emphasize that: Chinese technical assistance should build local capacities, and Chinese experts working in Africa should have the same standard of living as the local experts; economic cooperation should promote self-reliance and not dependency; and respect for the recipient's sovereignty should mean imposing no 'political or economic conditions' on recipient governments.[5] Thus, by 1965, seventeen of the thirty-eight African states had recognized China. Unfortunately, the campaign by the Chinese authorities to lure more African countries away from Taiwan was to be interrupted by the outbreak of the Cultural Revolution in 1966, a situation that Taiwan was able to exploit successfully.

In the early 1970s, however, China began an aggressive policy to reclaim ground lost in its attempt to establish diplomatic relations with African countries. More aid to African countries, continued support to liberation movements and an active diplomatic strategy in support of African and Third World efforts at the United Nations became central to Chinese foreign policy. As a result of these diplomatic efforts, the number of African countries recognizing China grew to thirty-seven by the early 1970s. Between 1970 and 1975, some sixteen African heads of states visited China. At the same time, Chinese aid to Africa grew from a low of US$428 million in 1966 to nearly US$1.9 billion in 1977 (US Central Intelligence Agency 1978).

The aggressive diplomatic strategy that China adopted from 1964 onwards was finally to result in major political gains. Thus in 1971 China finally secured a seat at the United Nations with the support of twenty-six African states. The number of African countries recognizing Taiwan also began to drop as the numbers recognizing China began to grow. Moreover, with the death of Mao Zedong and the subsequent policy shift towards economic modernization under the leadership of Deng Xiaoping, China entered a new era in world politics, culminating in the establishment of formal diplomatic relations with the United States in 1979. In an ironic twist, it is now India which is trying to follow in the footsteps of China as Indian officials go all out to extend India's economic and political influence in Africa (Zhang Hongming 2006).

China–Africa relations in the post-1970s reform period

In the early 1980s the policy of modernization and economic reform became the centrepiece of China's Communist Party under Premier Deng. The long-held ideology of maintaining a command economy began to receive less priority. This shift in China's strategy of globalization also began to influence the central goals and objectives of development assistance to poor countries. Should China's aid policy be driven by political/ideological criteria or should it be directed to promote China's economic interest? (Zhang Qingmin 2001). This debate ended with the new 'Four Principles on Sino-African Economic and Technical Cooperation' announced in 1983 by Premier Zhao Ziyang: *equality*; *mutual benefit*; *pursuing practical results*, adopting a variety of means; and *seeking common development* (G. T. Yu 1988b). Within the scope of the Eight Principles, these new adjustments were prompted by the weakening of ideological conditions and increasing attention being given to economic relations and the strengthening of humanitarian aid support (Huang Meibo 2007).

In the sixth National Foreign Aid Working Conference held by the State Council in 1983, it was emphasized that the working guideline should be *Liangli er xing* (China's aid to other developing countries should be dependent on its own capability), *jinli er wei* (and at the same time it should try its best) – the former meant materially, while the latter meant mentally (Shi Lin 1989; Lv Xuejian 1989: 70). Accordingly, grant aid was to be given only to the least developed countries, while the proportion of contract projects and technical services and the promotion of joint ventures were to be expanded substantially (Lv Xuejian 1989). Following these policy adjustments, China supported more than two hundred infrastructure projects in African countries in the 1980s. In total, the number of projects in Africa and West Asia exceeded 2,600, amounting to US$5.6 billion and employing some eight thousand Chinese labourers (Xie Yixian 1998: 449). In subsequent years, the proportion of infrastructure and technical assistance projects was increased substantially as these were deemed crucial to the social and economic development of recipient countries (Lv Xuejian 1989).

The central operative logic of Chinese aid has been that recipient countries must manage their own development and China's role should be limited to the transfer of technology and material resources. And one way of ensuring the sustainability of Chinese-funded projects in Africa is by helping countries to strengthen national management, including maintenance, follow-up and skills development (ibid.). In addition to project assistance through its bilateral channel, China began to provide development assistance through multilateral channels, such as the United Nations, during the 1980s. The idea was to take advantage of the strength of these better-resourced agencies, and it was felt that Chinese enterprises could also benefit from their involvement in these projects.

The most important experiences that one observes in Chinese development cooperation with Africa over the past three decades have been the recognition that close consultation with recipient governments and their constituencies is a prerequisite for the sustainability of projects and programmes; and the recognition that capacity-building should translate as real transfer of knowledge and skills, especially in those projects financed by China. These cardinal rules are far more important than the quantity of Chinese aid to Africa. Despite this recognition, however, many recent investments by China in Africa have been the subject of repeated criticism, including by several authors in this volume. In response, Chinese authorities have begun to respond to these criticisms and are now requiring Chinese firms operating in Africa to abide by internationally agreed norms on labour rights, working conditions and environmental standards. At the same time, major Chinese firms, such as Sinotel, with important branches in Zimbabwe and South Africa, have announced that they have joined the UN-sponsored Global Compact, a 7,000-member global corporate social responsibility initiative based on ten principles that the participating businesses have pledged to uphold in the areas of human rights, labour, anti-corruption and environmental standards.

The post-1990 reforms

In the 1990s, African countries accelerated the process of multiparty democracy and the liberalization of the economy under the watchful eyes of the IMF and the World Bank. The role of the state in the management of the economy was downgraded, while market forces were allowed greater freedom in the revitalization of African economies. With the trend towards liberalization and privatization in full swing, the Chinese government realized it would no longer be possible to insist on traditional cooperation between governments, that development aid should be directed towards invigorating private sector development in Africa and that the new policy should also enlist the participation of Chinese enterprise in African markets (Xu Jianping 1996).

Thus, in the working conference on foreign aid held in October 1995, the

State Council of China introduced new policies on foreign aid, whose aim was to encourage more qualified Chinese corporations to participate in overseas economic cooperation and technical assistance projects (Zhang Haibing 2007). This new approach was consistent with China's broad economic trade strategy of exploiting the opportunities made possible by the process of economic globalization (Li Yuliang 1999).

The second important reform was the decision to grant interest-free loans and subsidized export credits to African countries in order to promote Chinese trade and investment in Africa (Zhang Hongming 2006: 4–8). The first favourable loan project was signed with Zimbabwe in July 1995, and within three years China had signed fifty-six agreements on favourable terms with forty-three countries, including twenty-three African countries. Among the four largest projects were: the 100 million renminbi (RMBY) oil exploitation projects in Sudan; two textile factories in Tanzania and Zambia; a railway renovation project in Botswana; and a cement factory project in Zimbabwe. All these projects were believed to be mutually beneficial (Wei Hong 1999). The new approach in foreign aid has helped enlarge China's market share in Africa by stimulating Chinese export of construction and other heavy equipment and consumer goods, while it has imported strategic resources, such as oil and minerals, that China needs to feed its growing economy.

With the growth of its national strength, China has been willing to take on more external development commitments by extending various kinds of assistance to African countries. These include debt relief, preferential trade agreements, market access for African products into China and many more. Since the first Forum of China–Africa Cooperation, held in 2000, the list of preferential economic programmes has been expanded in subsequent forums.[6] Thus, over the past fifty years, China's development cooperation with Africa has gradually shifted from a preoccupation with the promotion of self-reliance, liberation and South–South solidarity to economic concerns, with the increasing integration of its economy into the capitalist world economy. In this new conjuncture, cultural diplomacy has become an important component of the new diplomacy of economic development in the context of globalization.

Reinventing cultural diplomacy in the service of globalization

Since the end of the 1990s, the cultural marketplace has become a new but overarching element in China's globalizing policy, deliberately designed to cultivate supportive international public opinion of China. The first goal of this culture-building movement is to present a positive image of China. Accordingly, large-scale cultural activities, such as the 2008 Olympic Games and Chinese cultural festivals, have become important avenues for showcasing China to the world. Since 2004, for example, the frequency of Chinese performing arts groups visiting Africa has increased dramatically, with twenty-two African countries receiving such visiting groups. In 2004, a number of cultural events were held in Beijing. Among these was the 'Meet in Beijing' arts festival, the 'Voyage of Chinese Culture to Africa' festival and the China–Africa Youth Festival (FOCAC 2003: 246).

The second official goal of cultural diplomacy is to anchor China's 'peaceful rise' and the ideal of a 'harmonious world' in the minds of the external world (Beijing Review 2005). Cultural diplomacy thus becomes an important tool to sell to the world the idea that China's economic rise should not be seen as a threat to the West, or – by developing countries where China has an interest in securing energy and other vital natural resources – as 'new colonialism' (X. Yu 2007).

The third political goal is related to the economic interest in developing China's cultural industry, in addition to the promotion of Chinese culture. The export of Chinese culture as something to be developed in its own right was beginning to receive special attention with the tabling of the White Paper on Programmes of Cultural Development as part of the State Council's eleventh Five-Year Plan, issued in September 2006. Interestingly, culture is not only being used to promote Chinese foreign policy; it has now assumed a particular economic role and has become an export sector that needs to be developed in its own right.

Key programmes for promoting Chinese cultural diplomacy

Many new channels of cultural cooperation have been explored and implemented. This chapter focuses on the six well-known programmes of cultural diplomacy:

Human resource training From 2003 to 2006, China trained more than 10,000 Africans in many sectors, including 3,700 government officials and 3,000 professionals.[7] Alongside the enormous increase in the number of scholarships (4,000 per year) announced at the Sino-African Summit held in November 2006, the Chinese government has promised to finish the task of training 15,000 Africans by 2010. Since the preferred way of providing education is in grant scholarships to African students, all kinds of training centres are mushrooming at many Chinese universities and colleges. Some of these training tasks are carried out by special African studies institutes, such as those at Beijing University and Zhejiang Normal University. Vocational schools specializing in training Africans (initiated by various ministries but sometimes financed by local governments or big companies) is also mushrooming.

Establishment of African Confucius Institutes The number of Confucius Institutes around the world is expected to grow from 100 in 2004 to 500 by 2010 as China expands its influence across the globe. The main task of the Confucius

Institute is 'to promote the teaching of Chinese as a foreign language and cultural exchanges and cooperation in education, culture and economics' (Confucius Institute Division 2007). As a national strategy for spreading cultural influence, the Confucius Institute has been constantly idealized in official discourse as symbolizing the start of China's peaceful ascent (Hunter 2006). It is not surprising that the government is devoting considerable resources in this area in view of the strategic position of Africa within China's overall foreign affairs.

Out of the 245 existing Confucius Institutes worldwide, only twelve are to be found in Africa, as of June 2008. These institutes are located in Egypt (two), Cameroon (one), South Africa (two), Zimbabwe (one), Nigeria (two), Kenya (two), Madagascar (one) and Rwanda (one) (Confucius Institute Division 2007). It is interesting to note that China, which once used to reject the ideology of tradition and privilege, is now intent on remobilizing traditional cultural resources in order to serve the current strategy of going global as it embraces economic globalization.

Organizing symposiums and forums The third new channel of cultural cooperation is the ever-increasing scholarly exchange and policy dialogue symposiums and forums attended by African scholars, artists, officials, diplomats and their Chinese counterparts. Some of the more prominent examples are: the Symposium of Sino-African Human Rights (Beijing, October 2004); the Conference of Sino-African Cooperation for Environmental Protection (Nairobi, February 2005); the International Symposium on African and Chinese Music (Beijing, October 2005); the Forum of Sino-African University Presidents (Zhejiang, November 2006); the Symposium of China and Africa, Shared Development (Beijing, December 2006). Compared with previous eras, when ideology was too often attached, these conferences, with focuses ranging from scholarly topics to music, journalism, environmental issues, education and even human rights, have contributed to establishing wide-ranging relationships in a softer yet possibly stronger and longer-lasting way, especially given the ever-increasing people-to-people contact.

The National Volunteer Project This project was officially launched in 2004 and the first eleven young Chinese volunteers were dispatched to Ethiopia in 2005. The aim of the programme, as stated by President Hu Jintao in 2006, is 'to encourage Chinese youth to participate in construction, medical, agricultural and teaching careers in Africa'. This was further elaborated in 2006 during the China–Africa Summit in Beijing when China announced a plan to dispatch some three hundred volunteers by 2010. All these volunteers are selected by the Association of Youth Volunteers under the central Communist Youth League and are given briefing courses on local customs and history before their departure. Thus, Chinese volunteers, considered to be the Chinese version of the Peace

Corps, are undoubtedly the most important medium for propagating Chinese culture in Africa (Kurlantzick 2007).

Municipal foreign policy and the Sister Cities Programme The fourth effective channel for strengthening cultural relations in recent years has been the Sister Cities Programme. Since the first relationship between Changsha (Hunan) and Brazzaville was established in 1982, seventy-three cities from twenty-eight African countries have entered into sister-city relationships with Chinese cities. The role of the programme as an important platform for strengthening economic ties with African countries was further emphasized during the 2006 China–Africa Forum and the May 2007 Sino-African Sister Cities symposium. The Chinese People's Association for Friendship with Foreign Countries is in charge of the day-to-day operations of the Sister Cities Programme.[8]

The African Cultural Visitor Programme An important channel initiated by China's Ministry of Culture is an exchange programme set up in 2006, designed to enhance mutual cultural understanding and cooperation between China and Africa by inviting African cultural personalities to visit and experience Chinese culture while China also sent artists to various African countries.[9] In 2007, this programme was officially named the African Cultural Visitor Programme, with 'cultural policy and its implementation in the market economy' as its theme, and specifically designed for ten African countries – namely, Senegal, Benin, Mali, the Republic of Congo, Madagascar, Tanzania, Zambia, Ethiopia, Botswana and Uganda.

In contrast to the one-way indoctrination of African visitors in the USA, candidates applying for China's cultural programme must – as a prerequisite – submit a paper and make a presentation at the conference on their own country's cultural management system, cultural policies, cases illustrating the results of implementing the cultural policies and the relation between domestic cultural policy and external exchanges.[10] The theme for the year 2008 was Domestic Cultural Development and External Cultural Exchange, and representatives from fifteen African countries were invited to participate at this event.[11] The African Cultural Visitor Programme has undoubtedly become a good way of promoting mutual cultural understanding and laying the necessary foundation for future cooperation between Africa and China.

Conclusion

Though one cannot deny the asymmetrical relationship between China and Africa, official Chinese policy always emphasizes strategic partnership, mutual benefit and respect for the sovereignty of African states. As development is still China's top priority in its relations with Africa, the most essential themes emphasized by the Chinese authorities are cooperation and co-development rather than the paternalistic language of development aid (King 2006). China always wants to present itself as a friendly developing country intent on contributing to the enhancement of the self-reliance capabilities of both Africa and China. Official Chinese policy makes no pretence that China is in Africa to help 'civilize the natives' or promote democracy, as is the case with Western development aid pronouncements.

A general historical review shows how China's traditional cultural diplomacy has developed and how it has opened different channels of cooperation in order to strengthen its economic and political ties with the African continent. As a result, both China and Africa have benefited politically and economically (Alden and Alves 2008). What is clear from the preceding analysis is that China's cultural cooperation precedes other forms of international cooperation.

As Tandon (2008) has succinctly argued: 'The conceptual starting point is not aid but development. The horse of development must be put before the cart of aid.' And the Chinese seem to follow this dictum rhetorically, although the motives and outcome might be quite different in reality. This historical fact must be understood in order to evaluate properly the relevance and effectiveness of Chinese aid to African countries.

5 | Engaging Africa: India's interests in the African continent, past and present

Sanjukta Banerji Bhattacharya

In the year 1900, Mohandas Karamchand Gandhi, who, apart from beginning his professional career as a lawyer in Africa, also debuted as an anti-colonialist nationalist campaigner for equality and justice on that continent. Gandhi once said that 'the commerce between India and Africa will be of ideas and services, not of manufactured goods against raw materials after the fashion of Western exploiters' (Mathews 1997). Today, in the twenty-first century, there is a twist in the tale: India–Africa relations relations have moved beyond those based merely on 'ideas and services' to a more pragmatic relationship that involves India's political, economic and security interests in convergence with and responding to Africa's developmental needs. Today, India provides not only a viable model of economic growth appreciable by the developing world; it is also a shining example of democratic consolidation and sustainability, rare in most post-colonial countries. One hundred and eight years after Mahatma Gandhi, Prime Minister Manmohan Singh, speaking at the first India–Africa Forum Summit in April 2008, elaborated on the theme of the growing and multifaceted India–Africa relations. He noted that this was a 'new chapter in the long history of civilizational contacts, friendship and cooperation between India and Africa', and the goal was to achieve 'economic vibrancy, peace, stability and self-reliance'. He further mentioned that he wished to see the twenty-first century as the 'century of Asia and Africa with the people of the two continents acting together to promote inclusive globalization'.[1]

In the context of the emerging vibrancy in India–Africa interactions, this chapter will first examine the nature of India's relations with Africa in the past, particularly between the 1950s and the 1990s; it will next analyse India's new terms of engagement with Africa from the 1990s, focusing on the economic, political and security aspects; and finally it will evaluate the challenges that India faces in this endeavour. It may be mentioned that India's relations with Africa are unique in one respect: there are three types of engagement in that it deals with Africa as a continent, it also has direct relations with the African Union (AU), and thirdly, it has relations with individual African countries on a bilateral basis. This kind of variety is not perceptible in India's relations with any other region. It should be emphasized here, however, that this chapter does not intend to delve into bilateral relations or relations with the AU. While Africa is a continent and India is only one country, there is a danger in generalizing about Indo–Africa relations and that the analysis might not put forth the complex and nuanced relationship between India and individual African countries.

India–Africa trade, past and present

Trade between India and Africa is said to go back to the fourteenth century (Tarling 1992: 186). It probably goes back even farther, however, as material evidence has been found to show that some form of contact had developed even before history was properly recorded. Mohenjodaro coins have been unearthed in Egypt, and the discovery of the port of Lothal in Gujarat, dating back to those times, implies that there may have been some form of seaborne trade going on between India's coast and that of ancient civilizations in Africa as early as 4,000–5,000 years ago,[2] though little or nothing is known about it and there is little historical evidence to prove it. Over the ages, there appears to have been a degree of population exchange as well between India and Africa, with people from India moving to Africa and vice versa. The pastoral Beja tribe of Sudan, that comprises around 5 per cent of the country's population, claim origin from India, and the language they speak has an affinity with Prakrit, which was prevalent in ancient India. On the other hand, India's Siddi community came from Africa around the tenth century, and today they can be found settled in the coastal regions of western India. During the time of the Sultanate (from c.1206 CE), and later during Mughal times – that is, from the thirteenth to the beginning of the eighteenth century – the presence of Africans (*habshis*) in the royal courts is well documented, with some of them playing important roles in the administration (Insoll 2003: 150).

More concrete evidence of shared exchanges goes back to colonial times, particularly because the continent and subcontinent shared colonial masters – the British, the French and the Portuguese. Mozambique became the staging ground for the Portuguese presence in Goa, while the British East Africa Protectorate that included Kenya and Uganda was originally administered from Bombay, which had been given to the British as part of a royal dowry by another European power. In a way, the British facilitated India's presence in Africa (though unwittingly) by sending thousands of Indians as indentured labour to work in plantations in South Africa, Mauritius and other African destinations. The result is that today there are approximately two million people of Indian origin in Africa (Government of India 2001). Subsequently, many Indians also went as traders, particularly from Gujarat, and settled down in different African countries, although they had closer affinity with states that were or had been under British colonial rule, perhaps because of the shared colonial language. Since India became independent, along with business entrepreneurs, there has been a growing presence of Indian professionals such as doctors, educationists and engineers in Africa. Again, while the preferred destination appeared to be the English-speaking states in the early years, with time, their numbers have begun to increase in the francophone states as well. These persons of Indian origin (PIO) serve as a vital link between India and their new home states in Africa.[3]

India's engagement with Africa took a new turn following decolonization. India became independent before most African states (South Africa and Rhodesia were decolonized, but they were under white minority rule; Ethiopia, on the other hand, had an African ruler), and its independence was achieved after a long struggle in which Mahatma Gandhi had played a pivotal role. Perhaps India's independence struck a chord with at least some of the nationalists who wished for freedom in Africa. More to the point, India's first prime minister, Jawaharlal Nehru, was a visionary who had actively participated in the Brussels Congress of Oppressed Nationalities organized by political exiles and revolutionaries from Asian, African and Latin American countries as far back as February 1927, and had from that time begun to think in terms of a common struggle against colonialism and imperialism (Gopal and Iyengar 2002; Brecher 1959). Even before independence, he had organized the Asian Relations Conference in New Delhi (1947), where he articulated his desire for unity among the struggling peoples of Asia (Government of India 1949).

Following 1947 and India's independence, Nehru emerged as the post-colonial world's leading voice against imperialism, colonialism, neocolonialism, racism and all forms of foreign aggression, occupation, domination, interference or hegemony – ideals that mirrored the views and aspirations of the newly independent countries of Asia and Africa. Nehru later became linked with a new organization, the Non-Aligned Movement (NAM), which reflected the problems and ideas of what soon came to be called the Third World. He was one of the driving forces behind the Bandung Summit of Asian and African states in 1955, which gave birth to the NAM, founded a few years later in 1961. The Bandung Conference helped to bring the developing nations of the two continents together and brought to the fore, for the first time, the community of interests that existed between India and Africa (Dikshit 1989). It is perhaps this coming together of leaders and ideas which facilitated the creation of NAM. It was not only Nehru and President Tito of Yugoslavia who were instrumental in its formation. President Nasser of Egypt and President Nkrumah of Ghana were the two important leaders from Africa who played a key role in the founding of NAM (Willetts 1978; De Silva 1983).

There was an ideological affiliation between India and Africa, which was evident in the anti-racism and anti-colonialism agenda of NAM. African concerns about apartheid were included in its programme and India ardently supported anti-racist movements in South Africa and Zimbabwe. The NAM began the Africa Fund in 1986 to help front-line states facing problems as a result of continued pressure by white minority regimes. India's initial contribution to this fund amounted to Rs 500 million, and this included Rs 25 million given by private and individual donors (Government of India 1993: 59). As a result of cooperation in this area, many resolutions condemning racism, colonialism and apartheid and supporting the self-determination of people were passed with overwhelming majorities in the United Nations General Assembly (UNGA). India, in fact, accorded diplomatic status to the African National Congress (ANC) in 1967 and to the South-West African People's Organization (SWAPO) in 1985 (Indian National Congress 1976: 92–6).

India's engagement with Africa was not restricted to an expression of ideological commonalities in the UNGA; it also had a strong political element in that it sought support against great-power bloc politics, which in a way was the rationale behind NAM. Many African leaders subscribed to this view, and the Organization of African Unity (OAU) had institutional affiliations with the NAM. At the same time it should be noted that some African countries were practically aligned with one bloc or the other, according to their own foreign policy imperatives, for most or all of the cold war period. As a result, total unity could never be achieved on matters hinging on East–West political issues in the UNGA. There was, however, strong unity of ideas on economic issues. Both India and post-colonial Africa faced developmental challenges, which in the 1960s and 1970s were analysed as stemming from the terms of international trade, which were seen as being shaped largely by the industrialized North. The Group of 77 (G77) countries, which included most African countries and India among others, voiced concerns about the unequal terms of trade and, in 1974, demanded a New International Economic Order (NIEO) that would improve the terms of trade between the North and the South, increase development assistance and reduce developed-country tariffs (H. Johnson 1976). According to Julius Nyerere, speaking at the fourth ministerial meeting of the G77, 'It was practical experience of the fact that legal independence did not mean economic freedom which made most of us think of cooperating with others similarly placed' (Braillard and Djalili 1986).

There was much solidarity on issues of economic deprivation and the demand for an NIEO, and a kind of Third World unity emerged vis-à-vis the North, with notions of South–South cooperation being voiced for the first time. At the time, however, the level of trade between India and Africa was low because India, like African countries, faced developmental challenges, and to sustain its economy, its trade – again like that of countries in Africa – was directed to the North, particularly to the former metropolitan country as well as the United States and, increasingly, the Soviet Union. Moreover, to help build up its infrastructure, heavy industries and commercial goods, and to protect these sectors from cheaper merchandise from the already developed states, India raised its tariffs and 'nationalized' many sectors of its economy. Many African countries followed suit for the same reason. This decreased the feasibility of trade between India and other countries of the South. Under the circumstances, the concept of South–South cooperation did not take on any practical shape.

India could and did cooperate in other areas, however, where it had built up its strength and there was potential for partnership. As early as 1964, India established the Indian Technical and Economic (ITEC) programme, which has so far trained over ten thousand Africans in Indian institutions in fields varying from agriculture and industry to management and diplomacy. India was also involved in several United Nations (UN) peacekeeping missions in Africa, beginning with the Congo in the 1960s. At another level, it was quick to share the benefits of its democratization experience when requested. For instance, Sudan's first parliamentary elections were conducted with the assistance and advice of Sukumar Sen, the then Chief Election Commissioner of India.

From idealism to pragmatism: India–Africa relations since the 1990s

The first four and a half decades of independent India's engagement with Africa were therefore based on ideological and idealistic principles and were mainly political. Following the end of the cold war, and with the introduction of India's economic liberalization programme early in the 1990s, India's foreign policy has moved away from Nehruvian non-alignment and Gandhian idealism to more pragmatic policies of attracting investment and expanding trade and investment with the African continent. India is particularly interested in acquiring ample supply of critical energy and raw material from Africa in order to fuel its growing economy and reduce poverty in the long term. India today is deemed to be an emerging economic power with enormous potential, and is viewed as a 'BRIC' country, a term coined by Goldman Sachs for what it perceives as the four largest emerging markets of the future: Brazil, Russia, India and China (O'Neill 2003, 2004). India's total estimated gross domestic product (GDP) for 2008 according to purchasing power parity (PPP) was US$3,267 trillion; its foreign exchange and gold reserves at the end of December 2008 stood at US$274.2 billion.[4]

India, in fact, now has the financial capacity to invest in other countries and a vibrant private sector. Companies like the Tata group, Ranbaxy, the Reliance group, the Birla group and Kirloskar have become multinational corporations in their own right. Indian companies like Infosys are now listed on the New York Stock Exchange, indicating the growing might of Indian multinational corporations in the world economy. India's major strength lies in the services sector, it being the second-largest exporter of computer and information services after the European Union (EU). At the same time, it has also developed considerable skills in manufacturing as well other sectors, including power, energy (conventional as well as alternative energy), mining and agriculture (Poddar and Yi 2007). The net result is that India's terms of engagement in the global economy can be, and are, different from the way they were in the cold war period. While political relations are, and have to be, important, economic considerations are increasingly becoming a major driving factor for multilateral and bilateral relations. And, as mentioned earlier, India's foreign policy has moved away from its former ideological basis and has become more pragmatic, with national interest being defined more in 'realistic' terms. Interestingly, the word 'security' has become the new mantra under globalization, taking on various hues, such as energy security, economic security, maritime security, environmental security, human security, food security and, of course, conventional security (Ganguly 2003a, 2003b; Nayar 2003; Mann 2000). India emphasizes its need for security on all these counts and more, and is ready to cooperate with both the developing and the developed world in the pursuit of its security goals.

In the newly globalizing world, however, power, whether political or economic, is still concentrated in the industrialized North. In the United Nations, China is the only Asian country among the permanent members of the Security Council, and this is significant because the concept of collective security and its legitimate use is largely concentrated in the Permanent Five. Economically speaking, the USA, the European Union (EU) countries and Japan are the biggest import and export partners for almost every country of the global South. The implication is that the direction of trade is still largely from the South to the North. There are, however, the first indications of a change in the new millennium, very minor currently, but predicted to increase in the future, as some developing countries are developing faster and are now emerging as middle powers economically and, to a lesser extent, politically, one such country being India.

It is necessary for India in its search for further economic growth and great-power status (among other things) to seek crucial allies, partner countries that are looking for developmental assistance, and invest in countries and sectors that will help satisfy its various security needs. It is only through a network of viable and mutually beneficial partnerships that it can hope to be recognized as a major emerging player in international relations both by the global South and the developed North. It is such partnerships which will increase its voice in international fora like the UN or the World Trade Organization (WTO). In the immediate post-cold-war period, the objectives of attracting investment, expanding trade and upgrading infrastructure led India to engage with the major powers and also to 'Look East'. While these regions continue to remain at the centre stage of India's foreign relations in the early years of the twenty-first century, India has begun to widen its scope and concentrate on other areas as well, and Africa is increasingly coming into focus, as illustrated by the first India–Africa Summit, which was held in April 2008. India has held no such summit with any other continental or even partly continental region so far.

India's re-engagement with Africa is on different terms than its earlier relations. While political concerns remain important, the economic content has increased in such a manner that one can speak of it in terms of genuine South–South cooperation, because the partnerships that are developing are for mutual benefit. The African continent contains large quantities of resources that India needs (Engineer and Parimi 2008); on the other hand, India has expertise in industry, mining, infrastructure building, information technology, pharmaceuticals, and so forth, which many countries in Africa seek; it can also provide low-cost solutions to poverty alleviation, and is ready to invest in industrial ventures, jointly or otherwise, that will help in the development of African countries and draw them into the international economy without being exploitative, on terms acceptable to both. South–South cooperation is increasingly being viewed by less developed countries as an alternative to North–South aid, which has mainly come to African countries, particularly in recent decades, with conditions attached – such as structural adjustment and political reforms – and at times has been used for political purposes. At the same time, investment by Western industrialized countries has been largely in the extractive industries in Africa and, as can be seen in the current development status of African states, has not led to any significant growth, development or building of basic infrastructure. Today's South–South cooperation is of a different nature, especially where India is concerned. It is more of a partnership whereby India also benefits. At the same time, India assists in building capacity and infrastructure and in training Africans in skills that, in the long run, will lead to the sustainable development of the continent.

India's intentions are borne out in deeds: India was the first Asian country to become a full member of the African Capacity Building Foundation (ACBF) and committed US$1 million to it to build capacity for sustainable development and poverty alleviation. It wrote off debt owed by African countries under the Heavily Indebted Poor Countries (HIPC) Paris Initiative and also restructured commercial debts. It began the Techno Economic Approach for Africa–India Movement, the TEAM-9 initiative with eight francophone African states to set up a mechanism for cooperation in bilateral and sub-regional projects with lines of credit (LOC) of US$500 million for those countries. The objective of such support is to build sustainable partnerships through development of institutional capacity in industry, agriculture and infrastructure. The initiative envisages transfer of technology and specific projects in agriculture, small-scale industry, rural development, pharmaceuticals, telecommunications and energy. India has also given a US$200 million LOC to assist the New Partnership for Africa's Development (NEPAD) initiative. India is the second-largest source of investment in Uganda, and Indian companies are the largest investors in Ghana. ONGC Videsh (OVL), the overseas arm of the state-owned Oil and Natural Gas Corporation (ONGC), has invested US$2 billion in Sudan's hydrocarbon sector, and this involves infrastructure-building as well.[5]

Private sector companies like Tata, Mahindra and Mahindra, Infosys, Grasim India Ltd and many others have also invested heavily in African countries. It is not only Indians who are welcoming Tata's new automobile, the Nano; African countries too are looking forward to the introduction of the inexpensive little car on Africa's roads. India is also cooperating in advanced technology, offering data from its remote-sensing satellites, and expertise to use the data application in different fields. The Pan-African e-Network, which has been launched recently, will provide satellite linkage with India's top schools and hospitals across Africa's fifty-three countries, thus providing cheap access to India's expertise through tele-medicine and tele-education. It will, at the same time, provide electronic linkage among these fifty-three countries. India is also a leading manufacturer of cheap generic drugs, especially those that are used to fight tropical diseases like malaria, cholera and tuberculosis. It is the biggest supplier of low-cost antiretroviral drugs to fight HIV/AIDS in sub-Saharan Africa, where this dreaded disease has wrought havoc. It has also invested in a farming initiative in post-conflict Mozambique, biofuels in western Africa and the textile industry in East Africa. These are attempts to put local resources to the best use for local benefit (Beri 2003: 216–32).

In education, the ITEC programme has already been mentioned (Pant 2007: 41–56). Apart from ITEC, the Indian Council for Cultural Relations (ICCR) gives full scholarships for higher studies in India, and many African scholars have taken advantage of these scholarships to obtain university degrees, including PhDs, from institutes of higher learning in India. At a more practical level, India's partnership plans include training local workers at the local level, thus contributing to the building up of human capital. For example, while India is gaining an entry into Angola's diamond trade, it has promised to open an institute for jewellery manufacture as well as a diamond-cutting and -polishing centre in Angola. Again, while Angola has offered a 30 per cent stake to India in its upcoming Liberto oil refinery, India has offered to set up a centre of excellence in petroleum technology in Angola as well as to construct a 300MW gas-based plant and to rebuild its railway infrastructure and financial sector. Angola's leading diamond company, Endiama, will also tie up with Tata Motors to manufacture its own commercial vehicles.

The vibrancy in India–Africa relations has increased further since 2008. In February, India announced a 60 per cent increase in aid over the next financial year, to US$20 million. At the India–Africa Project Partnership Forum held in New Delhi in March 2008, 150 projects worth US$11 billion were discussed and the EXIM Bank of India extended US$30 million in credit to finance Indian exports to Africa. At the India–Africa Summit of April 2008, the prime minister pledged US$500 in development grants over the next five to six years as part of the Aid to Africa budget of the Ministry of External Affairs (MEA). He also promised to double India's line of credit to US$5.4 billion from the US$2.25 of the previous five years. He also announced a Duty Free Tariff Preference Scheme for Least Developed Countries, which means that India will provide preferential market access for exports from fifty of the world's least developed countries, thirty-four of which are in Africa.[6]

This relationship is not just a one-way process. Mauritius has emerged as the largest African offshore investor in India. African companies are gradually entering into joint venture enterprises in India. For instance, Mumbai's international airport is being modernized in a million-dollar joint venture between India's GVK Group and the Airports Company of South Africa. Trade between African countries and India, too, has markedly increased as a result. Bilateral India–Africa trade grew from US$967 million in 1991 to US$30 billion in 2007/08. Africa's share in India's global trade increased in just four years from 5.8 per cent in 2002/03 to 8 per cent in 2006/07. Africa has many resources that can complement India's needs. To take the diamond industry as a case in point: India accounts for 90 per cent of the world's export of cut and polished diamonds; it is seeking close trade relations with Angola, Botswana, Congo and South Africa, which account for 90 per cent of the world's supply of rough diamonds. India is also looking at Africa to meet some of its energy needs (Muni and Pant 2005; Rumley and Chaturvedi 2005).

Africa has around 8 per cent of the world's known petroleum resources, and West African crude is known for its good quality. Nigeria already accounts for 10 per cent of India's oil imports. It is interested in further increasing its imports from Africa, particularly from Sudan and from the region around the Gulf of Guinea. It should be noted, however, that although India, like all other countries trading with Africa, is interested in Africa's resources, its interest is not merely in extracting these resources for itself at the expense of any given African country where the resource exists. It should again be emphasized that India believes in partnership, and this has led it to invest heavily in building infrastructure, such as roads and airports, and in training African personnel rather than bringing in its own. In the long run, the specific African country will benefit and will become economically sustainable.

India–Africa and new regionalisms

This new engagement is not limited to economic cooperation alone. Although the NAM is in terminal decline today and the term 'Third World' is hotly debated, there is no denying the fact that African countries and India can all be categorized as 'developing' and that there is a commonality of interests. The NAM is being replaced by more pragmatic groupings, such as the India, Brazil, South Africa (IBSA) Dialogue Forum, the Indian Ocean Rim Association for Regional Cooperation (IORARC), the Asia–Africa Summit, the Group of 33 (G33) bloc of developing countries in the World Trade Organization (WTO), among others. Although most of these south–south cooperation institutions face a great deal of criticism for being too slow or ineffective, they serve as a useful platform for developing tactical alliance and negotiation positions on key issues, such as global trade or climate change. Through such collaborative initiatives, stronger bonds are built among developing countries. In this respect, India has been one of the leading developing countries that has continued to champion the cause of south–south cooperation. This was particularly evident within the WTO, particularly when it comes to negotiations on the liberalization of agricultural trade. In the WTO, developing countries have put united pressure on the North on issues such as agricultural subsidies, which give unfair advantage to developed countries' agricultural commodities. In the UN, both AU countries and the Group of 4 (G4) want reforms of the Security Council. While they have so far hindered each other's efforts, the closer contact that is developing may help to bring them together on a common platform.

Another area of common interest lies in the sphere of conventional security (Beri 1999; Sheth 2008). Ninety per cent of India's trade volume and 70 per cent of its trade value comes by sea. Maritime security is therefore of utmost importance, given India's growing dependence on energy supply from the African continent. India established its first overseas surveillance facility in Madagascar in July 2007. It also reached defence agreements with several countries on the Indian Ocean Rim – Mauritius, Madagascar, Seychelles, Kenya, Mozambique and Tanzania – and stepped up joint military exercises with states in the region. It also held a joint naval exercise off Cape Town with South Africa and Brazil under an IBSA initiative in May 2008. Moreover, it held joint patrols off the coast of Mozambique during the AU summit of 2003 and the World Economic Forum of 2004. India is uniquely placed geostrategically and is a regional military power with outreach potential. The Indian army has trained officers from many African countries under the ITEC programme. It has also sent training teams to various countries, including Botswana, Zambia and Lesotho. As part of its defence cooperation efforts, it has supplied a small quantity of conventional arms for African patrol crafts to countries such as Mauritius and Guinea Bissau and light helicopters to Namibia. It also imports some weaponry from South Africa. Cooperation in maritime and other security initiatives with willing African countries is expected to grow.

India and China in Africa: competition or coexistence?

India faces several limiting factors, both internal and external, in its quest for bilateral and multilateral cooperation with African countries. From the domestic point of view, while Africa is now a focus of India's foreign policy, it is not the primary focus, and cannot be expected to be so, given India's growing economic and security cooperation with the US, the EU, and its Asian neighbours. The bulk of India's investments comes from the West, and most of India's exports are directed to the North. Other regions are also becoming economically important, depending on complementarities in trade and commerce and the level of sophistication in the production of industrial and manufacturing goods. Trade with African countries is improving rapidly but there is still a long way to go. So far as political relations are concerned, Western developed countries, particularly the USA, are still at the centre of India's foreign policy priorities, while still maintaining good relations with almost all developing countries. India's national interests link it to developed countries as wel. As an emerging middle power on par with the likes of China, India is now invited on a regular basis as an observer to the Group of 8 (G8) countries' meetings.

So far as the external arena in Africa is concerned, the main challenges here are posed by China and the USA. China's bilateral trade with Africa is around US$70 billion more than India's and it has also invested US$5.6 billion more than India in the continent. It is more or less interested in the same sectors as India is, and has successfully signed agreements with several countries. Its demand for oil and minerals has been a major factor in the growth of Sino-African trade. China went from being a net oil exporter to a net oil importer in the 1990s (it currently imports around 4.21 million barrels a day). It has been willing to buy stakes in Africa which are considered to be less profitable or 'too difficult' by the West, and as a result established a presence in countries like Sudan from the mid-1990s, when the country was mired in the north–south civil war. By 2005, when the north–south conflict ended with the signing of the Comprehensive Peace Agreement, China was buying 50-60 per cent of Sudan's oil exports buying 50–60 per cent of Sudan's oil exports. The state-owned China National Offshore Oil Corporation (CNOOC) is also active in Equatorial New Guinea, Chad, Gabon, Angola and Nigeria. China is also deeply interested in Africa's other mineral resources, such as copper, uranium, cobalt and gold. Apart from buying the Chambezi copper mines in Zambia, it has invested in copper and cobalt mines in the Democratic Republic of Congo and has built roads to facilitate exports (Junbo 2007).[7] It is also competing with India in the telecom sector – an area of strength for India. Its ZTE Corporation, which manufactures telecom equipment, has set up shops in Mali, Congo, Kenya and Nigeria, to mention a few. China also competes with India in the automobile sector, and, further, has a head start in the manufacturing sector.

China has a huge presence in Africa – it has 900 projects, and 800 companies are operating in various countries. It has sent 16,000 medical personnel to Africa, offered scholarships to 20,000 African students, and trained a large number of African professionals. Although India became a regional member of the African Development Bank two years before China (in 1982), China now holds more shares in the bank and has greater voting power. And in 2007, when the board of the African Development Bank chose to hold its first board meeting in an Asian city, it decided in favour of Shanghai rather than Mumbai

(Ramachandran 2007a). It should also be noted, however, that while China focuses on resource-based investment that largely advances its own interests, India engages in capacity-building. Indian firms also hire locally and train local Africans in maintenance and repair work, and as such are seen as more acceptable than Chinese investments by the local population. Moreover, China has a big advantage because the Chinese government is the major owner of most firms, while most of the Indian enterprises operating in Africa are private sector companies, whose capital funds are just a fraction of those of the Chinese state. One has to remember that the purchasing power parity of China's GDP was around US$8 trillion in 2008.[8] Questions have also been raised regarding unfair trading practices, such as providing below-market financing and using cheap Chinese labour to work in the mines in Africa. Questions have also been raised about the close connection between Chinese business interests and the country's foreign policy objectives. The Chinese government has further been accused of selling arms to countries with records of gross human rights violations in order to ease commercial deals. Much has been said and written about Chinese interests in Africa, and it is not the purpose of this chapter to examine this issue: what needs to be said here is that Chinese business and political deals are sometimes a challenge to India's relations with Africa.

On the other hand, India also faces stiff competition from the US when it comes to exercising influence in Africa. During the apartheid era, America's continued business cooperation with South Africa until the mid-1980s effectively countered the developing world's efforts to isolate that country economically. It was only after the imposition of US economic sanctions in 1986 that the apartheid regime made the move towards majority rule. In recent years, however, the USA has been increasing its presence in Africa. It is estimated that African crude will account for one-fourth of US oil imports by 2015. It is the major export partner for many African countries, overtaking France in some of the francophone states as well (White House 2001, 2002).

On the security front, the USA established the United States Africa Command (AFRICOM) in October 2007. Even earlier, it set up the African Crisis Response Force in 1996, which was soon replaced by the African Crisis Response Initiative (ACRI). Between July 1997 and May 2007, the US organized training for battalions (800–1,000 soldiers) in Senegal, Uganda, Malawi, Mali, Ghana, Benin and Côte d'Ivoire, apart from programmes such as training in psychological warfare, among others. After the terrorist attacks on the USA on 11 September 2001, the Bush administration boosted military investment in Africa, and ACRI became the African Contingency Operations Training and Assistance (ACOTA) programme. There is also the International Military Education and Training (IMET) programme, under which thousands of African officers have been trained in offensive and defensive manoeuvres, and millions of dollars have been spent (Abromovici 2004). Currently, the USA is training 200 members of the Nigerian navy and army, and as of March 2009 American naval ships have visited Senegal, Ghana, Cameroon, Nigeria and Gabon as part of the 'Africa Partnership Station' programme.[9] Not only is the USA competing for energy resources, but China's growing presence in Africa, in addition to issues relating to America's War on Terrorism – which may concern some unstable and 'failed' states in Africa and other countries in the Indian Ocean Rim region, as well as matters regarding the security of sea lanes, particularly off the Somalia coast – all appear to be focusing US attention on Africa in a subtle but sure manner. This engagement is somewhat different from earlier times. The USA is not a challenge in the direct sense of the term to India, but its engagement with Africa should be taken note of.

Apart from these potential challenges, India faces some problematic issues in Africa. There is a long history of labour unrest between ethnic Indians and indigenous Africans, especially in East African countries like Kenya and Uganda, where Indians settled more than a century ago. New areas of disharmony have also been emerging with India's growing presence. For instance, Indian steel-workers were abducted in Nigeria over a pay dispute with union members in October 2007. Moreover, India should be careful that the charges that are being levelled against China are not directed against it as well, because, despite its moral posturing, India, like China, also engages with some of the same regimes, charged with human rights violations. OVL secured a 25 per cent stake in Sudan's Greater Nile Oil Project (GNOP), despite the ongoing Darfur conflict, in which the government has been charged with instigating genocide-like killings. Moreover, India's trade with Zimbabwe, where the undemocratic and authoritarian Mugabe regime has been met with international condemnation, reached US$40 million by 2006.[10] While India has energy and food security requirements and, in the final analysis, national interest is placed above most other considerations, India has to be careful not to sully its record of economic cooperation for mutual benefit with African states and long-term sustainable partnership.

Conclusions

According to Prime Minister Manmohan Singh, speaking at the April 2008 summit of African and Indian leaders, the India–Africa partnership is 'anchored in the fundamental principles of equality, mutual respect and mutual benefit'. There has been a major shift in India's engagement with African countries from the 1948–91 period to the 2000–08 period. India now provides a vibrant market for African exports, resources for investment, finance for development and technologies for enhancing productivity. These are the things that normally help to engineer change in specific economies. Perhaps India, too, is becoming an engine of change and growth for African countries as they are being drawn, slowly but surely, into the mainstream of international exchanges on terms that are much more favourable than in earlier times. More needs to be done, however, and many more milestones have to be passed for the India–Africa partnership to be of greater significance and consequence in international relations. Respective strengths should be leveraged for mutual benefit and more preferential trade agreements with an eye to future free trade agreements should be worked out. Trade needs to increase to beyond US$100 billion in the next ten years to register a major shift away from the North–South direction and towards the South–South path. This will create greater leverage and a bargaining chip for developing countries in fora like the WTO, and a more equitable trading order could finally emerge.

Great strides have been made in India's re-engagement with Africa, not only in the economic sector but also at the political and security levels. The country has come a long way from Mahatma Gandhi's vision of a 'commerce of ideas' with Africa. India–Africa interactions today are more vibrant, encompassing political, economic, diplomatic, cultural, scientific and security cooperation; and there are great hopes of new horizons and greater friendships as India and Africa, and at another level Indians and Africans, come together to create new partnerships.

6 | Indian development cooperation with Africa

Pranay Kumar Sinha

Since the late 1990s there has been a major shift in Indian development cooperation policy towards Africa. Since India's independence the principle of South–South cooperation has been at the forefront of India's foreign policy towards Africa.[1] Now, in the first decade of the twenty-first century, India and Africa are prepared more than ever to re-establish economic and political relationships to promote their mutual interests. Furthermore, India's recent experience in reducing its aid dependency while moving in the direction of becoming one of the leading emerging economies in the world has played a central role in its foreign policy towards Africa. The government of India attaches greater importance to economic relations as the basis of renewed India–Africa engagement.

It is important to establish at the outset that India's apparent competition with China in Africa is also largely responsible for the dramatic shift in India's development cooperation strategy towards the continent. As Naidu, Vines and Campos and Bhattacharya (this volume) and Agrawal (2007) have argued, this competition focuses on three major issues: diplomatic influence, oil and markets for goods. It is, therefore, obviously clear that commercial interests have become embedded in India's assistance programmes.

The formation of Indian Technical and Economic Cooperation (ITEC) in 1964 kick-started India's bilateral assistance programme with its African and West Asian counterparts. Primarily, official aid was perceived as a means of countering the ever-increasing Chinese diplomacy in Africa (Beri 2003). But it is equally important to mention that even before ITEC was established as a development cooperation instrument, India had been involved in extending development assistance to other neighbouring countries since 1951, immediately after its independence.

India's African diplomacy in the post-cold-war period

The year 2003 proved to be the watershed in India's development assistance strategy, from the perspective of India both as an aid-receiving country and as a new emerging donor. First, the government of India (GOI) announced that the country would no longer accept foreign aid except from a few Western governments. This was followed by the repayment of approximately Rs 75 billion (US$1.6 billion), which India owed to fourteen bilateral donors (Times of India

2003). Second, India announced the establishment of the India Development Initiative to channel development aid to African and other developing countries. It immediately granted debt cancellation to seven heavily indebted poor countries (HIPCs): Mozambique, Tanzania, Zambia, Guyana, Nicaragua, Ghana and Uganda.[2] Another important event occurred in 2005, when India refused to accept any foreign aid for tsunami relief operations and started displaying its ambition to play a larger role as a donor by announcing it would be providing US$22.5 million of emergency reconstruction aid to other affected countries. Finally, in a 2007/08 budget speech, the GOI announced the establishment of the India International Development Cooperation Agency (IIDCA), which would bring all activities related to development cooperation under one umbrella (Ministry of Finance 2007).

India's current interest in courting African countries through aid and expanded trade and investment relations needs to be placed in the context of how Africa is being perceived by India, as well as by the international community, as an attractive continent with unlimited potential for trade and investment. The growing political stability, impressive economic revival and improved credit ratings of several African countries are behind the new thinking in India's active political and economic diplomacy towards the African continent.

It is important to look at how these new developments have translated into certain strategic interests that are shaping Indian development cooperation policy towards Africa. On the one hand, Africa has emerged as an important market for Indian goods and services as well as a vital element in India's quest for energy security. On the other hand, the potential of garnering political support from fifty-three African governments for India's bid to secure a permanent seat in the United Nations Security Council holds the key (Suri 2007: 507–26). Thus, India's engagement in Africa seems to be based on historical factors, economic as well as political interests that are being reflected in its development cooperation policy towards the African continent.

Indian development assistance outflow: volume and instruments involved

It is difficult to ascertain Indian development assistance outflow as a percentage of gross national income (GNI) as precisely as OECD aid-to-GNI ratios because these data are published neither by India nor by the OECD. Various aid analysts have attempted estimates and have come up with different figures. For example, Rowlands (2008) estimated that the Chinese aid-to-GNI ratio may have ranged from 0.01 per cent to 0.1 per cent, and India's ratio is roughly the same. Peter Kragelund, on the other hand, estimated it to be somewhere between 0.01 per cent and 0.02 per cent (Kragelund 2008: 555–84).

There are two development cooperation instruments through which India extends development assistance. The first is India's Aid and Technical Assistance

Programme, which is primarily managed by the Ministry of External Affairs, and the second is lines of credit (LOCs), which were managed by the Department of Economic Affairs (DEA), in the Ministry of Finance (MOF), until 2003/04. After 2003/04, this system was changed as the GOI stopped signing any credit agreements directly with the recipient country. Instead, it began to extend lines of credit through the Export-Import (EXIM) Bank of India. All LOCs are now managed by the EXIM Bank (Rao 2006).

Since there is no centralized agency which publishes Indian development assistance outflow data, an attempt will be made here to estimate the volume of India's government-to-government development assistance outflow. This is based on the data extracted from the Ministry of Finance expenditure budget over the last ten years (see Table 6.1). The objective of the framework followed in Table 6.1 is to disaggregate the outflow on the basis of loans and grants, which will reduce the distortion of the composition of Indian development aid as well as figures relating to different ministries involved in such outflows. It is also important to mention that the table does not reflect the LOCs that have been signed since 2003/04 and are being managed by EXIM Bank. This will be dealt with in the section below.

Volume and composition of aid

India's government-to-government development assistance outflow has been on the rise since 2000, and this includes grants and loans. As shown in Table 6.1, the total grants and loan outflow was Rs 9.2 billion in 1999/2000; the total reached Rs 26.99 billion in 2008/09. It is interesting to observe that India's grant outflow has been continuously on the rise for the last ten years. Grants now constitute approximately 75 per cent of India's development assistance. Over the past ten years, Rs 124.25 billion has been extended as grants, compared to Rs 46.69 billion as loans (Ministry of Finance 2007).

According to Table 6.1, the Ministry of External Affairs is the main conduit of delivery for India's development assistance, delivering 85.75 per cent (Rs 146.59 billion) of the total development assistance of Rs 170.94 billion offered by the GOI over the last ten years. The remaining 12.37 per cent (Rs 21.14 billion) is delivered by the Ministry of Finance. On the other hand, out of the total of Rs 124.25 billion grant aid delivered by India, approximately 95 per cent is routed through the Ministry of External Affairs and 5 per cent through the Ministry of Finance. Out of the total of Rs 46.69 billion delivered as loans, approximately 61 per cent is delivered through the Ministry of External Affairs, 32.5 per cent by the Ministry of Finance and 6.5 per cent through the Ministry of Commerce.

Development cooperation instruments employed

The two development cooperation instruments through which India extends its development assistance are the Aid and Technical Assistance Programme, the

TABLE 6.1 Indian development assistance outflow (in million Rs)

Year	Ministry of External Affairs			Ministry of Finance			Others*			All ministries		
	Grant	Loan	Total	Grant	Loan	Total	Grant	Loan	Total	Grant	Loan	Total
1999/2000	5,941	2,040	7,981	318	920	1,238	25	0	25	6,284	2,960	9,244
2000/01	7,168	2,758	9,926	335	1,005	1,340	25	0	25	7,528	3,763	11,291
2001/02	7,297	2,174	9,472	346	1,026	1,372	25	0	25	7,668	3,200	10,869
2002/03	9,288	2,544	11,832	412	3,146	3,558	20	2,985	3,005	9,719	8,675	18,394
2003/04	10,290	3,240	13,530	1,368	2,570	3,938	25	0	25	11,683	5,810	17,493
2004/05	13,264	2,989	16,253	629	2,717	3,346	20	0	20	13,913	5,706	19,619
2005/06	15,947	2,794	18,741	1,126	1,732	2,858	20	0	20	17,094	4,526	21,620
2006/07	15,015	352	15,367	644	1,256	1,900	21	0	21	15,680	1,608	17,288
2007/08	16,561	480	17,041	400	668	1,068	21	0	21	16,983	1,148	18,131
2008/09	17,301	9,146	26,447	381	148	529	23	0	23	17,705	9,294	26,993
Total	118,072	28,517	146,590	5,959	15,188	21,147	225	2,985	3,210	124,257	46,690	170,942
2009/10**	21,490	1,250	22,740	386	0	386	23	0	23	21,899	1,250	23,149

Notes: * Ministries of Agriculture, Shipping and Commerce ** Proposed budget
Source: Author's compilation (2009) based on revised budget figures of different years of GOI Finance Ministry's Expenditure Budget

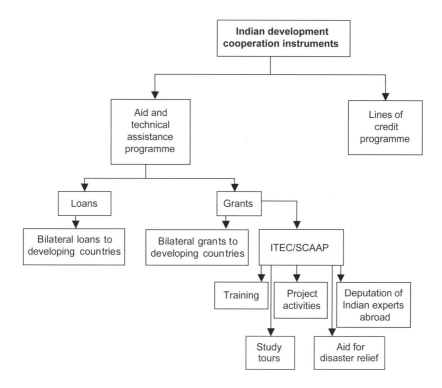

FIGURE 6.1 Indian development cooperation instruments

lines of credit (LOCs) and – last but not least – contributions to international organizations, which include multilateral bodies such as the UN and African Union peacekeeping operations.

India's Aid and Technical Assistance Programme

The Ministry of External Affairs (MEA) is the nodal ministry responsible for extending India's development cooperation in Africa through its various diplomatic missions. The Ministry of Finance and the EXIM Bank are the other institutions responsible for the execution of LOCs, and the following section describes their involvement in the process.

India's Aid and Technical Assistance Programme covers both the bilateral aid programme and the specialized capacity-building programmes. The bilateral aid programme is normally agreed upon by the Ministry of External Affairs and its African counterparts. There are agencies like National Small Industries Corporation (NSIC), Hindustan Machine Tools International Limited (HMTI), Water and Power Consultancy Services Limited (WAPCOS), Rail India Technical and Economic Services (RITES) and Central Electronics Limited (CEL) which have implemented bilateral programmes contracted by the MEA. During 2008/09, for example, forty-nine experts in the civilian and defence field were under

TABLE 6.2 India's aid and technical assistance outflows

Country/region	Outlay (in million Rs)						
	Revised estimate 2003/04	Revised estimate 2004/05	Revised estimate 2005/06	Revised estimate 2006/07	Revised estimate 2007/08	Revised estimate 2008/09	Budget estimate 2009/10
Bangladesh	20	3.3	52	20	60	6	8
Bhutan	696	768.65	1,131.11	541.8	731	1,205.92	961
Nepal	58.48	66.17	66.01	210	100	113	238
Sri Lanka	13.9	15.3	25	28.02	28	30	90
Maldives	3.9	3.2	13.2	6	19.5	504.7	7
Myanmar	2.1	6.21	22	40	20	35	45
ITEC and SCAAP	N/A	N/A	N/A	N/A	60	71	78
African countries	80	106.84	60.98	20	50	95	100
Other developing countries	151.21*	356.72*	503.83*	445.23*	240.08	215.75	36.55
Eurasia					20	18.82	48
Afghanistan					434	418.5	442.05
Total aid budget	1,025.59	1,326.39	1,874.13	1,311.05	1,762.68	2,713.69	2,053.6

Note: Includes Eurasia and Afghanstan
Source: Ministry of External Affairs, India, Annual Reports (various years)

secondment in seventeen African countries in various fields such as information technology, auditing, law, agriculture, statistics and democracy, public administration and pharmacology (Ministry of External Affairs 2008: 109).

The specialized capacity-building programmes include ITEC and SCAAP (Special Commonwealth African Assistance Programme), which have been established to promote cooperation and partnership for mutual benefit, and include training, project activities such as feasibility studies and consultancy services, deputation of Indian experts abroad, study tours and aid for disaster relief. Training includes both civilian and military training and is coordinated through the Indian missions abroad.

Under the ITEC and SCAAP programmes, participants are normally asked to seek nomination from their own ministries/departments or the Foreign Office, which will recommend the application to the Indian high commission or embassy in a particular country. After the grant of scholarship from the Indian Ministry of External Affairs, there are many institutes, such as the Administrative Staff College, that offer civilian training to the selected African participants (Ministry of External Affairs 2009). Army staff colleges and the Centre for United Nations Peacekeeping established in New Delhi are the other institutions involved in the provision of peacekeeping courses under SCAAP/ITEC programmes. ITEC training programmes normally involve the participation of 4,000 civil servants yearly in over two hundred courses and impart training in diplomacy, mass media, foreign trade, management, audit and accounts, banking, human resources planning, agriculture, rural development, small-scale industries, and computer and information technology.

As shown in Table 6.2, compared with India's aid and technical assistance programme to its neighbouring countries, aid to Africa is relatively small and does not exceed 5 per cent in any financial year. In the fiscal year 2009/10, a mere Rs 20.53 billion is allocated under India's aid and technical assistance programme. Out of this total allocation only 3.79 per cent is allocated for ITEC/SCAAP and 4.86 per cent is allocated for African countries (see Table 6.1, above). India has recently increased ITEC slots for African countries from 279 to 575 and the number of scholarships from twenty-one to sixty-six. On the other hand, lines of credit by the EXIM Bank of India to promote economic and business relationships between Africa and India are increasing, as will be discussed below.

India's lines of credit (LOC) programme

Another important but growing component of India's development cooperation programme to Africa is the lines of credit (LOCs) extended by the Export-Import Bank of India. LOCs are generally extended to overseas financial institutions, regional development banks, sovereign governments and other entities overseas, to enable buyers in those countries to import goods and services from India on deferred credit terms. A line of credit is not a foreign aid instrument, but rather

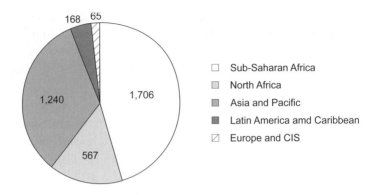

FIGURE 6.2 Indian lines of credit outlay *Source*: EXIM Bank
Annual Report 2008/09

an instrument for promoting international trade. It is used as a tool not only to enhance market diversification but also as an effective market entry mechanism for small and medium Indian enterprises. Indian LOCs are tied to the 'project exports' to the tune of 85 per cent of goods and services to be procured from Indian firms. In order to participate in the promotion of economic growth of these developing countries, Indian companies tend to participate in the execution of many projects, such as railways, information technology, power generation and transmission, buses, sugar mills and agricultural projects.

As of 31 March 2009, US$2.273 billion or 60 per cent of the total of EXIM Bank's operative portfolio of US$375 billion was operational in sub-Saharan Africa and North Africa. During 2008/09, the EXIM Bank extended twenty-five LOCs aggregating US$783.5 million, out of which US$479 million was extended to Africa (EXIM Bank of India 2008). New initiatives to double the existing levels of lines of credit to Africa to US$5.4 billion over the next five years, and a fresh grant of US$500 million in the area of capacity-building and human resource development, will only strengthen and enhance this development cooperation. The increasing volume of LOCs extended to African countries by the EXIM Bank is a good reflection of the private-sector-led thrust of India's Africa policy, which is mentioned by Renu Modi in her chapter in this volume.

Institutional arrangement for approving LOCs

The Ministry of Finance and the EXIM Bank are the two institutions responsible for the execution of the LOC programme. This section describes the approval process. Figure 6.3 outlines the institutions involved for the approval of LOCs and the steps in the approval process. This includes the following:

1 The Ministry of Foreign Affairs of the borrower country requests an LOC, submitting a pre-feasibility report on the proposed project, the estimated cost of project, its justification and the proposed repayment arrangement.

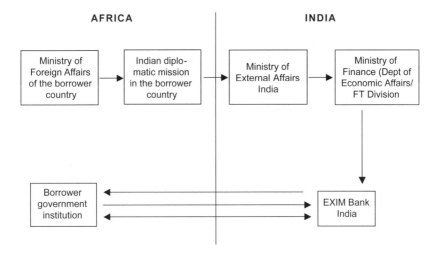

FIGURE 6.3 Institutions and activity flow chart for approval of an LOC
Source: Based on EXIM Bank of India guidelines for LOCs

2   The Indian diplomatic mission in the borrower country forwards the proposal with its recommendations/comments to the headquarters in New Delhi.

3   The Ministry of External Affairs, New Delhi, recommends the proposal to the Foreign Trade Division in the Department of Economic Affairs, Ministry of Finance, for appraisal.

4   The Foreign Trade Division in the Department of Economic Affairs, Ministry of Finance, examines the proposal, obtains internal approval and conveys approval of LOC and terms (interest rate, credit period) to the EXIM Bank.

5   The EXIM Bank, after seeking internal approval, conveys the offer of an LOC and the terms, and sends a draft of the LOC agreement to the borrower government/institution.

6   The borrower government/institution accept the terms of the LOC. It can accept the draft of the agreement or suggest changes and/or amendments to the EXIM Bank and thus the draft of agreement is finalized.

Finally the LOC agreement is signed between the EXIM Bank and the borrower government or institution. The borrower government/institution makes available the documents required to make the agreement effective and the EXIM Bank announces the approval of the agreement. Once the agreement for the LOC is signed by the EXIM Bank and the borrower government, the next stage is its implementation, which includes the approval of contracts/projects proposed under the LOC. There are two scenarios during this stage. First, the projects/contracts are identified prior to approval of the LOC/signing of the LOC agreement. The MOF-DEA approval letter will set out these projects. In the second scenario, projects or contracts are not identified prior to approval of the LOC or signing of the LOC agreement.

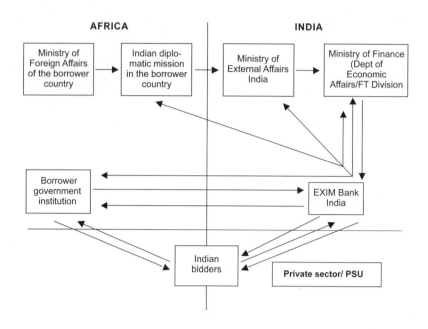

FIGURE 6.4 Institutions and activity flow chart after signing of an LOC
Source: Based on EXIM Bank of India guidelines for LOCs

Under such circumstances, procedures for approval of contracts (Figure 6.4) are as follows:

1 The borrower government/institution proposes a project concept/proposal to the Ministry of External Affairs, New Delhi.

2 The Ministry of External Affairs, New Delhi, recommends project proposals to the Foreign Trade Division in the Department of Economic Affairs (DEA), Ministry of Finance, which forwards them to the EXIM Bank.

3 The EXIM Bank examines GOI-recommended proposals in the light of the provisions of the LOC agreement. If these are found to be in line with all the requirements, it conveys approval for specific contracts/projects to the borrower government/institution, MEA and DEA.

4 After receiving approval from the EXIM Bank, the borrower government/ institution invites bids from Indian bidders.

5 After an evaluation of the awards and bids, the borrower government/institution refers the awarded contract for approval to the EXIM Bank.

6 The EXIM Bank examines the contract in the context of the provisions of the LOC agreement and may seek the following clarifications from the Indian exporter: (i) a list of sub-suppliers and their scope of work, (ii) delivery schedule and (iii) any other information considered necessary.

7 Finally, the EXIM Bank approves the contract and conveys this to the borrower government/institution, MEA, DEA and Indian exporter.

TABLE 6.3 Ongoing Indian development cooperation activities with African regional/multilateral bodies

Institution	Countries	Aid	Trade
African Union	53	Pan-African e-Network project – US$117 million grant under Aid-to-Africa Budget Programme	African Export-Import Bank – US$30 million LOCs from EXIM Bank NEPAD – US$200 million LOC from EXIM Bank
Southern African Development Community	14	–	Eastern and Southern African Trade and Development Bank (PTA Bank) – US$25 million LOCs from EXIM Bank
Eastern African Community (EAC)	10	–	East African Development Bank – US$5 million LOC from EXIM Bank
Economic Community of West African States (ECOWAS)	15	–	West African Development Bank – US$10 million LOC from EXIM Bank ECOWAS Bank for Investment and Development – US$250 million LOC from EXIM Bank
Common Market for Eastern and Southern African Countries (COMESA)	20	–	Overlap with EAC (East African Development Bank) and Eastern and Southern African Trade and Development Bank (PTA Bank)
Economic Community for Central African States (ECCAS)	11	–	–

Source: Author's compilation from EXIM Bank and Ministry of Commerce website

Development cooperation with African regional/multilateral bodies

India's bilateral aid programme is complemented by a multilateral approach whereby the government supports and cooperates with African regional institutions, such as the Africa Union, NEPAD and the five regional economic communities. This is expected to strengthen India's trade partnership with the African continent through participation in regional projects approved by NEPAD and the regional economic communities.

As shown in Table 6.3, it is important to observe that the tools of development cooperation that India employs with African multilateral and regional bodies come into both the aid and the trade categories. While the Pan-African e-Network project, worth US$117 million, is funded under the Aid-to-Africa Budget Programme, the LOCs are extended to the African EXIM Bank and other regional development banks such as PTA Bank and the East African and West African Development Banks (Pan-Africa e-Network 2009). These LOCs allow trading partners in their respective member countries to import Indian equipment, technology, projects, goods and services, on deferred credit terms.

In addition, India has also extended US$200 million dollars to NEPAD through EXIM Bank's lines of credit. It is important to state that these credit lines are not provided to NEPAD as an institution to administer. Instead, the loans are extended to African member countries individually to support commonly agreed regional projects, such as a regional road network or electricity grid. A similar process is adhered to in another initiative – the Techno-Economic Approach for Africa–India Movement, widely known as the TEAM-9 initiative. It is a regional cooperation mechanism set up by the government of India and eight countries in West Africa: Burkina Faso, Chad, Côte d'Ivoire, Equatorial Guinea, Ghana, Guinea Bissau, Mali and Senegal (see chapter by Modi, this volume).

There is also a cooperation arrangement with the International Finance Corporation (IFC) and the EXIM Bank under the African Project Development Facility, African Enterprise Fund, Technical Assistance and Trust Fund for providing consultancy support services in Africa. The EXIM Bank has been a partner institution in establishing the African EXIM Bank (Afreximbank) and the design and implementation of export finance programmes of industrial development in South Africa. Further, there is a strong relationship in terms of a co-financing agreement with the African Development Bank (Rao 2006).

India is also a signatory to economic treaties with regional entities such as the AU, NEPAD, SADC and ECOWAS. And according to Thomas Feus (2008: 6): 'India finds itself in harmony with the declared societal values of the AU and NEPAD, but agrees with China's position on absolute sovereignty, that is, not interfering in a country's domestic political affairs.'

Are Indian lines of credit concessional enough to qualify as ODA?

Indian lines of credit are granted on the basis of the Paris Club initiative and the World Bank classification. Except for countries with middle-level income and medium to high levels of debt (MILD), all other countries access these lines of credit on concessional terms. The grant element is 41.25 per cent for the highly indebted poor countries (HIPC) group, 35.11 per cent for countries having a low income and high levels of debt (LIHD) and 28.75 per cent for countries having a middle-level income and high levels of debt (MIHD).

TABLE 6.4 Terms and conditions of Indian lines of credit

Group	Interest (%)	Period	Grace	Grant element (%)
HIPC declared under the Paris Club Initiative	1.75 (fixed)	20	5	41.25
LIHD*	LIBOR + 0.5 (floating)	15	5	35.11
MIHD	LIBOR + 0.5 (floating)	12	4	28.75
MILD *	LIBOR + 0.5 (floating)	8–10	2–3	17.11–24.56

Note: *According to the World Bank Statistical Appendix 2003
Source: Ministry of Commerce, India

As OECD defines them, the concessional loans are 'extended on terms substantially more generous than market loans' and 'the concessionality is achieved either through interest rates below those available on the market or by grace periods, or a combination of these. Concessional loans typically have longer grace period' (OECD 2003). In the case of HIPC, the interest rate charged under the Indian LOC is 1.75 per cent at the fixed rate, with twenty years' repayment and a five-year grace period. The grant element constitutes 41.25 per cent of the loan, making it highly concessional (EXIM Bank of India 2008; Rao 2006). Thus, on the basis of the concessionality of loans, Indian LOCs targeted towards heavily indebted African countries definitely qualify as official development assistance (ODA) because they carry a grant element of at least 25 per cent.

But can Indian LOCs be technically considered as ODA?

As India does not adhere to OECD/DAC guidelines and extends LOCs as one of its development cooperation tools, it is important to understand what definition of development assistance they would fall under and whether they can technically qualify as ODA or not. Looking into the OECD's wider definitions of official development finance, it seems that they could either fall into the classification of ODA or officially supported exported credits (OSEC), depending on the purpose and concessionality element of the financial flows (OECD 2003).

As discussed above, Indian LOCs have qualified as ODA on the basis of their concessionality element as they carry a grant element of more than 25 per cent. Nevertheless, since the purpose of LOCs extended by India is to promote international trade through financing the export of goods and services, it is likely that they would fall into the category of OSEC and not ODA. It is important to explore how OECD/DAC segregates the issue of LOCs vis-à-vis the grant element/concessionality. It is interesting to note that OECD guidelines on ODA state that any 'lending by export credit agencies – with the pure purpose of export promotion – is excluded' from the category of ODA. Therefore, based on this guideline, Indian LOCs do not qualify to be termed as ODA.

Indian development cooperation: aid, trade and investment linkages

Before exploring the interlinkages between aid, trade and investment of Indian development cooperation in Africa, it is important to look again at the volume of Indian trade and FDI engagement in Africa. On the one hand, bilateral trade between India and Africa rose sharply to US$36 billion in 2007/08, which was a twelvefold increase since 2000/01. On the other hand, outward FDI flows to Africa during 2000–07 amounted to US$2.96 billion, an increase of 836 per cent compared with 1990–99. Interestingly, 56 per cent of such FDI has been in the manufacturing sector (chemicals, rubber, plastic and transport equipment were the top sectors), followed by 32 per cent in the service industry, with only 18 per cent in the primary sector – that is, raw materials (Pradhan 2008). Most of the FDI targeted towards the raw materials category was in the extractive sector – that is, natural gas and petroleum.

TABLE 6.5 Indian aid, trade and investment flows in Africa: geographical distribution (in US$ million)

Region	FDI flows	AfT lines of credit	Foreign trade	
			Export	Import
	2000–07	2004–Mar. 2009	2001–Dec. 2008	2001–Dec. 2008
North Africa	508	567	12,032	16,916
Southern Africa	24	1,706	13,948	24,165
West Africa	203		15,293	31,591
Central Africa	63		1,392	276
East Africa	2,170		15,483	1,745
TOTAL	2,968	2,273	58,148	74,693

Source: Pradhan (2008: 12–13); EXIM Bank of India (2008: 31)

Africa is an important market for Indian goods and services as well as a source of petroleum and other raw materials that India needs to run its growing economy. It is therefore important to explore whether Indian foreign aid has played any role in the massive increase in trade and investment between India and Africa. The task of answering this question is not an easy one, and it requires empirical evidence from the ground to substantiate it. The key challenge remains disaggregation of the composition of what India calls development assistance. At present, India's development assistance is a mixed bag of project assistance, purchase subsidies, lines of credit and technical training programmes. The absence of comprehensive definitions, measurements and accounting methods makes it difficult to adequately assess the real impact of different instruments of development cooperation on African development on the ground.

If it is not ODA then is it Aid for Trade?

As the purpose of Indian LOCs is to promote developmental activities as well as international trade through financing the export of goods and services, it is essential to see how this development instrument fares in the established international context. The question arises as to whether it is aid for development, or an instrument for promoting trade between India and Africa. It is important to remember that India was actively encouraging African countries to sign up to more LOCs while the OECD was simultaneously carrying out a policy dialogue with its non-OECD members to buy into Aid for Trade (AfT) as an engine of economic growth and poverty reduction (OECD 2006). This was organized on the basis of recommendations of the WTO task force to operationalize the AfT.

TABLE 6.6 Financing for trade (commitment in US$ millions current)

	2002	2003	2004	2005	2006	2007
AfT other official finance	11,412	11,904	9,986	14,176	20,234	27,305
AfT official development assistance	14,316	17,855	23,768	21,976	23,589	27,084

Source: OECD/WTO (2009: 54)

AfT, which includes other types of official finance as well as ODA, was found to be an integral component of financing for trade. As the figures in Table 6.6 are calculated only for OECD/DAC donor countries and not for emerging donors like India, it is possible that if India's LOCs were considered using the same yardstick, they would fall into the category of 'AfT other official finance' and be widely recognized as a trade instrument (OECD/WTO 2009).

What's the issue of tied aid vis-à-vis export credit?

The issue of tied aid in Indian lines of credit originates from the blurred line drawn between the way ODA and officially supported export credit is defined by the OECD. It is important to mention that, on the one hand, the development cooperation directorate of the OECD precludes export credits from being termed as ODA and, on the other hand, the trade and agriculture directorate of the OECD agrees that officially supported export credits cannot be considered as tied aid as long as they are in conformity with their agreed arrangement. Thus OECD/DAC members are agreeing to complementary policies for export credits and tied aid where export credit policies should be based on open competition and the free play of market forces. At the same time, tied aid policies should provide needed external resources to countries, sectors or projects with little or no access to market financing (OECD 2009: 17). At the moment it seems that India, like other Southern donors, is not interested in determining whether its lines of credit fall under the category of ODA or not. This is because extending such lines of credits is primarily considered as promotion of trade and investment under South–South cooperation rather than as foreign aid.

The role of Indian development cooperation in 'oil for infrastructure' deals

In its quest for energy security, India, like China, has also started striking 'oil for infrastructure' deals in Africa. As Obi, Naidu and Vines and Campos (this volume) eloquently elaborate, India has stepped up its diplomatic offensive in West Africa's Gulf of Guinea, where 70 per cent of African oil is extracted. It has gone toe to toe with the Chinese oil companies to win extractive rights from Angola, Nigeria and Gabon. In the recent past, Essar Oil Limited (in the Kenyan petroleum refinery sector), ONGC Videsh Limited (OVL) (in the oil and gas sector in Sudan), the OVL and Indian Oil Corporation (OIL-IOC) consortium (in Libya's hydrocarbon sector) and Mittal Energy Limited (MEL) (iron ore extraction in Liberia) have made natural resource deals. The 'resources for infrastructure' deal in Africa is best demonstrated in the case of a joint venture between OVL and MEL winning oil exploration rights in Nigeria in exchange for an investment of US$6 billion to construct an oil refinery and a power plant and to produce a feasibility study for a new east–west railway line (see chapter by Obi, this volume). Arcelor Mittal (formerly Mittal Steel) is also expected to invest US$1.5 billion in restoring the railways and port infrastructure in Liberia (see chapters by Obi and Vines and Campos, this volume).

All these investments are reported as being part of outward foreign direct investments. Whether technical assistance or LOCs are used to finance any of these investments is difficult to verify owing to the nature of classification of India's development cooperation data. While comparing Indian and Chinese national oil companies' presence in Nigeria and Angola, a recent Chatham

House report observed that 'India is both more risk-averse and more cautious about spending public money in the extractive sectors than China has been since India as a democracy is more accountable to its electorate' (Vines et al. 2009: 4). But as the competition between India and China for African resources heats up, it is possible that India's policy could change. Only time will tell.

Conclusion

In conclusion, it can be said that Indian development cooperation, which started out with the principle of South–South cooperation and mutual benefits, has changed over time and is now focused on promoting India's strategic and commercial interests in Africa. Moreover, the scattered approach in development is expected to be brought under one umbrella agency, namely the India International Development Cooperation Agency. This is a positive step forward and will enhance coordination and efficiency in the delivery of aid.

Indeed, compared to that of traditional DAC donors and even of China, the volume of Indian development assistance outflows is quite small. On the other hand, the volume of export credits (LOCs) to Africa is growing year by year, though still not at a comparable level with China's. As a recent report by the US–China working group pointed out, China's EXIM Bank has extended several oil-backed loans worth US$4.5 billion to Angola for reconstruction projects in the petroleum sector. The EXIM Bank financing also brings together a host of other Chinese construction and oil companies in a coordinated way to dominate the Angolan market (Levkowitz et al. 2009). This coordinated approach by the Chinese state is likely to put pressure on the government of India to take a more proactive approach to counter Chinese influence in Africa. This would necessarily mean pouring more money into Africa and giving African states more generous trading terms and more aid and credits on concessional terms.

It is too early to accurately assess the real impact of India's development cooperation with Africa. More empirical research is needed to explore the following questions: what are the interlinkages between the three development cooperation channels, i.e. aid, trade and investments, and how are they targeted towards the different sectors of African economies – the primary, secondary and tertiary sectors? Are they targeted towards extraction of raw materials, manufacturing of goods or the service industry? And finally, what are the development outcomes or the policy implications, especially in terms of growth, distribution, governance and environment in the recipient countries? For now, however, it is clear that the broad thrust of India's development cooperation policy towards Africa has been to increase the country's geopolitical influence and to promote India's private business interests in the continent.

PART THREE

China and India's growth surge in Africa

7 | China and India's growth surge: the implications for African manufactured exports

Alemayehu Geda and Atnafu G. Meskel

Most studies of the impact of the Asian drivers are on Latin America and Asia, studies on African being limited. As Goldstein and co-authors (2006) noted, the sheer size of the Asian drivers, their phenomenal rate of growth and their growing economic and political power mean that they will reshape the world economy and change the rules of the game. Thus, it is likely that they will transform past relationships in a number of key respects, bringing both challenges and opportunities not just for the major trading partners in OECD countries, but also for developing countries such as those in Africa; and thus, the need to understand their interaction with Africa.

The rise of China and India is both a threat and an opportunity for Africa. Trade between Africa and China surged from US$3 billion in 1995 to US$32 billion in 2005 and about US$55 billion in 2007, although Africa makes up only 2.3 per cent of China's world trade. This trade is expected to double by 2010. For some African countries exports to China are becoming a significant share of their world exports. As key net importers of commodities from Africa, this means that global commodity markets are likely to be the main channels through which the impact of China and India's ascendancy has been (and will be) felt on the African continent (Eichengreen et al. 2004). African countries that export labour-intensive manufactures may also face competition in the third market where China and India are active – this seems a potential threat to Africa. There are also opportunities for some countries to increase exports to China and India as incomes in China and India increase (Jenkins and Edwards 2005: ii). But we do not know exactly what the balance of these challenges is and what opportunities exist in Africa.

According to Goldstein and co-authors (2006), the limited available empirical studies of Africa along these lines include those by Jenkins and Edwards (2005) and Stevens and Kennan (2006). The former combines a disaggregated trade analysis with a framework to assess trade–poverty linkages, whereas the latter estimates the impact of China on African countries' trade balance and draws a tentative list of African 'losers' and 'winners' from China's rise in the international trade arena. The study by Kaplinsky et al. (2006) is also inconclusive. They summarized the trade, production and foreign direct investment

(FDI) and aid-related impact of China and India on Africa in terms of direct (both complementary and competitive) and indirect (both complementary and competitive) impacts, and noted that it is difficult to conclude whether the impact is positive or negative across countries and sectors. The availability of studies is even weaker in the case of India (Alemayehu 2006). This chapter aims to help close this gap in the literature.

Modelling the China–Africa relation in manufacturing exports

There are two major questions that this chapter attempts to address. First, we ask whether African exports are displaced by Chinese and Indian export growth in the third market. If the answer to this question is yes, then the growth of China and India could be a threat or a challenge to Africa. It may not be a major threat, however, if African countries are stepping into the manufacturing export space that is left by China and India. This leads to the second major question of this chapter: are African countries indeed stepping into this space as China and India move up the technological ladder? In this chapter the first question is addressed using the 'gravity model' approach, while the second question is handled using the 'flying-geese (FG) model'. We attempt to offer a fairly comprehensive answer to these questions based on the result of the two models.

Are African exporters being displaced by China and India?

To examine whether the Asian drivers are displacing the African exporters in the third market, we employ a gravity model as given by Equation 1 below. The gravity model has been widely used to study the determinants of bilateral trade flows among trading countries, beginning with pioneering applied econometric work by Tinbergen (1962) and Pöyhönen (1963). The model is formed on the central idea that income and distance between countries are respectively positive and negative determinants of bilateral trade. The model we used will have three fundamental determinants of bilateral trade volume: (a) export supply capacity, captured by income and income per capita of the exporting country; (b) import demand captured by income and income per capita of the importing country; and (c) resistance or attraction captured by distance and well-known gravity model variables such as border sharing. These fundamental determinants are augmented by the local (exporter) country effect, and the time (business cycle effect) as given by Equation 1 below.

$$InM_{ijt} = \beta_0 + \beta_1 ChEXP_{it} + \beta_2 InIndEXP_{it} + \beta_3 InGDP_{it} + \beta_4 InCAPM_{it} + \beta_5 InGDPX_{jt} +$$
$$\beta_6 InCAPX_{jt} + \beta_7 InDIST_{ijt} + \beta_8 InAreap_{ijt} + \beta_9 Broader_{ijt} + \beta_{10} Comlang_{ijt} +$$
$$\beta_{11} Comcol_{ijt} + \beta_{12} Colony_{ijt} + \beta_{13} ImpCorrup_{it} + \alpha_i + \lambda_i + \varepsilon_{it}$$

where:
M_{ijt} imports of country i from the African country j at time t
$ChEXP_{it}$ exports of China to third market i at time t

$INDEX_{it}$ exports of India to third market i at time t

GDP_{it} real GDP of the importing country i at time t

$CAPX_{it}$ real per capita GDP of the importing country i at time t

$GDPX_{jt}$ real GDP of the exporting country j at time t

$CAPX_{jt}$ real per capita GDP of exporting country j at time t

$DIST_{ijt}$ ristance between i and j at time t

$Areap_{ijt}$ product of country size/area of country pairs i and j a time t

$Broader_{ij}$ binary dummy which is unity if i and j share a land border, zero otherwise

$Comlang_{itj}$ binary dummy which is unity if i and j share a common language, zero otherwise, at time t

$Comcol_{ijt}$ binary dummy which is unity if i and j were ever colonials with the same colonizer, zero otherwise, at time t

$Colony_{ijt}$ binary dummy which is unity if i ever colonized j or vice versa, zero otherwise

$ImpCorrup_{it}$ importer's corruption index at time t

α_i the exporter country effect

λ_t the time (business cycle effect)

ε_{ijt} white noise disturbance term

Based on the UN Economic Commission for Africa (UNECA) reporting system a total of thirteen countries that export clothing and accessories are selected using probability sampling. We have used the pooled data consisting of six importing countries regarded as the third market (France, Nigeria, Uganda, the UK, the USA and Zimbabwe), thirteen exporting countries (Algeria, Burkina Faso, Côte d'Ivoire, Gabon, Ghana, Kenya, Lesotho, Madagascar, Niger, Rwanda, South Africa, Tunisia and Zambia), for the sample period 1995–2005. The thirteen countries constitute 73 per cent of the African exports of clothing and accessories recorded during the study period.

Empirical results As can be read from Table 7.1, over the period 1995–2005 China's exports of clothing and accessories significantly displaced African exports of the same from the third market with a statistically significant elasticity coefficient of minus 2.25. On the other hand our result shows a positive elasticity of 2.1 for India. Thus Indian manufacturing exports are found to complement African exports of this commodity in the third market. This may entail a rather close link between Indian and African manufacture-exporting firms compared to that between Chinese and African firms. This requires further study, however, using micro-level data.

Given the above evidence that China's exports of clothing and accessories are driving out African exports from the third market, it is interesting to ask which African exporters are facing severe competition from China. By looking at country-specific dummies, we note that Niger, Zambia and Burkina Faso

TABLE 7.1 G2LSLS IV regression result: dependent variable log of third market imports

Explanatory variables	coefficient	t-ratio	P-value
Log of China's export	−2.25	-3.69	0.00
Log of India's export	2.08	4.64	0.00
Log of importers' real GDP	0.33	0.70	0.49
Log of exporters' real GDP	−1.91	−1.00	0.32
Log of exporters' real GDP per capita	−1.50	−1.57	0.12
Log of importers' real GDP per capita	0.23	0.22	0.83
Log of distance between importer and exporter countries	−1.18	−4.52	0.00
Log of importer and exporters' land area product	2.04	3.58	0.00
Importer corruption index	0.81	1.35	0.18
Common border between importer and exporter countries	1.73	2.24	0.03
Common language between importer and exporter countries	1.69	2.92	0.00
Importer and exporters being colonized by common colonizer	0.13	0.30	0.76
Importer post-1945 colonization of exporters	1.96	2.76	0.01
α − Exporter-specific dummy for Algeria	−10.68	−2.32	0.02
α − Exporter-specific dummy for Burkina Faso	−14.87	−2.79	0.01
α − Exporter-specific dummy for Côte d'Ivoire	−8.70	−2.59	0.01
α − Exporter-specific dummy for Gabon	−8.70	−3.32	0.00
α − Exporter-specific dummy for Ghana	−11.74	−2.63	0.01
α − Exporter-specific dummy for Kenya	−7.54	−2.16	0.03
α − Exporter-specific dummy for Lesotho	−9.75	−1.49	0.14
α − Exporter-specific dummy for Madagascar	−11.03	−1.49	0.03
α − Exporter-specific dummy for Niger	−19.92	−3.17	0.00
α − Exporter-specific dummy for Rwanda	−11.78	−1.98	0.05
α − Exporter-specific dummy for South Africa	−2.37	−0.40	0.69
α − Exporter-specific dummy for Tunisia	−0.04	−0.01	0.99
α − Exporter-specific dummy for Zambia	−16.88	−3.43	0.00
1995 − time-specific dummy for year 1995	−3.74	−2.07	0.04
1996 − time-specific dummy for year 1996	−3.18	−3.60	0.00
1997 − time-specific dummy for year 1997	−1.90	−2.33	0.02
1998 − time-specific dummy for year 1998	−2.62	−3.04	0.00
1999 − time-specific dummy for year 1999	−2.45	−3.05	0.00
2000 − time-specific dummy for year 2000	−0.94	−1.31	0.19
2002 − time-specific dummy for year 2002	1.32	1.88	0.06
2003 − time-specific dummy for year 2003	0.87	1.17	0.24
2004 − time-specific dummy for year 2004	2.51	2.71	0.01
2005 − time-specific dummy for year 2005	3.04	2.66	0.01
Constant	16.13	0.32	0.75
R2 within 0.3711	0.37		
Between 0.9404	0.94		

Overall 0.5002; Waldchi2(36) 964.72; Number of observations 858; Prob>chi2 0.0000; Sigma _U 0; Sigma_e 4.103549; Rho 0 (fraction of variance due to Ui)

are the three most vulnerable exporters of clothing and accessories, followed by Ghana, Algeria, Gabon, Côte d'Ivoire and Kenya, which also experienced a displacement effect from China (see Table 7.1). Looking at these exporters, we note that, except for Zambia, Ghana and Kenya, most of the affected countries are the former French colonies. This may suggest a possible effect of colonial history in determining export performance and hence third-market effect.

It can be read from Table 7.1 that the early years (1995–99) were characterized by higher displacement of African exports from the third market than the later years. The displacement effect, however, was declining up to 1999. In fact, the years 2004 and 2005 did show complementary effects. This result may also be related to the effect of the African Growth and Opportunity Act (AGOA), which was passed in 2000 and gave African countries unlimited duty-free and quota-free access to the US market for clothing made with US materials in eligible African countries. China and India have been particularly keen to exploit the opportunities provided by AGOA by actively investing in the beneficiary sectors of AGOA-eligible African countries. This may have created a channel for African exports and the Asian drivers' exports to complement each other in the third market. This underscores the importance of focusing on the dynamics of the impacts as the effects may vary across time.

Is Africa stepping into the export space left by China and India? The 'flying-geese' theorem

Even though Africa may be displaced by the surge in China's and India's export growth in the third market, it may still benefit from this growth, if Africans are stepping into the manufacturing export space left by the Asian drivers as the latter move up the technological ladder of manufacturing exports.

A theoretical framework that helps to see this is what is called the 'flying-geese' (FG) theorem (see Kojima 2000; Ozawa 2001; Cutler et al. 2003; Kasahara 2004, among others). In this theorem latecomers successfully adopt a strategy of entering sectors in which they have a rising comparative advantage and import technology from a more mature economy whose advantage in that industry is declining. The latter in turn invest in newer industrial projects using more advanced technology and know-how in which they have an innovative edge (Rana 1990: 244).

In this study, the degree and nature of export specialization association between Africa and the Asian drivers is thus evaluated by estimating the Spearman's rank correlation (SRC) coefficients of revealed comparative advantage (RCA) between the Asian drivers and Africa in the world market of manufacturing products. On the other hand, the revealed comparative advantage index (RCAI) compares a country's world export shares of the commodity in question with the total exports of the country in question (Mahmood 2001). If a country's share of world export of a particular commodity is greater than the country's share of world exports of all commodities, the RCAI will be greater than one (Lutz 1987; Rana 1990; Dowling and Cheang 2000; Mahmood 2001). The SRC coefficient is widely used to analyse the degree of association between two variables and is given by Equation 2 (see, for example, Dowling and Cheang 2000; Mahmood 2001).

$$SRC = 1 - \frac{6}{N(N^2 - 1)} \sum_{i=1}^{N} D_{RCAIi}$$

Where:

SRC = the Spearman's rank correlation coefficient
N = the number of observations or product group categories
D_{RCAIi} = the difference between any pair of RCAI ranking of two countries

In the next section, using the FG theoretical framework, we address the following questions: (i) whether there is evidence of industrial development through shifting comparative advantage in African clothing and accessories manufacturing (Lutz 1987); (ii) whether there is a shift in comparative advantage from China and India to Africa in clothing and accessories manufacturing (Dowling and Cheang 2000; Mahmood 2001); and (iii) whether this is beneficial to Africa. The sign and magnitude of the SRC will give us an implication of shifting comparative advantage between the African exporters of clothing and accessories relative to that of China and India.

Empirical results A data exploration of the trend of RCAI for each country reveals the following major points. First, in the period 1995–99 RCAIs declined for most of the African exporters in our sample (with minor exceptions for Rwanda, Gabon and Ghana). On the other hand, the RCAI vectors of China and India were moderately stable. This means that India's and China's investment during this period had a negative impact, *resulting in displacement* of local firms in Algeria, Burkina Faso, Côte d'Ivoire, Lesotho, Madagascar, Niger and Zambia.

In the period 2000–04, however, RCAIs for African exporters varied. For Gabon, the RCAI was initially rising, then declining after 2002, while for Ghana it was initially volatile but declined at the end. For Tunisia, it was stable. The RCAIs for Kenya and South Africa show consistent and significant rises after 2002. On the other hand, the RCAIs of China and India declined moderately from their value in the year 2000, even though the level (of values) of exports of China and India has been rising. We conclude that China's and India's *investments in the latter years have had a complementary effect*, particularly for Tunisia, Kenya and South Africa.

Given the above result, it is useful to examine whether increases in RCAI were beneficial in terms of African exporters gaining comparative advantage. This will be so if the world demand for clothing and accessories is shown to be growing fast. We used the growth rate of world imports during 1995–2004 as a proxy for the growth of world demand for clothing and accessories. Positive correlation between the changes in the RCAI vectors during a given period and the growth rate of a particular country's share of world demand would mean that the country had successfully gained comparative advantage in commodities that have growing world demand. A negative sign would mean that the country gained comparative advantage in a declining industry (Rana 1990). Since Kenya and South Africa were the countries that gained comparative advantage, we focus our analysis on them. We found that the correlation coefficient between the RCAI and the growth in world demand of manufacture export vectors was 0.32 and −0.056 for Kenya and South Africa respectively. *Thus, Kenya was gaining comparative advantage in the study period while South Africa was gaining comparative advantage in a declining industry.*

Having this evidence, we further explored whether South Africa has moved from manufacturing of clothing and accessories to a higher rung on the ladder of industrial development as the FG theory would predict. To test this, the Spearman's rank correlation (SRC) between RCAI vectors of each of the thirteen African exporter countries on the one hand and China and India on the other is calculated for the period 1995–2004. A negative and statistically significant coefficient suggests that the recipient country/group of countries replaces the source recipient country/group of countries, thus indicating unidirectional shifts in comparative advantage (Dowling and Cheang 2000). In this context, a negative sign would mean Africa is increasing its industrial development. The result of this analysis is given in Table 7.2 below.

TABLE 7.2 Spearman's rank correlation coefficient between the RCAIs of African exporters and the Asian drivers (China and India)

No.	African exporter	China		India	
		Rho	P-value	Rho	P-value
1	Algeria	0.25	0.49	0.23	0.52
2	Burkina Faso	0.50	0.14	0.49	0.15
3	Côte d'Ivoire	0.57	0.08	−0.22	0.55
4	Gabon	−0.36	0.31	−0.06	0.87
5	Ghana	0.27	0.44	−0.07	0.85
6	Kenya	0.65*	0.04	0.24	0.50
7	Lesotho	−0.08	0.82	0.50	0.14
8	Madagascar	0.19	0.60	0.71*	0.02
9	Niger	0.85**	0.00	0.62*	0.06
10	Rwanda	−0.05	0.90	−0.24	0.50
11	South Africa	−0.67*	0.04	−0.14	0.69
12	Tunisia	−0.16	0.65	−0.11	0.76
13	Zambia	0.14	0.70	−0.13	0.71

Notes: * Significant at 5 per cent   ** Significant at 1 per cent

From the table, we note that Kenya, Madagascar and Niger are the African exporters with a positive and significant SRC. The SRC between Kenya and China is 0.65 and significant at 5 per cent while the SRC between Madagascar and India is 0.71 and significant at 5 per cent. Between Niger and China and Niger and India, SRCs are 0.85 and 0.62 respectively and both significant at 5 per cent. *Thus, we conclude that these countries' manufacturing exports did not receive comparative advantage from China and India to undergo substantial structural change in manufacturing.*

Niger, Madagascar and Kenya, in order of importance according to the degree of their comparative advantage, are moving in the same direction as China and India. The SRC between South Africa and China, however, is −0.67 and significant at 5 per cent. *Thus we conclude that South Africa has received comparative advantage from China, has undergone a substantial structural change in the clothing industry and has moved to the next stage of industrial development. This makes South Africa a 'leading goose' in the African region.*

In the case of South Africa, the available evidence on the linkages is well documented. As Rogerson (2000) puts it, the decade (1990–2000) was noted as a period when the clothing sector in South Africa underwent a metamorphosis as protected domestic manufacturers gave way to a market that was increasingly exposed to international competition. In the view of the National Clothing Federation of South Africa, in the year 2000 the clothing sector in South Africa was undergoing dramatic change and was in the process of entering the global market (ibid.: 694). The implications of this finding for the rest of Africa need to be further examined by an in-depth country study that takes into account both the direct and indirect impact of the Asian drivers on the country in question.

Conclusion

This chapter has attempted to quantify the possible impact of China and India on Africa, using the case of manufacturing exports of clothing and accessories. First, we found that China and India affect Africa differently. Their impact is also found to vary across time. In the early years of the study period, particularly before the year 2000, the overall impact of China was to crowd out African labour-intensive manufacturing exports. India, on the other hand, has been complementing the African exports of labour-intensive manufacture in the third market.

However, *the overall impact of China and India seems to be that of complementarity during the later years of the study period.* This is open to two different interpretations. First, it could be that during the early years, Africa was importing consumer goods that did not have a production-enhancing effect on manufacturing in China, while also competing in the third market with China, whereas it was importing capital goods or skills from India that augmented African manufacturing production. The complementarity effect during the later years in the study period may imply that Africa has been importing production-augmenting capital goods or skills and technology from both China and India.

The other reason may have to do with the African Growth and Opportunity Act of May 2000, which provides duty-free and quota-free access to the US market to SSA's textile products made from US fabrics, yarns and threads (Nouve and Staatz 2003). Obviously, duty-free access to SSA's exports to the USA would mean that the duty-free importing by the USA offsets high initial production costs in Africa, which enabled Africa to compete with China and India on the US market. Interestingly, Chinese and Indian firms were active in investing in Africa to exploit this opportunity at this time.

The second major finding is that the impact varies across countries. The source of these variations could also be different. But one source of variation seems to be colonial history. This could be read from the fact that (i) the dummy variable for the importer's colonization history of the exporters is significant and positive and (ii), except in the case of Tunisia, the country-specific dummies for former colonies of France are significant and negative. This could provide evidence of how little the destinations of African exports have changed from the colonial period. Once these markets become open to China and India's exports, it is possible that African manufacturing exports will be crowded out from these markets.

The third finding, using the FG theoretical framework of industrial development, was evidence of a significant shift in comparative advantage from the Asian drivers to Africa. Other empirical studies (see, for example, Rogerson 2000) have also shown that South Africa has gained comparative advantage and has undergone substantial structural change in its manufacturing and trade. Be that as it may, given that different African countries are affected by China and India differently, and owing to the dynamic nature of the impacts, it will be difficult to offer specific suggestions as to how to design an optimum strategic policy that could enable African manufacturing exporters to maximize the benefits while minimizing the risks. We offer the following two important conclusions.

First, *in the world where China and India are rearranging the global economic order dynamically, the outcomes of the traditionally received wisdom of trade liberalization and industrialization policies, such as a simple export promotion strategy, may be dubious.* This is particularly true in a situation where African exporters of labour-intensive manufacturing commodities adopt endowment-based trade policies, and yet our econometric estimate, using the gravity model, offered evidence that China's labour-intensive manufactured exports are crowding out similar African commodities from the third market. This underscores the need to rethink African trade and industrial policies in general and the continent's interaction with China and India in particular.

On the other hand, the negative impact of SSA dependence on primary commodity exports is reflected in three interdependent phenomena: a decline in terms of trade, instability of export earnings, and absolute decline in levels of demand and supply (Alemayehu 2002, 2006). This situation might be changing. In the first place, China's and India's growth is creating a demand surge for African commodities. The continent need not be left worse off, however, as has been the case historically, once the boom ends. Thus, deals must be made to sustain it – through, for example, downstreaming linkages and local partnership (World Economic Forum 2006: 11).

What is important for Africa may not relate to the static gain and loss but to the future industrialization of Africa and the space left by China and India (Kaplinsky et al. 2006; see also Alemayehu 2006). In this regard it is important to think about and act on the possible impact of the Asian drivers' trade and perhaps also the related FDI impact in locking African countries into the primary commodity sector, especially in the long run. Moreover, the demand boom for commodities may lead to problems of management of such resources (such as the Dutch Disease effect and possibly conflict among the political elite), which should be a central policy issue. *Despite the possible threat alluded to above, however, there is a need to change from a defensive mind-set about China and India to one that is more embracing, and one in which the Africans determine the terms of engagement* (see also World Economic Forum 2006: 12).

Africans need to develop the dynamic capability to scan changing environments, to develop appropriate strategic responses and to implement these strategies effectively (Kaplinsky et al. 2006). This may include the possibility of exploiting joint ventures with the Asian drivers as well as identifying niches for African exporters. There is also the need to actively seek investment linkages with the drivers as well as locating one's country so as to benefit from being part of certain industrial supply chains with the drivers.

Second, *for Africa to benefit from a shift in comparative advantage from China and India, it is important to understand the long-term trend of the growth of world demand for the commodities in which Africa is gaining comparative advantage.* Otherwise, it is possible that Africa gains comparative advantage, but in commodities in which the growth rates of world demand are declining, implying that Africa is not benefiting from this shift in comparative advantage.

Finally, we caution readers that this study has examined only one aspect of Africa's interaction with China and India. This is only a single channel through which the impact of the Asian drivers could be transmitted to Africa. Other channels, however, such as FDI, governance and aid, are open to research. Furthermore, Chinese and Indian investments in some sectors, such as mining, the domestic market and the impact of such investments on income and poverty reduction in Africa are areas for future research. Specific country-based studies are fundamental to charting mutually beneficial interaction between African countries and emerging economies such as those of China and India.

8 | Chinese investment in African network industries: case studies from the Democratic Republic of Congo and Kenya

Peter Draper, Tsidiso Disenyana and
Gilberto Biacuana

Africa's development needs are enormous; the question is whether China's African safari can be harnessed to address them. Initial debates on this subject were characterized alternately by euphoria (at last a power to challenge former colonizers) and hysteria (China's footprint is exploitative). In recent years the debate has become more measured and nuanced, and overall opinion seems to be shifting to the positive side of the pendulum, albeit with reservations concerning governance issues.

This chapter contributes to the debate by drawing on two case studies of Chinese investment in Africa: communications in the Democratic Republic of Congo; and solar energy in Kenya. Both represent service sectors crucial to the functioning of modern economies which are highly relevant to Africa's pressing development priorities. Our point of departure is that African economies lack the capacities to develop these network services in the short to medium term; hence Chinese foreign direct investment (FDI) has the potential to build them competitively. A subsidiary question is whether the modus operandi of Chinese multinational corporations (MNCs), in collaboration with the Chinese state, undermines these potential gains. The chapter considers the general nature of Chinese outward FDI via an assessment of the literature on FDI by emerging market MNCs (EMMNCs). Next some empirical evidence relating to China's outward FDI thrust into Africa is presented. Our two case studies are presented in light of the lessons learned from the review of EMMNC literature and patterns of Chinese FDI into Africa. The final section presents our conclusions.

Outward FDI: motivations and entry modes

Dunning (1973; see also 2001) identified three primary motivations for FDI. First, extending ownership of proprietary assets abroad. This ownership motivation is conventionally taken to extend to acquisition of resources abroad, or 'resource-seeking'. Second, MNCs could invest in order to establish offshore production platforms and leverage specific locational advantages such as access to cheap labour or local distribution networks in order to integrate their activities globally. Conventionally this is known as 'efficiency-seeking' investment. Location advantages could also be considered as deriving from the home market and constitute country-specific advantages (CSAs) based on resource endowments – a factor clearly at play in China's global economic emergence. Third, the process of extending firm-specific advantages (FSAs) abroad is known as 'internalization'. This process can in turn give rise to ownership advantages, by extending economies of scope and scale in production through FDI (Dunning 2001: 175). In addition to Dunning's characterization MNCs could engage in FDI in order to overcome barriers to entering the market in question, for example high trade tariffs, in a process conventionally termed 'market-seeking'. Other motivations might include the need to diversify risk, such as avoiding trade barriers in third markets, or the necessity to pre-empt negative policy environments both at home and in host countries. In the case studies we examine, we note that both patterns are based on Chinese country-specific advantages rather than firm-specific advantages.

While the traditional motivations for outward FDI still hold true, it is important to acknowledge that outward investment from EMMNCs is taking place in a very different global economic setting to that characterizing the early growth of traditional MNCs in the post-Second World War environment. Of particular salience are the intense pressures that globalization poses, driven in particular by domestic and international market liberalization, and the transport and information communications technology (ICT) revolutions (J. Matthews 2006; Sauvant 2008; UNCTAD 2006). Put simply, the world is a much more competitive place now than ever before. In addition, EMMNCs face many challenges that limit their capacity to compete despite the many opportunities that globalization offers. Despite the fact that they enjoy certain advantages – e.g. cheap disciplined labour force and sometimes strong government backing – EMMNCs lack management talent and possess weak intellectual capital which prevents innovation and inhibits supply-chain management. Moreover, many of these companies face hostility from host-country citizens since they sometimes do not comply with internationally recognized labour, environmental and governance standards (Boston Consulting Group 2006a).

In this light Akyut and Goldstein (2006: 20) argue that EMMNCs internationalize not on the basis of FSAs, but rather on building one. This is consistent with Rugman and Jing Li's (2007) view that EMMNC investment is largely based on CSAs rather than FSAs. J. Matthews (2006; cited in Akyut and Goldstein 2006: 21) posits that EMMNC outward FDI motivations are different in character from the traditional FDI framework. He argues that EMMNCs internationalize in order to build leverage; based on organizational, not technological, innovation; and in terms of entry modes characterized by building linkages with incumbents rather than internalization. Furthermore, Dawar and Frost (1999: 129) argue that not many EMMNCs will make the transition to 'Contender' status (see Figure

Competitive assets

		Customized to home market	Transferable abroad
Industry globalization process	High	**Dodger** focuses on a locally oriented link in the value chain; enters a joint venture or sells out to an MNC	**Contender** focuses on upgrading capacities and resources to match MNCs globally, often by keeping to niche markets
	Low	**Defender** focuses on leveraging local assets in market segments where MNCs are weak	**Extender** focuses on expanding into markets similar to those of the home base, using competencies developed at home

FIGURE 8.1 Positioning for emerging market companies *Source*: N. Dawar and T. Frost (1999) 'Competing with giants', *Harvard Business Review*, March/April

8.1), and will thus remain unable to develop niche markets and/or become truly globally competitive.[1] Much depends on the extent of 'globalization pressure' experienced by particular sectors; in our two case studies this is especially high in telecommunications but less so in solar energy.

In general Chinese multinationals seem to lack the systems integration skills critical to pursuing internationalization to its maximum advantages. As Rugman and Jing Li (2007: 36) argue: 'Chinese firms tend to be protected, resource-based, labor intensive, low technology, and inefficient firms.' Most large Chinese state-owned enterprises (SOEs) are in the early phases of restructuring, and it will take time for them to build up international positions (Buckley et al. 2007: 499). The technological dynamism in the Chinese home market is arguably largely confined to small and medium enterprises (SMEs) linked to foreign MNCs (Rugman and Jing Li 2007).

Hence it is likely that the Chinese outward FDI thrust will remain relatively tenuous and state-linked for the foreseeable future.[2] Rugman and Jing Li (2007) argue that Chinese firms will continue to remain reliant on joint ventures with Western firms, but these carry the risk of entrenching technology dependence as they would generally be the junior partners (in the technological sense). While international acquisition of technology remains an option, their lack of experience in innovative activities makes it difficult to recognize and absorb all the potential value of acquisitions. Moreover, Chinese enterprises lack the managerial capabilities to integrate foreign acquisitions in order to develop dynamic capabilities. In short, their ability to transfer technology to African countries will remain very limited for some time to come.

From the above, several implications are apparent when it comes to Chinese investment in Africa. First, it is likely to be dominated by resource-seeking linked to the Chinese state's strategic interests, thus conforming to the broader pattern of FDI flows into the continent (Alden and Davies 2006). Second, efficiency-seeking FDI is unlikely to feature since African manufacturing production platforms are not readily available outside of South Africa and are not generally competitive with what Asia can offer. At best, Chinese multinationals will likely focus on expanding into African markets using competencies developed at home; indeed, this is the clear story that emerges from our case studies. In other words, we would expect Chinese MNCs outside of the resources sector to engage in outward FDI on the basis of strong country-specific advantages (CSAs) – generally very low-cost structures[3] – and to seek alliances in their target markets in doing so. Hence their competition with established MNCs in African markets should take the form of price differentiation, rather than product differentiation or technological leadership.

Patterns of Chinese investment in Africa

Table 8.1 shows that the sectoral distribution of China's total outward FDI stock is concentrated in the services sector, although the primary sector has gained prominence in recent years.

TABLE 8.1 Sectoral distribution of outward Chinese FDI stock, 2003–06

| | 2003 | | 2004 | | 2005 | | 2006 | |
	US$ mil	%	US$ mil	%	US$ mil	%	US$ mil	%
Primary	6,370	19.2	8,876	15.2	9,163	16	18,718	24.9
Agriculture, forestry, husbandry and fishery	470	1.4	834	1.9	512	0.9	807	1.1
Mining, quarrying and petroleum	5,900	17.8	5,951	13.3	8,652	15.1	17,902	23.9
Secondary (manufacturing)	2,070	6.2	4,538	10.1	5,770	10.1	7,530	10
Tertiary	24,782	74.6	33,454	74.7	42,272	73.9	48,778	65
Lease and business services	2,070	6.2	16,428	36.7	16,554	28.9	19,464	25.9
Wholesale and retail	6,530	19.7	7,843	17.5	11,418	20	12,955	17.3
Transport and storage	2,020	6.1	4,581	10.2	7,083	12.4	7,568	10.1
Others	14,162	42.6	4,602	10.3	7,218	12.6	8,791	11.7
TOTAL	33,222	100	44,777	100	57,206	100	75,026	100

Source: OECD (2008: 136)

Table 8.2 reveals that China's outward FDI thrust is concentrated in Asia, particularly in Hong Kong, and in offshore financial centres in Latin America. Africa accounts for a negligible proportion of the overall total. This figure challenges the perception that China is recolonizing Africa.

TABLE 8.2 China's OFDI outflows – regional distribution (stock), 2003–06

	2003		2004		2005		2006	
	US$ mil	%	US$ mil	%	US$ mil	%	US$ mil	%
Asia	26,603	80.1	33,480	74.8	40,954	71.6	47,978	63.9
Hong Kong, China (share of Asia)	24,632	92.6	30,393	90.8	36,507	89.1	42,270	88.1
Latin America (as share of LA)	4,619	13.6	8,268	18.5	11,470	20	19,694	26.3
3 offshore financial centres (as share of LA)	4,268	92.4	7,829	94.7	10,934	95.3	18,977	96.4
Europe	487	1.5	677	1.5	1,273	2.2	2,270	3
Africa	491	1.5	900	2	1,595	2.8	2,557	3.4
North America	548	1.7	909	2	1,263	2.2	1,584	2.1
Oceania	472	1.4	544	1.2	650	1.1	939	1.3
TOTAL	33,222	100	44,777	100	57,206	100	75,026	100

Source: OECD (2008: 136)

Nonetheless, China is becoming a very important trading partner and an important source of FDI for Africa (Besada et al. 2008). In keeping with other source countries investing in the continent (OECD 2008: 110), FDI flows to Africa from China are concentrated on a few resource-rich African states with the primary motive being to gain strategic control of natural resources to support China's economic growth (Alden and Davies 2006; Besada et al. 2008). Yet commercial motives are becoming more important as China tries to gain market share for its manufactured goods in Africa (UNCTAD 2007a; OECD 2008: 110–13) and to expand its share of target services markets, especially in construction linked to Chinese government official development assistance (ODA) (OECD 2008: 111–12). Overall China's ODA flows to Africa are approximately double FDI flows and provide reassurance to Chinese investors wary of operating in what are perceived to be risky markets (ibid.: 114–15).

Historically, China's FDI flows into Africa have mainly been in the form of equity joint ventures with local enterprises. This form of entry and ownership allowed Chinese firms to exercise some degree of control over local operations while avoiding outright ownership and exposure to political and commercial risk. From the mid-1990s onwards, however, wholly owned enterprises via mergers and acquisitions, directed at developed markets in particular, replaced jointly owned ones (ibid.: 74). This applies particularly to large Chinese MNCs, with small and medium enterprises generally establishing sales offices in target markets (ibid.: 74–5). The motives for investing directly include direct access to the market, increased market penetration, securing access to natural resources, reuse of idle equipment from the parent firm in China and to circumvent import quotas imposed on Chinese products (UNCTAD 2007a: 59). The last motive was particularly pertinent before 2005, when the Multi-fibre Agreement was still in force; nonetheless, the various preferential trading schemes available to African countries are attractive to those Chinese companies wishing to engage in risk diversification.

The impact of Chinese investment: case studies from Kenya and the DRC

Considering the dynamics described above regarding the nature of Chinese enterprises, what are their likely contributions to African development? Other than the natural resource sector, what are the beneficiary sectors? Would Chinese firms be interested in investing in 'network services' crucial to Africa's development priorities? We try to answer these questions by analysing Chinese investment in the telecommunications and solar energy sectors in Kenya and the Democratic Republic of Congo (DRC).

Telecommunications in the Democratic Republic of Congo: the case of two Chinese companies[4] Mobile telephony has proved particularly liberating in Africa, where fixed-line coverage is still weak or non-existent. In most of the continent, mobile phones have arrived not as competitors to fixed lines but as a long-awaited solution to the frustration of communications isolation. The International Telecommunications Union (ITU) reported that Africa had shown the strongest growth in mobile phone usage over the previous two years, with an impressive 39 per cent annual subscription growth between 2005 and 2007, with the result that 90 per cent of all African telephone subscribers today use mobile phones rather than landlines.

Mobile phone operators in the DRC are targeting a penetration rate of 50 per cent, implying fivefold growth to over thirty million users (Personal interview 2008a). For this to be achieved, mobile phone reception will need to expand further, and the barriers to entry will have to come down further too, to make mobile telephony affordable to more people. Happily for the industry, both of these requirements are indeed happening, and a 50 per cent penetration rate looks distinctly possible within the next decade.

A major difficulty is that the 2002 Telecommunications Law is poorly drafted and even contradictory in places, resulting in ambiguities of interpretation, particularly regarding the key question of the division of powers and competencies between the Post and Telecommunications Regulatory Authority (ARPTC), the Office of Post and Telecommunications (OCPT) and the Ministry of Communications. The ambiguities have created opportunities for veteran, wily bureaucrats in the OCPT to stymie the bureaucratically inexperienced ARPTC's efforts to carve out its rightful regulatory territory. Adding to the difficulties, during the transitional government period until 2006, the minister of communications was from a different political camp to the regulator. The result, according to insiders, has been a long-running, debilitating turf struggle between the ARPTC and OCPT, sapping much of the energy they needed to do their actual work.

Another important aspect in the government's relations with the mobile telecommunications sector is that the state has a direct shareholding in one of the companies operating within it. Creative Communications Technology (CCT) officials were unsurprisingly adamant that the OCPTC's holding a stake in their company afforded it no unfair competitive advantage. Indeed, one CCT official privately argued that it left the company at a disadvantage, because instead of injecting equity, the Congolese state was 'always asking for money' (Personal interview 2008b). Another significant competitor disagreed, however, alleging that CCT's relationship with the Congolese state had enabled it to negotiate significant, hidden and probably illegal tax breaks.

There are two Chinese companies involved in a significant way in the DRC telecommunications sector: Zhong Xing Telecommunications Company (ZTE) and Huawei. The economic objective of both ZTE and Huawei's investments in the DRC is to create and develop a market for their products, primarily through the establishment and servicing of new base stations. In addition, several of the other European companies operating in the telecommunications sector have major Chinese subsidiaries, such as the France-based Alcatel-Lucent corporation, which supplies equipment to Vodacom Congo. It is also a major shareholder in China-based Alcatel Shanghai Bell.

Regardless of where any given telecommunications service provider comes from, the chances are that its equipment, from handsets to base stations, was made in whole or in part in China and was relatively cheaper than equipment from other established companies such as Ericsson and Nokia. The low price of Chinese manufactured telecommunications equipment makes handsets affordable to more people, and particularly the poor, and also means telephone service companies get more equipment for their money, which translates into wider coverage for all consumers.

Zhong Xing Telecommunications (ZTE) ZTE appears to have been encouraged by the Chinese political authorities to form its joint venture with the Congolese government, which it duly did in late 2000. In one sense, it was the result of a political decision by the Chinese state and promises made to former president Laurent Kabila that China would enter into a joint venture with the Congo Office of Post and Telecommunications (OCPTC). The agreement stipulated that the OCPTC hold a 49 per cent stake in Congo China Telecom (CCT), with the 51 per cent balance held by Chinese telecommunications giant Zhong Xing Telecommunications Company (ZTE). At the same time, China's Export Import (EXIM) Bank, in which the Chinese state also plays an influential role, provided a 'concessional' loan of 80 million yuan renminbi to CCT to enable it to establish itself as a business (People's Daily 2000), which has principally consisted in purchasing all its equipment from ZTE. Succinctly stated, it would seem that ZTE's aim in the DRC, as elsewhere in the continent, has been to supply and instal equipment.

CCT has said its aim is to increase its share of the market to 20 per cent by 2010 (Personal interview 2008b). The company's strategy to achieve this target is to maintain extreme price competitiveness, improve its marketing and at the same time expand its geographical presence in the country. Indeed, CCT's net profit on inter-network calls in April 2008 was far lower than all its competitors'. The average net profit per minute for CCT's main rivals was US$0.096, more than four times CCT's profit. This huge difference has prompted the concern among CCT's competitors that the company enjoys unfair advantages owing to its close tie to the Office of Post and Telecommunications. This relationship, they argued, has enabled the company to avoid taxes on its imports of a wide range of goods, a charge denied by CCT officials and the Chinese embassy in Kinshasa.

As mobile telephony penetrates deeper into the ranks of the Congolese poor, the price sensitivity of the market will surely rise, and CCT will be well placed to benefit. CCT's experience in the DRC demonstrates that Chinese multinationals expand into markets similar to those of the home base, using competitiveness developed at home. The strategy is aimed at capturing a market niche primarily focused on the millions of African poor who now constitute the largest potential consumers.

Huawei's entry into the DRC Life in the DRC, by contrast, has been much more straightforward for Huawei. Huawei arrived in the DRC four years after ZTE, in 2004, free from any political obligation to either the Congolese or Chinese governments to take on commitments that were not in line with its commercial objectives. Huawei won the contract to be Tigo's equipment supplier in 2006, carrying out its first installation for the company in March that year. Tigo officials have indicated that the contract was won mainly on price, with Huawei's quote being significantly lower than the competition's. For Tigo users and anyone who wants to phone them, Huawei's price power has meant the Tigo network being able to expand faster and farther than would otherwise have been possible. And for users of other networks, the price challenge posed by Huawei will keep the prices of Alcatel and Ericsson (Huawei's competitors) lower than they might otherwise have been, again to the consumers' benefit.

The Tigo contract is substantial; by mid-2008 Huawei had apparently installed 450 sites, with eighty more coming soon. The first phase of development is supposed to be followed by a second phase in which Huawei plans to instal a further 400 sites. An Alcatel official conceded that Huawei was very competitive on price, but cited quality and service as two areas where Alcatel considered itself to have the edge (Personal interview 2008c). One senior Tigo official conceded privately that Alcatel might have a point. Not content with the Tigo contract alone, Huawei is also bidding aggressively to win the lucrative Vodacom (the company with the largest market share) equipment contract from Alcatel.

China's price power in telecommunications equipment appears to be an unambiguous good for the DRC in particular and Africa as a whole. The Chinese expansion will not pose any adverse impact on domestic manufacturing, since Africa does not manufacture telecommunications equipment. This is in contrast to many other sectors, and particularly the textile industry, where the benefits to African consumers of cheap Chinese clothing are mitigated by the disastrous impacts on African textile manufacturing, which can have significant implications for employment levels (Draper et al. 2006).

One key criticism levelled against the two Chinese telecommunication companies has to do with their poor labour practices. CCT and Huawei have both acquired reputations in the DRC for paying lower salaries and offering worse working conditions than their European counterparts. Thus while Congolese politicians, like many of their counterparts across the continent, wax lyrical about the multiple advantages of China's 'new model', the reaction of the local workforce it employs seems to be to hanker after the old one. It seems one of the ironies of history that it has taken a Chinese company to encourage Congolese trade unionists to sing the praises of Belgian business, which had for decades been emblematic in the DRC of the exploitative colonial regime.

The laissez-faire approach of the Chinese government regarding CCT and Huawei stands in apparent contrast to the important role it is playing in the negotiation of a complex and controversial minerals-for-infrastructure deal between the Congolese government and mining parastatal Gécamines on the one hand, and China's EXIM Bank, Sinohydro Corporation and China Railway Group Ltd on the other. At an economic level, the deal delivers mineral resources for which the Chinese economy has a huge appetite, a new African market for Chinese construction and other companies, plus an interesting project for the liquidity-rich EXIM Bank. Politically, if the deal succeeds it will be hailed as proving there is a viable Chinese alternative to typical Western and Bretton Woods institution loans, which have never managed to deliver much infrastructure to the DRC. The implications of this would be enormous, though first the deal must deliver to both parties' satisfaction, and it remains to be seen whether this happens.

Solar energy in Kenya The energy sector in Kenya is facing chronic challenges, including a weak power transmission and distribution infrastructure due to limited investments in power system upgrading. As a consequence, the economy has been experiencing high electrical power system losses estimated at 20 per cent of net generation, extreme voltage fluctuations and intermittent power outages at a rate of 11,000 per month, which cause equipment and material damage, including losses in production. These power system weaknesses contribute to the high cost of doing business in Kenya. Other challenges include low per-capita power consumption at 121 kilowatts per hour (kWh) and low countrywide electricity access at 15.3 per cent of the total population and 3.8 per cent of the rural population (Kenya Ministry of Energy 2004).

Owing to these challenges a substantial number of institutions and people have turned to alternative technologies in order to access electricity; solar energy constitutes one alternative. The Kenyan market is important for a number of reasons. First, it is the most dynamic and largest private-sector-led photovoltaic (PV) market in Africa as measured in per capita of solar home systems units in use. Second, the Kenyan market has now become a driver of East African regional solar PV home system sales (Duke et al. 2002). Third, the Kenyan market represents a promising policy and development model because of its private-sector-led development of clean energy technologies. This source of energy has not been fully fitted with solar panels, however, owing to a number of factors, including the relatively high cost of systems and lack of standards.

Consequently, Beijing Tianpu Xianxing Enterprises and Electrogen Technologies have entered into a 9 billion Kenya shilling (Sh) (US$140 million) partnership to build a solar panel factory in Nairobi – considered to be the first in the Horn of Africa (Munyao 2008). The Beijing Tianpu Xianxing Group specialize in researching, developing, designing, manufacturing and marketing of products such as solar energy water heaters, solar energy semi-finished pipes, vacuum pipes, heat pipes, solar energy electricity generators and air heat pumps (Duke et al. 2002). The company's products have been awarded the Certificate of Operating High Technology. Its annual production capability, for example, is 300,000 luxury solar energy water heaters, 3 million glass vacuum pipes, superconducting heat pipes and double-vacuum glass superconducting heat pipes, 100,000 square metres of super-absorbing platmodules, and 200,000 million vacuum pipe and superconducting heat pipe modules. The company enjoys a good reputation in the manufacturing of solar energy swimming pools, solar energy light/heat, photo-electricity, air heat pumps and ecological architecture projects. Furthermore, it has been constantly improving production technology and researching new products. Its products, for example, have been sold to the United States, Japan, Germany, Holland and South Africa, among other countries (ibid.).

These attributes reflect China's growing investment and capabilities in solar power technologies. These are driven by China's legendary pollution that has made many Chinese cities inhospitable places to live in. There is intense international pressure for China to take on major carbon emission reduction commitments as as was evident during the Copenhagen UN climate summit. *Business Week* (2007) notes that by 2010 China hopes to be generating and consuming about 300 megawatts of solar energy, roughly equivalent to what Japan, the world's second-largest consumer of solar energy, used in 2006. This is part of a broader target to generate 10 per cent of its total energy requirement from renewables by 2010 (Financial Times 2007a). Nevertheless, the industry still has a long way to go. While Chinese companies account for a third of the world's solar cell production, the industry is heavily reliant on overseas supplies of polycrystalline silicon, or polysilicon, a key material used in solar cell production. The solar cell production industry is dominated by seven companies which guard their technologies closely. Furthermore, up to 2006 Chinese solar cell makers exported 90 per cent of their products to Germany, Japan, the USA and other countries.

Yet as *Business Week* (2007) and the *Financial Times* (2007a) note, just as the focal point of global TV and personal computer manufacturing has shifted to China, solar panel and cell production could be next. There are large-scale Chinese plans to invest in the production of polysilicon, with their target being to produce 25 per cent of world supplies by 2010 (Financial Times 2007a). Domestic regulations in China currently, however, are not favourable to inducing the large coal-based energy suppliers to invest in renewable technologies – a fact the government is aware of and wishes to change. Consequently, most of the current and projected domestic demand comes from rural electrification projects – a fact of great relevance to this case study.

The Kenya solar project will be implemented through Pan-African Technologies, a jointly owned company in which Beijing Tianpu Xianxing has a 70 per cent interest, and the latter will raise US$100 million (Sh7 billion) from its internal resources. The company's local partner, Electrogen Technologies, is expected to take up the remaining fraction of the financing plan in cash and kind, including US$40 million (Sh2.8 billion) in cash and three acres of land along Nairobi's Mombasa Road, where the factory is to be erected. The move is expected to position solar as a key source of energy in Kenya by making it more affordable to millions of consumers who do not have access to the national grid, and also to those who depend on the unreliable national electricity grid for their energy needs.

At a glance, an opportunity for profit in a growing market is the key motive for Tianpu's expanding footprint in Kenya. Indirectly, there is an attempt to spur the growth of the local and regional solar energy market by making solar home units easily accessible and affordable. The quest for operational control and to circumvent political and commercial risks associated with such an investment might explain the joint-venture entry mode preferred by Tianpu.

Once built, the factory will source the materials required locally, reportedly create at least two hundred jobs locally, and see the inclusion of a number of expatriate Chinese technicians to assist in training and launching the project. 'Because they will be locally manufactured, Pan-African's products will cost less than the currently available imported options, with a typical system retailing for Sh5,000 [US$77] rather than Sh20,000 [US$310],' said Mr Munyao. Local solar retailers and distributors[5] concur that the proposed solar panel manufacturing factory could see the prices of solar panels drop by up to 70 per cent as domestic companies currently largely import their solar merchandise from abroad, especially from China. Pan African is eyeing East Africa as a key market and wants to interest the government in a partnership to provide solar panelling for its planned upgrade of slums in Kenya.

While the potential for solar energy to meet some of Kenya's most pressing development needs is evident, the existing legal and regulatory frameworks governing energy sub-sectors are inadequate and there is no specific law to regulate the management of renewable energy sub-sectors. As a result there are no existing laws regulating domestic versus international investors in renewable energy. To encourage wider adoption and use of renewable energy technologies, however, and to enhance their role in the country's energy supply matrix, the Kenyan government has designed incentive packages to promote private sector investments in renewable energy and other off-grid generation. For example, value-added tax on solar panels and accessories was removed in 2007 (Imitira 2008). These incentives are targeted at solar home systems consumers only, however, and are not sufficiently attractive to induce the much-needed investment to ensure sustainable renewable energy generation and transmission. The phenomenal growth of PV in Japan, Germany and elsewhere is almost entirely due to incentive support from governments. For example, the incentives in the United States include a 30 per cent federal investment tax credit for solar energy.

In conclusion, the proposed partnership between China's Tianpu Xianxing Enterprise and Kenya's Electrogen Technologies provides a good means of helping to fulfil the country's aspiration to extend electrification to its poor population through the use of solar energy. This relationship has potential spin-offs not only for domestic suppliers and end users, but for the region as a whole. In many respects, the types of products that China produces or invests in tend to complement African needs, and the low-price structure tends to favour the African poor.

Concluding observations

It is clear that African development needs, insofar as the DRC and Kenya are representative, are huge in the telecommunications and energy sectors – both sectors in which China has major established capabilities. In both cases presented here, market-seeking motivations are the driving force for Chinese companies, although politics and the Chinese state played a role initially in the DRC. Needless to say, there are major domestic regulatory challenges in the DRC with substantial implications for entry modes for Chinese companies. In Huawei's case, the company seems to prefer servicing the market by in-sourcing the product from China – a rational choice given the presumed challenges involved in establishing large-scale manufacturing facilities in the DRC.

In terms of impact it is clear that in both cases the rural poor should benefit unambiguously. That is because both the telecommunications companies in the DRC and the solar energy company in Kenya specifically target the rural poor, tailoring their offerings to their circumstances. To some extent – but we would argue this is relatively minor, considered from the economy-wide standpoint – workers have experienced more difficult working conditions than might otherwise be the case. In both cases, though, there were no established domestic producers to displace; rather, in the case of telecommunications in the DRC, Chinese MNCs are feeling the heat in a competitive process that reinforces the broader benefits of lower prices for poor consumers.

In short, China's outward investment thrust, while growing strongly, will remain relatively limited for the foreseeable future. China's outward investment thrust in some sectors is of advantage to Africa. This implies that African states must become more strategic and use this opportunity to build local productive capacities.

9 | The role of India's private sector in the health and agricultural sectors of Africa

Renu Modi

As India's economic engagement with the African continent continues to grow, there has been a slight shift in the diplomatic language of the Indian government. On the one hand, the rhetoric of South–South cooperation and Third World solidarity rings loud in official statements of the Indian government in its dealings with Africa. On the other stands the reality of the quest for markets, investments, resources and energy by the Indian private sector. While the rhetoric of South–South cooperation has not completely disappeared, it is being developed in a different manner to promote economic interests in Africa in the context of South–South solidarity and win-win partnerships between India and Africa, as clearly expressed in the final communiqué of the April 2008 India–Africa Summit. This shift is partly attributed to the critical role being played by India's influential private sector in the world economy and India's new role as a major power with significant leverage in shaping global politics.

This chapter examines the relationship between the Indian state, the Indian private sector organizations under the stewardship of the Confederation of Indian Industries (CII),[1] the publicly owned Export-Import (EXIM) Bank of India[2] (hereinafter, the Bank), and the captains of major companies in shaping the direction and content of India's growing engagement in Africa. We examine this development through a closer look at the annual business meeting, or conclave, organized by the CII and the EXIM Bank. Since 2004, the CII and the EXIM Bank, in collaboration with the Ministry of Foreign Affairs, have organized five major meetings that brought together key Indian and African private sector organizations, the EXIM Bank and government representatives to discuss and review the progress made in deepening economic engagement between India and Africa. The focus of the study is largely on the non-extractive sectors, which have so far received little attention in the steadily growing literature on India–Africa economic engagement.

It is important to note at the outset that the Indian strategy of engaging Africa is in contrast to the Chinese policy towards Africa, which has been directed centrally by Chinese state authorities since the adoption of the so-called 'Go Out' policy (*zou chu qu*) in 2001 – the year China joined the World Trade Organization – to make Chinese state-owned enterprises (SOEs) internationally competitive.

The policy reduced red tape to make procedures more outward-looking and receptive to foreign direct investment, and entitled certain Chinese state-owned enterprises to tax incentives, cheap loans, direct or indirect subsidies, and various types of support (Wu and Chen 2001). The Chinese state sees the Chinese transnational companies as vehicles for consolidating China's geopolitical position and ensuring access to natural resources for industrial production as well as to new markets (Wang 2002; Schuller and Turner 2005). And as India and China compete vigorously to win the hearts and minds of Africans, which one of these two strategies – the Chinese or Indian model of engagement – will gain the upper hand is matter of speculation, and it will be many years before we know the real answer.

Indian investments in Africa

Both the government of India (GOI) and the private enterprises are engaged in trade and investments on the African continent. The significant state-owned enterprises include Telecommunications Consultants India Ltd (TCIL), Indian Telecom Industries (ITI) Ltd, Rail India Technical and Economic Services (RITES), Konkan Railways, IRCON International Ltd, Oil and Natural Gas Corporation (ONGC) Videsh Ltd (OVL), Bharat Heavy Electricals Ltd (BHEL) and others.

Private companies like Kirloskar Brothers Ltd (KBL), the Tata group, Mahindra and Mahindra (M&M), Larsen and Toubro (L&T), National Information Informatics Technology (NIIT), Angelique International, Overseas Infrastructure Alliance (India) Pvt. Ltd (OIA), Kalpataru Power, Mohan Exports, Jaguar Industries, Shapoorji Pallonji and several others have a significant and long-established presence on the African continent. Fortis, Escorts, Apollo, for example, in the health sector are recent entrants. Business houses like the Tata group have had a presence in Africa since 1976 in the transport, information technology, hotels, mining and telecom sectors.

In addition to the above-mentioned official government initiatives, the Indian private sector organizations have been very active since 2004 in augmenting government, institutional and private initiatives and forging stronger private–public partnerships (PPPs) and joint-venture investments between African and Indian firms. There have been five India–Africa Project Partnership Conclaves (hereafter, the Conclave) held in India since 2004, in addition to several regional conclaves across Africa, such as the two regional conclaves in Senegal and Tanzania in 2008 (CII-EXIM Bank 2009). The Conclave was a landmark event and connected 483 African delegates with 318 Indian counterparts to take stock of the progress made and address their future needs. The meeting was attended by Indian and African representatives from the banking sector, government and private enterprises. The Indian participants included, *inter alia*, EXIM Bank, CII, the Ministry of External Affairs (MEA), academia, representatives of government enterprises and private business houses.

The target sectors where Indian and African mutual business interests have been identified by the Indian and African business communities are: agriculture, agro-processing, construction, railway infrastructure and rolling stock, consultancy, minerals, transport infrastructure (such as roads, waterways, ports and airports), power and non-conventional energy resources, healthcare, pharmaceuticals, institutional capacity-building, information and communications technology (ICT), iron and steel, education, water and sanitation, low-cost housing and community building, oil and gas, turnkey manufacturing projects, tourism, small and medium enterprises (SMEs), biotechnology and consumer goods.

Indian private investments in Africa and the role of the EXIM Bank

One key institution that has played a critical role in facilitating the entry of Indian private sector companies into the African continent has been the Export-Import Bank of India. The Bank has advanced the Indian private sector's development agenda in Africa through offering lines of credit (LOCs) at concessional rates to several institutions and agencies in Africa to support project financing. Of the total LOCs extended globally, 61 per cent have been provided to the Africa continent (Dalal 2009: 61).

These LOCs supplement the 'Focus Africa' programme of the GOI. EXIM Bank has extended sixty-six LOCs totalling US$2.25 billion in forty-seven African countries (EXIM Bank 2009b: 13). The LOCs have facilitated access to affordable industrial machinery for production, technology transfer and improved value addition for primary products, and have helped create employment at the user end (CII-EXIM Bank 2009: 19). Earlier the Bank extended LOCs for the purchase of agricultural equipment (such as tractors and harvesters from India), the setting up of small and medium-sized agro-processing plants, motor pumps or irrigation equipment, and the setting up of sugar industries to countries across the continent, including Angola, Burkina Faso, Chad, Côte d'Ivoire, Gambia, Ghana, Ethiopia, Lesotho, Mali, Niger and Senegal. Agriculture and related projects, such as development of irrigation, sugar plants and purchase of agricultural equipment, constitute about 30 per cent of the EXIM Bank's total approved LOCs (Dalal 2009: 62). The Bank has also been the key source for the development of SMEs in a number of African countries.

In addition, the Bank has also provided loans for cement plants in the Democratic Republic of Congo (DRC); energy projects in Ethiopia, Mali, Mozambique, Rwanda and Sudan; transport projects in Angola, Mali, Senegal and Sudan; investments in rural electrification in Burkina Faso, Ghana and Mozambique; and the construction of the seat of presidency in Accra, Ghana. In terms of value, Sudan is the leading recipient of LOCs extended by the Bank, and some one hundred Indian companies operate in the country (CII-EXIM Bank 2009; Dalal 2009: 60–64). At the 2009 Conclave two MoUs were signed, between the

COMESA Business Council (CBC) and CII to promote economic activity, and for a $25 million-dollar LOC to Burkina Faso for rural electrification.

The Bank has also opened offices in Durban and Dakar, to support the growing Indian investments in southern and western Africa respectively. To facilitate the increasing Indian investments in eastern Africa, the Bank has negotiated with the government of Ethiopia to open a regional branch, which is scheduled to start operations by the end 2009 (Modi 2009a). Ethiopia has emerged as an important destination for Indian investments in several sectors, mainly agriculture and health.

Despite the diversified nature of India's investment in Africa, the available literature on India–Africa economic relations so far has focused on India's engagement in the energy and extractive sectors (see Naidu, Bhattacharya, Vines and Campos, and Obi, this volume). In the following section, we examine the scope of Indian engagement in Africa in the non-extractive sectors – mainly agriculture, agro-processing and health – through private sector initiatives that directly affect the lives of millions of Africans. The two sector case studies are illustrative of the expansive Indian economic engagement in Africa.

Indian FDI and trade in the African agricultural and agribusiness sector

Food security is an important area of collaboration between India and Africa, two predominantly agrarian economies. This is a sector which has been identified by the New Partnership for Africa's Development (NEPAD) as a priority area where Indian FDI can play a critical role. India has been successful in building an impressive food security system for itself. India's expertise and farm technologies in the field of 'green revolution' could be shared with African countries to enable them to become the world's food basket (CII-EXIM Bank 2009: Recommendation 7; see also Sinha, this volume).

NEPAD has identified agriculture as a 'sustainable solution to hunger and poverty in Africa' and emphasized the role of agriculture as an 'engine of growth' (CAADP 2009). The development of agriculture and food security is of high priority to NEPAD as this sector employs 65 per cent of Africa's labour force and accounts for 32 per cent of gross domestic product. Food security is needed for achieving the Millennium Development Goals of halving poverty by 2015 (World Bank 2006). According to NEPAD's Comprehensive African Agriculture Development Programme (CAADP), each African country is expected to spend 10 per cent of its budgetary resources on agriculture (CAADP 2001). Not many countries have been able to meet these expenses, however. External investments such as India's FDI can help meet these targets and generate employment and raise productivity. Given its good track record in pioneering the successful 'green revolution' in the early 1970s, India can provide low-cost appropriate technology to increase agricultural productivity in food and raw materials in Africa.

At the 2008 India–Africa Forum Summit, the president of Tanzania and chairman of the African Union (AU), Jakaya Mrisho Kikwete, echoed the position of NEPAD and stated, 'Currently Africa's agriculture is peasant agriculture, traditional, plagued with low levels of production. If we are able to increase productivity in African agriculture, Africa would not only be able to feed itself, but have huge surpluses to sell to the world. India has the technology and the skills, which if made available to Africa certainly it will help implement the African Green Revolution' (VOA 2008). Indeed, Tanzania, a major trading partner for India, received a LOC of $40 million for financing the export of agricultural equipment from India to Tanzania in 2008/09 (EXIM Bank of India 2009d: 34).

The Indian private sector has responded to the call from African governments to invest more in the African agricultural sector in order to raise the productivity of peasant farmers, raise income levels and reduce poverty in the process. Among India's expanding investments in the African agriculture sector are the following:

Indian farm equipment in Africa Some of the Indian companies engaged in the agricultural sector in Africa – the Mahindra and Mahindra (M&M) group, KBL, Angelique International – supply customized agricultural equipment such as small tractors, drilling and irrigation equipment and machines for small and medium-sized agro-processing units that are appropriate and affordable for smallholdings. The US$6 billion Indian company, the M&M group, the third-largest producer of tractors in the world, is setting up a US$1 billion tractor plant in Tanzania which will serve as a base for the supply of tractors in East Africa (Said 2009). M&M also supplies tractors to several African countries and has set up assembly lines in West Africa, the Gambia, Mali, Nigeria and Senegal.

Another Indian firm, KBL, deals with agricultural and agro-processing equipment and has had a presence in over twenty-five African countries over the past three decades. It supplies pumps and valves and spare parts to the Kagera sugar plant and diesel engines and water pumps in Tanzania to help the country achieve 'food security through water management'. In addition to spare parts and valves, etc., KBL also provides energy audits to reduce energy and maintenance costs to sugar plants such as East Africa Sugar Industries Ltd and the South Nyanza Sugar Company Ltd in Kenya, Kinyara and Kakira Sugar Works and Sugar Corporation of Uganda Ltd in Uganda and Metahara and the Ethiopian Sugar Factory in Ethiopia (web.kbl.co.in/kbl_internet/images/downloads/sectoralleaflets/Sugar.pdf).

Indian investments in Senegal With a projected rise in population from 12 million today to 15 million by 2012, modernizing agriculture to fight poverty and hunger is high on the political agenda of the Senegalese government (Harsh 2009; McKeon 2009; World Bank 2006; KBL 2008). Currently, agriculture contributes 13.5 per cent to the country's GDP (AfDB/OECD 2008). At the same time, the total available cultivable land is limited. Therefore, the only solution to the problem of food sufficiency in this semi-arid country is to increase the acreage of irrigated land, and leading Indian companies are playing a critical role in helping Senegal tackle the problem of low agricultural productivity.

KBL is the leading supplier of water pumps for irrigation to Senegal. In 2005, KBL made site visits to this Sahelian country and is working in a phased manner to irrigate 80,000 hectares and cultivate 1 million metric tonnes of rice in the next five years and attain food sufficiency by 2012/13, and thus save resources on imports as well as feed the additional population of 5 million. KBL signed a contract with the Senegalese Ministry of Agriculture for 2,394 water-pump sets and accessories complete with installation and commissioning worth US\$27 million, which were supplied under the LOC provided by EXIM Bank India. As a result of the enhanced irrigation, mainly in the Northern Valley and the Casamance region, Senegal can now meet 40 per cent of its rice demands locally as compared to 19 per cent prior to the implementation of the project (Dalal 2009: 64). The company's advertisement byline reads 'Food sufficient Senegal ... a dream soon to become a reality!' This is an example of the critical and noteworthy contribution by Indian private investment to an African country that has been a net food importer (KBL 2008).

Indian investments in Ethiopia Agriculture is the mainstay of Ethiopia's economy and accounts for half of the country's GDP, 60 per cent of its exports and 85 per cent of total employment. The country is vulnerable to droughts and is considered one of the most food-deficient and aid-dependent countries in Africa. Therefore, investments in agriculture are critical for building self-sufficiency in food grains, employment generation and poverty alleviation. To further this objective, the government of Ethiopia plans to bring 5 million hectares of land under cultivation by the year 2010. It has set aside 1.6 million hectares of land for commercial farming in sugar cane, tea, cotton, palm oil, coffee, soya bean and sesame. A further 800,000 and 300,000 hectares in the Oromia and the Amhara regions respectively were in the process of being parcelled out. Foreign firms from China, India and Saudi Arabia have invested in these farms (Tadesse 2009).

Indian investments in the Ethiopian small and medium-scale agribusiness sectors are significant. By the end of 2008 Indian investments in Ethiopia were about US\$4.15 billion, of which more than 50 per cent were in the agricultural sector, including floriculture (G. Singh 2009; Ethiopian Embassy 2008). The Indian embassy in Ethiopia lists 414 companies that have invested in Ethiopia as of 30 December 2008 (Embassy of India in Ethiopia 2009). Of these 414 companies, eighty have investments in agriculture and related sectors. The biggest investment in the agricultural sector has been by a Bangalore-based company,

Karaturi Global Ltd, the world's largest grower of roses, which has acquired 3.4 million hectares of land on a long-term lease from the government of Ethiopia at the rate of US$14 dollars/hectare per annum and has started cultivation on about 11,700 hectares in Bako. The company will invest US$250 million over the next five years. An additional 40,000 hectares of land were brought under cultivation in mid-2009 to produce maize, rice, vegetables and long-gestation crops like oilseeds, sugar cane and cotton. In lieu of the concessions granted for land, the company will invest in importing farm equipment and in the construction of schools and healthcare facilities as part of its corporate social responsibilities (CSR) (Hindu Business Line 2008a). Small and medium-scale processing units will also be installed to add value to the commercial crops.

A significant line of credit to Ethiopia was announced in 2006 amounting to US$65 million to support rural electrification projects, and in 2007 US$640 million for the development of the sugar sector (Fortune 2009). The establishment of the Tendaho sugar factory and the expansion of the Finchaa and Wonji-Shoa factories with an investment of US$100 million, awarded to the Delhi-based company Uttam Sucrotech, will help Ethiopia produce large amounts of sugar both for export and domestic consumption (Thaindian 2009). Other Indian investments in the Illubabor region are in the tea sector, in the cotton farms to support the textile sector, and in *jatropha* plantations to support biodiesel plants. India has also provided a Duty Free Tariff Preference Scheme under which Ethiopian agricultural products can enter the Indian market on lower tariffs. It is expected that these projects will generate employment for 100,000 people (G. Singh 2009).

Large-scale agricultural investments by Indian firms such as Karturi in Ethiopia, Kenya and other countries have not been free of controversy and were the subject of a critical editorial in the well-respected *Economist* magazine. Critics see Indian investment in Africa's agricultural sector as 'neocolonialism' and 'land grabbing' by speculative enterprises whose interest is to meet the food security needs of India itself (Economist 2009: 60–62). But India's agriculture minister, Mr Sharad Pawar, has described it as 'business and nothing more' (Nelson 2009).

In the author's opinion the terms 'neocolonialism' and 'land grabbing' are inaccurate for two main reasons. First, the land acquired, mainly on long lease, has been by the invitation and with the facilitation of the host country. Second, it is premature to rush to conclusions, as farming by the foreign investors has only just begun. Given the background that only 14 per cent of Africa's 184 million hectares of arable land is under cultivation and 21 million hectares are in a state of 'accelerated degradation', an impetus to agriculture through FDI might augur well for the continent (FAO 2008). But as Joachim von Braun of the International Food Policy Research Institute argues, the best way to resolve the conflicts and create a 'win-win' situation is for foreign investors to sign a code of conduct to improve the terms of deals for the locals (Economist 2009: 62). This is the sort of issue on which NEPAD, through the CAADP, should develop an Africa-wide code of conduct by which any supplier of FDI to Africa should be required to subscribe. The crucial issue that needs to be addressed is securing the future of the original inhabitants of these tracts of land that are being now allotted by the African state governments to foreign investors. 'New rules were needed because some investments reportedly were leading to evictions, sudden losses of farm and grazing lands, and greater competition for water resources' (Kanter 2009). The state-backed large-scale investments in land definitely need to include the locals as stakeholders in the project who are provided with either employment and a share of the produce or adequate compensation and rehabilitation that goes beyond mere relocation.

The author feels that Africa certainly needs to be in the driver's seat and formulate regulatory mechanisms and negotiate terms that promote social equity and pro-poor policies that are equally the objectives of the states and the African Union at the continental level, so that the foreign companies do not act like 'pirates', but rather provide support for the granaries of the host country as well and benefit the local populace in terms of employment opportunities on farmlands and in agro-processing units owned by foreigners. The business model has to be transparent and on a 'win-win' basis within the framework of South–South cooperation for the partnership to be long lasting, sustainable and development oriented. Some reputed and established companies, such as Tata, KBL, Mahindra and Mahindra and others, have already incorporated good CSR in their business ethics in India, and it is hoped that they will do the same in their business operations in Africa.

In the final analysis, however, the controls have to come mainly from the African host governments. Unfortunately, there are no stringent controls imposed by the Indian government, at the moment, on how Indian private companies should behave in Africa. The African states have to be discerning and vigilant and provide contracts to companies that further the twin objectives of poverty alleviation and employment generation on the African continent, and not those companies that have deep pockets and can share a significant percentage of the largesse with African elites. Given the nature of the current African elites that control the levers of power, the role of African civil society and the people at large is immeasurable. They need to ensure through collective action that any company that operates to their disadvantage should not be allowed to work their lands.

Indian private sector FDI in the African healthcare sector

Indian engagement is growing at an accelerated pace in the sunrise sector of healthcare and medicine through medical tourism of Africans to India, the setting up of business partnerships with hospitals in Africa and the export of high-quality Indian pharmaceuticals to African countries.

Medical tourism[3] Health infrastructure is in a shambles on the African continent, owing mainly to lack of expertise, finance and governance. Internationally accredited, high-quality and relatively low-cost medical services are seen as 'cost-effective' and suitable for the average African consumer with a limited budget who cannot afford to purchase high-end products. The Indian medical sector's marketing line is 'first-class treatment at Third World prices'. The identical socio-economic status of the population of India and Africa, knowledge of English as a medium of communication and a convergent disease profile, with the most common ailments being hypertension, heart disease, diabetes, kidney and orthopaedic problems, and cancer, make India a preferred destination since the cost of medical treatment is much cheaper there than in the UK or the USA (Modi 2009b). Having the facilities closer to home is undoubtedly advantageous, however, in terms of immediate access to medical facilities and regular follow-ups. To overcome the shortage of healthcare facilities, some of the African countries are exploring the possibility of Indian investments in pharmaceuticals, hospitals and export of medical skills in the form of PPPs in their home countries.

Hospitals and health centres The Chennai-based Apollo Group of Hospitals, with an extensive network of hospitals in India and abroad, was the first private hospital group to offer its consultancy services to hospitals in West Africa, in Ghana and Nigeria in 2003/04. Apollo has been the project consultant for a 100-bed multi-speciality hospital in Ghana. In 2004, Apollo tied up with Hygeia Nigeria, which owns the largest health maintenance organization (HMO), with over two hundred hospitals and clinics in the country (Apollo Hospital, Bangalore 2009). Apollo has the distinction of successfully treating 60,000 foreign patients from across the world in the past five years. It also has the Joint Commission International (JCI) accreditation which is considered the gold standard for American and European hospitals, defined in terms of excellent patient care and safety (Apollo Hospitals, Indraprastha Apollo Hospitals, New Delhi 2009).

Since 2000 Apollo has been the largest provider of telemedicine in India. In Nigeria, Apollo has assisted in capacity-building through upgrading the skills of medical personnel and has introduced state-of-the-art techniques that are used by the Apollo chain of hospitals in India. It has also worked to 'improve [the] clinical and administrative process and also train doctors in super speciality disciplines and provide telemedicine support' (Hindu 2004). Currently the Tanzanian government has been exploring the possibility of collaboration with the Apollo Group and the Bangalore-based Narayan Hrudalaya hospital, mainly to improve the quality of cardiac care in the country.

In March 2009, the New Delhi-based Fortis Healthcare Ltd and Clinique Darne, Mauritius's largest private hospital owned by CIEL, a Mauritius-based investment company, launched their new collaborative enterprise and set up the now renamed 'Fortis Clinique Darne'. Fortis also has JCI accreditation and follows protocols found in the best global hospitals. The 400-bed multi-speciality hospital includes world-class facilities for cardiac problems. It will enable people in the neighbouring countries to get treatment in Mauritius without having to travel farther abroad. Fortis offers capacity-building of local medical and para-medical, nursing and support and service staff through training and education in the medical practices adopted in its hospitals in India (Clinique Darne 2009). Apollo and Fortis hospitals are among the twelve super-speciality hospitals that are a part of the Pan-African e-Network telemedicine programme, which offers live tele-consultation services to African patients through the use of electronic information communication and technology (ICT).

Pan-African e-Network As part of its Aid for Africa Programme, the Ministry of Foreign Affairs in India launched the Pan-African e-Network project on 26 February 2009. The e-Network shares India's quality healthcare with its African counterparts despite the distance between India and the African continent. Ethiopia's Black Lion and Nkempte hospitals were linked with the Care Hospital in Hyderabad as a part of the pilot project, which was launched in July 2007, and following the success of the test project the e-Network has been introduced to a total of fifty-three member states of the African Union to improve healthcare (Modi 2009c: 56–8). In addition, Indian exports of medicines have provided access to quality drugs at reasonable prices in Africa.

Export of pharmaceutical products The contribution of the Indian pharmaceutical sector to the African medical sector is significant. India exports vaccines, antibiotics, penicillin, medicaments of alkaloids or derivatives, medicaments of other hormones, vitamins, anaesthetic medicaments of mixed/unmixed products, adhesive dressings, wadding, gauze, first-aid kits, etc., to several African countries.

India exported US$1,064.8 million worth of pharmaceuticals in 2007/08 (including to countries of North Africa) as compared to about US$398.8 million in 2003/04. Pharmaceuticals, the third-largest export item to Africa, account for a total of 8 per cent of India's exports to Africa (including North Africa), according to the Director General of Commerce Intelligence and Statistics of the Ministry of Commerce and Industry (CII-EXIM Bank 2009: 11–12). To illustrate, in 2004 India was the leading country for the export of pharmaceutical products to Ethiopia, which were worth more than 138.1 million birr (about US$16.4 million) and accounted for 21 per cent of total pharmaceutical imports into the country. India's share of exports declined the following year, however, and it ranked third among exporting countries next to France and the USA (Embassy of India in Ethiopia 2006: 4). Ranbaxy Laboratories Ltd was one of the first Indian pharmaceutical companies to set up base in Africa, way back in 1977, when it entered into a joint venture in Nigeria. Kenya, Sudan, South Africa, Nigeria and other countries are major importers of Indian pharmaceutical products.

Today Ranbaxy offers a range of products – anti-infective, cardiovascular and, most significantly, antiretroviral (ARVs). The company has an agreement with the Clinton Foundation and is the key provider for the treatment of the life-threatening HIV/AIDS (CII 2005: 42–4). Other companies, such as Aurobindo Pharma, Cipla, Dr Reddy's, Hetero and Wockhardt, also export ARVs to Africa at affordable prices and save the lives of millions of poor Africans. At present there is no competition for these drugs from any other Asian country, including China (Padmanabhan 2003). Cipla is credited with introducing the 'dollar-a-day' treatment that dramatically transformed life-saving drug access for HIV-infected people around the world at an affordable rate and challenged the dominance of Western pharmaceutical companies, which sold drugs for HIV/AIDS at a much higher price. In the context of global recession there has been a severe downturn in the external donor funding from which the bulk of the HIV/AIDS budget is sourced.

In view of the budget cuts in several AIDS-affected countries, and the imperative for continued treatment, Indian low-cost generics are the only alternative for affordable healthcare in terms of this life-threatening disease. Currently, Africa accounts for over 15 per cent of India's total generic exports, worth US$6 billion annually. West Africa alone accounts for US$200 million worth of exports of Indian generics. However, opportunities for increasing the exports of Indian drugs to Africa face new challenges. India is faced with the challenge of countering the supply of spurious anti-malarial and other drugs labelled 'made in India' that have been traced to China (Economic Times 2009). Amid the above challenges there are opportunities for trade and investment in this sector of mutual interest to India and Africa. With the Indian sectors ready to invest in the healthcare sector, it is now the responsibility of the African governments to further explore and strengthen engagements in the medical sector, and negotiate terms that work towards meeting their social objectives as well.

Conclusion

Economic relations between India and Africa are buoyant, and this is largely the result of the active role being played by the Indian private sector, with strong support from a more pro-business Export-Import Bank of India. The India–Africa connection has progressed far beyond Bollywood, cricket and the cultural and historical ties that have bound the two regions for over two centuries. It is now firmly entrenched in economic complementarities of trade and investment. Several African delegates at the 2009 Conclave stated that their business trip to India was like a 'homecoming', as many of them were either educated in India or had been taught by Indian teachers back home, and therefore regarded

Indian companies favourably. Unlike Chinese state-owned enterprises that receive tremendous state support and guidance, however, the Indian private sector agents are succeeding in doing business in Africa based on the quality of the products and services they offer at competitive prices and the reputation they have built over many years.

Indeed, as Bhattacharya (this volume, Chapter 5) points out, Africans and Indians have been trading with each other since the fourteenth century, and more concrete evidence of shared cultural and economic exchanges goes back to colonial times. In contrast to the case of China, these historical links, in addition to the presence of a significant Indian diaspora in Africa, are important factors that could give India a significant advantage over China. Several Indian companies that have established a footprint in Africa, such as the Tata group, have expanded business through the 'African Indians' who are familiar with the business modalities of Indian companies and their work ethics and also with the African business terrain. Needless to say, these advantages have not been fully exploited given the dynamics and parameters of state–society–private-sector relations in a democratic country such as India. While the contours of a systematic India–Africa engagement have been defined by the government of India through a number of policy initiatives, such as the 'Focus Africa Programme' and the Team 9 Initiative, many of these initiatives are implemented by different agencies with conflicting interests and constituencies. To date, India does not have a dedicated independent development assistance institution (Sinha, this volume, Chapter 6).

For these initiatives to have a real impact on the promotion of India's economic and geopolitical interests in Africa, the Indian state must be in the driver's seat and mimic the Chinese way of catalysing investments in Africa. For the Indian private sector to succeed in doing business in Africa and elsewhere in the world, it requires elaborate and proactive state support which does not exist at the moment, at least in a coordinated way. There are some plausible explanations for this. First, the democratic set-up of India, which is an advantage in the long run, can also fetter business because of long-winded and bureaucratic procedures which can slow down state involvement in private sector activities abroad. Moreover, complete freedom of the press and their reach implies that transparency in business contracts needs to be maintained. The challenge for the Indian state is how to actively support India's private enterprise in Africa while staying firm on the need to uphold the principles of democracy and corporate social responsibility in the areas of labour standards, environmental sustainability and respect for human rights. Emulating the Chinese way of accelerating investments in Africa should not mean that India should follow current Chinese business practices in Africa, which have scant regard for issues of human rights and the kind of governance adhered to by dictatorial African regimes.

10 | Navigating Chinese textile networks: women traders in Accra and Lomé

Linn Axelsson and Nina Sylvanus

China's interests in African resources, as well as intensified trade, aid and investment links, have been widely noted in the vast literature on China–Africa relations. Emerging Chinese competition in Africa's urban trading economies, however, has received less attention. In this chapter we attempt to address this gap by looking at two case studies to highlight the booming Chinese textile trade in Ghana and Togo and how local women trading in printed textiles engage, challenge and navigate Chinese textile competition.

Ghana and Togo are particularly interesting cases to consider, since they are not only central marketplaces in the region but are also linked through a long intersecting history in the printed textiles trade. While Ghana was historically the place where these fabrics were introduced from Europe during the early colonial period, Togo's women traders, referred to locally as the 'Nana-Benzes', took over the role played by Accra's powerful traders (the 'Mammies'), and began monopolizing this trade from Lomé by the late 1950s. From the mid-1960s onwards, Ghana developed its own textile industry and trade was accordingly redirected towards locally produced textiles. This strategy did not produce the desired result of protecting the market dominance of Ghanaian industry and traders in wax-print textiles.

With the implementation of donor-mandated International Monetary Fund (IMF)/World Bank 'structural adjustment programmes' by the governments of Ghana and Togo from the mid-1980s onwards (in the context of the debt crisis), local markets were opened for external competition, which paved the way for massive penetration of the textile market by Chinese traders. We conclude that the liberalization policies of the 1980s and 1990s that both Ghana and Togo pursued, rather than any deliberate policy by the Chinese government, account for the dramatic penetration of Chinese textiles into the West African market. The massive Chinese penetration of West Africa's trading economies has sparked much debate and has unleashed conflicting interests over formerly protected market spaces in both Ghana and Togo. In this context, the capacity of the state to protect national markets is being questioned. This chapter explores these shifts and tensions by considering how both Ghanaian and Togolese traders are responding to the entry of these new Chinese textile networks.

The politics of trade, women traders and textiles in Togo and Ghana

West African women's long background in trade (Robertson 1976), as well as their dominance of regional distribution networks and economic independence, has produced a large literature, especially since the 1970s (Arhin 1979; Clark 1994; Coquery-Vidrovitch 1997; Darkwah 2002). This literature portrays women traders as economically and politically influential while simultaneously drawing attention to the way women in trade negotiate their identities as traders and their right to earn a living in response to economic and political decisions at various scales.

Throughout history Ghanaian traders have been able to make use of their role as distributors of essential commodities to negotiate their positions within Ghanaian society. Textile traders have maintained a particularly strong position within the hierarchies of local trade. Indeed, female traders in Ghana played an important role in the 1940s' and 1950s' national liberation movement. Their networks across the country enabled efficient fund-raising and campaigning, and traders were largely responsible for the Convention People's Party (CPP) win in the first election (Manuh 1985, in Clark 1994). After independence their sheer number made market women an important resource base of voters. Traders' abilities to provide illegal supplies to fill the gaps in the officially authorized system for distribution gave traders leverage vis-à-vis the state (Clark 1994).

Similarly, in Togo, a group of wealthy textile traders involved in the import of European wax prints were active participants in the independence movement and largely sponsored nationalist political parties (Heilbrunn 1993; Cordonnier 1987). Lomé's Nana-Benzes would soon transform Lomé into a regional centre of textiles, which took over Accra's position in the region in the late 1950s. The converging interests of a dozen of these women and their combined social and economic capital provided the context for their establishment as an informally, yet oligopolistically, functioning market association that operated freely under the former colonial radar. In the early 1960s these women entrepreneurs would display themselves in expensive Mercedes-Benz cars, hence the term Nana-Benz to describe them.

The profits generated during this period placed this group of entrepreneurs in a powerful, coveted position. When General Gnassingbé Eyadéma came to power in 1967 after a military coup and instituted one-party rule under the Rally of the Togolese People (RPT), he used the lucrative textile trade as a façade for its political authority. Thus his regime worked as a 'gate-keeper' (F. Cooper 2002) to these women's activities by providing them with trade licences, low-turnover taxes and the region's lowest re-exportation taxes, as well as a particularly interesting foreign investment code that turned Lomé into a booming trade hub during a period when Ghana, as well as most of its neighbours, faced political instability. In return, the textile elite offered political support to the regime via public appearances with the president and the chairing of the women's wing of the RPT, the Union National des Femmes Togolaises (UNFT).

Ghana Since independence in 1957 Ghana's political history has been marked by shifting modes of government. In 1981 Flight Lieutenant J. J. Rawlings took over power in a military coup. Plagued by financial difficulties, Rawlings began negotiations with the World Bank and the IMF in 1983, and Ghana began to implement a series of market-oriented economic reforms to kick-start the economy, as well as reduce Ghana's huge external debt (Ayee 2007; Boafo-Arthur 2007; Tsikata 2007). Ghana's market was opened wide and the protection afforded to the local textile industry was removed. The most important outcome of the neoliberal project for the traders was therefore the partial state withdrawal from the textile sector (Clark 1994; Hutchful 2002). At the same time, reduction of public sector expenditure has increased competition between traders dealing in home-made and imported textiles (Aryeetey 1994). In a situation in which the domestic textile industry struggled to keep a strong position, Ghana's textile traders have had to respond to the competition between home-made and imported textiles from China.

Though initially described as the 'model for adjustment', the Ghanaian economy and industry quickly deteriorated in the 1980s, with substantial falls in industrial growth. The textile-manufacturing sector was hit particularly hard (Hutchful 2002). Weakened by economic instability under the Rawlings regime and structural adjustment, the Ghanaian textile industry was seriously affected by Chinese competition in the 1990s. Thousands of workers were made redundant as factories closed their doors (Quartey 2006). The retreat of the state from the management of the national economy and the institutionalization of free market norms with little regulation thus paved the way for a massive penetration of the Ghanaian textile trade, ironically by state-subsidized and state-supported Chinese-made textiles.

Togo Togo's position as West Africa's 'entrepôt' began to crumble in the late 1980s. The Togolese state apparatus was weakened by a series of events: a severe contraction of the national economy and the imposition of a structural adjustment programme that necessitated harsh belt-tightening measures; the devaluation of the regional currency (the CFA); political instability as the demand for democratic change became more pronounced; and the partial disengagement of France's Africa politics. The Togolese regime gradually lost its political support from France and other Western allies (Piot 1999).

Political contestation intensified in the early 1990s when the long-serving dictator, President Eyadéma, was temporarily expelled from power as a result of a national conference. A significant number of second-generation textile traders sided with the opposition during the time of the transitional government and they played a key role in the struggles leading to Togo's first democratic elections. But when the transitional government attempted to dismantle Eyadéma's RPT, the president and his supporters struck back and began to target Lomé's market women and their businesses. Eyadéma wanted to make an example of them, for they had abandoned him during the transitional period. Their shops were vandalized and looted by Eyadéma's men. Yet street protests continued and large-scale strikes in southern Togolese cities paralysed the country's economy for almost eighteen months (Heilbrunn 1993; Nwajiaku 1994). Many textile traders left the country for fear of repression.

In a surprise move, Eyadéma fraudulently returned to power in 1993 in the face of massive opposition from the citizenry. When Togo's big-time traders returned to Lomé after the 1993 elections, the economic environment had changed profoundly. Unilever, which had controlled the textile trade since the colonial period, withdrew from the country and sold its subsidiaries to the Dutch manufacturer Vlisco. The latter broke with Unilever's policies, rooted in the arrangements that had long secured the oligopoly of Lomé's textile traders. With the decline of Togo's reputation as a stable and prosperous country, and Cotonou's rise as a new trade hub for textiles, Lomé was adversely affected.

The devaluation of the regional currency, the CFA, was another setback for Lomé's Nana-Benzes, whose textile empire began to decline. With the rapid exposure of Togo's economy to external competition, the weakened Togolese entrepôt state has never recovered fully from the economic slump and political crisis. Benefiting from the region's declining purchasing power, fuelled by the devaluation and 'deregulated' market space, Chinese textile networks found a fertile ground for expansion while providing an alternative source of accumulation to the entrepôt state.

With the withdrawal of long-established state regulations that previously favoured local trade networks, Lomé was literally transformed into a market open to any potential business the regime could benefit from. During this period of flux, long-standing trade hierarchies have been challenged, if they have not been replaced by new enterprising traders. These mutations were further enhanced in 2005 when Eyadéma died after thirty-eight years of single-party rule. Within hours of his death, and with the backing of the military, Eyadéma's son, Faure Gnassingbé, was installed in power in violation of the constitutional law. The already unhinged state apparatus entered a new phase of reorganization, fuelling a context of uncertainty for Togo's economic elites. It is in this post-succession climate that textile traders, both old and newly emerging ones, compete to navigate the recomposed structures of a globalized market economy.

Navigating Chinese penetration of local markets: a tale of two traders

In this section, we examine how two women traders in Lomé and Accra negotiate their positions in a situation of global trade liberalizations, especially by exploring the traders' active engagement with and responses to China's presence in the market. We are suggesting that the current influx of Chinese prints provides new opportunities for some traders to circumvent the hierarchical organization in the long-standing trade networks based on European and Ghanaian wax prints as well as in Ghanaian wax and fancy prints. It also suggests that Ghanaian and Togolese traders actively strategize in navigating the new spaces in the competitive textile sector. The conflicting strategies indicate that we cannot simply speak of distinct groups of traders with clear-cut ways of relating to the entry of Chinese prints into the informal trading economy, just as we cannot speak of 'one' Chinese strategy in this market.

The ethnographic portraits to follow focus on the historical and contemporary conditions that have encouraged a Togolese businesswoman and a third-generation Ghanaian textile trader to trade in Chinese textiles. These snapshots are intended to nuance our understanding of how local players engage with China as an economic partner as well as to highlight some of the tensions involved in this new trade relationship.

Marketing Chinese knock-offs in Lomé – Solenne Solenne, the thirty-four-year-old chief executive officer (CEO) of Wax Nana Benz (WNB), is a US-trained economist who recently returned to her native Togo. She entered the textile market in 2007, despite being an outsider to the textile trade establishment that has been in the hand of Lomé's Nana-Benzes.[1] Her associates, whose names she does not provide, although she insinuates that these figures are linked to the current regime, are in full support of her marketing approach, unprecedented in Togo. Numerous billboards decorate the streets of Lomé and daily TV commercials preceding and following the evening news are part of the high-visibility advertising strategy that Solenne uses.

Solenne views herself as the defender of Togo's cultural heritage, which she considers to be represented in these fabrics. She appears determined to restore Lomé's prominent role in the region's textile trade. In a recent interview she gave in the West African women's magazine *Amina*,[2] she engages in a highly ambivalent discourse. She claims she is seeking to revolutionize the textile market. She correctly states that Togo's market is currently faced with high costs and counterfeiting problems. To counteract these trends, she wants to return to the Togolese what they 'own and deserve'. Solenne then engages in a dialogue in which she praises the historical role of Lomé's Nana-Benzes in creating a market for European-produced wax prints. Although her broad-brush historical picture of this trade lacks many elements, she concludes that the textile and wax designs are the intellectual property of the Togolese. In a nutshell, her message is the following: Lomé's Nana-Benzes have created this market, the fabrics belong to the Togolese and thus she is entitled to copy them as a service to her compatriots. This, she considers, is the fundamental difference between her WNB product, her company's mantra, and the many Chinese copies that 'invade' the market.

Her rhetoric elegantly takes on the issue of international copyright law, which she disregards, stating that the Dutch and British patents expired after fifty years, and the textile designs are therefore in the public domain. Solenne is wrong here, since these firms have extended their patents. Ironically, the pattern on the billboard, a seventy-year-old design owned by the Dutch, and which Chinese competitors have long copied, was not even in production by WNB when they started the advertising campaign. If her marketing techniques are innovative, her narrative deeply resonates with the regime's nationalist 'authenticity' discourse of the 1970s (Toulabor 1983). Authenticity and heritage are concepts thrown back into question in today's global marketplace, as her marketing strategy powerfully captures. While Solenne had benefited from the distortion of long-held trade and value hierarchies brought on by the post-crisis vacuum, her inexperience in this market segment and her quest for unrealistic profit margins nevertheless constitute a serious handicap to her success.

Cha Chi Ming, a Hong Kong Chinese group that entered the African print market in the late 1960s (with factories in Nigeria and Ghana), revealed that WNB produces at a government-owned factory in south-eastern China. Cha Chi Ming used this factory to produce one of its own brands for almost a year. Indeed, the group began producing in China in 2004 (in addition to its African factories) in response to increased Chinese–Chinese competition in the African market. Yet WNB moved into its site of production in China by literally buying itself into this factory, placing large orders that monopolized the factory's printing facilities, de facto pushing Cha Chi Ming out. The latter insinuates that political strings are likely to have been pulled between the Chinese and Togolese governments in order for the production site of a Chinese public company to be taken over. This may even suggest that Solenne operates as a puppet for a more powerful network of political figures, who are testing the Chinese trade's potential as an alternative source of income for the state's ruling elite.

Regardless of the many rumours that circulate in the market, and which link her company to the regime, her entrepreneurial strategy is rooted in what Togo's former market queens performed to perfection: the monopoly principle. WNB indeed aspires to establish a monopoly over wax prints as Solenne's primary strategy is to impose her brand in the market and maximize profits. And even if she has key connections to a faction of the regime, the multiple changes in the local, regional and international environment have been so profound that it has indeed become impossible to reconstitute a locked system of mutual benefits via a monopoly position. In spite of her legacy discourse, Solenne's trajectory differs sharply from that of the Nana-Benz generation. If her business is not very successful despite high visibility – and is de facto likely to disappear if prices and quality are not adjusted – she nevertheless manages to use her role as CEO as a political strategy. Her brand, and thus her name, covers the streets of Lomé, advertising her image to the public.

Adapting to new circumstances in Accra – Ruth Ruth operates a shop together with her sister at Rawlings Park in central Accra. Her shop is located inside a large warehouse called Ghana Chinese Commodities Wholesale Town. Today the building hosts several textile shops, many of which specialize in imported textiles, and a number of businesses operated by Chinese traders who sell suitcases, T-shirts, posters, artificial flowers, bedspreads, pillows and pillowcases, among other items.

Ruth is a third-generation textile trader. Her grandmother first started the business at Accra's main Makola market. Because of the tightly regulated economic environment, locally produced (and European) textiles were for a long time the main options available to Ghana's textile traders. Consequently, the textile trade in Ghana remained in the hands of a few powerful market 'Mammies' who gained their influential position owing to their capacity to control distribution of locally produced textiles. With time, distribution strategies have diversified, allowing a varying number of traders to hold the position of distributor for the local textile producers.

While part of the textile trade relocated within central Accra when a new market was built in 1986, some remained in the vicinity of the former market space. When Ruth's mother took over the family business she opened a shop at the former market, now redesigned as a car park named Rawlings Park. Before retiring, however, Ruth's mother relocated to the shop inside the Chinese Commodities Town. When Ruth came into the family business to work with her mother in the late 1980s, her mother held the position of distributor for Ghana Textiles Printing (GTP), Ghana's most esteemed textile company. After the move from the former shop, however, Ruth found that GTP no longer sold well as it used to. Given that the business was fairly small, she found it difficult to rely on one source only. One of Ruth's first business decisions as the head of the family business was therefore to withdraw from the position of being distributor for GTP. This business decision repositioned Ruth and she now depends on other sources for her supply of textiles and wax prints.

At this time Chinese textiles are becoming popular in Accra. Ruth therefore decides to diversify the business by engaging in trade in several different brands of textiles, including Chinese-made copies. This business strategy links her up with women like Solenne, even if the latter operates on a much larger scale. Lomé's free port has positioned Togo as a West African centre for Chinese textiles, as it did before for European textiles. Given Ghana's continued high import duties on textiles, many of Accra's traders have found Lomé an appealing alternative link to Chinese textiles. Given that all overland imports of textiles from Togo have been illegal since 2005, however, textiles from Lomé are generally referred to as contraband. Furthermore, as imitating Ghanaian and European designs is common practice among the new Chinese textile producers, one of Ghana's leading textile producers has organized raids at the market to bring traders who deal in imitations of Ghanaian designs to court. To trade in these textiles therefore involves certain risks. Having been arrested several times for selling counterfeits, Ruth has to learn new ways to engage in the Chinese trade without supporting illegal imports. Today she chooses carefully the importer that she buys from to ensure that the importers approve their designs with the Ghana Standards Board and that the goods are legally imported through Ghana's Takoradi port. Thus, Ruth differentiates between different types of Chinese textiles. Original Chinese designs that enter Ghana through the port are accepted, whereas smuggled imitations are labelled as damaging to the nation.

Ruth, like most traders, expresses support for the Ghanaian textile industry and welcomes cooperation with the textile producers to prevent trade in counterfeits in the future. Many traders feel ambivalent about the transition to marketing Chinese textiles. In many cases they are closely linked to the Ghanaian textile companies via their husbands, who are employees of those companies. To trade in Chinese textiles also means that they part with the tradition and the legacy of the influential women who once participated in introducing wax prints to the West African market. In redefining their identities, traders have to juggle their anti-Chinese rhetoric and everyday economic interests.

Previous contradictions involving foreign influences in Ghana's trading economy have been associated with the presence of foreign traders (Akyeampong 2006; Garlick 1971; Peil 1974) and have included elements of 'othering'. Levantine traders in particular have been subjected to hostile resistance (Garlick 1971). In the case of printed textiles, traders of Chinese origin do not operate visibly at the market. Rather, the process of 'othering' of the Chinese prints trade is concentrated on the commodity. Yet the discourses that emerge around the inflow of Chinese textiles share many characteristics with those during the conflict in the 1950s and 1960s when Levantine traders were legally banned. Today Ghanaian textile companies and their workers are portrayed as hard working and law abiding, competing against large-scale Chinese manufacturers engaged in illegal modes of production (including production of counterfeits and use of child labour). Networks for the import and distribution of Chinese prints are also associated with illegality (including smuggling and tax evasion). When talking about Ghanaian (and European) prints, people particularly emphasize their high quality. Chinese prints, on the other hand, are associated with poor quality. Furthermore, Chinese business strategies are often referred to as unethical.

Ruth's trajectory illuminates several changes in Accra's trading landscape since the introduction of Chinese textiles on a large scale. Today positions are altered, and most traders choose to diversify their businesses to include Chinese textiles in their selection of wares. Ruth's story also reveals the ambivalent attitude many traders have towards the inflow of Chinese textiles in their market.

While it is an economic opportunity not to be missed, they are still faced with the difficulty of constructing their identities as Ghanaian traders together under these new circumstances.

Conclusions

The chapter began by providing a historical context for understanding Ghanaian and Togolese women's strategies in the new trade in Chinese prints. In considering the trajectory of the post-colonial state and its conflicting and shifting relationship with women traders, the chapter sketched out the entangled historical, political and economic dynamics that contributed to the entry of Chinese prints into these markets. If these transformations have created opportunities for local agents, otherwise excluded from this long-standing and highly protected market segment, the shift to China has nevertheless brought about tensions and ambivalence. It becomes necessary to look at power relations within and between informal trading networks to better understand the workings of Chinese–African involvement. The notion of one Chinese presence in West African markets may thus be misleading, as our cases suggest. While Chinese traders have no shops in the Accra market, there are numerous Chinese shops in the Lomé market, suggesting a high degree of variability in China's presence. Local traders thus link up in different ways to Chinese traders or manufactures, depending on the context.

While the introduction of Chinese textiles has produced increased links between Ghanaian and Togolese trade networks, it also shows how local traders adopt different strategies. Both case studies have illustrated how traders find ways either to remain faithful to their historical legacy or to challenge that same legacy when engaging in trade with China. In the Togolese case, the legacy of the Nana-Benzes and their position in society appears as crucial in Solenne's redefinition of herself as a 'modern' defender of that heritage. Solenne's strategy appears to be insufficient, however, in the light of a transformed Togolese political and economic context. New entrepreneurs such as Solenne are unlikely to receive the kind of political support the Nana-Benzes were granted. Her chance to benefit from this trade derives, rather, from the contradictions between competing Togolese political networks and their visions for themselves. While one faction appears to rely on generating its income primarily via port taxes with Chinese mass imports, the faction supporting Solenne appears be attempting to establish a new Chinese trade monopoly in order to boost their finances.

The narratives used by traders in both Togo and Ghana to legitimize their economic decisions are highly ambiguous. In Togo, both Chinese traders and their products are often identified as suspicious. Many stories circulate in the market, suggesting the immoral nature of Chinese traders and the way they have led to the Togolese buying these new, yet defective, products. Similarly, in Ghana, an anti-Chinese rhetoric is projected on to the commodity itself, but rarely on to the person selling it; while the reverse is the case in Togo. Since it is mainly Ghanaian and Togolese women who are associated with the inflow of Chinese textiles to Ghana, the 'Chinese threat' is rather indistinct and there is a no obvious scapegoat to blame for any decline in business. In both cases, however, the discourse about China is used for similar purposes: to justify economic adaptation to new circumstances in Lomé and Accra.

PART FOUR

The conflict–development nexus:
a precarious balance!

11 | China and Africa: towards a new security relationship

Kwesi Aning

Since the 1960s, the Organization of African Unity (OAU) sought to deal with its security crises through its institutional frameworks. The ability of the OAU to fulfil this expectation, however, was at best minimal. As a result, the transformation of the OAU into the African Union (AU) in 2002 imposed new expectations and duties on the new organization. These related mainly to the AU's capacity to respond to and resolve Africa's conflicts. While the public rhetoric about conflict resolution was frequent, the actual capacity to deliver troops on the ground and respond credibly to the security challenges posed by new forms of war has proved challenging to the AU.

Concomitant with this development was a resurgent China, which sought to flex its new-found muscles and exert power and influence on the African continent. While discourses about China's Africa engagement have concentrated mainly on resource extraction, this chapter argues that new forms of relationship with Africa, especially with its flagship multilateral institution, the AU, are beginning to emerge. One such area of engagement is that of peacekeeping and helping to 'stabilize' conflict areas.

This chapter examines China's peace and security policy with respect to Africa in general and the African Union in particular. Specifically, the chapter examines China's endeavours in contributing to resolving or worsening the crisis in Sudan. Moreover, the AU's relationship with China is examined, especially in relation to China's peacekeeping activities on the continent. The analysis is then placed within the context of the interaction between security and non-political interference, which is then followed by an attempt to explain China's success in Africa.

Background to China's Africa engagement

China's Africa policy can be succinctly characterized as a policy of continuity and change: a policy that seeks to apply influence without interference. This relationship has gone through several changes over the years. During the cold war era, Sino-African relations were characterized mainly by a policy of anti-Soviet rhetoric and the extension of support to the anti-Portuguese nationalist movements in Angola and Mozambique (Saint-Paul 2004). Sino-African ties

145

slowly turned a corner in the 1980s, and gathered steam in the 1990s. This was evident in the dramtatic shift from the political rhetoric of solidarity and anti-colonialism to a relationship founded on economic imperatives and political-security calculations (Vines 2006; Ampiah and Naidu 2008; Hanson 2008). The result is that Africa has perhaps become the most significant testing ground for the expression of Chinese soft power.

The year 2006 marked the 'year of Africa' in China's diplomacy. China's 'new' African policy, adopted by the Chinese government in January 2006, describes the basic principles that should guide the new strategic partnership as follows. First, this relationship should be mutually beneficial to all parties, and must be based on sincerity, friendship and equality. This is a relationship which states China's adherence to the principles of peaceful coexistence, and respects African countries' independent choice of development path (Wenping 2007). Second, China's Africa engagement is based on mutual benefit, reciprocity and common prosperity. It means that China supports African countries' economic development and is committed to cooperation in various forms for the prosperity of both sides (Anshan 2007). Third, this emerging relationship is premised on mutual support and close coordination, which includes a commitment from China to strengthen cooperation with Africa in multilateral systems and to appeal to the international community to give more attention to questions concerning peace and development in Africa. Fourth, both parties seek to learn from each other by exploring the foundations for common development, which includes deepening exchanges and cooperation in various social fields and supporting African countries by enhancing capacity-building, and deepening collaboration for sustainable development (FOCAC 2003).

The crucial questions that ought to be answered are the following. Are Sino-African relations just opportunistic and based on an ad hoc momentum, or is this relationship a reflection of a real, nuanced strategy based on conflict and cooperation with countries on the African continent? How does China's peace and security engagement in Africa relate to its broader strategic and economic interest in Africa?

Expressions of soft power? From 'resource grab' to a mutually beneficial relationship?

Since 2005, China has been engaged in an unparalleled series of diplomatic offensives towards Africa 'promising more trade, cheaper loans and no political interference' (Chan 2007). In spite of suspicions on the part of Western countries about China's intentions (Brooks and Shin 2006), it is beginning to play a critical role also in the political calculations and equations of the AU and several of its member states. This new engagement is bound to transform Africa's international relations in a profound way.

In situating the political and strategic dimensions of China's Africa policy in its right perspective, it is crucial to understand that the Taiwan question – that is the non-recognition of Taiwan by African states – may not necessarily be the primary element of the African strategy of the People's Republic of China (PRC) (Taylor 2002a). While Taiwan is now on the back burner, its role in the United Nations (UN), and that dimension of its international relations with Africa, remains a critical point. This is because Beijing can offer its African partners a 'diplomatic package' thanks to its triple status as a developing country, a former colony and a great power able to carry its weight in the arena of world politics (Niquet 2006).

A good illustration of China's ability to exploit its Big Five Power status on the UN Security Council is its role in discussions of the Darfur case at the UN Security Council, demonstrating China's 'soft power' political leverage in Africa (Wenping 2007: 29). The above point is important and needs to be disaggregated. It must be understood that China's attitude to conflict resolution in Africa, according to Large, '... reflects contrasting priorities and economic interests'. Large argues further that, although Beijing regularly cites conflict resolution in Africa, this is far from being a central or direct plank in China's Africa engagement. In fact, in its 2006 Africa Policy, just one paragraph is devoted to this issue (Large 2008a). Actually the 'peace and security' section of the January 2006 White Paper does not represent a proactive approach to conflict resolution in Africa. Rather, it shows a preference for classical bilateral military cooperation, and to that end

> China will promote high-level military exchanges between [the] two sides and actively carry out military-related technological exchanges and cooperation. It will continue to help train African military personnel and support defence and army building of African countries for their own security. (People's Republic of China 2006)

In spite of this, however, there is an increasing engagement in peace support operations (PSOs) by China in a few African countries, exemplified by its activities and engagements in countries such as Liberia and the Democratic Republic of Congo (DRC), though these have elicited minimal international responses, unlike its engagement in Darfur. According to China, it has contributed almost ten thousand troops to UN peacekeeping activities since 1990. As of 2008, a total of 1,963 Chinese peacekeepers were serving on UN missions, which is higher than for any permanent member of the United Nations Security Council (UNSC) (Zhongying 2005). There are several reasons for China's peacekeeping engagement internationally and in Africa specifically. While there have been assertions that China's engagement is not humanitarian but rather protects authoritarian regimes and supplies them with arms, there are other more pertinent reasons for this shift (Curtis and Hickson 2005; Chan 2007). Three core reasons have been identified to explain this shift. First, this trend reflects China's overall effort to be responsive to international expectations; second, its stepped-up activity is part of President Hu Jintao's calls for 'new historic missions' in the twenty-first century; and third, it appears that participation in peacekeeping activities abroad carries important military applications and lessons (Gill et al. 2006).

In terms of placing China on the African diplomatic and PSO map, the international interest in China's Darfur operation – both negative and positive – certainly surpasses that of any other Chinese engagement in Africa on the security front. But the argument about China's Africa, AU and Sudan engagements have to be evaluated at two levels: first one needs to consider the bilateral aspect of China's relations with Sudan and then the multilateral aspect of its relations with the AU. The argument here is that what drives China's policy is that it eventually chose the multilateral approach (that is, support for the AU initiative) in order to preserve its bilateral relations with Sudan, which it highly values. It may not be so apparent at first, and creates the impression that by engaging the AU, China was shifting its attention away from Sudan. Rather, China's embrace of the multilateral approach hardly means a radical break in its bilateral relations. Rather, the AU was exploited to provide a veneer of authenticity to its policy in Sudan and to deflect attention and criticism (Large 2008a).

During the Darfur crisis, China has officially supported the regime in Khartoum, and offered critical diplomatic support. Furthermore, it has provided weaponry and has insulated the Khartoum regime from economic pressure and human rights accountability. At the UNSC, its strategy has been to dilute the language of resolutions and to frequently abstain from voting (Large 2007: 7). For example, on the occasion of the adoption of the crucial UN Security Council Resolution 1706 (related to the deployment of the hybrid AU–UN operation in Darfur), on which voting took place on 31 August 2006, China abstained, along with Qatar and Russia (United Nations 2006). Indeed, China's abstention signalled to Khartoum that it would face no prospect of urgent or forceful implementation of Resolution 1706 (E. Reeves 2007: 3). Despite its final abstention, there was a subtle shift in Beijing's approach to Sudan and the Darfur crisis, which was noticeable during the debate in Council over the final wording of UNSC Resolution 1706.

For the first time, China publicly encouraged Khartoum to allow UN peacekeepers into Darfur and called for a 'comprehensive political solution' to the crisis. The tipping points for this decision were interrelated processes. First, China prior to this vote had publicly cast itself as playing a 'constructive role' in Darfur (African Union Peace and Security Council 2006; Haselock 2008). Second, in that regard China followed this changed strategy when, in May 2007, Liu Guijin was appointed special representative for African affairs with a brief to facilitate a political solution to the Darfur crisis (Large 2007: 8–9). According to Ambassador Liu Guijin, China has 'tried every means ... [both] positive and constructive [to elicit changed behaviour in the Sudan]'. As a result of this change in approach, a two-pronged strategy was initiated – an indirect approach (from New York)[1] and a direct one (Guijin's Khartoum engagements), which contributed to ensuring Sudanese 'flexibility' in meeting the demands and expectations of the international community.

As much as China values its economic relationship with Khartoum, including its lucrative arms trade and central role in Sudanese oil production and exploration, another explanation for Beijing's subtle shift in emphasis was the unsurpassed importance it attached to the success of its hosting of the Beijing Summer Olympic Games in 2008 (Farrow and Farrow 2007; Kristoff 2006; E. Reeves 2007: 10). China's gradual acceptance of its role as a world power and its development of a more long-term economic and diplomatic perspective have also contributed to this change (Large 2007: 9). Needless to say, questions still linger about China's long-term motives in Africa and its commitment to democracy and human rights (Amosu 2007: 2).

China and the African Union

On the whole, China does not have a holistic programme of engagement with the AU, and neither does the AU have a policy framework of its own on how to engage China constructively. Rather, there is a bilateral approach that enables China on the one hand and the AU and its member states on the other to deal with each other. More importantly, China does not have the same approach with all African countries. China is astute in its African diplomacy in the sense that it knows perfectly what it can get from each state. Consequently, it adopts different approaches and not a one-size-fits-all approach in Africa. Furthermore, China has different levels of engagement with different countries of the continent, and sometimes no relations at all. It depends on the internal dynamics and the economic strength of its African partner. Certainly for China, there is no doubt that its aid to both the AU and its member states is premised on the 'principles of sustainability and mutual benefit rather than charity' (Wenping 2007: 34).

There is as yet no clarity about the extent to which both the AU and its member states are fully aware of China's instrumentalist and realist approach to its relations with Africa, which are usually framed within rhetoric of developmental humanitarianism. While China is constantly reassessing and adapting its policies to the shifting realities of African realpolitik, the African Union and most of its member states do not seem to have a coherent policy towards China. In fact the African Union lacks a consistent official China policy, which results in a weakening of its own and its member states' ability to negotiate with China. This lack of coherence in strategy has been recognized and has been rhetorically addressed since September 2006, when an AU experts' meeting on the subject opined that 'the African Union should be the fulcrum of the emerging Strategic Partnership and should be able to define the continent's interest more coherently and clearly'. Basically, the argument is that Africa needs a strategy on how to engage China from a position of strength (Amosu 2007: 4).

These concerns about policy incoherence between the AU and China are being addressed through the recently signed memorandum of understanding (MoU) between the AU and China. This deals with several facets of their cooperation, including but not limited to infrastructure, business negotiations, the financial and material support to the AU's peacekeeping mission in Darfur, and good governance. Then chairperson of the AU, Alpha Oumar Konare, during the signing of the MoU, stated that 'the consolidation of the friendship between China and the African Union should be done in a respectful manner for the interest of all' (African Union 2008). In the subsequent discussions, the AU argued that Chinese involvement in Africa should not be limited to the economic sector but should also seek to bring peace and unity in conflict-ridden African countries. Consequently, China is building its peacekeeping capacity. There is now a Civilian Peacekeeping Training Centre in Langfang and an International Relations Academy in Nanking; a new peacekeeping training centre will open in Huairou in mid-2009 to help centralize and better coordinate Chinese peacekeeping activities.

In what areas is China engaging the AU in its security-related activities? China's commitments with the AU have taken place, among other contexts, within the context of the Forum on China–Africa Cooperation (FOCAC). Basically, these include:

- US$11 million in aid to help with the humanitarian crisis in Darfur;
- US$1.8 million to the AU's peacekeeping mission;
- supporting the Kofi Annan Plan in November 2006 to bring peace to Darfur;
- 315 peacekeepers/engineering corps in Darfur;
- US$300,000 to the Kenyan Red Cross in January 2008 after an AU appeal for support;
- US$300,000 to the AU to assist with the African Union Mission for peace-keeping in Somalia (AMISOM) in August 2007;
- the appointment of a substantive special adviser/envoy to the AU and Sudan;
- the establishment of the Forum on China–Africa Cooperation (FOCAC) in 2000; and
- the provision of 435 soldiers, nine police officers and fourteen observers for the United Nations Mission in Sudan (UNMIS) from 2006.[2]

Although Chinese involvement in UN peacekeeping operations is relatively short and dates back to the early 1980s, in 2006 China ranked twelfth in the list of troop providers. Despite a steady growth in the number of Chinese troops participating in peacekeeping operations, China continues to express reservations (as it did in the case of UN peacekeeping in Sudan) about the decision to dispatch a peacekeeping mission into a conflict zone without the prior consent of all parties to the conflict.

TABLE 11.1 Ranking of countries by size of troop contribution to UN peacekeeping missions, as of 31 December 2006

Country	Number of troops
Pakistan	9,867
Bangladesh	9,681
INDIA	9,483
Jordan	3,820
Ghana	2,694
Nepal	2,607
Uruguay	2,586
Italy	2,462
Nigeria	2,408
France	1,988
Senegal	1,881
CHINA	1,666

Source: United Nations, 'Ranking of military and police contributions to UN operations', Department of Peacekeeping (www.un.org/Depts/dpko/dpko/contributors/2006/dec06_2)

What does the geography of Chinese engagement with the AU and its member states in terms of security demonstrate? One critical area where such bilateral engagements have increased is the exchange of intelligence as well as joint training programmes to address both traditional and non-traditional security areas. An important area where a more multilateral approach would have been useful, however, is terrorism. Here, the AU's African Centre for Study and Research on Terrorism (ACSRT) in Algiers, Algeria, would have been useful, as this institution fulfils part of the AU's Plan of Action on terrorism. It is becoming clear, however, that because most African states perceive bilateral relations as more profitable than a multilateral approach, they are reluctant for the African Union to take a lead in these negotiations.

The key AU–China project is currently the construction of a new modern conference centre at the AU headquarters, which is scheduled for completion by mid-2010 and is estimated to cost US$150 million. This project forms part of China's Eight Point Proposal supporting African development.

Defining a new partnership? The intersection between security and non-political interference

To appreciate China's Africa policy, one needs to understand its various facets. Thus, according to Niquet (2006), Chinese interests are a matter of developing trade by increasing aid 'without political conditions' within a non-interference policy that accepts the survival of authoritarian regimes, persuading the international community to increase its support, and defending Africa's position on the world stage. But given the fluidity of certain issues (especially security) in Africa, and the speed with which they can change, it is important to be aware that China is also examining how best to regulate and align its policies to reflect African realities.

But China's African concerns go considerably deeper, spanning both classical and non-traditional security issues. The classical security issues relate to its engagement with peacekeeping, the transfer of arms to African states and diverse support offers, as discussed above. The Chinese are increasingly engaging in non-traditional security issues, however, such as maritime and oil security, both in the Central African Republic (CAR) and Sudan. In its Africa Policy document, China also pledges to support conflict resolution efforts by the AU and other regional organizations, urges the UN to follow suit, and guarantees continuing support to and participation in UN peacekeeping operations in Africa. Commitments are made to judicial and police cooperation in combating crime, corruption and illegal immigration, as well as closer cooperation in fighting 'terrorism, small arms and light weapons (SALW) smuggling, narcotics trafficking and transnational economic crimes as part of the China–Africa cooperation plan'.[3] In fact, as Chan puts it, the Chinese are not just about everywhere, they are in most places Western nations are not. The Chinese diaspora runs everything from grocery stores and building material shops to restaurants and corner stores in even the most remote provincial towns throughout Africa. Beijing has zeroed in on pariah states like Sudan, where Western firms are either barred by sanctions or constrained from doing business because of concerns over human rights, repressive policies, labour standards and security issues (Chan 2007: 3–4).

What prospects for a new and dynamic partnership?

China is at a comparatively early stage of engagement in Africa. But any evaluation of China's relationship with the AU and its member states must take account of the fact that its policies are driven by its long-term strategic interests and its perception of its rising international status. Although the AU has elaborate peace and security mechanisms, it lacks the necessary cohesion and resources to utilize them effectively. This is because the AU is still in a state of flux. Legitimacy and credibility will come to the AU only if and when it manages to build its own capacity to represent the interests of the African people, while helping to enhance standards of living. There is still uncertainty about the AU's ability to take full advantage of the new peace and security partnership with China. The policy options that are available for developing coherence and capacity within the AU should take place within the EU–AU capacity-building project, including enabling the recruitment of professionals with policy skills.

In China–Africa relations, there is not only a psychological resonance, but also an emotional aspect. Africa does not have any suspicions about Chinese motives, or if it does, these are outweighed by the practical benefits of the relationship. Africa does not feel threatened because China too has been through the experience of colonialism, occupation and exploitation. Africa has a long memory regarding colonization, and this is beginning to play a role in its relationship with China.

Most African countries look to China as a nation that has a peculiar endogenous developmental approach, namely 'development built from within' – a process they can identify with and learn from. China's economic prowess and self-promotion as an alternative to Western hegemony has, therefore, won Beijing friends throughout Africa. As Zimbabwe's president Robert Mugabe stated: 'we are looking to the east where the sun rises, and have turned our backs on the west where the sun sets' (Hilsum 2005). Indeed, for African states, China's presence has opened new avenues of flexibility and manoeuvrability previously denied to them by the excessive conditionality imposed by Western financial institutions and governments since the early 1980s, limiting their policy space.[4] But more important is the manner in which economic engagement is also beginning to impact on new peace and security relations in terms of China's deepening involvement in African peace and security issues.

The new China–Africa partnership symbolizes a new economic and diplomatic 'cold war' on the African stage. Therefore, if France, the United States, the United Kingdom and others want to maintain a semblance of their earlier predominant influence on the continent, they have to re-engage with Africa, but in a way that differs from their past relationship.[5] Some commentators even raise the issue of the modalities of collaboration between the United States and China on African matters (Gill et al. 2006; Lyman 2005). For example, the importance and centrality of Africa's emerging peace and security architecture and China's deepening role in these processes were exemplified on the occasion of the negotiations pertaining to the Africa–EU dialogue follow-up mechanism. During the negotiations, the European contingent initially asked its African counterpart for regular briefings on the state of dialogue between Africa and its other partners, in particular China, India and Brazil. The draft communiqué finally adopted by the Africa–EU Ministerial Troika Meeting held in Accra, Ghana, on 31 October 2007 stated:

> In order to ensure coherence and complementarity with the work of other international actors, including emerging partners, Africa and the EU recognize the need to broaden their cooperation with third partners through enhanced tripartite dialogue. Similarly, both parties recognize the importance of triangular cooperation for the development of the two continents.[6]

The emergence of China, Brazil and India as competitors to Europe on the African continent has jeopardized 'old' Europe's historical and socio-economic and political influence. The China–Africa relationship has definitely given greater political leverage to Africa in the Africa–EU dialogue. While this dialogue opens new vistas for engagement with China, it is operationally wider than that, because it affects relations with the EU, the USA, France and the UK, which have traditionally been Africa's economic, political and security partners. Similarly, this will also shape broader relations with India, which has a considerably longer relationship with Africa and has shared and participated in peacekeeping ventures with several of the AU's member states. But we should look at this emerging partnership in a much more nuanced way. Only time will tell whether China is indeed a better partner than the West, and whether Western concerns are justified.

Conclusion

China's Africa engagement reflects the emergence of new power dynamics in the global economy. But it nevertheless raises a critical question: to what extent is China's presence in Africa different or more of the same? And to what extent do these new international relations benefit Africa economically while also increasing the involvement of Africa's international relations in security issues? There is no doubt that because of China's history and approach, it is perceived as a friend that does not come with the heavy baggage of other powers, precisely because of its earlier support for liberation movements. Furthermore, there is wide recognition of the fact that China's foreign policy makes a conscious effort to respect Africans as partners, and thus this redefined relationship provides windows of opportunity within and through which African states can also redefine themselves in relation to their security issues. It may be too early to discuss what the lasting impacts of China's new Africa engagement will be, but there is no doubt, based on the foregoing, that its robust engagement with the African Union is spurring the AU's traditional partners, especially the EU, to engage more with the organization.

12 | The Darfur issue: a new test for China's Africa policy

He Wenping

The ongoing conflict in the Darfur region of Sudan and China's growing economic engagement in that country, particularly in the energy field, has put China's Africa policy in the spotlight. Since China and Sudan have had a long tradition of friendship and close political and economic ties, there has been an unreasonable expectation from the international community that China alone can influence the position of the Sudanese government on this sensitive matter. The international controversy over Darfur has put China's long-held foreign policy of 'non-interference' on a collision course with the new international principle of the 'responsibility to protect' and the campaign by Western governments and some non-governmental organizations to impose a 'sanctions regime' on the government of Sudan.

In this chapter, we argue that, as far as the Chinese government is concerned, the principle of 'non-interference'should not be interpreted as unwillingness on the part of China to take on the 'responsibility to protect'. As a matter of fact, in recent years China's Darfur policy has shown more and more flexibility and the 'non-interference' policy itself is also undergoing changes. Given the complexity of the Darfur issue and the volatile north–south relations in Sudan, the 'engagement approach' endorsed and pushed by China is more constructive than the punitive 'sanction initiative' being pushed by the West for bringing about stability and peace in Sudan.

Darfur: a complicated issue

Since early 2003, the crisis in Darfur has grabbed international attention thanks to the special attention devoted to it by Western human rights organizations, the media and politicians (Amnesty International 2006; Kristoff 2006; Large 2007). The protracted political crisis has also called into question the growing involvement of China in Sudan and the extent to which China's economic engagement, particularly in the energy field, indirectly emboldens the Sudanese government relentlessly to prosecute the conflict in Darfur. Western governments and human rights groups continue to argue that China's strict adherence to its policy of 'non-interference' amounts to nothing less than direct complicity in fuelling the crisis in Darfur (Amnesty International 2006;

International Crisis Group 2002). The questions that must be asked are the following. What are the root causes of the crisis in Darfur? Does China really have any leverage over Sudan? What steps has China taken in recent years to resolve the Darfur crisis?

Located in western Sudan, Darfur is home to some eighty ethnic groups, the great majority of which are either Arab or African. The former group is nomadic and is distributed over the north of the area, and the latter is made up of agricultural ethnic groups inhabiting the central and southern parts. Apart from occasional conflicts over land and water, the two groups coexisted more or less peacefully until the early 1970s, when a severe drought drove Arab tribes from northern Darfur and from neighbouring countries like Chad to central and southern Darfur, leading to an increase in population from 3 million twenty years ago to its current level of 6 million. This factor, combined with famine and the collapse of the fragile ecosystem, began to accentuate disputes over land and water. According to some Sudanese scholars, the number of intra-group conflicts jumped from three in 1968 to twenty-one by 1998 (Takana 1998).

The conflicts over life-sustaining resources such as water and land were further exacerbated by deliberate political exclusion of the southern Sudanese by the northern-dominated central government in Khartoum. The imposition of strict Islamic sharia law across the whole of Sudan by the regime in Khartoum was the straw that broke the camel's back. It fuelled political resentment and gave birth to armed resistance movements which demanded political autonomy from the north. One of the most prominent of these militant movements is the Sudan People's Liberation Movement (SPLM), which, after decades of brutal civil war, finally came to an accommodation with Khartoum with the signing of the Comprehensive Peace Agreement in 2005, which laid out a road map for sharing power, including self-determination for the south.

Just as the deadly conflict in south Sudan was coming to an end, the conflict in Darfur broke out, engulfing neighbouring countries such as Chad, the Central African Republic, Libya and Uganda. Arab militias, known as the Janjaweed, began to mete out cruel punishment to Darfurians. In the face of the mass atrocities being committed against defenceless civilians, and the failure of the Sudanese government to protect Darfurian citizens, a concerted humanitarian response was mounted. On their part, Darfurians began to arm themselves to repel the incursion by the government-supported Janjaweed militias (Ronalsen 2007; Murphy 2007). The two prominent military fronts were the Sudan Liberation Army (SLA) and the Justice and Equality Movement (JEM). In February 2003, the two armed forces launched a large-scale anti-government campaign demanding autonomous rule. The involvement of neighbouring countries such as Libya, Chad and the Central African Republic was to complicate the situation further as political discord existed between them and Sudan. The expansion of the conflict has caused large numbers of casualities in Darfur, although estimates are difficult to obtain. The estimated number of people who died in the conflict varies from a low of 10,000 (given by the Sudanese government) to a high of 70,000, according to an estimate by the World Health Organization. More than a million people have been displaced. The conflict in Darfur has resulted in the worst humanitarian crisis in decades.

Darfur and the debate on 'genocide'

The failure of the Sudanese government to protect Darfurian citizens from the daily onslaught by Arab militias promoted a great deal of debate in Western capitals. Many humanitarian groups began to accuse the Sudanese government of complicity in 'genocide'. In the United States, some right-wing Christian organizations and anti-Arab interest groups in particular began to lobby hard for the Bush administration publicly to label the atrocities in Darfur 'genocide' and crimes against humanity (Birchall 2006). From the point of view of the Bush administration and the critics of the Sudanese government, this would permit the USA and the international community to impose sanctions against the al-Bashir regime and lay the grounds for UN intervention under the principle of 'responsibility to protect' (de Waal 2007; Udombana 2005). Though couched in the language of 'responsibility to protect', it was not too difficult to detect the anti-Islam and anti-Arab motives of the Bush administration and the 'Save Darfur' coalitions. But in the political environment of post-9/11 America, the indifference of the al-Bashir regime towards the people of Darfur in itself justified a hard-line position against Sudan on the part of the international community. It is in this respect that one needs to examine China's role in the Darfur crisis, and see whether Beijing has any tricks in its diplomatic bag to persuade the al-Bashir regime to comply with international norms and standards in addressing the Darfur conflict.

The United Nations, the African Union and the European Union had all refused to use the term 'genocide' to describe the crisis in Darfur; the UN in particular had categorized the issue as a humanitarian crisis (Cornwell 2005). Despite this, the US Congress went ahead and passed a resolution in July 2004, describing the Darfur crisis as 'genocide' and instructing the administration promptly to impose sanctions on Sudan (Associated Press 2007b). This led to the internationalization of the Darfur issue (Farrow and Farrow 2007; A. Reeves 2007). According to William Engdahl (2007): '[G]enocide was the preferred theme, and Washington was the orchestra conductor ... only Washington and the NGOs close to it use the charged term "genocide" to describe Darfur. If they are able to get a popular acceptance of the charge [of] genocide, it opens the possibility for drastic "regime change" intervention by NATO and de facto by Washington into Sudan's sovereign affairs.'

The Bush administration put forward a number of sanction initiatives in the UN Security Council, but none of these resolutions was adopted owing to disagreement among the permanent members of the Council. For example, in September 2004 the UN Security Council passed Resolution 1564, which condemned the mass killing of civilians in the Darfur region, but stopped short of imposing oil sanctions if Khartoum did not act to stop the killing. China abstained from the vote and threatened to veto any further move to impose sanctions. While the Bush administration and its supporters had tried to present China as the stumbling block in Sudan, Chinese officials pointed out that the real intent of the United States in the Sudan was quite different from what it appeared to be on the surface. As William Engdahl has rightly pointed out, 'Oil, not human misery, is behind Washington's new interest in Darfur' (Engdahl 2007). China's position throughout has been that diplomacy is a much better tool to resolve the crisis in Darfur than the threat of sanctions and attempts to isolate the Sudanese government. Moreover, the Chinese position has been that the US interest in Sudan (despite the rhetoric of humanitarianism) is motivated by two factors: its determination to prosecute the war on terror, given the strategic location of Sudan in the Horn of Africa; and the search for a secure supply of energy, of which Sudan has plenty.

Darfur and its 'links' with China

Many Western governments and non-governmental organizations have consistently advanced the view that, in its relations with the government of Sudan, China is simply pursuing its own economic interests and ignoring the human rights situation in Darfur. Therefore, they argue, China bears some responsibility for the worsening humanitarian crisis in Darfur, and should start to behave as a responsible stakeholder on the international stage.[1] As the date for the 2008 Beijing Olympic Games approached, the 'Save Darfur Coalition' and many politicians intensified their campaign to put pressure on China by calling for a boycott of the Beijing games (Farrow and Farrow 2007; Cullen 2007).[2] Furthermore, in May 2007 over one hundred US Representatives wrote to the Chinese president, pointing out that if China did not take measures with regard to Darfur, the 2008 Beijing Olympic Games might be jeopardized (H. Cooper 2007).[3] Thus the spotlight was put on China, but the criticism was one-sided and hypocritical as there were many other countries heavily involved in the Sudanese oil sector, such as India and Malaysia, whose governments were spared the same kind of criticism.

Lost in the political blame game is China's role in transforming the Sudanese economy through its comprehensive economic cooperation strategy with Sudan. With increased revenue from oil, the government of Sudan was able to gain considerable room to manoeuvre politically, which enabled it to reach political accommodation with its arch enemy, the Sudan People's Liberation Army (SPLA). Without the improved economic situation, considerably aided by Chinese investment in the oil sector, the signing of the Comprehensive Peace Agreement (CPA) in 2005 would not have been possible. The CPA stipulated a fifty-fifty revenue-sharing formula between Khartoum and Juba (the capital of south Sudan).

China–Sudan economic relations

First of all, the strong economic recovery in Sudan is closely linked with China's involvement. China and Sudan enjoy a traditional friendship. Since diplomatic ties were established between them in February 1959, the relationship has developed smoothly. The first trade treaty between the two governments was signed in 1962. In terms of the oil industry, China's energy cooperation with Sudan has dramatically improved Sudanese oil capacity. Chinese companies started to prospect for energy resources in Sudan in the mid-1990s. By the end of 2003, their investment totalled US$2.7 billion, with which they laid 1,506 kilometres of oil pipelines, and built a crude-oil processing plant with a capacity of 2.5 million tons a year and several gas stations (Blair 2005; Goodman 2004; Thompson 2005). With Chinese investment, Sudan transformed itself from an oil-importing country into an oil-exporting country.

More importantly, with China's help Sudan established its own oil industry, consisting of prospecting, exploitation, refining and transportation facilities and sales networks. As a result, oil production has risen from 2,000 barrels per day in 1993 to 500,000 barrels per day today. Crude oil exports amounted to roughly 84 per cent of total exports in 2006 (Gadir 2007). And Sudan's economic growth rate has been maintained at around 8–12 per cent annually, which ranks as one of the best growth rates among north-east African countries. The inflation rate has also dropped from 135 per cent in the 1990s to 5 per cent in 2006. Meanwhile, annual income per capita has increased from US$280 to US$1,080. Foreign exchange reserves reached US$1.44 billion at the end of April 2005. Sudan then had the capability to repay the loan provided by the International Monetary Fund (IMF) and Sudan's voting rights in the IMF were restored in 2000 (EIU 2005).

Chinese oil companies not only provide employment to local people, they have been engaged in other kinds of projects that directly benefit local communities. For example, by the end of 2006 China National Petroleum Corporation (CNPC), China's largest oil producer, had spent over US$32 million on building schools and hospitals and drilling water wells in the country, benefiting over 1.5 million local people.[4] CNPC has invested in the construction of twenty-two primary schools and helped 65,000 people receive education. Meanwhile, the company has also provided millions of dollars for Sudanese students to study at undergraduate and postgraduate level in China, or receive short-term training.[5]

Oil revenues, positive economic growth and the birth of the CPA

Lost in the debate over Darfur is the significant contribution of China in the revival of the Sudanese economy and the effect this had on accelerating the peace process in south Sudan. As stated earlier, the development of Sudan's oil industry with China's help had a direct impact on the ability and willingness of the central government to reach an accommodation with the Sudan People's Liberation Movement, leading to the signing of the CPA in 2005. While diplomacy and international mediation were a critical part of the peace process, the resolution of the north–south conflict would not have gone that far without the improved economic situation of Sudan as a result of windfall oil receipts. According to Hamad Elneel A. Gadir, deputy secretary-general of the Sudanese Energy and Mining Ministry: '[O]il has become a main factor for development, peace and unity in Sudan. Sanctions against Sudan are sanctions against Sudan's development, peace and unity' (Gadir 2007). Sudan's president Omar al-Bashir also extolled the success of Sino-Sudanese energy cooperation when he said: 'No CNPC, no oil industry in Sudan, not to mention the peace in the south and north of Sudan.'[6]

According to the statistics given by the Sudanese Energy and Mining Ministry, the total oil revenue from 1999 to July 2005 reached US$15 billion. Oil income accounted for 53.7 per cent of national fiscal revenue in 2003. Only as a result of the oil revenue could the NPC-dominated central government in the capital, Khartoum, and the SPLM-led autonomous Government of Southern Sudan (GoSS) finally reach the deal over resource-sharing, consisting of a fifty-fifty split, after an allocation of 2 per cent of the revenue allocated directly to the oil-producing regions themselves. At present, the Ministry of Finance and National Economy publishes a monthly report on oil revenue, which is prepared with assistance from the Energy and Mining Ministry and southern officials. According to the data given by the Ministry of Finance and National Economy, the GoSS had received US$473 million in oil revenue in the first five months of 2006. During this period, the south's reported monthly share of oil receipts increased from US$72 million in January to US$112 million in May (EIU 2006: 24). And according to Andrew S. Natsios, US Special Envoy to Sudan in 2006/07, as of early 2008, some US$3 billion in oil revenues had been transferred to the south's treasury. The south's economy is beginning to boom (Natsios 2008: 80). Therefore, there is no doubt that the increased oil income received either by the central government in Khartoum or the GoSS in the south had greatly eased the budgetary constraints in both the north and the south and improved people's living standards as a whole. And that is very helpful for the consolidation of the CPA.

'Non-interference' and the 'responsibility to protect'

The principle of 'non-interference' has been one of the Five Principles of Peaceful Coexistence guiding China's foreign policy since the First Afro-Asian Conference in Bandung, Indonesia, in 1955. It is also embraced in the Charter of the United Nations[7] and other international legal documents. While China has moved increasingly towards a market-based system, the principle of 'non-interference' remains constant and been reiterated in many important official documents, including the January 2006 *China's African Policy* (People's Republic of China 2006; Taylor 1998). China believes that upholding non-interference and offering unconditional aid are important to its efforts to develop lasting relations with Africa. China is careful not to interfere in African countries' internal affairs, giving full respect to the right of African countries to manage their own internal affairs independently (Ping 1999: 179). For China, this principle is not theoretical; it is informed by its own history, which was marked by repeated Western interference in Chinese domestic affairs.[8]

In the context of the Darfur crisis, the relevance of this important principle has been questioned by the Western media and the Bush administration, and has put the Chinese leadership on the defensive as it tries to balance its belief in the principle of 'non-interference' and the demands of the international community that it abandon this principle. As Belgian scholar Jonathan Holsag has put it, 'Darfur exigently tested China's diplomatic agility. It compelled Beijing to veer between its traditional norms and economic interests on the one side, and on the other side the international pressure and the need for long term stability' (Holsag 2007). While insisting that 'non-interference' does not imply unwillingness to protect, Chinese diplomats were quick to point out that the principle of 'responsibility to protect' is a coded expression deliberately crafted by the United States and its friends to justify intervention in Sudan with the explicit goal of bringing 'regime change' and maintaining US hegemony in the region (de Waal 2007; Abbas 2007). Moreover, Chinese policy-makers also point out Washington's hypocritical moralizing when in fact, since the early 1980s, the USA and its Western allies have been interfering in the internal affairs of African countries through conditional lending and debt structures all in the name of market reform. As a result, African development has been stunted in the process; the role of the African state in the management of the economy has been significantly reduced; and poverty has been exacerbated. This amounts to recolonization, not development.

China, Sudan and the United Nations

While insisting on and strictly abiding by the principle of 'non-interference', China has become more and more active in joining the international effort led by the UN for conflict resolution and peacemaking in Africa. Since the late 1990s, China has dispatched a total of nearly two thousand peacekeeping troops to eight African countries and ranks first among the five permanent members of the United Nations Security Council in terms of contribution to peacekeeping operations (Yuan 1998).

With respect to Darfur, China has shown more pragmatism and flexibility since 2007. Apart from appointing a Special Envoy to Darfur and increasing humanitarian assistance to the region, China actively began to pressure the Sudanese government to cooperate with the international community and to allow the deployment of UN peacekeepers to Darfur, but only with the consent of the regime in Khartoum (Reuters 2006). By doing so, China was able successfully to pacify the international community while maintaining good relations with the government of Sudan. Given its position in the global economy, it cannot afford to alienate its important trading partner, the United States, and its important oil supplier, Sudan. Seen from a broader perspective, China's actions in the case of Darfur are a demonstration of its commitment to act as a responsible global stakeholder in a complex world where issues are interconnected and difficult to disentangle.

The 'engagement approach': China's constructive role

On the Darfur issue, there are two major allegations levelled at China by the Western media and international organizations: first, China has objected to using sanctions against Sudan when the UN Security Council has discussed the Darfur issue; and second, China has not done enough to pressure the Sudanese government to change its stance. On the contrary, China has been active in search of pragmatic solutions to the crisis in Darfur, despite relentless criticism from the West. China believes that regional and international conflicts should be settled through diplomatic means such as dialogue and negotiation. It argues that sanctions are counterproductive and that those hit hardest by sanctions are the common people, not the authorities. Sanctions and strong-arm tactics against Sudan will succeed only in complicating matters (Thompson 2004). According to Chinese Special Envoy to Darfur Liu Guijin: 'Too much pressure or expanding sanctions will not be helpful for the peaceful settlement of the issue, but [will] further complicate the situation, and many previous cases had already proved that issues like Darfur would never be properly addressed without the country's internal political process.'[9]

It is important to acknowledge from the outset that China's adherence to the principle of 'non-interference' does not mean that Beijing is unwilling to take on the 'responsibility to protect'. The key difference here is that China supports legitimate intervention only if it meets the following criteria: first, the intervention should not violate the concerned state's sovereignty; second, the intervention must gain the authorization of the United Nations; third, the UN force must secure an invitation from the concerned state; and finally, the UN mission should use force only when all other options have proved ineffective (Carlson 2004; A. Reeves 2007). In defence of this position, the Chinese authorities point to the disastrous failure of the US invasion of Iraq in the name of 'protecting' the 'human rights' and 'freedom' of the Iraqi people, which took place without the support of the United Nations (Bellamy 2005; de Waal 2007). China believes that, in the case of the Iraqi invasion, the United States did not fully exploit all diplomatic avenues and instead chose a bilateral approach over multilateral means. In the end, its actions generated a great deal of resentment from Iraqi citizens, paving the way for internal insurrection by the Iraqis against what they came to regard as an occupying power rather than a liberating force.

Since the emergence of the Darfur issue, China has been in constant communication with the relevant people, playing mediator, promoting dialogue between top leaders, dispatching envoys and discussing the problem in the UN General Assembly (Russel and Wallis 2007). President Hu Jintao held discussions with Sudanese president Omar al-Bashir on the Darfur issue during the Beijing summit of the Forum on China–Africa Cooperation in November 2006 and his visit to Sudan in February 2007. Furthermore, China participated in a conference held in the Ethiopian capital Addis Ababa in November 2006 involving representatives of the five permanent members of the UN Security Council, the African Union and Sudan. Former UN secretary-general Kofi Annan outlined a three-phase plan (the Annan Plan) to offer assistance to African Union troops stationed in Darfur. In the first phase, the UN would send in military equipment valued at US$21 million, and dispatch nearly two hundred personnel as intelligence officials and counsellors. In the second phase, the personnel and equipment sent to the African Union troops should reach a certain level; in the third phase, a UN–AU united force should be established in Darfur with 17,000 soldiers and 3,000 police, under the command of the UN (United Nations 2006; African Union 2006a). China supports the Annan Plan, and believes it is practical and acceptable to Sudan.

Owing to China's constructive efforts and its endorsement of the Annan Plan, the Sudanese government announced that it would agree to the deployment of a hybrid UN–AU peacekeeping force in Darfur. This was subsequently reflected in Resolution 1769, passed by the UN Security Council on 31 July 2007. This would have been unimaginable without China's constructive diplomatic engagement (Large 2007). Moreover, China is committed to going beyond words and taking action. In order to promote the implementation of UN Resolution 1769, China has dispatched 315 Chinese military engineers to Darfur as part of the first group of UN peacekeepers to be sent there. China has offered assistance valued at a total of 80 million yuan (US$10.93 million) to the Darfur region, and donated US$1.8 million to the peacekeeping organizations of the African Union.

In addition to its support of the Annan Plan and its behind-the-scenes diplomatic manoeuvring in the passing of Resolution 1769, on 10 May 2007 the Chinese government appointed Ambassador Liu Guijin as the special representative on African affairs (Associated Press 2007a). Prior to Ambassador Liu's appointment, China had previously dispatched five Special Envoys to Darfur to study the situation on the ground in order to help the authorities in Beijing develop appropriate strategies towards Sudan. This clearly shows the importance the Chinese government attaches to Africa, and particularly to the Darfur issue at present. After assuming office, Ambassador Liu immediately made a five-day trip to Sudan, and discussed the plight of Darfur with high-ranking Sudanese leaders, so as to accelerate the political settlement of the issue and afford local people a better life and security.[10] *The Economist* applauded China for publicly applying more pressure on the Khartoum regime.

As Andrew S. Natsios has stressed, 'engagement is now the only policy that has any chance of success' (Natsios 2008: 89). The unpleasant history of relations between Khartoum and the West, however, has naturally made the leaders in Khartoum believe that the West is out to depose them and facilitate Sudan's break-up. And unfortunately, the arrest warrant issued by the Hague-based International Criminal Court (ICC) to Sudanese president Omar al-Bashir in early March 2009 seems the latest evidence of what feeds this anxiety. Owing to the deep-rooted mistrust between Khartoum and the West, China has the advantage of being able to serve as a bridge-builder and message-transmitter bringing its engagement approach to the Darfur issue. And China has indeed played this role and made a great contribution in this direction.

The ICC's verdict and the future of Darfur

Some people may think that the Darfur issue is complicated enough without the Hague-based ICC stepping in and, ironically, making it even more complicated and difficult to resolve. In the middle of July 2008, ICC chief prosecutor Luis Moreno-Ocampo charged Sudanese president Omar al-Bashir with genocide and crimes against humanity and asked the court to issue an arrest warrant for al-Bashir. In early March 2009, the ICC issued the warrant, targeting a sitting president of a state for the first time in the modern history of international relations.

On the surface of things, it may seem that the ICC has finally made an important step forward in judicial justice. But in reality the move was in the wrong direction, and even set the peacemaking effort promoted by all stakeholders in Sudan two or three steps back. On the one hand, the verdict has stimulated wide-ranging outrage in Sudan as well as in some Arab and African countries. President al-Bashir and the high-level persons around him have criticized the verdict as part of a Western conspiracy and a 'neocolonialist' plan aimed at effecting 'regime change' in Sudan. There is no doubt that the verdict has pushed al-Bashir farther into the camp of hardliners in his party and will help the ruling elite in Khartoum consolidates its hold on power. The rebel group in Darfur will likely be encouraged by the verdict and will probably step up their attacks or increase their demands at the negotiating table. We have now seen the Khartoum government expel a dozen foreign aid agencies, including Britain's Oxfam and Save the Children, the US-based Care, the International Rescue Committee and Médecins Sans Frontières. The departure of these aid agencies will cause a huge shortage of manpower and resources for humanitarian assistance in Darfur. Once again, the poor people in Darfur are the ultimate victims of the ICC verdict.

The ICC verdict even helped to push the outside stakeholders into two different camps. The African Union and the Arab League both reacted strongly to the verdict and suggested the indictment could destabilize the region, worsen the Darfur conflict and threaten a troubled peace deal between the north and the south. By contrast, the European Union has urged the Sudanese government to cooperate with the court while the USA has called for all sides to exercise restraint. China, of course, opposes any acts that could disrupt efforts to realize peace in Darfur and in Sudan, and backs the call by African and Arab nations to suspend or even revoke the warrant.

The future of Darfur, as well as the whole situation in Sudan, is becoming more and more unclear and challenging since the ICC verdict. With the approaching presidential election in 2009 and the referendum in 2011, peace in Darfur and stability in Sudan depend completely on the joint endeavour of all the stakeholders in and outside the country. Given the complicated nature of the crisis in Darfur, inextricable from the deterioration of the ecosystem and the involvement of religion and politics as well as inside and outside forces, the Darfur issue is not a simple one that can be solved either by China or any other country alone. The complicated nature of the conflict could make a quick resolution difficult, and the world should prepare itself accordingly.

Conclusions

The success of China's 'quiet diplomacy' in Darfur does not mean that Beijing should not make a reassessment of its policy in Sudan and Africa in general. Globalization and Africa's own progress have altered the strategic and political circumstances on the continent and this will continue to influence China's foreign policy projections in Africa. For example, with the transformation of the former Organization of Africa Unity (OAU) into the African Union, the OAU's principle of 'non-interference in the internal affairs of member states' has been replaced by the AU's principle of 'non-indifference', that is 'conditional intervention in member states' internal affairs'. In Article 4 of the AU Charter, sovereign equality and non-interference are stressed; the same article emphasizes, however, 'the right of the AU to intervene in a member state in grave circumstances, such as war crimes, genocide and crimes against humanity'. This demonstrates a realization by African nations that conflict in one area of Africa can affect neighbouring countries, and that collective responsibility is required for a strong and stable Africa. Consequently, China is exploring how to adjust to Africa's new policies in a new era (Gill and Reilly 2000).

In the light of the ICC's decision to indict President al-Bashir for genocide, the situation in Darfur remain precarious. While China has worked hard for the regime in Khartoum to accept UN peacekeeping operations on its soil, it remains unconvinced by the international community's narrow focus on peacekeeping to the exclusion of permanent peace by addressing through peaceful means the root causes of the Sudanese conflict, which are both political and historical. As former US Special Envoy to Sudan Andrew S. Natsios has rightly pointed out, 'Washington spends a disproportionate amount of its staffing and budgetary resources on resolving the crisis in Darfur rather than on supporting the Comprehensive Peace Agreement.' As General Martin Luther Agwai, the commander of the hybrid AU–UN mission (UNAMID) in Darfur, has put it succinctly: 'Without a new peace deal, even with the force numbers we are bringing into Darfur, it will still be a big task because you cannot keep peace if there is no peace deal.'[11] This imbalance must be redressed urgently, because peace cannot be achieved in Darfur if it is not secured between the north and the south. It is exactly this same message which China has been trying to get across to the international community, with little success. Failure to address this contradictory position will no doubt send wrong signals to the protagonists and will harm efforts to bring peace to the country as a whole.

13 | China and Zambia: between development and politics

Fredrick Mutesa

The Sino-Zambian bilateral relationship has flourished, despite policy and ideological shifts in both countries. Not surprisingly, all the three presidents who have run Zambia since the country attained political independence from British colonial rule in 1964 have fondly referred to Zambia's relationship with China as an 'all weather' friendship. This is no mere euphemism or empty slogan. To fully comprehend the value that Zambia places on the relationship, one needs to appreciate the geopolitics of southern Africa at the time that Zambia gained independence. The new nation of Zambia was born as a beleaguered state, flanked by hostile white minority regimes on its eastern (Mozambique), southern (Rhodesia) and western (Angola) borders that were all opposed to the principle of black majority rule.

Zambia's support for black liberation movements in the region made it vulnerable to military and economic destabilization from the white minority regimes. This vulnerability was exacerbated by the country's dependence on trade routes that ran through the same countries whose regimes it was opposed to. As a result, in the late 1960s Zambia requested assistance from multilateral financial institutions and Western countries to construct an alternative lifeline to the Dar es Salaam seaport, through friendly Tanzania. This request was turned down on the pretext that the project was not economically viable. It was China which stepped in to construct the 2,000-kilometre-long Tanzania–Zambia railway (Tazara), when the country's traditional donors refused to come to its aid. The great Uhuru (freedom) railway, therefore, has remained as an enduring symbol of China's dependability as Zambia's ally. For its part, Zambia stood shoulder to shoulder with China in its diplomatic efforts to gain acceptance as a member of the international community. It was Zambia, for instance, which co-sponsored the United Nations General Assembly resolution in 1971 to restore China's seat on the Security Council. Successive Zambian governments have also been consistent supporters of the one-China policy.

In the course of a little over three decades since the Sino-Zambia 'all weather' friendship was cemented, the southern African geopolitical situation has radically changed and Chinese society has undergone great transformation. Black majority rule has come to all of southern Africa, and China has abandoned its rigid socialist economy of the first three decades of its revolution for a more robust free market economy. The collapse of the socialist bloc in the late 1980s and early 1990s has also resulted in a greatly altered global balance of forces. The world has moved on from the bipolar world of US–USSR superpower rivalry to a unipolar one in which neoliberalism has been the main ideological driving force behind the new globalism. In this, vastly different, world of the twenty-first century, former allies, as well as antagonists, have found that they have to respond to a different logic in the manner in which they engage with each other. For the first time since Sino-Zambia diplomatic relations were established, the 'all weather' friendship between these two nations seems to have hit turbulence. This historical background needs to be taken into account when one considers the latest phase of Sino-African relations in general and Sino-Zambian relations in particular.

The scope and content of Sino-Zambian bilateral ties

Sino-Zambian economic relations span the entire trade, investment and aid spectrum, and conform to a clearly discernible pattern that reinforces Beijing's policy of accelerating China's economic growth and helps to satisfy its huge appetite for resources to fuel this growth. At the same time, these relations present Zambia with an alternative way to negotiate terms of forging inter-national economic relations, different from that of the Washington Consensus. Unfortunately, there is no clear evidence to suggest that the government of Zambia has a well-elaborated framework and time frame to make this a reality. Therefore, if there are any flaws in Sino-Zambian relations, the larger blame lies at the doorstep of the Zambian government for failing to seize the initiative.

Development cooperation For ease of analysis, this study has made a distinc-tion between development cooperation, foreign direct investment (FDI) and trade. In practice, however, it is difficult to tell when one form changes into another. This study therefore takes it for granted that in the way China extends development assistance, it is not the easiest of things to delineate aid from investment and trade.

Mwanawina (2007) has compiled one of the most comprehensive datasets on the nature of Chinese development cooperation with Zambia. Table 13.1 indicates that, by 2006, China had committed itself to financing about forty development cooperation projects in Zambia. Some of these were extensions of ongoing bi-lateral agreements between the two countries. According to Mwanawina, over the period 1967–2006 the loans amounted to 1,413.79 million renminbi (RMBY).

A further round of development cooperation agreements between China and Zambia was announced by President Hu Jintao during his February 2007 visit to Lusaka. These included construction of a football stadium in Ndola and a hos-pital in North-Western Province, establishment of an agricultural demonstration

TABLE 13.1 Chinese engagement in Zambia, 1967–2006

Year	Type	Amount (million)
1967	Economic and technical cooperation	RMBY 41.36
	Loan, construction of Tazara	RMBY 484
1974	Economic and technical cooperation	RMBY 100
1979	Loan, 12 locomotives	RMBY 5.58
1986	Loan, Tazara spare parts	RMBY 5
1987	Loan, assorted spares and road rehabilitation	RMBY 50
1988	Economic and technical cooperation	RMBY 50
1990	Economic and technical cooperation	RMBY 30
1992	Loan	RMBY 30
1993	Economic and technical cooperation	RMBY 50
1995	Grant, cash, relief food and general goods	US$1.2
	Grant, implements and sports goods	RMBY 3
	Loan, new government complex	US$8
1997	Economic and technical cooperation	RMBY 30
	Loans	RMBY 50.6
1998	Grant, relief food	US$0.2
	Grant, medicine	RMBY 0.2
	Five water pumps	RMBY 2
	Economic and technical cooperation	RMBY 20
1999	Grant, relief food	US$0.2
	Grant, office equipment	RMBY 4
	Loan, FM transmitters in seven provinces, Tazara locomotives; overhaul, technical training	RMBY 52
	Economic and technical cooperation	RMBY 30
2000	Grant, equipment for National Assembly	RMBY 1
	Economic and technical cooperation	RMBY 30
2001	Grant, cash for OAU	US$0.5
	Loan	RMBY 100
	Grant, goods to OAU and web printing press	RMBY 6.9
	Economic and technical cooperation	RMBY 20
2002	Loan, FM transmitters for seven provinces, new government complex and special loan	RMBY 120.9
	Grant, maize	4,500 tonnes
	Economic and technical cooperation	RMBY 30
2003	Grant, web printing press	RMBY 0.55
	Economic and technical cooperation	US$6
2004	Economic and technical cooperation	US$7.1
	Loan, Tazara	US$11
2006	Loan, Tazara	US$10
	Grant, relief food	US$1
	Economic and technical cooperation, extension of radio transmitters	RMBY 3.8
	Economic and technical cooperation, anti-malaria medicines	US$0.2

Source: Mwanawina (2007: 7)

centre and an anti-malaria centre, construction of two schools in rural areas, supply of anti-malaria drugs, provision of about forty scholarships tenable in China, training seminars and workshops in China for about three hundred people per year, provision of Chinese agricultural experts, young Chinese volunteers and doctors, and a loan for construction equipment.[1]

In addition to project aid, China has also granted debt relief to Zambia. Zambia's debt to China was said to stand at US$217 million as of 12 December 2006, making China the highest non-Paris Club provider of loans to Zambia (ibid.: 10). During his visit to Zambia in February 2007, President Hu expressed China's willingness to cancel some of the debt owed to it by Zambia. Subsequently, an initial amount of US$11 million was cancelled, with the possibility of more to follow.[2]

African leaders find Chinese development assistance attractive because it is based on a 'no strings attached' policy, in line with Beijing's espoused policy of 'non-interference' in the internal political affairs of its cooperating partners. Critics have, of course, cited this as a major weakness in Chinese development assistance because it can also serve as a smokescreen for supporting nations considered as pariah states. In the case of Zambia, as we shall see later, non-interference was breached in the country's September 2006 presidential elections when the Chinese government openly threatened to cut economic ties with Zambia in the event of victory by the country's leading opposition leader, Michael Sata of the Patriotic Front.

Bilateral trade Another field in which Sino-Zambian economic ties are developing very fast is bilateral trade relations. Shoute (2007) writes: 'Bilateral trade in the early 1990s had been only 20 million dollars, but in 2005 it reached 300 million dollars, partly thanks to China's tax exemption on Zambia's commodities. In the first 10 months of 2006, it reached 290 million dollars, an increase of 20% compared with the same period of 2005.' According to the embassy official interviewed by this writer, China has zero-tax-rated about 442 goods from Zambia in order to promote trade between the two countries.[3] Critics, however, doubt Zambia's ability to increase the range of goods entering the Chinese market because of the country's lack of manufacturing diversity (Schatz 2007). Not surprisingly, while Zambia's bilateral trade is concentrated in a few commodities, China's exports to Zambia are increasing rapidly in diversity. Zambia's main exports to China are tobacco, cotton, sugar, coffee and copper. On the other hand, China's export basket to Zambia consists of Chinese textiles, apparel, food items, electronic goods and automobiles. Zambia enjoys a trade surplus with China, mainly because of China's bulk purchases of Zambian copper. With the rapidly diversifying Chinese export basket to Zambia, the gap is likely to narrow quickly.

The growth of Sino-Zambian bilateral trade has been received with mixed feelings. On the one hand, there are those who point to the benefits to consumers of competitively priced Chinese goods, which are relatively affordable by the local population. On the other hand, critics decry what they perceive as dumping of poor-quality government-subsidized goods that in some sectors, particularly the textile and apparel sectors, are killing the local industry and throwing people out of employment.

Investments China has become the third-largest investor in Zambia after South Africa and Britain. The importance of Zambia as an attractive destination for Chinese investment was further underscored during President Hu Jintao's February 2007 visit to Lusaka. President Hu announced that his government had chosen Chambishi in Zambia's mining heartland of Copperbelt Province as the site of the first of three to five Multi-Facility Economic Zones (MFEZs) that China intends to establish in Africa. He further informed his Zambian hosts that China was looking to spend a total of US$800 million in the form of FDI over a three-year period to make the scheme operational. The Chambishi MFEZ is also expected to create about 50,000 new employment opportunities for Zambians by 2010. With these projections, there is no doubt that China is poised to become a very important player in the Zambian economy.

Like development cooperation and trade, Chinese investments in Zambia also span all sectors of the economy, including agriculture, construction, engineering, health, manufacturing, mining, services and tourism (Koyi and Muneku 2007). Chinese investments have also penetrated the small-scale trading sector, where Indians and indigenous Zambians previously held sway. It is the natural resource sector, however, to which the bulk of Chinese investments in Zambia have gone. Unfortunately, a number of thorny key issues have come to be associated with these investments. The complaints include the following.

The issue of *'poverty' wages* has dogged Chinese investments in Zambia from the outset. In comparison to investors from the West and India, Chinese employers have been noted for paying their Zambian employees wages that are way below the minimum wage of 268,000 kwacha (K) or approximately US$70 per month. At the Chinese-owned Collum coal mine in the Southern Province of Zambia, for instance, workers were reported to be getting as little as US$2 a day or US$60 dollars a month (Dixon 2006). This is the same amount that the World Bank uses to classify people living in poverty. There were similar sentiments echoed by employees of Non Ferrous Company (NFC) Africa Mining in Chambishi. Bennet Sondashi, for example, lamented: 'I work 30 days a month and I get K180,170,200 ... US$50–US$60 a month' (Wilson 2006). Rayford Mbulu, president of the Mineworkers Union of Zambia (MUZ), also revealed that at BGRIMM, a sister company to NFC Africa Mining, the highest-paid employee in one section received K158,000.[4] According to Koyi and Muneku (2007): 'Chinese FDI has tended to generally exert a downward pull on wages, thereby worsening the living conditions of the workers.'

Closely related to 'poverty' wages is the issue of *disparities in wages and salaries* between Chinese and Zambian workers performing the same tasks. In this regard, the story of the defunct Zambia–China Mulungushi Textiles (ZCMT) is illustrative. ZCMT was a China–Zambia joint venture, with the Chinese government holding majority shares. The general manager was Chinese, his deputy was a Zambian and there was an assistant general manager who was Chinese. The Chinese assistant general manager was being paid about K17 million while the Zambian deputy general manager was getting K3.5 million. According to the Zambia Congress of Trade Unions (ZCTU) general secretary, 'the salary difference between the Chinese assistant general manager and the Zambian deputy general manager was very ridiculous'.[5]

Exploitative working conditions were reported by Zambian employees in Chinese enterprises across the country. Workers complained of working long hours without breaks and of having few days off. In July 2006 there was a dramatic clip during the main news bulletin on the state-owned national television, Zambia National Broadcasting Corporation (ZNBC). Alice Simango, then deputy minister of Southern Province, following numerous complaints from the public, went to inspect conditions under which Zambian employees at the Chinese-owned Collum coal mine worked. She openly wept on national television when she saw emaciated and ill-clad employees with no protective clothing emerging from underground. The government was forced to close the company for three days. Chinese managers, however, apparently do not see anything wrong with the near-forced-labour conditions under which their employees work. Take the view of Lui Peng, general manager of China's largest construction company in Zambia, the state-owned China National Overseas Engineering Corporation, for example:

> Chinese people can stand very hard work. This is a cultural difference. Chinese people work until they finish and then rest. Here they are like the British, they work according to plan. They have tea-breaks and a lot of days off. For our construction company that means it costs a lot more. (McGreal 2007)

China is reported to have the worst mining *health and safety records* in the world (Range 2005). Going by the tragic fatalities that have taken place at NFC Africa Mining and its sister company BGRIMM, it is difficult to dispute this unsavoury conclusion. One suggestion has been that the high copper prices have provoked a tendency to push machinery to the limit in order to boost production. This profit motive leads to lack of investment in safety and health measures.

Chinese investors in Zambia have also been associated with flouting of *labour laws*. Several factors could explain this. First, many Chinese investors have difficulty conversing in English. Second, the government is also to blame because of the overgenerous incentives that are given to foreign investors in Zambia. This causes some investors to behave as though they are above the law. Third, lack of robust institutional capacity and underfunding have contributed to the inability of labour standards inspectors to go round factories and business premises to check whether employers are complying with the requirements of the law.

Opinions are divided on the issue of *backwards and forwards linkages* with regard to Chinese investments in the Zambian economy. In the textile sector, ZCMT at its peak was credited with creating a market where no fewer than 5,000 cotton farmers supplied the factory with raw materials. With regard to the mining industry, however, the picture is quite different. Opposition Patriotic Front president Michael Sata has accused large-scale Chinese firms in Zambia of bringing Chinese business cartels into the country to ensure that they source only from fellow Chinese suppliers (Sata 2007). As one contractor put it very succinctly, 'Zambians are left to scramble for the scrap that is left at the master's table' (Koyi and Muneku 2007).

Another key complaint targeted at Chinese investors is that they have a tendency to bring *unskilled and semi-skilled Chinese labour* into the country to perform very menial tasks which Zambians are able to do. Zambian law requires that for any foreign person to be issued with a work permit, the authorities must be satisfied that such persons are bringing skills that cannot be sourced locally. Similarly, Chinese operators of small-scale enterprises such as trading stands in markets and the rearing of chickens are resented for crowding out small-scale local operators. The argument of critics of unrestrained immigration of Chinese nationals is that a human influx of such magnitude is harmful to the livelihoods of the local people.

Non-Ferrous Company (NFC) Africa Mining plc: a case study

In this section, we examine the case of Chinese investment at firm level in the mining sector, where the bulk of Chinese investment has been channelled. The case study will examine issues related to employment, wages, occupational health and safety standards, and corporate social responsibility. It is, however, important to place China's role in the Zambian mining sector in perspective. Though China is often cited as the main culprit in the deterioration of working conditions in the Zambian mining sector, the story is much more complex and pre-dates China's entry into the industry. As clearly demonstrated in Peter Kragelund's chapter in this volume, China's entry into Zambia has been facilitated by the liberalization of the Zambian economy over the past twenty-five years under the watchful eyes of the IMF and the World Bank. The liberalization and privatization of the Zambian economy have been accompanied by drastic changes in labour market practices. Privatization has entailed right-sizing the workforce, which in practice has meant downsizing. As a result, by 2004 the number of mineworkers in direct employment had declined to 20,000, from a peak of 62,222 in 1976 (Frazer and Lungu 2006: 21).

NFC Africa Mining plc is situated in the small town of Chambishi near Kitwe, Zambia's second-largest city, about four hundred kilometres north of the capital, Lusaka. In July 1998, the mine was bought by a Chinese state-owned enterprise known as Non-Ferrous Metal Industries. In Zambia, the company began operating as NFC Africa Mining plc–Chambishi. The Zambian government, through the Zambia Consolidated Copper Mines (ZCCM)–Investment Holdings, retained a 15 per cent minority shareholding.

The company was sold for a US$10 million cash payment, with a further feasibility commitment of US$10 million over a three-year period and another conditional investment of US$110 million over five years (Lungu and Mulenga 2005). Before its privatization, the company had ceased production and was on a 'care and maintenance' programme operated by a skeleton staff of workers retained from the former state conglomerate, ZCCM. The new Chinese owners pledged to bring the mine back into operation and achieve a production capacity of 3,000 tons of ore per day, and later increase this to 9,000 tons per day, depending on the results of further exploration work on the Chambishi West and Chambishi South-East ore bodies. In October 2007, the Chambishi West ore body was officially opened at a ceremony officiated by Zambia's vice-president, Rupiah Banda. This newly opened mine is estimated to have total reserves of about 34 million tons with a copper grade of 2.03 per cent. The forecast annual output is 1 million tons and the mine has an estimated service life of twenty-five years.[6]

At the time that NFC Africa Mining plc commenced operations in 1998, it inherited 112 employees who had been retained for the 'care and maintenance' programme. The company is now reported to be employing 2,100 employees, a major boost in livelihoods in a location faced with high unemployment figures. Meanwhile, the newly opened Chambishi West ore body is projected to provide about 1,500 employment opportunities for the local population.[7] Naturally, one would expect that such a development would be received with delight by the local people. This, however, is not the case. There is a widely reported anti-Chinese feeling among the locals. This has to do with the quality of jobs that the Chinese investors are providing for the people.

Casualization of the workforce is reported to be rife at NFC Africa Mining plc. The new mine-owners have opted to keep the labour force that is directly employed by them to a minimum. Instead, they employ workers on fixed-term rolling contracts and hire the rest from contractors who are subcontracted to undertake projects in the industry. The latter two categories of employees are paid far less than those who are directly engaged by the mining companies.[8] Statistics indicate that of the initial 112 employees on permanent contracts retained from ZCCM, only fifty-two have remained (Frazer and Lungu 2006: 49). NFC Africa Mining has directly employed 687 workers on contracts that vary in duration from one to five years. Another one hundred or so employees taken on directly by the company are classified as casual workers, with the lowest pay and the worst conditions of service. There are 1,093 workers employed indirectly via two Chinese subcontracting firms. The company also has 180 Chinese employees on permanent contracts. The senior management team comprises eleven staff members, of which only one is Zambian.

A major consequence of casualization is denial of workers' rights, particularly the right to belong to a trade union. There are two unions in Zambia that represent mineworkers: the Mineworkers Union of Zambia (MUZ) and its breakaway sister union, the National Union of Miners and Allied Workers (NUMAW). Rayford Mbulu, president of MUZ, told participants at a workshop organized to discuss the social and economic impact of Asian FDI in Zambia that his union had been holding discussions with the Ministry of Labour and Social Security (MLSS) about outlawing contract labour, casual labour and labour hire.[9] He argued that employees in these categories have no social security. The unions have also experienced serious problems organizing membership among casual and contract workers. Without union membership, casual workers are at the mercy of company management.

'Poverty' wages are another contentious issue at NFC Africa Mining plc. According to Koyi and Muneku (2007), NFC Africa Mining plc pays the lowest wages of all the mining companies in Zambia, and employs the majority of workers on casual and fixed-term contracts. Another source affirms that, despite an agreement recently reached with unions to bring pay scales at the mine in line with the national minimum wage, employees doing similar work at other mines are paid more (Dixon 2006).

In July 2006 there were violent protests at NFC Africa Mining plc in which five protesting workers were shot at. The workers turned violent after management failed to pay salary increments that were agreed to in negotiations with workers' representatives. There are conflicting reports as to who exactly shot at the workers. One account says that four protesting workers were shot at by a Chinese manager and one by the police. Another version of the protests attributes the shooting and wounding of all five protesting employees to armed police officers who were called in to quell the demonstrations. A commission of inquiry set up to investigate the circumstances of the shooting has never made its findings public. Meanwhile violent protests over poverty wages by workers continue to rock NFC Africa Mining plc, the latest being the riots of March 2008 involving 500 workers which resulted in injuries to seven workers, including one Chinese national who lost his teeth in the fracas, and damage to company property valued at US$200,000.[10]

Another area of concern at NFC Africa Mining plc is that of *occupational health and safety standards*. A tragic accident at BGRIMM explosives factory in October 2005, which left fifty Zambian workers dead, is the worst disaster in the mining industry since the mines were privatized. This has only served to reinforce the view that safety standards in China's mines are among the worst in the world and that Chinese companies have exported low pay and hazardous conditions to Africa and elsewhere.[11] All the fifty workers who perished in the BGRIMM disaster were casuals with no compensation schemes. Albert Mando, general secretary of NUMAW, said that injuries were common at NFC Africa Mining and that workers were afraid to complain because they were hired on one-year contracts and could easily be fired.[12] According to Rayford Mbulu, president of MUZ, accidents in the mining industry in general have increased since privatization, with at least two employees per month dying.

Corporate social responsibility is another area where NFC Africa Mining plc has failed to match the standards set by the former ZCCM. ZCCM used to operate what has been termed a 'from cradle to grave policy' (Lungu and Mulenga 2005; Frazer and Lungu 2006). ZCCM inherited a model of corporate social responsibility which started during the colonial period and developed it further to cater for all the needs of the mineworkers and their families. This included provision of free medical care, education, water and sanitation, recreational facilities, housing, roads, garbage collection, electricity, and food supplements. ZCCM built and managed schools, clinics and hospitals in the mine townships. When the mines were privatized, the new private owners resisted taking over this responsibility and facilities were passed on to ill-equipped municipal councils that had no capacity to continue providing the services. As a result, in most mining townships, including Chambishi, infrastructure has fallen into a state of disrepair and families now have to pay for most services that they previously accessed freely. At a time when there are few people employed, this has meant severe hardships for the residents of mine townships.

In terms of provision of health services, NFC Africa Mining, like other mine-owners, has allowed the fifty-two unionized workers taken over from ZCCM and their families access to free medical services at nearby SINOZAM hospital, another subsidiary of the company. Contract workers, on the other hand, are allowed to nominate only one family member to access the medical services at the hospital. For an average Zambian family of six, this means that the majority have no access to health services (Frazer and Lungu 2006: 50).

It is issues such as the ones highlighted above which have generated great resentment towards Chinese investors in Zambia. The residents of Chambishi Mine Township welcomed the takeover of the mine by new Chinese owners in 1998 because of the prospects of new employment opportunities which this development presented. Their hopes, however, have turned into disappointment because of precisely the issues discussed above. The quality of jobs, type of wages and care for the families of the miners have all turned out to be far below what the same workers had experienced under ZCCM's 'from cradle to grave' policy. It is these negative experiences which have dampened the expectations of the population regarding the proposed US$800 MFEZ and the promised 50,000 new job opportunities in the Chambishi area, which, it has been claimed, will bring prosperity to the suffering citizens of Zambia.

Conclusions

The issue of Chinese investments in Zambia is highly sensitive and emotive. It has become divisive and has polarized Zambian society. The most outspoken critic of Chinese investments in Zambia is the opposition Patriotic Front president, Michael Sata, who refuses to call the Chinese investors, preferring to refer to them as 'infesters' (Schatz 2007). Meanwhile, the government of President Mwanawasa and his Chinese partners continue to emphasize that the Sino-Zambian bilateral relationship is a 'win-win' situation.

In the run-up to the 2006 September tripartite elections, Sata and his Patriotic Front politicians campaigned very strongly on the anti-Chinese platform. Sata, who is widely believed to have been funded by the government of Taiwan through its embassy in neighbouring Malawi, had threatened to deport the Chinese and establish diplomatic relations with Taiwan. This move drew a rather sharp response from the Chinese government, which has always prided itself on following a policy of non-interference in the internal affairs of partner nations. The Chinese ambassador in Lusaka addressed a press conference at which he challenged Sata to clarify his position on Taiwan. Some media accounts reported that the envoy threatened that Beijing would cut ties with Zambia should Sata win the elections. Many observers interpreted this threat as tantamount to trying to influence the outcome of the elections. President Mwanawasa publicly appealed to the Chinese to rescind their decision and gave assurances that their investments in Zambia were safe.

In the ensuing elections, President Mwanawasa won with a comfortable majority of no less than 40 per cent, but Sata came second with 29 per cent, winning all parliamentary and local government seats in Lusaka and the urban Copperbelt Province, home to the majority of Chinese investments in the country. This outcome indicates that Sata's anti-Chinese rhetoric resonated well with the feelings of the population in the areas where the Chinese presence is most visible.

The anti-Chinese feelings in Zambia run high and are close to xenophobic proportions. This was evident during the visit of President Hu Jintao in February 2007. First, the University of Zambia, which is situated on the main route from the airport, was cordoned off by armed police in riot gear because of fear on the part of government authorities that the students were planning to protest to Hu on the issue of Sino-Zambian bilateral relations. Second, the police stopped former workers of the closed ZCMT, who were planning to protest to Hu on the continued closure of the factory and non-payment of workers' dues. Third, and most important, the high point of President Hu's visit to Zambia was to be a trip to the Copperbelt, where he was scheduled to lay a foundation stone at the site of a proposed 40,000-seat stadium to be built with Chinese aid in Ndola and also officially launch the US$800 million Chambishi MFEZ. This important leg of the visit was cancelled because of planned demonstrations by the residents of the province, which is also a Patriotic Front stronghold.

In conclusion, it is important to put the overseas expansion of China in its historical and economic perspective. To begin with, China's rapid economic growth has mainly been driven by its low-cost labour force. This is one of the main factors that have caused many Western multinational corporations to rush to invest in China. China runs a market economy superintended by a communist system that does not tolerate dissent from the official line. It is not surprising that China is exporting the same production relations to countries where it is spreading its economic tentacles. Naturally, this has resulted in a kind of 'clash of cultures'. But China is not doing anything different from what other capitalist countries practised during the era of primitive accumulation. What has compounded the situation in developing countries, such as Zambia, is that recipient governments of Chinese aid and investments are desperate to augment limited domestic savings by means of external resource mobilization. In the process, most countries have extended overgenerous incentives to foreign investors which have meant that, in the short to medium term, citizens are not able to see any benefits of playing host to these investors.

PART FIVE

The scramble for African oil and resources

14 | African oil in the energy security calculations of China and India

Cyril Obi

This chapter explores the place of African oil and gas supplies in the energy security calculations of two emerging global powers: China and India. This is against the background of the recent figures that show that, within a decade, China has moved from being an oil exporter to the world's second-largest importer of oil (overtaking Japan), while India has also moved to the position of the world's fifth-largest importer of oil. While China imports about 46.05 per cent of the oil consumed domestically (Xinhua News Agency 2008), India imports about 70 per cent.

The story, however, does not end with the surging demand for oil imports from the rapidly expanding economies of China and India; it goes on to include investments by their state-owned oil enterprises (SOOEs) and companies keen on cashing in on the opportunities in Africa's largely untapped oil potential (relative to other regions of the world), by investing in a region where, until very recently, Western oil multinationals held undisputed sway.

At the heart of the rise in demand for Africa's energy resources is the quest by oil-dependent global powers such as the United States, Japan and the countries of the European Union (EU) to diversify the sources of crude oil and gas supplies away from the volatile Middle East region. China and India are the latest to join this scramble to secure access to stable supplies of oil and gas to fuel their economies. Concern over energy security has, therefore, been central to the Africa policy of both Western and emerging powers (Yergin 2006: 69; Toman 2002: 1.3).

What the foregoing implies is an increased interest, on the part of both Western and emerging powers, not just in Africa's oil but also in the long-term stability, security and governance of Africa's 'petro-states' as sources of supply. It also suggests a much greater inflow of resources to these states – with attendant political and developmental outcomes. Given that China and India are both 'newcomers' to the African oil scene, their calculations and strategies for gaining entry, partnering with African petro-states, and competing as well as cooperating with each other in various African oil-producing countries go a long way to shaping the nature and outcomes of the China–India–Africa triad, whose ramifications will in turn go a long way to contributing to Africa's fortunes in the present and the future.

China in global energy security

In analysing China's energy security calculations, it is important to note that China was once an exporter of oil, but by 1993 it had become a net importer of oil. Estimates place China's oil imports to the tune of 30 per cent of domestic consumption in 2000, and it is projected that by 2010 the figures could rise to 40–50 per cent of domestic consumption (Dannreuther 2003: 197). This relates to its high level of economic growth, put at an average of 9 per cent a year for close to two decades, which greatly increases its energy demands – progressively met by imports.

Although China imports most of its oil from the Middle East, it is keen to expand and diversify its sources of supply by seeking oil investments in Central Asia, Africa and South America, closer Sino-Russian cooperation, and also by exploring the construction of pipelines to supply oil from neighbouring states such as Kazakhstan (Jakobson and Daojiong 2006). While Downs (2004: 23) defines China's energy security challenge as 'its growing oil deficit', Jakobson and Daojiong (2006: 61) are of the view that the country's vulnerability lies in its 'dependency on international sea lanes, mostly controlled by the United States'.

Arguing that the Chinese leadership considers 'China's energy security strategically too important to be left to market forces alone', Zhao (2008: 207–8) justifies the greater reliance on the state-centred approach. At the forefront of this state-led oil diplomacy are the Chinese state and Chinese SOOEs and their overseas subsidiaries, which are currently at various stages of transformation along 'market-friendly' and transnational lines: China National Petroleum Corporation (CNPC), China Petroleum and Chemical Corporation (SINOPEC),[1] and China National Offshore Oil Corporation (CNOOC). These companies operate across the world, seeking oil investments.

This also underscores the point of a strong linkage between the 'securing of stable supplies of oil and China's national security'. In this regard, Zhao (ibid.: 208) notes that 'China has developed a series of diplomatic and administrative measures to enhance China's energy security by deepening political and diplomatic relationships with all energy producing nations and aggressively investing in oilfields and pipelines around the world to directly control overseas oil and gas reserves'. It is therefore clear that China's oil diplomacy is intimately connected to its energy security calculations as an emergent power in a rapidly globalizing post-cold-war world. In this regard, it seeks to diversify its sources of supply, of which the Middle East accounts for an estimated 60 per cent, by intensifying its oil diplomacy towards increasing supplies from Africa (now estimated at 30 per cent), the Asia-Pacific region, South America, Russia and Kazakhstan.

China's strategic energy security calculations in Africa

In the past decade and a half China has been increasingly engaged with African states in its quest for oil and other commodities. Providing a perspective on the oil factor in Sino-African relations, Hanson (2008) posits: 'China has developed a twin-pronged strategy towards energy investments. First it has pursued exploration and production deals in smaller, low-visibility countries such as Gabon, Equatorial Guinea, and the Republic of Congo (Brazzaville). Second, it has gone after the largest oil producers by offering integrated packages of aid.' China is keen to couch this engagement in the rhetoric of strategic partnership, to show that, far from being a 'fair-weather friend' or exploiter (differentiating itself from Western imperialist countries), it has remained consistent and sincere in its support of and friendship with Africa over a long period (Guijin 2007).

It should be pointed out that although oil is a major and obvious source of Chinese interest in Africa, it is far from being the only one (Taylor 2007: 938). During a state visit to Nigeria in April 2006, the Chinese president, Hu Jintao, clearly outlined the '... five pillars of a proposed new type of Sino-African strategic partnership: China and Africa should strengthen political mutual trust; China and Africa should strengthen win-win economic cooperation; China and Africa should increase cultural interaction; China and Africa should strengthen security cooperation; and China and Africa should maintain close coordination in international affairs' (Xinhua News Agency 2006). These goals were further reiterated by the Chinese leadership during the November 2006 Forum on China–Africa Cooperation (FOCAC).

Chinese policy-makers and scholars are often quick to reject the criticism that China's engagement with Africa is 'resource-driven and exploitative' (Wenping 2007; Xinhua News Agency 2007; Li 2007: 69–93), insisting it has consistently taken a path of 'cooperation with Africa on the basis of sincerity and mutual benefit'. In the words of He Wenping, the director of the African Studies section of the Chinese Academy of Social Sciences in Beijing: 'African countries have more choices with China's coming, which to an extent gives them greater say on their own resources' (quoted in Xinhua News Agency 2007).

China's energy diplomacy to some extent is hinged upon the position that China has a lot more to offer resource-rich African countries, on better terms and with more (developmental) benefits for the producer states, than Western mining companies and their home governments, which have benefited immensely from the wanton exploitation of Africa's resources. Chinese oil companies operate in the following countries: Algeria, Gabon, Angola, Nigeria, Republic of Congo (Brazzaville), Namibia, Ethiopia and Kenya. It is also believed that Chinese companies have oil interests in Chad, Mauritania, Niger and Equatorial Guinea. In this chapter, the focus will be on Africa's largest oil producers: Angola, Sudan and Nigeria.

Angola Angola is Africa's largest oil exporter to China and the country's second-largest trading partner in Africa. It accounts for about 13 per cent of China's oil imports. As Taylor recalls (2007: 947), on the heels of a visit by the Chinese vice-premier, cooperation agreements were signed, 'three of which related to oil' – a long-term supply contract, joint evaluation of an offshore oil block, and a joint venture to buy out Shell's interest in one of Angola's offshore oilfields – largely in exchange for aid and soft loans. Placing this in perspective, Hanson (2008) notes that 'in Angola, which exported roughly 465,000 barrels of oil per day to China in the first six months of 2007, Beijing secured a major stake in future oil production in 2004 through Sinopec with a US$2 billion package of loans and aid that includes funds for Chinese companies to build railroads, schools, roads, hospitals, bridges, and offices; lay a fibre-optic network, and train Angolan telecommunication workers'. In 2005 SINOPEC also reached a joint-venture agreement with the Angolan state oil corporation, Sonangol, for the exploration of some offshore oil blocks (see the chapter by Alex Vines and Indira Campos in this volume for a detailed analysis of Sino-Angolan relations).

International uproar was caused by the granting of a low-interest loan of US$2 billion to Angola by the Chinese EXIM Bank, payable over seventeen years, with a written agreement to supply Angolan oil and award some contracts to China, after the Angolan government had stopped negotiations with the International Monetary Fund (IMF) over the latter's insistence on transparency and accountability clauses. This action raised concerns that China, by deploying a 'no-strings-attached' strategy in its economic relations, was flouting international business practices and providing resources to 'corrupt' African governments. For its part, however, the Angolan government felt it was within its rights to reject the IMF's rather interventionist conditions, while noting that the loan was needed for its post-war reconstruction efforts.

Sudan China's first major oil investment in Africa was in 1996 in Sudan, where CNPC (40 per cent) joined Petronas (30 per cent), Sudapet (5 per cent) and Araxis, later Talisman, then India's Oil and Natural Gas Corporation Videsh Ltd (OVL, 25 per cent) to form the Greater Nile Petroleum Corporation (GNPC). This followed the withdrawal of Chevron Oil in 1992, later followed by the exit of other Western oil companies owing to increased domestic pressures and US sanctions on the Sudanese government for human rights violations. CNPC commenced operations in three oil blocks in southern Sudan in the following year and began to export oil from the country in 1999 (Large 2008c: 95). Apart from owning the largest investments in CNPC, China has also assisted Sudan with oil infrastructure, including the construction of an oil pipeline to the Red Sea, as well as an oil refinery. CNPC also featured in Sudan's second oil consortium, Petrodar, in which it had 'a 41 per cent share and SINOPEC 6 per cent to develop two oil concessions' (ibid.: 95–7). A construction subsidiary of CNPC also got the contract to build an oil pipeline to transport oil from the new oilfields to Port Sudan. Sudan is presently believed to be Africa's third-largest oil producer, accounting for about 9 per cent of China's oil imports.

China's engagement with Sudan has, like its involvement with Angola, drawn a lot of international criticism. China has been accused of providing resources, arms and diplomatic support to a government that is seen as corrupt and complicit in human rights violations in Darfur. Its claim that it operates on the principle of non-interference has only attracted more criticism of its 'resource diplomacy' in Africa. In this regard, China is beginning to take a second look at its strategies, and learning fast about how to tread carefully on rather slippery diplomatic terrain (see the chapter by He Wenping in this volume for a more detailed analysis).

Nigeria China's entry into the oil sector in Nigeria (Africa's largest oil producer) is fairly recent. Petro-China signed a contract in 2004, valued at US$800 million, with the Nigerian National Petroleum Corporation (NNPC) – the state oil company – to supply 30,000 barrels of crude oil per day to China (Mbachu 2006: 79). That same year, SINOPEC signed two agreements with NNPC to develop five exploration wells, and signed two others with the Nigerian Petroleum Development Corporation (an NNPC subsidiary) and the Nigerian Agip Oil Corporation (NAOC) to develop two oilfields (Taylor 2007: 636).

China's 'entry' coincided with visits by the Nigerian president, Olusegun Obasanjo, to the country in August 2001, September 2004 and April 2005, and reciprocal visits by the Chinese president, Hu Jintao, to Nigeria in July 2002 and April 2006, followed by the signing of cooperation agreements and contracts. Thus, in 2005, CNOOC bought a 45 per cent stake in a Nigerian oil-for-gas field for US$2.27 billion and also purchased 35 per cent of an oil exploration licence in the Niger Delta for US$60 million in April 2006 (IRIN News 2006). This was after the Indian government had failed to give ONGC approval for its bid for the same oil block on the grounds that it was too 'risky' (Asian Times 2006). This sale to CNOOC was later challenged in court by the owner of the Apo oil-for-gas field – South Atlantic Petroleum Ltd (SAPETRO) went to court seeking the revocation of the lease granted by the state to CNOOC. It should be noted that the acquisition of the oilfield by CNOOC (which later compensated all the parties to the contract) 'was its largest in the world, and guaranteed the company 70 per cent of profits from oil plot 246' (Obi 2008: 422). Following President Hu Jintao's visit to Nigeria in 2006, 'Chinese oil companies also benefited from being allocated, and given the right of first refusal for, four oil blocks (two in the Chad basin and two in the Niger Delta)', valued at US$4 billion (ibid.: 422). It is also important to note that Nigeria's president, Umaru Yar'Adua, visited China in March 2008, almost a year after he was elected into power.

While some estimates put Chinese investments in Nigeria at US$10 billion, it is difficult to estimate the current value of Chinese oil investments in the country, as some of the 'oil-for-infrastructure' deals reached under the administration of former president Obasanjo (1999–2007) have been suspended, pending investigations by the Yar'Adua administration. Also of note is the suspension of the US$8.3 billion railways modernization contract awarded to the China Civil Engineering and Construction Corporation (CCECC) in 2006.

Many experts agree that the threat posed by the Chinese to Western oil interests in Africa is often exaggerated as 'Chinese companies hold under 2 per cent of Africa's known oil reserves' (Hanson 2008). As Downs (2007: 44) notes, 'most of the African assets held by China's NOCs (national oil companies) are of a size and quality of little interest to international oil companies (IOCs). In fact, many of these assets were relinquished by the IOCs.' For instance, in Sudan, the exit of Western oil companies was followed by the entry of Chinese, Malaysian and Indian oil companies, while in Angola the state's rejection of Western aid conditionalities paved the way for the acceptance of Chinese aid, and the takeover by a Chinese oil company of an oil block formerly leased by a Western oil company. Chinese oil companies are entering oil-rich African countries through state-led resource diplomacy and low-cost development aid.

The growing profile of China in Africa reached a significant milestone on 4/5 November 2006, marked by the holding of the third Ministerial Meeting and First Heads of State Summit of the Forum on China–Africa Cooperation (FOCAC) in Beijing. FOCAC also served to reinforce China's African policy based on the five principles of peaceful coexistence and the recognition of the 'one China' principle as 'the political foundation for the establishment of China's relations with African countries and regional organisations' (China Report 2007).

According to Naidu and Corkin (2006: 4), the Chinese leadership proposed a robust development assistance package for Africa, based on: 'US$3 billion in preferential loans and US$2 billion in preferential buyers' credits over the next three years; the doubling of its 2006 aid assistance by 2009; initiating a China–Africa development fund that will reach US$5 billion to encourage Chinese companies to invest in Africa'. At FOCAC, China's rhetoric was couched 'in terms of its interests in assisting Africa in its development efforts. No Chinese speaker mentioned China's appetite for African oil' (Orr 2006: 6).

China has also taken advantage of the 'nationalist' instincts of, and invitations by, African elites seeking national development, and integration into a global system on more equitable terms. This has been against the background of the 'demonstrative effect' of Chinese aid, which, unlike Western aid, does not come with much conditionality, some of which impinges on the recipient's sovereignty. Apart from the socially harsh consequences of the policies of the 'Washington Consensus' in Africa, the opening up of the engagement space by the arrival of emerging powers from the global South on the African scene has provided African countries with greater leverage to negotiate more beneficial external relations.

India's strategic energy security calculations in Africa

As with China, energy security is at the forefront of India's strategy in Africa. India's unprecedented growth rate of 8 per cent in the last decade has led to growing oil imports, presently put at 30 per cent of domestic energy needs, but which are expected to increase to 90 per cent by 2025 (Hate 2008). India's energy engagement with Africa is premised on the understanding that one of the most critical challenges facing a rapidly industrializing and developing economy is the need to diversify and increase the supply of energy. India imports 'almost 70 percent of its oil' (Sharma and Mahajan 2007: 40), and is engaged in the quest for oil and gas from all parts of the world, including Africa. Also relevant are diversification from dependence on oil supplies from the volatile Middle East, and the low sulphur content of Africa's oil, preferred by Indian refineries. Within official circles, the concern with energy security is fairly recent (Madan 2006: 13).

Other concerns underpinning India's energy security include its growing energy dependence in the face of rapidly growing energy consumption and demand (it is projected to be the world's third-largest consumer in two decades' time), the debate over the feasibility and cost of a nuclear energy option, scant domestic production of oil, geopolitical uncertainty (in the Middle East, the Indian Ocean region and Africa), 'stoking fears of a possible supply disruption', social stability within India, and its aspirations to regional and global power (ibid.: 14–16). With respect to Africa, Indian policy-makers have recognized the risks posed to their energy security calculations by the intense competition from other energy-hungry states. This, among other considerations, has encouraged India to revive and step up its engagement with Africa (Bajpaee 2008; Ramachandran 2007b; Blakely 2008).

It is in the foregoing context that India's SOOEs have intensified their quest for access to Africa's oil. These include: the Oil and Natural Gas Corporation (ONGC), Oil India Ltd (OIL), Indian Oil Corporation Ltd (IOC), Bharat Petroleum Corporation Ltd (BPCL) and the Gas Authority of India Ltd (GAIL). While they have achieved some modest success in Angola and Sudan, Nigeria provides 'almost 15 per cent of India's total oil imports', ranking the country as second only to 'Saudi Arabia as India's largest oil supplier' (Sharma and Mahajan 2007: 41; Beri 2005: 381).

Underscoring the importance of India's engagement with Africa, the country hosted its first India–Africa Hydrocarbon Conference and exhibition in New Delhi in November 2007. Thus Africa, and Nigeria in particular, is writ large in India's oil diplomacy and quest for energy security as the country emerges as an Asian and global industrial power. Although India's ONGC-Mittal Energy Ltd (OMEL) did benefit from the oil-for-infrastructure deals by being allocated three oil blocks by the Obasanjo administration, it is not clear whether any progress has been made in developing these oil blocks in the face of the suspension of most of the deals by the Yar'Adua administration. It is therefore difficult to come up with exact figures for Indian oil investments in Nigeria. The picture is also further complicated by the revocation in January 2009 of two oil blocks previously awarded to the Korean National Oil Company (KNOC) and their reallocation by the federal oil regulatory body, the Department of Petroleum Resources, to ONGC-Videsh. This decision to hand the oil blocks to the Indian company has been challenged and has become a subject of litigation as KNOC has taken the government to court to reclaim the revoked rights to the oil blocks.

Anand Sharma, Indian minister of state for external affairs, underscored India's perception of Africa's oil potential thus: '[I]t has been projected that Africa would add 38 per cent to global oil contributing a further four million barrels of oil per day by 2010. Nigeria, Angola and Algeria have huge prospects. Apart from oil, Africa has a huge potential for Liquefied Natural Gas (LNG) and it produces over 50,000 Metric Tonnes (MTs) per year' (Sharma 2008). Unlike China, India does not have the huge resources to expend on its oil diplomacy in Africa (Thakurta 2008). Sharma is, however, clear about the attraction that Africa's hydrocarbons hold for India, as an additional factor for the 'renaissance' in Indo-African relations.

The need to respond to China's 'edge' in the race for energy security with regard to Africa is also confirmed by another Indian researcher (Beri 2007: 306), who notes that, 'as India's economy grows, the search for scarce energy and other natural resources has brought India in direct competition with China in Africa. This was quite visible as China outbid India in Angola and Sudan.' On the other hand, Indian oil companies lost out in Nigeria not because of their inability to compete with Chinese oil companies, but as a result of a deliberate effort on the part of the Indian government when it stepped in to prevent an Indian oil investment that was considered to be risky. This gave the Chinese the opportunity to seal the deal with no contest.

One of India's strategies in response to the 'Chinese threat' is to position itself as a true partner and old friend of Africa, which seeks to help it develop on a win-win basis. The other is to 'offer economic aid, assistance in finding low-cost solutions to poverty, and improved business relations' (Hate 2008). Linked to this is the role of the Indian diaspora in exploring its traditional and community links with the continent to promote Indian business and trade (Shukla 2008). Also of note is the role of the Indian private sector 'in strengthening Indian goodwill in the continent' (Hate 2008). This came out in the pledges made to African leaders by the Indian leadership during the India–Africa Summit. Also, in October 2007 the Indian prime minister paid a visit to critical African countries, including – in the first such state visit by an Indian prime minister to the country in forty-five years – Nigeria, the largest African supplier of oil to India, as a form of shuttle diplomacy directed at a strategic engagement with Africa's largest oil producer (African Oil Journal 2007). While India's Africa policy is not fundamentally different from that of China – one of non-alignment and South–South cooperation (see chapters by Naidu Sanjukta in this volume) – India's strategy is to present itself differently by emphasizing its long-standing solidarity, 'political goodwill and equal partner approach' and a focus on sharing low-cost appropriate technology, expertise, education, human resource development and information technology (Shukla 2008 and Modi, this volume).

India has attempted to distance itself from the resource diplomacy of the Chinese, which it presents as having 'exploitative designs' on Africa. Quoting a high-level Indian military researcher, *Africa-Asia Confidential* notes that 'unlike China, India is pursuing a more inclusive, people-oriented policy in Africa where its historical connections and well placed Diaspora are incrementally helping it expand its influence'.[2]

The strategy has played out in two events recently hosted in New Delhi. They are the India–Africa Hydrocarbon Conference held in November 2007 and the India–Africa Forum summit held in April 2008. In the special address at the hydrocarbon conference, Shri Murli Deora, the Indian minister for petroleum and natural gas, put forward India's offer to 'partner with African nations in their progress by offering its expertise in the upstream and downstream sectors through technology, training, investments, research and development' (FICCI 2007).

A year later, the Indian prime minister, Manmohan Singh, in his opening address to the first India–Africa Forum summit, told his audience, including fourteen African presidents and heads of government: '[W]e visualize a partnership that is anchored in the fundamental principles of equality, mutual respect and mutual benefit.' This same view is echoed in the Delhi Declaration issued at the end of the summit.

The foregoing, though it captures India's rhetoric as an 'alternative' to China in the context of mutually beneficial South–South cooperation with Africa, still does not preclude the reality that its energy security calculations towards the continent are framed by the consideration that 'Africa provides a reliable alternative of sustained fuel supplies to a world confronted with huge shortages' (Sharma 2008). Thus, although Indian oil companies were 'outmanoeuvred' by their Chinese counterparts in oil bids in Nigeria, Sudan and Angola, where Chinese oil companies offered higher amounts for oil bids and won,[3] the Indian government and oil companies have learnt to restrategize and are gaining entry into Africa's oilfields.

In Nigeria, for example, after losing out earlier in an oil bid to China (owing, as explained, to the obstruction of the bid by the Indian government, which considered it too risky), India resorted to an aid-for-oil strategy and succeeded in getting a US$6 billion investment to establish an oil refinery, power plant and railway lines in Nigeria, through a joint venture oil company, ONGC-Mittal Energy Ltd (OMEL).[4] In the May 2006 Oil Licensing Round in Nigeria,

OMEL won two oil blocks, OPL 279 and OPL 285, after committing to invest in a 180,000-barrels-per-day oil refinery, a 2,000-megawatt power plant and an east–west railway line that will run from Lagos to Port Harcourt (Alike 2008; Global Insight 2007). IOC, another Indian oil company, also secured a deal to import Nigerian oil.

Apart from the deals with Nigeria, ONGC and OVL[5] have invested US$2 billion in Sudan, Libya, Egypt, Gabon, Côte d'Ivoire and the Nigeria–São Tomé Joint Development Zone. Although operating at a lower level, and with less strategic drive and fewer resources than China, India has been very pragmatic in gaining a foothold in Africa's oilfields, as part of a broader strategy of diversifying the sources of its energy supplies, ensuring the security of supplies, and gaining more influence on the global stage.

It should be noted, however, that India's pragmatism in relation to the pursuit of its energy security also includes cooperation, where necessary, with China. This is also consistent with its policy towards its regional neighbours in Asia, with whom India seeks to 'evolve a common energy security that could mitigate the vagaries of the global market' (Kumaraswamy 2007: 350). Examples of countries where Chinese and Indian oil companies have cooperated include Sudan, Iran, Colombia and Syria.

In Sudan, ONGC joined CNPC as part of GNPOC, which produces the bulk of Sudanese oil, by acquiring the shares of Talisman Oil in 2003. The same year, OVL and CNPC formed another partnership to develop the Malut basin oilfields in Sudan, making India a major stakeholder in Sudan's oil industry. It should be noted that the Export-Import Bank of India played a role in supporting OVL's foray into Sudan's oilfields.

Apart from being engaged in oil diplomacy with Africa, China and India have been involved in a 'softer' form of the projection of power, involving fighter aircraft and arms sales, contributing peacekeepers to conflict zones and the sending of 'security advisers/defence attachés' to certain African countries. Of note also is the presence of their navies in the Indian Ocean alongside the East African and southern African coasts, along which international oil shipping lanes pass en route from Asia to the Middle East and other parts of the world. While it has been suggested that both countries may nurse suspicions about each other's designs in the region, it is clear this cannot be separated from their competing interests in Africa, alongside those of Western powers, including the United States.

Conclusion

Africa's place in the energy security calculations of China and India brings out in bold relief the rather fluid and complex outcomes that can proceed from 'Africa's moment' in a rapidly globalizing post-cold-war world. Even though the West appears to be losing out to its latest rivals on the continent, the extent of 'Eastern' penetration of Africa has been exaggerated – often to good effect, although the West remains clearly dominant in Africa's economies. For example, some of the oil-for-aid deals between China and Angola and Nigeria later turned out to be problematic. As Hanson (2008) notes, '… in Nigeria Chinese state-owned CNPC's $2 billion investment in an oil refinery has fallen through, and in Angola, new reports suggest that work on the country's railroads halted or encountered serious delays'. The reasons for these reversals are embedded in the allegations of non-transparency and overpricing that have dogged the oil-for-infrastructure deals, and the determination of the Angolan government to diversify its sources of finance and investments and open up to both Western and Asian sources (see the chapter by Alex Vines and Indira Campos in this volume). Also, the Chinese Petroleum Corporation (CPC), which in 2007 was allocated OPL 294 in Nigeria, in a joint venture with Starcrest Nigeria Energy Ltd, after pledging a US$100 million investment in independent power projects in exchange for the oil block, lost out for unclear reasons, after its Nigerian partner swapped OPL 294 for OPL 291, and dropped CPC for Addax Petroleum (Alike 2008). Also of note in understanding China's pursuit of its energy security is the need to go beyond the assumption that all the actions of Chinese oil firms in Africa are state-directed from Beijing, and that these firms do not operate as competitive profit-seeking corporate actors.

The idea that China is sweeping the stakes in the African energy sector, or that African countries are uncritically accepting 'Chinese gifts' in exchange for oil, needs to be systematically rethought. It is a more complex relationship. This partly calls for deeper studies, on a case-by-case basis, of the impact of Chinese oil-for-aid packages and oil investments in Africa. This becomes more pertinent as the intensified competition for resources, energy and markets in Africa gains wider global ramifications. Of note, in this regard, are the ways in which the West's securitization/militarization of trade, energy and development in Africa will play out vis-à-vis the 'soft-power' ambitions of the Asian giants in Africa (Cohen 2008).

It is also clear that the policy of non-interference alone, as the case of Sudan shows, will not be enough to stave off criticism that China's resource diplomacy is complicit in the support for human rights abuses and corruption in some African states. Although India has not been in the spotlight like China, it is not clear that its strategy is radically different from the Chinese strategy, or the ambiguous policies of the Western powers in Africa. As with China's, several of India's oil deals in Nigeria have turned out not to be as rosy as initially thought, with little to show after the initial euphoria (Wong 2008). This can be seen from the recent recommendation of a Nigerian House of Representatives committee investigating some of the oil-for-infrastructure deals/contracts under the Obasanjo presidency, asking for their cancellation, where most of the contracts have already been suspended or abandoned (Africa-Asia Confidential 2009).

It is unlikely that the competing Chinese and Indian interests will lead to any form of conflict over Africa's resources. What we are confronted with could be explained as a three-way relationship involving the West, particularly the USA, the EU and Japan; Asia, that is China and India; and Africa – with Western and Asian countries all competing and cooperating at different levels simultaneously, and all claiming to be friends of Africa, keen on helping it to develop. Perhaps what we are beginning to see with the case of China and India are the early signs of emerging global powers combining economic, political, strategic and cultural tools of diplomacy to pursue their permanent interests in Africa in the context of a strong Eastern axis of a transforming global capitalist order.

There is no doubt that the unprecedented growth rate that African countries have enjoyed in recent years as a result of the commodity boom is in part due to increased investments and demand from China and India. Africa may want to bask in the 'glory' of this moment, as a long-neglected 'beautiful bride', now being courted by the world's established and emerging powers – for her resources, markets and potential influence. But this may all turn out to be counterproductive if a clear strategic African vision remains missing. As Naidu (2007: 295) rightly cautions, 'if Africa has to ensure that there are mutual gains in this "new strategic partnership", then surely it must set the rules of engagement with China and not vice versa'. This applies not only to Sino-African relations; it applies equally to Indo-African relations.

15 | China and India in Angola

Alex Vines and Indira Campos

Angola has enjoyed a period of sustained peace since April 2002 and held legis-
lative elections in September 2008 – the first since 1992. From having one of the
most protracted conflicts in Africa, Angola has within six years become one of
the most successful economies in sub-Saharan Africa. With the war now over,
rapid post-conflict reconstruction has become the government's priority. The
People's Republic of China (China) has in particular played an important role
in assisting these efforts, and this has to date eclipsed Indian efforts to obtain
energy concessions (Vines and Campos 2008; Vines et al. 2009).

China's growing role in Angola has generated debate and speculation. From
both the Angolan and Chinese perspectives, the relationship is pragmatic and
strategic. On the occasion of the Chinese prime minister's visit to Angola in June
2006, President dos Santos stated simply that 'China needs natural resources
and Angola wants development'.[1]

The year 2008 marked the twenty-fifth anniversary of the establishment of
bilateral relations between the two countries (Centre for Chinese Studies 2007;
Fandrych 2007; Taylor 2006). With the war now over, the Angolan government
has deployed revenues from oil towards post-conflict reconstruction. China has
been an important partner in these efforts. Chinese financial and technical
assistance has kick-started over one hundred projects in the areas of energy,
water, health, education, telecommunications, fisheries and public works. On
the occasion of Chinese prime minister Wen Jibao's visit to Angola in June
2006, Angolan president Eduardo dos Santos described bilateral relations as
being 'mutually advantageous' partnerships that were 'pragmatic' and had no
'political preconditions'.[2]

The growth of bilateral ties has been spectacular. During the 1990s, the value
of bilateral trade ranged between $150 million and $700 million. In 2000 it
exceeded $1.8 billion, and by the end of 2005 it had increased to $6.9 billion.
Within a year it had nearly doubled to $12 billion, making Angola China's largest
trading partner in Africa (with South Africa now second). The bulk of bilateral
trade has been made up of oil exports, while official Chinese imports remain
smaller, consisting mostly of food products and consumer goods. Angola's trade
with China expanded at its fastest rate in 2008, with bilateral trade reaching an
estimated $25.3 billion. This represented a 79 per cent increase on the level of

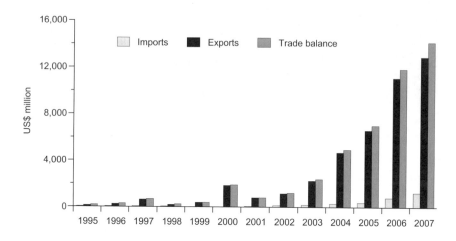

FIGURE 15.1 China–Angola trade volume (1995–2006) *Source*: Xinhua
China Economic Information Service

trade in 2007 and was primarily driven by high oil prices. In 2008 Angola was the second-largest source of crude oil for China (after Saudi Arabia), providing 28.89 million metric tonnes (543,533 barrels per day). This accounts for over one-fifth of China's total trade in Africa. By 2009, China had also facilitated loans to Angola amounting to at least $13.4 billion (or, according to some estimates, up to $19.7 billion).

The impact of this relationship is very visible in Angola, with Chinese construction sites spreading across the country. In 2006 nearly 15,000 Chinese resided in Angola with work visas. In 2007 there were over 22,000, and by 2008 this Chinese community had grown to almost 50,000, according to Chinese officials (and according to Angola's Service of Migration and Foreigners, 40,000 of these were working on the official bilateral infrastructure projects). By comparison, in 2008 a reported 10,400 Angolans applied for visas to visit China, according to the Chinese embassy in Luanda.

In 2008 Angola's TAAG Airlines and Air China began regular flights between the two countries. Flights to Angola today are full of Chinese workers and busi-

TABLE 15.1 Number of visas issued to Chinese nationals (2004–07)

Year	Work visas	Dependants	TOTAL
2007	22,043	57	22,100
2006	14,283	39	14,322
2005	1,952	18	1,970
2004	192	49	241

Source: Angolan Ministry of the Interior, 2007

ness people and, despite the global economic slow-down, the number visiting Angola in 2009 continues to grow.

Political and diplomatic relations

China's involvement in Angola dates back to the early years of the anti-colonial struggle through its support for the three major liberation movements in the country: the MPLA, UNITA and the FNLA. At that time the Cultural Revolution was raging in China and relations were defined by cold war politics.

The Chinese initially refused to recognize Angola's independence, and formal diplomatic relations between Beijing and Luanda were established only in 1983 after China distanced itself from supporting the then UNITA rebels and recognized the ruling MPLA as the governing party. The first trade agreement was signed in 1984, and a Joint Economic and Trade Commission followed. Relations between Angola and China improved gradually in the 1990s, and Angola had become China's second-largest trading partner in Africa (overtaking South Africa) by the end of the decade, mostly because of defence cooperation. In October 1998, President dos Santos visited China, seeking to 'expand bilateral ties'. He visited Beijing twice in 2008.

Following the end of the conflict in 2002, China's relationship with Angola shifted quickly from a defence and security basis to an economic one. Relations between China and Angola reached an even higher level on 2 March 2004, when China's Export-Import Bank (EximBank) pledged the first $2 billion oil-backed loan to Angola to fund the reconstruction of shattered infrastructure throughout the country. Since then, cooperation between the two countries has been characterized by frequent bilateral visits of important state officials, aimed at strengthening the partnership further. These visits have contributed to the normalization of bilateral relations and have resulted in the signing of various political, diplomatic, economic, cultural and social agreements.

Since 1993, Angola has maintained an embassy in Beijing, and in April 2007 increasing investments in Hong Kong led Angola to open a consulate there; in November 2007 an Angolan consulate was also opened in the former Portuguese colony of Macau.

Financial and economic cooperation

Increased political activity between Angola and China has enabled bilateral economic ties to progress quickly. This relationship has often been misunderstood. China's EximBank is increasingly making use of this deal structure – known by the World Bank as the 'Angola mode' or 'resources for infrastructure' – whereby repayment of the loan for infrastructure development is made in natural resources. This approach follows a long history of resource-based transactions. In the case of EximBank, the arrangement is used for countries that cannot provide adequate financial guarantees and allows them to package together natural resource exploitation and infrastructure development. According to the World Bank, these loans offer on average an interest rate of 3.6 per cent, a grace period of four years and a maturity of twelve years. The only unique thing about the 'Angola mode' is that Chinese engagement has been quick and loans have been large. Angolans argue that, over time, China's investment in the Democratic Republic of Congo will probably become more significant than its investment in Angola.

The bulk of Chinese financial assistance in Angola is reserved for key public investment projects in infrastructure, telecommunications and agro-businesses under the Angolan government's National Reconstruction Programme. The China Construction Bank (CCB) and China's EximBank provided the first funding for infrastructure development in 2002.

Financial relations between China and Angola grew in late 2003, when a 'framework agreement' for new economic and commercial cooperation was formally signed by Angola's Ministry of Finance and the Chinese Ministry of Trade. On 21 March 2004, the first $2 billion financing package for public investment projects was approved. The loan, payable over twelve years at a deeply concessional interest rate, was divided into two phases, with $1 billon assigned to each. The terms of the loan are Libor plus a spread of 1.5 per cent, with a grace period up to three years.

The second phase of this loan funded implementation of seventeen contracts, involving over fifty-two projects, some of which were unfinished projects from the first phase. Although education remains a priority, the second phase also supports fisheries and telecommunications projects. By the end of 2008 many of these projects were under way.

In May 2007, an extension of $500 million was negotiated with EximBank to finance 'complementary actions' to first-phase projects that had not been budgeted for. In September 2007, agreement for a further oil-backed loan of $2 billion was signed in Luanda by Angola's finance minister, José Pedro de Morais, and China's EximBank president Li Ruogu. This new credit line funds an additional one hundred projects approved by the Council of Ministers in November 2007.[3] Conditions attached to Chinese exports were relaxed, but the local content rules for reconstruction were tightened to ensure greater local participation.

Project proposals identified as priorities by the respective Angolan ministries are put forward to the Grupo de Trabalho Conjunto, a joint committee of the Ministry of Finance and the Chinese Ministry for Foreign and Commercial Affairs (MOFCOM). Having recently emerged from war, the Angolan government considers every project a priority, and therefore there are rarely any disagreements between the two parties regarding the projects being put forward. MOFCOM has in the past suggested further areas of development where it feels China can provide important know-how, such as in telecommunications and fisheries, which were not included in the first phase.

For each project put to tender, the Chinese government proposes three to four Chinese companies. All projects are inspected by third parties not funded by the credit line. A multi-sectoral technical group, GAT (Gabinete de apoio tecnico de gestão da linha de crédito da China), oversees the implementation of projects financed by the EximBank credit line, ensuring fast and efficient completion of the projects. Sectoral ministries are in charge of managing these public works and making certain that sufficient staff (nurses, teachers, etc.) are trained.

The loan operates like a current account. When ordered by the Ministry of Finance, disbursements are made by EximBank directly into the accounts of the contractors. Repayment starts as soon as a project is completed. If a project is not undertaken, no repayment is made. Revenue from oil sold under this arrangement is deposited into an escrow account from which the exact amount towards servicing the debt is then deducted. The government of Angola is free to use the difference at its own discretion. By all accounts Chinese loans of at least $13.4 billion have been agreed.

Angolan officials admit that falling oil prices have forced them to cut back on some of their $42 billion infrastructure plans for 2009. China's ambassador to Angola, Zhang Bolun, met President dos Santos on 17 February 2009, after which he signalled that China was considering further financial assistance for infrastructure that would be 'properly implemented and protected from the world crisis'. It is clear that since the legislative elections in 2008 the Angolan government has new priorities. Rapid post-conflict infrastructural development is less pressing, and delivering on some of the MPLA's election promises, such as diversification of the economy away from its dependence on oil and providing better services in health and education, is higher up the agenda. The global economic downturn has also introduced cost-cutting and a focus on greater efficiency in government agencies.

The importance of these issues became even more apparent at the fourth session of the bilateral Angola–China Commission in March 2009, at which Chinese and Angolan officials committed themselves to increased financial cooperation by agreeing to put in place an investment guarantee scheme (emulating an earlier US agreement to the same effect). At the meeting China also offered a 'non-reimbursable credit' (i.e. a grant) worth $34.15 million. China is clearly seeking to secure more oil concessions but it is also under pressure to furnish better local content provisions in contracts for its companies. Chinese government officials believe that oil-backed loans are the most beneficial arrangement as they offer the greatest security, and have regularly indicated their preference to their Angolan counterparts. The Angolans, however, seem to continue to want to move away from the 'Angola mode' approach.

China International Fund Ltd In 2005, China International Fund Ltd (CIF), a private Hong Kong-based institution, extended $2.9 billion to assist Angola's post-war reconstruction effort. This credit facility is managed by Angola's Recon-struction Office, Gabinete de Reconstrução Nacional (GRN), which is exclusively accountable to the Angolan presidency. CIF has its headquarters at a Hong Kong address that also hosts a portfolio of other business ventures tied to Angola, including Sonangol Sinopec International, China Sonangol International Ltd (CSIL) and China Beiya Escom International Ltd. CIF was created in 2003 and appears to be the construction arm of Hong Kong-based Beiya (now Dayuan) International Development Ltd, the parent company of China Angola Oil Stock Holding Ltd, which trades Angolan oil. CSIL is 70 per cent beneficially owned by New Bright International Development Limited and 30 per cent by Sonangol E.P. Ms Lo Fong Hung, Ms Fung Yuen Kwan, Wu Yang and Manuel Vicente, the president of Sonangol, are the directors of CSIL (Levkowitz et al. 2009).

GRN was set up in 2005 to manage large investment projects and ensure rapid infrastructural reconstruction prior to national elections. Headed by a military adviser to the president, General Helder Vieira Dias 'Kopelipa', GRN was designed to provide work for demobilized military in order to bring new dynamism to the reconstruction effort. It was also created on the assumption that the ministries would not have the organizational and technical capacity to manage the large inflows of money directed to the National Reconstruction Programme. According to a senior government official close to the presidency, GRN projects are valued at somewhere around $10 billion. CIF was meant to provide the funds to undertake these projects. How these funds were to have been allocated across projects remains unclear, however.

Many GRN projects came to a standstill in 2007, drawing a lot of media speculation. Although it was reported that CIF had some difficulties in raising funds to complete the projects, a GRN technician admitted that a lack of plan-ning on the part of GRN also contributed to many construction projects failing to start. As he explains: 'we went ahead with projects pressured by a strict time deadline and did not take into account the forward planning that is required in a country like ours ... We overlooked crucial elements such as the fact that our ports would not be able to cope with the increased amount of material being imported for these projects.'[4] Chinese construction firms have also complained about CIF cajoling contractors into taking part in projects in Angola, routinely delaying payment for completed work and keeping rates as low as possible.[5]

As a result, some of the funds from the second EximBank loan have been used to continue the major programmes of GRN, but the Ministry of Finance was forced to raise $3.5 billion in domestic funding by issuing treasury bonds. This is a new departure for Angola as Angolan funds are for the first time being used to finance Chinese firms to ensure completion of these projects.

Behind the CIF loan there is an opaqueness that can be traced back to the first loan in March 2004. In 2007, CIF's opacity attracted renewed media attention. A Chinese construction company, Zhejiang Hangxiao Steel Structure Co. Ltd, came under investigation by the China Securities Regulatory Commission (CSRC) for suspected stock price rigging in deals related to Angola, and it suspended its trading of stock on 19 March. Suspicion about the company followed a statement in February by Hangxiao that it had signed a $4.4 billion contract to sell CIF construction products and services for its 'Residents Heaven' public housing projects in Angola. In March, China's Ministry of Commerce published a report that Hangxiao Steel had defended its handling of $4.4 billion in contracts but that CIF 'had failed to supply Hangxiao with details of its contracts with the Angolan government'.[6] Unusually for the CSRC, on 22 March it made public a statement on the case, urging the Shanghai stock exchange and the local regulatory bureau to investigate as well. The Zhejiang Provincial Securities Regulatory Commission said it had launched an investigation.

In May of the same year, CSRC fined the Shanghai-listed construction company, management and leading shareholders, a combined $95,000 for failing to follow legal procedures in the release of financial information, which led to the jailing of two Hangxiao employees and one associate for insider trading charges. Trading in Hangxiao shares was suspended twice in July 2007, and in August, in a statement to the Shanghai stock exchange, Hangxiao stated that although construction of its first phase of building was under way, it was not yet able to secure confirmation of follow-up construction, and the dispatch of extra workers to Angola had been cancelled.

On 17 October 2007, in Luanda, the Angolan Ministry of Finance issued a statement denying any misuse of Chinese funds. They also published details of the lines of credit managed by the ministry.[7] Although this is a welcome development, more disclosure is needed, especially regarding the GRN, as many of the larger Chinese infrastructural projects are managed out of this office. In contrast to projects undertaken by the Ministry of Finance, it is unclear how much money is directly managed by the GRN, how funds are allocated among projects, and how much money has so far been spent.

Bilateral trade

Commercial trade between China and Angola has grown remarkably in recent years. Crude oil represents over 95 per cent of all Angolan exports and it is also China's main Angolan import. Over the last six years, China has been the second-largest importer of oil from Angola behind the United States, representing roughly 9.3 to 30 per cent of Angola's total oil exports.[8] Despite the US lead in the imports of Angolan oil, since 2002 Angolan oil exports to China have increased sevenfold, compared to only 3.5 times in the case of the United States.[9] Angolan oil imports now represent over 18 per cent of China's total oil imports, and this proportion was increasing until the global economic downturn.

In recent years, Chinese imports to Angola have also seen a significant increase. In 2004, China became Angola's fourth-largest trading partner at $194 million, up from being its seventh-largest trading partner the year before. In 2006, China kept its position despite the fact that Chinese exports to Angola quadrupled, with steel and iron bars, batteries, cement and automobiles as the principal imports.[10] In 2007, China surpassed Brazil and South Africa as the second-largest trading partner behind Portugal. In 2008 it became the largest trading partner.

Despite the rise in the value of both imports and exports in the period analysed, Angola has consistently run a large trade surplus with China, owing to the rapidly rising rate of Chinese oil importation. With the increase in infrastructural projects and the greater competitiveness of Chinese exports compared to European exports in Angola, it is expected that in the next few years the penetration of Chinese products in Angola will rise significantly, equalling the level of Portuguese imports.

Foreign direct investment

In addition to trade, China has significantly stepped up its FDI to Angola in recent years. While the largest Chinese operations in Angola are concentrated in oil exploration, there has been an overall dramatic increase in non-oil Chinese FDI to Angola. Between 2005 and 2007, fifty projects, valued at $73.6 million, were approved by the National Agency for Private Investment (ANIP) and were under way by Chinese companies. In 2006/07, the number of Chinese businessmen requesting visas to Angola increased by 30 per cent.[11]

Some Chinese firms engaged in projects tied to Chinese credit lines are establishing themselves in Angola after completion of their projects. The growing participation in construction reflects the urgent need for infrastructure. Local capacity is weak, and the Chinese have a record for quality construction, completed more quickly and cheaply than rivals can offer.

Extractive industries

China has shown its greatest interest in Angola's extractive industries. Following the opening of China's first credit line to Angola in March 2004, China Petrochemical Corp., better known as Sinopec Group, acquired its first stake in Angola's oil industry, 50 per cent of the BP-operated Block 18. Sonangol Sinopec International (SSI) is a joint-venture enterprise owned by Sinopec with Sonangol and Hong Kong-based Beiya (now Dayuan) International Development. Although BP's former licence partner Shell had agreed to sell its stake to India's state-owned Oil and Natural Gas Corporation (ONGC), the Chinese, on their first involvement in the Angolan oil industry, sidelined ONGC with an offer that media sources estimate at $725 million.[12] The company reportedly spent an additional $1.5 billion on the development and exploration of the block.[13] Both CNPC and CNOOC in late 2008 indicated their interest in buying Marathon Oil shares from its offshore Block 32 as part of an asset sale programme. On 17 July 2009, it was announced that Marathon had entered into a definitive agreement with CNOOC and SINOPEC. Both companies would purchase an undivided 20 per cent participating interest in the production-sharing contract and joint operating agreement in Block 32 for $1.3 billion, effective from 1 January 2009, subject to government and regulatory approvals. In an echo of what occurred when Shell tried to sell its oil assets to ONGC of India in April 2004, in September 2009 Sonangol said that it was invoking its right of first refusal and would be taking over this equity. It is now probable that this 20 per cent participating interest will be offered by Sonangol during the next oil block licensing round.

TABLE 15.2 China's exploration and production assets in Angola

Block(s)	Company	Year acquired	Share (%)	Partners (%)
15(06)	SSI	2006	20	ENI Angola EXPL. [OP] (35), Sonangol P&P (15), TOTAL (15), Falcon Oil (5), STATOIL (5), Petrobras (5)
17(06)	SSI	2006	27.5	TOTAL [OP] (30), Sonangol P&P (30), Falcon Oil (5), ACR (5), Partex Oil & Gas (2.5)
18(06)	SSI	2006	40	Petrobras [OP] (30), Sonangol P&P (20), Falcon Oil (5), Grupo Gema (5)
3/05 & 3/05A	CSIH (SSI from 2007)	2005	25	Sonangol P&P [OP] (25), Ajoco (20), ENI Angola EXPL. (12), SOMOIL (10), NAFTGAS (4), Ina-Naftaplin (4)
18	SSI	2004	50	BP [OP] (50)

Partner companies' countries of origin: Italy (ENI); Angola (Sonangol P&P, ACR, Grupo Gema, SOMOIL, Falcon Oil Holding Angola SA); France (TOTAL); Croatia (Ina-Naftaplin, NAFTGAS); UK (BP); Norway (STATOIL); Japan (Ajoco); Portugal (Partex)

Source: Sonangol (2008)

This is not the first time that the Chinese have encountered setbacks in Angola. The Lobito oil refinery Sonaref negotiations, for example, collapsed in early 2007 with Sonangol declaring it would manage the project on its own. Manuel Vicente, president of Sonangol, criticized the Chinese in the Angolan media, claiming that 'we can't construct a refinery just to make products for China'. This would suggest some resistance on the strategy of locking in supplies through long-term contracts, which China has applied elsewhere. According to Chang Hexi, the Chinese economic counsellor in Luanda, however, the negotiations over the refinery were deliberately obstructed by the Chinese negotiators because they were not genuinely interested in the deal (Centre for Chinese Studies 2007).

A special relationship?

From Angola's perspective, the Chinese provide funding for strategic post-conflict infrastructure projects that Western donors do not fund. Chinese financing offers better conditions, lower interest rates and longer repayment time than commercial loans. Non-Chinese credit lines that Angola had secured in 2004 demand higher guarantees of oil, with no grace period and with high interest rates.

Chinese financing was provided when concessional funding was not available for Angola. Relations between the international financial institutions and Angola had been poor for years. The recurrent episodes of hyperinflation and stabilization had prevented any lasting accord with the IMF. Relations with the World Bank were also limited to emergency and humanitarian assistance projects in the absence of an agreed framework with the IMF. At the end of the war in 2002, the IMF and many Western donors wanted Angola to negotiate a Staff-Monitored Programme (SMP) and show good performance for three trimesters before being eligible to receive financial support. A SMP would give credibility to Angola's economic policies and open the way for a donor conference to raise funds to rebuild the country. The Angolan government, however, felt it could not agree to IMF conditionalities, and after multiple rounds of consultations they announced that they would no longer seek to conclude an IMF agreement. This was not the first time: agreement with the IMF had collapsed several times previously during cycles of high commodity prices (Hodges 2001).

For the Angolan government this new cooperation brings significant advantages to the country, helping to support economic growth. As a commodity-based economy emerging from twenty-seven years of conflict, Angola was in desperate need of new partners and a new source of FDI. China provides a new model of cooperation, based on credit lines, economy and commerce, which contrasts with Western efforts of cooperation based on aid attached to conditionality.

China also offers Angola cheap technological transfer opportunities. These tend to be more suitable for Angola than those from Europe or the United States, where the technological gap is bigger and the opportunities more expensive. Currently, sixty-six students are benefiting from scholarships from the Chinese government.[14] According to the Chinese embassy in Luanda, twenty-three scholarships were offered to Angolan students in 2007 to pursue undergraduate and postgraduate studies in China. The Chinese government has also offered numerous short-term courses to Angolan employees and government officials in areas such as health, education, fishing and enterprise management and administration. In 2007 alone, more than one hundred Angolans went to China to participate in these courses.

Impact on poverty reduction

Although this is not easily measured, Chinese investment has contributed to poverty reduction in Angola. The construction and rehabilitation of electrical and hydroelectrical infrastructure by the Chinese has expanded electricity access to over sixty thousand new clients in Luanda. The rehabilitation of water supply systems across the country has granted thousands of people access to clean water.

The rehabilitation of roads, bridges and rail networks has provided access to parts of the country that had been disconnected by the war and facilitates commercial activities. The rehabilitation of the rail system across the country will benefit people commuting into towns and ease the transport of goods across the whole southern African region. Lastly, the rehabilitation of hospitals, health centres, schools and polytechnic institutes will provide access to education and health for many communities that for years had been deprived of it. The government of China has also agreed to send eighteen doctors to Angola. The doctors are to stay in the country for two years and provide medical assistance as well as training to local doctors. Nevertheless, serious human capital challenges remain despite the effort of the government to train professionals in these fields.

Putting it into context

The scale of the Chinese loans directed to infrastructure reconstruction is large, but Angola's developmental needs are even larger. In his address to the OPEC summit in November 2007, President dos Santos stated that 'Angola needs over $20 billion to guarantee its reconstruction'.[15] Not surprisingly, the Angolan government is extending its credit lines to other commercial partners. Traditional partners like Portugal and Brazil remain fully engaged in Angola's post-war reconstruction.

The need to diversify sources of financing further and at the same time sustain existing dependence on Western technology has triggered the government into strengthening its relationship with the Paris Club. In late 2006 and early 2007, Angola paid the bulk of its principal interest, estimated at around $2.5 billion, to Paris Club creditors. In November 2007, the issue of overdue interest arrears of about $1.8 billion was also resolved, with the government pledging to repay the outstanding amount in three tranches by 2010. The agreement with the Paris Club clears the way for the normalization of Angola's relations with the rest of the world. This is already evident, with the World Bank doubling its funds to Angola in 2007 and Spain pledging $600 million for Angola's reconstruction in late November 2007. Other donors, such as Canada, France, Italy and Germany, have also expanded their credit lines.

Angola's post-conflict behaviour reflects Luanda's pragmatic policy of avoiding any rigid adherence to dogma. President dos Santos made this point clear in his 2008 New Year's address to the diplomatic corps by stressing that the

Angolan government plans to reinforce its bilateral and commercial relationships with other countries: '... globalization naturally makes us see the need to diversify international relations and to accept the principle of competition, which has, in a dynamic world, replaced the petrified concept of zones of influence that used to characterize the world'.

China has offered Angola in the short term things others do not offer, such as rapid infrastructure development, which is important to the Angolan government in a pre-election context. A more businesslike relationship is now emerging, although the global economic downturn has resulted in Luanda's diversification efforts being cut back. Unusually, President dos Santos visited a foreign country twice in 2008 – China, in order to secure new credit lines and shore up Chinese support.

India and Angola

Although India was one of the first countries to recognize the MPLA government in 1975, following support of nationalist movements against Portuguese colonialism, its footprint is tiny in Angola compared with China's. India set up its resident mission in Luanda in September 1986 and Angola its embassy in Delhi in 1992.

Despite this, bilateral visits were initially infrequent. Prime Minister Rajiv Gandhi's visit in May 1986 led to the signing of a bilateral trade agreement in October 1986 in New Delhi. President José Eduardo dos Santos visited India in April 1987 and a series of officials have visited India since. Visits became more regular after 2004, when oil and diamond diplomacy took off as part of the global commodities boom. João Miranda, then foreign minister of Angola, visited India in May 2006 and met Anand Sharma, minister of state for external affairs, Kamal Nath, minister of commerce and industry, and Shri Murli Deora, minister for petroleum and natural gas. He met a cross-section of businessmen at a meeting arranged by the Confederation of Indian Industry and visited the facilities of several leading companies engaged in the software, automobiles, agricultural equipment, transportation, railways, energy and mining sectors. Anand Sharma, minister of state for external affairs, visited Luanda in June 2007 to discuss cooperation in the fields of oil, geology and mining, agriculture, health, education and tourism. Sonangol sends some thirty to thirty-five students each year from its subsidiary Sonaship for training as sailors in Madras. President dos Santos met Indian prime minister Manmohan Singh at the G8 summit at L'Aquila in Italy in July 2009.

Trade with India is small – mainly in meat, pharmaceuticals, dairy products and machinery. Indian companies such as Tata, Mahindra & Mahindra and others have had business interests in Angola for some years. The Indian community in Angola is tiny, numbering around one thousand. India's main import from Angola is crude oil and its state-run oil refiner Indian Oil Corporation

(IOC) estimates that for the financial year starting April 2009 it will buy 60,000 barrels/day (compared with 30,000 barrels/day in financial year 2008/09).

TABLE 15.3 India–Angola trade (US$ million)

Period	India's exports	India's imports
1999/2000	5.80	0.00
2000/01	5.15	0.00
2001/02	25.02	0.01
2002/03	37.31	7.20
2003/04	70.55	0.00
2004/05	67.26	0.91
2005/06	151.66	3.25

Source: Indian embassy, Luanda

Lines of credit extended by India include $40 million for rehabilitation of Angolan Railways by RITES, $10 million for purchase of tractors and $5 million for the agriculture sector by credit extended by the EXIM Bank of India.

India has tried to get an oil acreage in Angola. ONGC's bid for an Angolan oil block failed at the last moment in 2004 when its offer of US$310 million for infrastructure development could not compete with a massive US$725 million from China. India hopes to do better in a future Angola licensing round, however, and in July 2008 India's oil minister announced that ONGC had qualified to bid as an operator in the next licensing round and would consider jointly bidding with Angola's national oil company Sonangol.

In May 2007 President dos Santos offered India a 30 per cent stake in the Lobito oil refinery when the Indian minister of state for external affairs, Anand Sharma, visited Luanda. This offer has not been taken forward but ONGC-Videsh has been designated as the company to deal with oil issues.

India's diamond diplomacy seems more successful. The Angolan state diamond company, Endiama, has agreed to do business directly with the large Indian diamond industry, while India is looking at opening an institute for jewellery manufacturing in Luanda. India's minister of state for commerce, Jairam Ramesh, visited Angola in April 2009 to set up an initiative for the direct import of diamonds. India seeks direct links with supplier countries, cutting out the middlemen. As part of diversifying and beefing up the supply of rough diamonds, Jairam Ramesh visited the CEO of Endiama, which promised to send a team to Mumbai to begin the process of setting up an office there. This would enable direct sales of rough diamonds by Endiama to Indian companies in 2009. Endiama has also invited Indian mining companies to explore and develop diamond mines in Angola.

Conclusions

The Chinese seem to be settling in for the long haul in Angola. Although both China and Angola stand to benefit from the increased economic cooperation, the relationship also raises new policy challenges for Angola. India, on the other hand, is trying to catch up but lacks the financial muscle that China enjoys. It hopes, though, that an Angolan strategy of diversification will allow it to gain a market foothold, and Sonangol's intervention in September 2009 to block the sale by Marathon Oil of participating interest in oil Block 32 to CNOOC and Sinopec will give Indian officials hope that they may yet succeed (Vines et al. 2009).

China's massive credit lines to finance infrastructural development also raise important questions related to the sustainability of these projects. Without downplaying the importance of the schools, hospitals, dams, roads and bridges that are being built around the country, there is legitimate concern about the government's capacity to maintain such investments after their completion, taking into account the country's enormous deficiency in human and institutional capacity. Although the government is making efforts to train people, it would be unrealistic to think that they train people as quickly as they build infrastructure. Furthermore, with Angola's low level of technology, there is the threat of long-term dependence on China. This was recently witnessed when the central air conditioner of the newly renovated Ministry of Finance broke down and spare pieces to fix it had to come from China. The government will need to focus more attention on planning and organization to ensure the sustainability and transfer of know-how – or risk relying on the Portuguese and others returning in the near future to rebuild what the Chinese have just completed.

China's growth into an economic powerhouse has pushed global commodity prices to unprecedented highs, which has contributed to Angola's rapid economic growth in recent years. Although the commodity boom favours the economy – and in particular the reconstruction effort – it poses very severe challenges for economic management. Reliance on oil exports may contribute to real exchange appreciation, preventing diversification into more labour-intensive sectors such as manufacturing and agriculture (the so-called Dutch disease). This may have implications for the government's efforts to diversify the economy beyond oil. Angola needs to take explicit steps to counteract the dangers posed to existing and future capabilities in industry.

The inflow of money and credit lines from China gives Angola's rulers the ability to resist pressure from Western financial institutions for transparency and accountability. Yet this should not be exaggerated, as Angola has said it will continue to work with the IMF on technical assistance. Recently, the government published substantial amounts of new data on the oil sector that go far beyond what several members of the Extractive Industries Transparency Initiative (EITI) have disclosed. The investigation and US$52,000 fine by the China Securities

Regulatory Commission (CSRC), imposed on the Hangxiao Steel Structure Company Ltd in 2007 for suspected stock price rigging, are significant and show that the Chinese are concerned with limiting corrupt practices. There does not appear to have been an investigation of its Hong Kong-registered partner CIF, however. Nonetheless, Angolan civil society and some international NGOs and Western governments have raised concerns regarding transparency in the use of Chinese funds. The US$2.9 billion extended by CIF and its management through GRN have, in particular, been opaque.

The Ministry of Finance's October 2007 statement about Chinese funds reflects diverse opinion in Luanda. More disclosure is needed, especially regarding GRN and its relationship to CIF. This would be a good issue for the CSRC to investigate further, especially in terms of CIF and its dealings under Chinese law. In Angola new research into the Chinese relationship, such as that undertaken by the Catholic University, could also provide more information on such deals, which could then be used by parliamentarians, civil society groups and the media. It is clear that there is a growing trend in Angola towards governmental disclosure. Appraisal of what becomes of the Chinese loans and investment is an important part of Angola's post-conflict development.

16 | The price of 'openness': towards Chinese economic control in Zambia

Peter Kragelund

This chapter argues that the advance of Chinese enterprises in Africa is not only the result of deliberate Chinese policies to gain access to resources and markets but also the consequence of liberal African investment policies imposed by Western donors since the early 1980s. Led by the international financial institutions (IFIs) Africa – in the middle of a deep economic crisis – embarked on a series of Economic Recovery Programmes (ERPs), which ultimately aimed to correct imbalances between government spending and government revenues, and thereby raise African economies' productive capacity. The most widespread measures used included trade liberalization, exchange-rate liberalization (devaluation), fiscal and monetary reforms, public enterprise reforms, and deregulation of investments, labour and prices (Bennell 1997; Cockcroft and Riddell 1991). A critical aspiration of the ERP model was persuading foreign investors to invest in African economies and thereby expand the production capacity, increase foreign exchange earnings and create employment. Therefore, any serious analysis of the rise of China in Africa must *consider the strategic role of the Chinese state as well as the historical legacy of host-country investment policies.*

Western donors and the shrinking capacity for autonomous investment policies

The post-1994 creation of a New International Trade Regime implies that the policy liberalizations embarked upon in the late 1980s and the beginning of the 1990s in Africa are difficult to turn back. Moreover, the agreements covered by the World Trade Organization (WTO) have made it difficult for African countries to pursue their own (protectionist) trade, industrial and investment policies. Although the international system still lacks an agreed regulatory framework for all aspects of FDI (comparable to the WTO regarding trade), the WTO covers many aspects of FDI. Most importantly, the Trade-Related Investment Measures (TRIMs) govern global FDI flows, but aspects of FDI are also covered by, for instance, the Agreement on Trade-Related Aspects of Intellectual Property Rights and the General Agreement on Trade in Services. The TRIM agreement essentially seeks to '... outlaw host governments' use of most "discriminatory" investment pre-conditions or performance requirements in relation to foreign investors' (Gibbon 2002: 105). In short, the TRIMs agreement bans certain performance requirements related to local content, mandatory technology transfer and export requirements.

Of greater importance for the governance of FDI, however, are bilateral investment treaties (BITs), which provide protection for investors via binding investor-to-state dispute-settlement mechanisms, and double taxation treaties (DTTs), which provide foreign investors with tax-issue security and stability and hinder double taxation of corporate incomes. The number of BITs and DDTs has increased rapidly in recent years, indicating increased competition for FDI, especially among developing countries. BITs take many forms but they usually include principles central to the New International Trade Regime, namely that of most-favoured nation (privileges provided to one foreign investor must be provided to all investors) and national treatment (foreign investors may not be treated worse than domestic investors). Moreover, they include paragraphs to guarantee repatriation of profits and free transfer of capital, seek to apply international standards regarding fair and equitable treatment of foreign investors, and include guarantees of compensation for any expropriation. In addition, some BITs include bans similar to the bans included in the TRIMs regarding local content, employment and technology transfer (UNCTAD 2007b; Neumayer and Spess 2005).

Both the TRIM agreement and the BITs represent an interference with the sovereignty of host governments, essentially contracting the policy space for developing countries. In the words of Wade (2003: 622), the New International Trade Regime '... ties the hands of developing country governments "forever" to the North's interpretation of a market opening agenda'. Essentially, the ability to design and customize investment policies to augment desired benefits and minimize negative effects of FDI has shrunk. The very advantages of FDI to developing countries compared to other financial flows – that is, its role in transferring technology and managerial knowledge, providing access to international markets and building export capacity – may therefore not materialize.

External actors, FDI and the Zambian economy

As elsewhere in Africa, the IFIs also played a crucial role in the transformation of the Zambian economy. While foreign investments played a major role in the development of Zambia's copper-dominated economy just after independence, this situation radically changed when, in April 1968, at Mulungushi Rock, President Kenneth Kaunda launched a series of economic reforms. The original aim of these reforms was to Zambianize the private sector, but the end result was rather a shift from private to public ownership (Kaunda 1968; Burdette 1988).

Basically, these reforms ended the era of foreign investments in Zambia. Simultaneously, international demand for copper declined, ore grades deteriorated, and the state-owned mines faced technical problems. This immediately resulted in a slowdown of the Zambian economy at large, soon to turn into a major financial crisis, and then a long-standing relationship with the IFIs from the mid-1980s onwards. Unable to service its huge external debt, Zambia embarked upon an economic liberalization programme, which aimed to make room for the private sector to kick-start the economy (Saasa 1987). Private investors, however, did not react positively to these measures as they had lost faith in the Zambian economy (Rakner 2003). Therefore, the incentives that were given to FDI as part of the restructuring programmes in the 1980s did not result in the emergence of a vibrant domestic private sector.

In fact, Kaunda did not pay particular attention to the role of foreign investors in the 1980s, but the passing of the 1986 Investment Act, which allowed foreign investors to retain part of their foreign exchange earnings, gave them export incentives and preferential tax rates, and full exemption from tax on dividends for five years (Saasa 1987). This situation, however, changed just prior to the 1991 presidential elections, when parliament passed the 1991 Investment Act. This act, among others, allowed foreign investors to retain 100 per cent of the foreign exchange earnings for three years while simultaneously being exempted from company tax and custom duties for the same length of time. Thereby, the 1991 act deliberately offered generous incentives to foreign investors intending to set up new foreign-exchange-earning ventures in Zambia.

The new Chiluba-led government basically continued these policies. It perceived liberalization – the IMF way – as a means of attracting foreign investments (Baylies and Szeftel 1992). Moreover, encouraged by the IFIs, the government decontrolled foreign exchange in order to encourage foreign investments, and the Investment Code, passed in parliament in 1993, basically reinforced the 1991 act. In 1996, as a condition for extension of a World Bank loan, the Chiluba-led government passed a new Investment Act. This act introduced minor restrictions on tax holidays and duty-free import of capital goods, but more importantly it established the Zambian Investment Centre (ZIC) to assist (foreign) companies to invest in the Zambian economy in the wake of the widespread privatization programme.

By the same token, the IFIs, assisted by prospective investors, pressed the Zambian government to pass the 1995 Mines and Minerals Development Act, which gave foreign investors particular incentives to invest in the mines. The act stipulated, for instance, that investors were exempted from customs duties on imported capital equipment while simultaneously they could reduce income taxes by deducting investments from the profit. Moreover, it paved the way for confidential 'Development Agreements' between the Zambian state and the investors, in which the terms of the privatization of the Zambia Consolidated Copper Mines were specified. In the same vein, the IFIs used Zambia's position as a Highly Indebted Poor Country to force it to privatize other strategically important state-owned enterprises (SOEs) (Lungu 2008; Larmer 2005; Rakner

). The impression of a very liberal investment climate 'encouraged' by the IFIs therefore remains.

Currently, FDI in Zambia is governed by the ZDA Act, 2006, passed in May 2006 and effective from 1 January 2007. Thereby, the ZDA (Zambia Development Agency) effectively replaced ZIC. Even though the ZDA Act introduces stricter rules on the minimum investment and employment creation requirements to obtain a Zambian resident permit, it still offers investors a very liberal investment climate. The act does not, for instance, stipulate any requirements regarding local content, technology transfer, equity, employment or use of subcontractors for foreign investors, even if such investors are encouraged to commit to local participation; it allows investors to repatriate any capital investments freely, and send home profit, dividends, interest, fees and royalties; and it permits foreign nationals to transfer wages earned in Zambia.

The most recent incentive to attract foreign investors is the passing of the Multi-Facility Economic Zones (MFEZ) Regulations, which were first launched in the 2007 budget speech. The law allows the establishment of MFEZs throughout Zambia. Companies that are located in these zones enjoy special incentives, including duty-free imports of raw materials, capital goods and machinery for five years. So far three MFEZs have been approved. One, financed by Japan International Cooperation Agency, is located in Lusaka. It encourages Malaysian and Indian companies to set up joint ventures with Zambian companies. It is tellingly called 'Triangle of Hope'. The second, located a stone's throw from the Chinese-owned Chambishi mine in the Zambian Copperbelt, called the Zambia–China Economic and Trade Cooperation Zone (ZCCZ), is exclusively for Chinese companies, and the third – basically a sub-zone of the ZCCZ – is located in Lusaka East (Personal communication, Lusaka, 15 February 2008).

The scope of Chinese investments in Zambia

As in any other African economy, the quality and availability of FDI data in Zambia are poor, and data on Chinese FDI are even poorer. Neither Chinese nor Zambian sources provide us with anything but aggregate (often contradictory) figures. Hence, as of 2006 more than two hundred Chinese companies had invested in Zambia, making the stock of Chinese FDI reach US$570 million, according to an official source (Personal communication, China House, Lusaka, 25 January 2008), but only 143 Chinese investments had been approved by the ZDA by the end of 2006. Nonetheless, they do point to the growing importance of Chinese investment in relation to total investments as well as in relation to other foreign investors. By 2006, China was the third-largest investor in terms of FDI stock in Zambia – surpassed only by Great Britain and South Africa – but if one looks at the most recent FDI flows it becomes clear that China will become even more important in the near future.

Chinese investments are not confined to resource-extraction activities – as one would assume based on news bulletins. In fact, only eight Chinese companies are directly involved in mining activities in Zambia. The remainder of the Chinese companies invest in other sectors of the economy. In addition to the ZDA-approved investments, Table 16.1 lists the Chinese companies that are members of the Association of Chinese Companies in Zambia (ACCZ). The total number of Chinese companies had reached 175 by the end of 2006. Table 16.1 also shows that fewer than 5 per cent of the Chinese companies in Zambia have invested (directly) in the mining sector; the rest have invested in manufacturing (43 per cent), services (21 per cent), construction (16 per cent), agriculture (13 per cent) and timber (2 per cent). Concealed in the ZDA categorization, however, is the fact that the majority of investments in the manufacturing sector are mining related. For instance, the BGRIMM Explosives (US$5.6 million), the Chambishi Copper Smelter (US$199 million) and the Sino-Metals Leaching Plant (US$12 million) investments are all registered as manufacturing investments, even though they are clearly related to the mining industry. In fact, they are all subsidiaries of the same company, China Nonferrous Metal Mining Group, which also owns China's largest mine in Zambia, the Chambishi mine in the Copperbelt. In total, therefore, mining-related activities make up at least 70 per cent of the value of all registered Chinese investments in Zambia (see Bastholm and Kragelund 2009).

TABLE 16.1 Sectoral distribution of Chinese companies in Zambia

	Number of companies	ZDA-certified companies	ACCZ members	Non-ZDA-certified ACCZ members	ZDA investment pledges (US$ million)
Agriculture	23	21	8	2	10
Construction	28	20	14	8	35.5
Manufacturing	76	74	9	2	299
Mining	8	7	3	1	22.2
Services	37	21	21	16	11.9
Timber	3	0	3	3	0
TOTAL	175	143	58	32	402

Table 16.1 is not complete, as not all Chinese companies are registered either by the ZDA, the ACCZ or the line ministries. Numerous Zambian-run shops – especially in and around the large markets – are in fact owned by Chinese businessmen. Furthermore, the table does not include the small manufacturing and construction companies set up by former employees of large-scale Chinese companies that have not registered their activities with the Registrar General's office (Personal communications, Lusaka, 30 January 2008 and 20 February

2008). Lastly, some companies, especially in the construction sector, are *de jure* Zambian – that is, a Zambian citizen owns more than 51 per cent of the company's shares, but in fact the Zambian partner is used only as a front in order to win tenders specifically targeted at Zambian small and medium-sized enterprises. Hence, these companies are de facto Chinese (Personal communication, Lusaka, 25 February 2008).

Catalysing investments in Africa: Chinese state support for FDI

The spread of Chinese companies throughout Africa is rendered possible not only by liberal investment policies but also by support and guidance from the Chinese state. Chinese outward FDI (OFDI) was virtually non-existent until the political and economic reforms in the late 1970s. As a result of the changing political discourse in China vis-à-vis the outside world, in August 1979 the Chinese State Council allowed certain companies to invest overseas. This political change became the starting point for emerging Chinese OFDI and together with the high rates of economic growth of the past three decades has sustained its growth.

The reforms, however, did not immediately lead to growth in OFDI. Although some Chinese OFDI did take place in the 1980s and 1990s, the determining factor for its growing importance worldwide was the so-called Go Out policy, implemented by the Chinese government in 2001 to make Chinese enterprises become internationally competitive players. The Go Out policy aimed to reduce red tape and entitle certain firms to tax incentives, cheap loans, direct or indirect subsidies and various types of support from state institutions in China and in host-country contexts (Buckley et al. 2007; Wu and Chen 2001).

Even though Chinese SOEs have been dominant players in Chinese OFDI – and were among the intended beneficiaries of the Go Out policy – Chinese provincial and private companies are now playing an increasingly important role in OFDI (see Kragelund 2009: 644–61). Notwithstanding their ownership structure, these companies are instruments of Chinese foreign policy, and the central government plays a determining role in directing the FDI activities of the SOEs. The transnational activities of SOEs provide access to natural resources for industrial production, as well as to new markets, as China's industrial capacity in many industries now exceeds domestic demand. SOEs can circumvent import quotas; their FDI activities also result in the transfer of technological and managerial capabilities into the Chinese economy from more advanced economies and thereby strengthen Chinese national competitiveness. Moreover, the Chinese state sees these companies as vehicles for consolidating China's geopolitical position (Wang 2002; Schuller and Turner 2005).

China's Go Out policy is by no means the only way in which the Chinese state supports these companies. China has set a whole series of initiatives in motion to support Chinese enterprises willing to invest in Africa. First and foremost, the launch of the Africa Policy in January 2006 set the framework for current and future Sino-African relations, kick-starting the Year of Africa. The policy, *inter alia*, points to the importance of economic cooperation between China and Africa, and states:

> The Chinese Government encourages and supports Chinese enterprises' invest-
> ment and business in Africa, and will continue to provide preferential loans
> and buyer credits to this end ... [and] will continue to negotiate, conclude and
> implement the Agreement on Bilateral Facilitation and Protection of Investment
> and the Agreement on Avoidance of Double Taxation with African Countries.
> (People's Republic of China 2006)

Second, in June 2007 the Chinese government launched the China–Africa Development Fund, which will help well-established and reputable Chinese companies in investing in Africa. Third, the government (in collaboration with Chinese companies) is in the process of setting up overseas economic and trade cooperation zones in African countries. Two such zones have been launched in Zambia (Kragelund 2009), a contract has been signed for another zone in Mauritius (Ancharaz 2009) and China is likely to establish even more in Tanzania and Nigeria (Davies 2008b).

Moreover, the Chinese state facilitates Chinese OFDI by offering low-interest loans directly as well as indirectly to Chinese enterprises: directly via the Bank of China (BOC), and indirectly via non-commercial banks such as the Export-Import Bank of China, the State Development Bank and the Agricultural Development Bank. All of these banks, but in particular the non-commercial banks, are closely involved in the Chinese state's large infrastructural development projects in African countries. In addition, to create a secure investment climate overseas, by June 2007 China had signed BITs with twenty-eight African countries[1] – representing almost 50 per cent of the total BITs signed by China in the past decade. According to Berger (2008: 20ff.), the content of these BITs shows that '... China generally agrees to international standards of FDI protection and thus to the current liberal global governance regime for FDI shaped by developed countries' policies'.

The Chinese state, however, does not confine itself to these general types of support in order to facilitate the further growth and expansion of Chinese companies in Africa; it also establishes institutions in the host economies aimed specifically at guiding and helping Chinese transnational companies. In Zambia, the most important institution is the Chinese embassy and in particular the Economic Counsellor's Office, which, via diplomatic attention and development aid to prestige projects, facilitates a positive attitude towards Chinese investments among the political elite. Moreover, it provides investors with investment opportunities, maintains essential contacts with Zambian authorities, and makes inter-Chinese cooperation in Zambia possible.

Of importance also is the Chinese Centre for Investment Promotion and Trade (CCIPT) and the ACCZ, established as a consequence of the implementation of the Go Out policy. Both were established by political decree and both seek to smooth Chinese companies' progress in Zambia. While the CCIPT currently mostly identifies suitable investment projects and provides practical support to newly established Chinese companies, the ACCZ essentially functions as the Chinese chamber of commerce in Zambia, taking care of the interests of Chinese companies, communicating and promoting the cause of Chinese investors, and educating its members in Zambian rules and regulations. Likewise, the Zambian branch of BOC, set up in 1997 by political decree, helps to pave the way for large-scale Chinese investments in Zambia, especially in the mining and construction sectors, by offering cheap loans for capital investments; it also eases the day-to-day banking operations of almost all Chinese companies in Zambia.

Lastly, the establishment of the US$900 million ZCCZ in the Copperbelt, with an expected fifty to sixty Chinese companies (Burke et al. 2007), as well as the US$500 million sub-zone in Lusaka, is a manifestation of the support that the Chinese state gives Chinese companies in Zambia. The overall aim of these Chinese MFEZs is to build export hubs for locally produced Chinese goods. In order to fulfil this aim, the Chinese state constructs the essential infrastructure and erects the required buildings within the zones, all financed by Chinese development aid and carried out by Chinese companies. Moreover, it provides cheap loans via BOC (or any of the other four main banks in China) to potential investors in the zones.

Conclusion

Chinese transnational companies have become increasingly active in African economies, but data from Zambia show that we have to modify our general perception of these investments as solely comprising resource-seeking activities. First, as pointed out in this chapter, Chinese companies come in all shapes and sizes. Among the first companies to return to Zambia were SOEs and provincial companies with previous experience of Chinese development aid projects. Only later did mining and related enterprises arrive in Zambia. Second, Chinese corporations are not the only mining companies in Zambia. In fact, the Zambian mining sector is dominated by British and American transnationals rather than Chinese ones. Third, they do not differ radically from other resource-extractive industries in Africa (UNCTAD 2007c). And finally, they do not operate in a vacuum: alongside the arrival of mining-related Chinese companies several private Chinese companies of all sizes have chosen to invest in Zambia. They are not only pursuing raw materials. Many have been pushed out of China owing to increasing demands for technological capabilities and low profit margins in China. They did not choose Zambia per se, but found that investment codes were liberal and that the institutional set-up supported them. Thus, they aimed to benefit from the existing combination of liberal investment codes, close networks and lack of local competition. A simple explanation based on the need for resources for the 'factory of the world', therefore, is not sufficient to account for the rapid growth of Chinese transnational companies in African economies, even though securing access to resources is indeed an important aspect of official Chinese OFDI policies.

Similarly, the literature on China in Africa tends to suggest that lack of other investors is a deciding factor for Chinese enterprises' successful presence in African economies. Put differently, the literature states that Western companies have avoided certain African economies owing to fear of bad governance and political instability. Thereby, they have paved the way for Chinese SOEs that are governed neither by shareholder doctrines and high returns on investments, nor by corporate reputation. This chapter shows that this is only one of several factors explaining the phenomenon of China's presence in Africa. Of importance, too, are the deliberate policies of the Chinese state to support Chinese OFDI. Although the scale may be different, other countries also support their corporations operating in Africa (Alden and Davies 2006). The Chinese way of catalysing investments in Africa, therefore, is not exceptional. Moreover, neither the Go Out policy nor the support to Chinese transnational companies in host economies is confined to Africa. Rather, they are part of China's global rise. This casts into question the uniqueness implicit in most current literature on Sino-African relations.

Moreover, the literature tends to forget the role of the West – especially that of Western donors – in the rise of Chinese transnational corporations in Africa: without the very liberal investment climate in Africa, to a large extent imposed by the IFIs, China could not have pursued its grand policies of vertical integration to control full value chains. Instead, Chinese companies would have had to link up with other companies. Likewise, China could not have established exclusive investment and trade zones for Chinese companies throughout Africa (Davies 2008b), but would compete on equal terms with domestic (and other foreign) companies. Lastly, the liberal investment policies (alongside the highly politicized nature of current Sino-African relations) have enabled thousands of small-scale Chinese traders to establish in and around the main markets in Lusaka, driving out the domestic private sector (Konings 2007).

Consequently, traditional explanations do not sufficiently account for the presence of Chinese companies in Africa in general or Zambia in particular. In order to understand what is happening we have to take both push and pull factors into account. Push factors include not only deliberate OFDI policies but also fiercer competition and lower profit margins at home. Similarly, pull factors comprise not only natural resources, large untapped markets and possibilities of learning to internationalize, but also liberal investment codes and limited domestic competition.

Hence, if African development is indeed a priority for Western observers, they should stop pointing the finger at Chinese transnational corporations and instead assist African host economies to maximize the benefits of the current upward trend of Chinese investments. Rather than putting more emphasis on liberalizing African economies, Western donors should help African governments to make use of the, albeit small, policy space in the form of the temporary exemptions and longer implementation periods that exist within the New International Trade Regime for most African countries. An efficient use of this policy space to build local subcontracting schemes, combined with broad-based capacity-building in the domestic private sector – funded, for instance, by windfall taxes on rising commodity prices – could enhance the more positive effects of Chinese (and other foreign) investments in Africa, and thereby curb Western criticism of Chinese interest in Africa.

PART SIX

Conclusion

17 | Countering 'new imperialisms': what role for the New Partnership for Africa's Development?

Fantu Cheru and Magnus Calais

As we begin the second decade of the twenty-first century, the balance of power in the world economy looks quite different from what existed barely two decades ago. The shift from bipolarity to multipolarity has ushered in a new set of international alignments, potentially making a definitive break with some of the post-Second World War institutions and practices (NIC 2008: 47). The emergence of China and India, new trilateral formations such as the Brazil, Russia, India and China (BRIC) Forum, the India, Brazil, South Africa Dialogue (IBSA) and a profoundly transformed G20 forum in the aftermath of the current global financial crisis present both challenges and opportunities to the African continent. As the preceding chapters have shown, a high volume of trade revenue and investment from China and India have come to represent a significant source of funding to African governments which previously, albeit to varying degrees, have been reliant on official development assistance (ODA) flows from the developed countries (UNCTAD 2007a: 56). The central question posed in this concluding chapter is the following: *how can African countries harness these new relationships with China and India and avoid being subordinated in a neocolonial type of relationship reminiscent of the past century with Europe?*

Enter the New Partnership for Africa's Development (NEPAD), adopted by the African Union as a framework for Africa's renaissance (NEPAD 2001). NEPAD's aim is to articulate an authentic, African-owned and African-driven development agenda and to strengthen the continent's bargaining capacity with its external development partners. This chapter scrutinizes whether the NEPAD framework can be used as a platform to negotiate effectively with Africa's external development partners, including China and India, in order to create conditions of globalization that are favourable to Africa. Given the character of the ruling classes in charge of most African states, and the weakness of civil society organizations, can NEPAD be transformed as a powerful platform for engaging China and India from a position of strength (Adesina 2002; Adesina et al. 2006; Bond 2002; S. Matthews 2004; Söderbaum and Taylor 2008: 13–31)?

The tortured history of Africa's regional integration experience

The issues of economic integration and cooperation have occupied a central place in the pan-African politics of independent African countries since the establishment of the Organization of African Unity (OAU) in 1963. From the early days of decolonization to the present moment, the aim of African unity and integration has been the same: to end Africa's marginalization in the world economy and to chart an independent development path through collective self-reliance and South–South cooperation (Nkrumah 1963; OAU 1980; African Union 2006b). With the adoption of the Lagos Plan of Action in 1980 by the African heads of state, regional integration and cooperation received a major boost, and in successive years a number of regional economic integration schemes were initiated, ranging from the Preferential Trade Area (PTA) at the lower end of the integration spectrum to Economic Union at the upper end (Agubuzu 2004; Anyang' Nyongo'o 1990).

Many of these regional integration schemes generally sought to expand the growth of intra-regional trade by removing tariffs and non-tariff barriers; strengthen regional development through the promotion of economic sectors, regional infrastructure and the establishment of large-scale manufacturing projects; remove barriers to free movement of labour, goods and services; and promote monetary cooperation. During this period, many African countries implemented highly interventionist and protectionist trade regimes, motivated by fiscal concern and the protection of domestic industry in the context of an import-substitution industrialization strategy (UNECA 2004; Adedeji 2002).

Unlike the economic integration schemes in other parts of the world, regional economic communities in Africa have not succeeded in accelerating growth or trade between member states (C. Johnson 1995; Lyakurwa et al. 1997). Intra-African exports as a proportion of the continent's total exports amounted to only 7.6 per cent in 2000 as against 17.2 per cent for Latin America, a region which has not been as active as Africa in the promotion of cooperation and integration (Elbadawi 1997; Longo and Sekkat 2004; Lyakurwa et al. 1997). Over the period 2004–06, intra-African exports represented 8.7 per cent of the region's total exports. Intra-African imports, on the other hand, represented 9.6 per cent of total imports (UNCTAD 2009). There have been no noticeable changes in the composition of trade that would suggest that integration has led to any significant structural change in the economies concerned (World Bank 1989; Yeats 1999).

Time and space do not permit a full exposé of the reasons why many regional integration efforts in Africa have failed. Among the factors accounting for the poor performance, however, are the following:

- lack of effective political leadership and the unwillingness of political elites to surrender sovereignty of macroeconomic policy-making to a regional authority (such as COMESA, SADC, etc.), with legal powers to enforce treaty obligations;

- serious institutional and bureaucratic challenges, including the lack of co-ordination and harmonization of policies and regulations at the regional level, and non-implementation of agreed decisions (Cheru 1989, 2002; UNCTAD 2009);
- lack of complementarities of production structures since member states export nearly similar primary products and import manufactured goods from their main trading partners, the EU and the US (UNCTAD 2009: 14; Alemayehu and Kibret 2002: 11);
- lack of a compensatory mechanism for gains and risks (Asante 1997; Lee 2003; UNCTAD 2009: 15), so that the weakest members suspect that stronger countries will take advantage of them;
- unwillingness by African governments to break colonial ties as the aid budget now constitutes a high percentage of the national budget, further adding to the lack of strong political commitment and macroeconomic instability (C. Johnson 1995: 213; Lyakurwa et al. 1997: 176);
- Africa's regional economic integration process is characterized by a multi-plicity of schemes and overlapping memberships and mandates. Of the fifty-three countries in Africa, twenty-seven are members of two regional groupings, eighteen belong to three, and one country is a member of four. Multiple arrangements and overlapping membership tend to lead to poor implementation of agreed goals and failure to harmonize policies among participating countries (UNECA 2004, 2008).

Moreover, early African integration efforts were further hampered by the dramatic collapse of African economies in the early 1980s, which necessitated a radical shift away from an inward-looking regional strategy and towards ration-alization and liberalization of trade regimes at the national level. The outward-oriented focus of structural adjustment implied closer integration of the continent into the world economy (Cheru 1989; Mkandawire and Soludo 1999). In short, the old concept of 'closed' regional integration advocated by the Lagos Plan of Action (LPA) in 1980 was to give way to the new concept of 'open' regional integration, which emphasized the liberalization of trade and investment regimes (Akopari 2008: 86; NEPAD 2001). This ideological shift was further consolidated with the conclusion of the Uruguay Round of trade negotiations, which gave birth to the World Trade Organization in 1996, and later, in 2001, the signing of the Cotonu agreement, which paved the way for the ACP–EU partnership agreement. It is in this political environment that the renewed interest in regional integration in Africa emerged after the 1990s. It is here that one must locate the ideological roots of the African Union (AU) and its development arm, the New Partnership for Africa's Development (NEPAD) (Ikome 2007; Adesina et al. 2006).

Revival of regionalism in Africa in the post-1990 period

As Africa entered the 1990s, a number of internal and external factors brought to the forefront the need to revive the regional integration agenda in continental policy discussions. The formation and strengthening of various regional blocs outside of Africa, such as the EU in Europe, the North America Free Trade Area (NAFTA) in North America and MERCOSUR in South America, the Free Trade Area of the Americas (FTAA) and the Asia Pacific Cooperation Agreement (APCA), convinced African leaders to accelerate the pace of African unity and integration more seriously if the continent was to avoid further marginalization (Cheru 2002; Ikome 2007).

The Abuja Treaty, signed at the OAU Summit in June 1991 with the aim of establishing an African Economic Community (AEC) by 2027, with a common currency, full mobility of factors of production, and free movement of goods and services among African countries, is indicative of Africa's resolve to become an important player in global economic relations. The implementation of the treaty was to be a six-stage process lasting thirty-four years (Sunmonu 2004: 63–71; African Union 2000). A decade later, in 2001, policy discussions on regional integration moved one step further with the transformation of the Organization of African Unity (OAU) into the African Union (AU), as well as the launch of a new economic blueprint for the continent – the New Partnership for Africa's Development (NEPAD) (African Union 2000; NEPAD 2001).

Interestingly, the renewed interest in regional integration in Africa has come from two opposite camps: local capitalist firms (for example, South African capital), comprador elites and institutions like the World Bank, which see enormous opportunities in more 'open' but tightly integrated regional markets (World Bank 1989, 2000); and some African governments and civil society organizations, which advocate 'strategic' regional integration as offering the possibility of greater national and continental leverage vis-à-vis both European and emerging-market economies and the need to protect local industries from a hostile international trading environment. Of these two perspectives, the first (that is, the neoliberal model of open integration) remains dominant in shaping the trajectory of Africa's economic integration. The World Bank (2000) in particular believes that regional integration should not become a means of salvaging failed import-substitution industrialization programmes; rather, the strategy should focus on creating open markets harmonized with ongoing structural adjustment programmes at the national level. This thinking, which assigns a greater role to market forces and a minimal role for the state, permeates the NEPAD framework (Adesina et al. 2006; Keet 2002).

NEPAD: a new beginning or another 'false start'?

In order to achieve the goals of economic growth and poverty eradication, NEPAD has identified three interrelated components. The first component provides the preconditions for sustainable development, which include: the peace, security, democracy, good governance initiative; the economic and corporate governance initiative; and the subregional and regional approaches to development (NEPAD 2001: 16). The second component provides NEPAD's sectoral priorities: bridging the infrastructure gap; the human resource development initiative; the agriculture and environment initiative; and the culture and science/technology initiative. The key focus has been on the provision of essential regional public goods (such as transport, energy, water, disease eradication, environmental protection and regional research capacity) (ibid.: ch. 7). The third component concerns the mobilization of resources, including capital flows and market access initiatives. The focus here has been on rationalizing the institutional framework for economic integration, by identifying common projects compatible with integrated country and regional development programmes, and on the harmonization of economic and investment policies and practices.

Within the framework offered by the NEPAD initiative, African regional economic communities (RECs) are designated as the key institutions for the implementation of NEPAD's programmes. These include: the Arab Maghreb Union (AMU), the Common Market for Eastern and Southern Africa (COMESA), the Economic Community of Central African States (ECCAS), the Economic Community of West African States (ECOWAS), the Southern African Development Community (SADC) and the Intergovernmental Authority on Development (IGAD). In order to ensure full implementation of the NEPAD programme of action, strengthening the capacities of regional and subregional institutions is considered a key priority.

What distinguishes NEPAD from the early articulation of regional integration by the Organization of African Unity? In terms of ideology and practice, regional integration in the post-structural adjustment decades of the 1980s and 1990s is conceived not as a counter-hegemonic project to deflect the ill-effects of globalization on weak and vulnerable African economies, but as a necessary vehicle to accelerate Africa's integration into the global economy. While the LPA of 1980 emphasized collective self-reliance and assigned a central role to the state in controlling and managing the commanding heights of the economy, NEPAD emphasizes a market-driven integration strategy, with the state playing a central role in creating a more market-friendly environment (OAU 1980; Taylor 2002b: 61–84; Adesina 2002: 17; Adejumobi 2003; Agubuzu 2004; Bond 2002).

Second, unlike the earlier African regional integration initiatives that stressed the need for African states to have unfettered sovereignty over domestic issues of governance, NEPAD, by establishing a politically intrusive peer review mechanism – the African Peer Review Mechanism (APRM) – recognizes the need to restrain politically unresponsive and unaccountable African governments (NEPAD 2003; Mohammed 2009; Mohiddin 2009). In so doing, the architects of NEPAD believe that reforming domestic institutions and processes of governance will increase the prospects for NEPAD's implementation. In short, the APRM is a means by which NEPAD hopes to lock otherwise unresponsive African governments into regionally agreed norms and standards, including those defined in regional economic initiatives.

The limits to NEPAD: an evaluation and the way forward

Whether NEPAD is an appropriate platform to deal effectively with the emerging giants or the traditional African partners in the West depends on its effectiveness in addressing the following issues: whether economic integration should be 'open' or 'closed'; whether integration should be state driven or market driven; and whether economic integration should precede political union or vice versa (Akopari 2008: 86). While many of its stated goals are well intentioned, the development vision and the economic measures that NEPAD promotes for the realization of its goals are flawed.

First, NEPAD subscribes too much to the neoliberal theories of liberalized trade as being a necessary and sufficient engine of growth, providing the necessary stimulus of international competition for domestic industrial development. While identifying a complex web of internal policy shortcomings, the framework offers little by way of remedial actions designed to tackle the negative consequences of exogenously imposed conditions, such as trade barriers and unnecessarily high vulnerability to market fluctuation, and the endless conditionality through which Africa's international relations are governed (Oxfam 2002; Mkandawire and Soludo 1999). Instead, NEPAD continues to advocate structural adjustment policy packages that have been used over the preceding two decades and overlooks the disastrous effects of those policies (Adesina et al. 2006: 33–61; Anyang' Nyongo'o et al. 2002). The architects of NEPAD failed to articulate the need for Africa to participate more 'strategically' and 'selectively' in the global economy.

Second, NEPAD ignores the central role of corporations, non-governmental organizations and actors in the informal economies in shaping the trajectory of regional development in Africa and the complex relationships between these non-state actors and contemporary globalization (Yeates 2007; Söderbaum and Taylor 2008; Shaw et al. 2007). Instead, it privileges an external partnership (that is, the G8–NEPAD dialogue) over the need to catalyse local actors and mobilize local resources to drive the African development agenda. Consistent with NEPAD's neoliberal philosophy of open markets and deregulated economy, it has focused a lot of energy on expanding partnerships with a number of countries and multilateral bodies, and has entered into bilateral investment and trade treaties with the EU, the United States and China (UNCTAD 2009: 12–13). The multiplicity of agreements and obligations with a multiplicity of international actors is hardly a sign that an authentic and unified African development agenda is on the horizon. Rather, the opposite is true: the reinforcement of the hostile external environment and the further weakening of African capacity to respond collectively from a well-informed position (Keet 2007; Adesina et al. 2006: 277).

Third, NEPAD has no clear strategy on how to mobilize resources within the continent to achieve its goals. Instead, it has prioritized foreign assistance and partnerships, in the context of the NEPAD–G8 dialogue, as the locomotive force for economic take-off in Africa (Adesina et al. 2006; Accra Declaration 2002). To meet its resource mobilization goal, NEPAD has emphasized the centrality of domestic governance reform as a means of reversing the negative image of Africa in the external world as a bad place to do business. In so doing, NEPAD hopes to garner greater ODA flows and debt relief from the Western powers, and attract foreign investment by assuring potential private investors that their long-term interests in Africa will be protected (Adejumobi and Olukoshi 2009: 8–9; Nnadozie 2009; IPA 2002).

While NEPAD's strategy of 'charming the donors' might have produced some 'empty pledges', the important task of catalysing the domestic private sector, commercial banks, savings associations, pension funds, national stock exchanges and diaspora groups to drive Africa's economic transformation has not been given the attention it deserves. For example, long before foreign capital started coming into China, domestic savings and remittances from abroad were the only sources of financing to kick-start the Chinese economy. To the extent that NEPAD relies heavily on donor ideas and resources to drive the African renaissance, this will only limit its capacity to pursue an independent, African-owned and African-driven development agenda.

To conclude, a careful reading of the recent history of economic development in the newly industrializing countries of East Asia (including China) points up the significant role of the state in national development. In these successful countries, the role of government has been to develop a mix of macroeconomic, structural and social policies to enable the producers to become more productive; to protect them from unfair competition from outside; to regulate and deregulate the market appropriately; and to organize research, finance and transport, so as to enhance the competitiveness and the productivity of local actors engaged in the global economy (Wade 1990; C. Kay 1989). The Asian countries also implemented far-reaching land reform programmes, invested heavily in human capital and infrastructure, and instituted redistributive social policies to address structural inequalities. The centrality of this argument is missing in the current NEPAD development framework. Finally, for African countries to be able to engage with the Asian giants on an equal footing, a new and transformed NEPAD, with a considerable authority and administrative capacity to present a unified African position vis-à-vis the G20, BRIC (Brazil, Russia, India and China), the USA and the European Union is an absolute necessity.

Countering Chinese and Indian 'imperialism': what is to be done?

African strategies to engage China and India from a stronger platform and a better-informed position will have to be implemented at multiple levels –

national, subregional and *continental* – and the formulation of such strategies must involve the full participation of domestic private sector actors, civil society organizations and other non-state actors (Acharya and Johnston 2007: 10). As Shaw and co-authors (2007), Söderbaum and Taylor (2008) and others have argued, regional development in Africa today is more a function of corporate strategies and complex and multifaceted informal processes and cross-border exchanges involving a multitude of non-state actors than the endless and ineffective intergovernmental negotiations and declarations. In the pages that follow, we identify the key aspects of national and regional strategies that African governments must put in place to create conditions for domestic private sector actors to succeed and, more importantly, to counter or minimize the ill-effects of Chinese and Indian penetration of African economies.

Action at the national level: engaging China and India

Properly functioning national economies are certainly a necessary condition for effective regional integration arrangements and for countering the negative effects of Chinese, Indian and European penetration of African economies. The first line of defence against external domination of African economies by China and India is the national context. This is essential since NEPAD, as it is currently formulated, does not give Africa sufficient leverage to break free from the Western-led neoliberal diktat (Adesina et al. 2006: 33–61) or the ability to negotiate with China and India from a position of strength. What happens at the national level, therefore, becomes more important. This requires the presence of a strong, effective and development-oriented state that is capable of articulating a national development vision that is 'empowering and liberating' in close consultation with broad societal actors at the national level (Rodrik 1994a; Sunkel 1993; Mkandawire 2001).

The alternative to the 'Washington Consensus' is what Charles Gore (2000) aptly refers to as 'strategic integration', and Cheru (2002) dubbed 'a guided embrace of globalization'. Terminology aside, the concept of 'strategic integration' draws its inspiration from East Asian developmentalism (Wade 1990; Rodrik 1994b; Evans 1998) and Latin American neo-structuralism (Sunkel 1993; ECLAC 1995; French-Davies 1988). The key assumption of 'strategic integration' is the belief that growth and industrialization in poor countries cannot be animated using a general blueprint as expounded by the advocates of neoliberal globalization. Instead, policy measures have to be adapted to initial conditions and the external environment, based on an analysis of the strengths, weaknesses, opportunities and threats that each country is confronted with. In addition, a policy of strategic integration must include appropriate macroeconomic, structural and social policies.

The central concern of 'strategic integration' is policy autonomy. As Martin Khor (2001: 37) has succinctly argued, 'developing countries must have the ability, freedom and flexibility to make strategic choices in finance, trade and investment policies, where they can decide on the rate and scope of liberalization and combine this appropriately with the defence of local firms and farms'. African countries need this policy space in order to exercise institutional innovations that would enable them to experiment with alternative development strategies that are pro-poor, and environmentally and socially sustainable. If any government does not have such freedom to define its own development path, it will never be able to give meaning to the concept of citizenship, democratic representation and the full realization of economic, social and cultural rights (Mkandawire 2001; UNCTAD 2007e). In this regard, there is a lot that African countries can learn from the successful development experiences of the newly industrializing countries of East Asia, which were able to pull millions of people out of poverty in a relatively short period of time (Wade 1994; Haggard 1994; Rodrik 1994b). Among measures that support 'strategic integration' are:

Pro-poor macroeconomic policy For economic growth to be pro-poor, maintaining a stable macroeconomic policy – reducing fiscal deficits and inflation – is critical for generating growth and for ensuring the full utilization of production capacity and encouraging the pace of domestic capital formation. This requires the adoption of a range of measures to improve the supply capabilities of the economy and specific sectors within it to assist domestic private agents to acquire increased international competitiveness. Such policies could include targeted subsidies, lower interest rates, protection of infant industries through import and export controls, maintaining exchange rate stability, and instituting managed liberalization as opposed to indiscriminate liberalization of the domestic economy. Monetary, trade and financial policies can also be supplemented with human resource and infrastructure development that supports the productivity of local enterprises (Wade 1994; Haggard 1994; Rodrik 1994b).

Moreover, the policies adopted should support 'strategic opening to world markets' as opposed to 'indiscriminate opening', as advocated by the apologists of neoliberal globalization. Such opening to external markets should be decided on the basis of how they support the national interest in terms of promoting economic growth and structural change (Wade 1994; Rodrik 1994b: 35–9; Mkandawire and Soludo 1999; Cheru 2002). It would involve a mix of sectorally neutral as well as selective policies. In other words, strategic integration involves deliberate state intervention to strengthen national political capacity in the face of a polarizing logic of world order, which undermines such capacity.

Creation of strategic alliances between governments and business sectors Successful developing countries have been those that have shaped a constructive, mutually supportive relationship between the public and private sectors, rather than those that opted either for the primacy of the market or the primacy of the state. Therefore, transformational change in Africa requires the simultaneous participation of the three major elements of society: the private sector, the developmental state and civil society (C. Johnson 1995; Cheru and Bradford 2005). The role of the development state is to articulate a common vision of national development objectives and to outline strategies on how these can be achieved through formal and informal ties with the private sector (Haggard 1994: 94). The state, in consultation with private sector actors, puts in place a range of policy measures designed to improve the supply capabilities of both private enterprises and publicly owned strategic industries to identify and acquire competitive advantages. Such measures might include: technology policy; financial policy; human resource development; physical infrastructure development; and industrial organization and competition policy. In short, the aim is to manage the state–market–society nexus as effectively as possible. This, of course, requires the enhancement of state capacity rather than state minimization.

Social policy and the distributional dimension Social policies need to be integrated into national economic policies, and this would in turn serve to legitimize the role of institutions/governments. The main focus for a more equitable and inclusive growth process is wide asset ownership and the expansion of productive employment. Important policies in this regard are: agrarian reform and rural development; investment in education and critical infrastructure; targeted social protection and social insurance; support for small and medium enterprises, particularly through financial policies; and broad-based human development through social provisioning of basic needs and health services (Haggard 1994: 91–3; Rodrik 1994b: 16; UNCTAD 2007d: 57–74). Similar policies were credited for the spectacular economic growth that the East Asian countries experienced in the early stages of their development. The main focus of the strategies has been to develop the domestic market adequately, and support key sectors so as to adopt competitive market-viable behaviour within an initially protective framework, before opening them up to external market forces. In other words, if the market is to function effectively, it requires elaborate state guidance.

In summary, engaging China and India from a position of strength is more an outcome of clear and deliberate strategic national policies than ineffective intergovernmental treaties drawn up by the African Union or NEPAD. Through well-crafted domestic policy measures, African states will be in a position to dictate the behaviour and activities of Chinese and Indian investors at the national level so that their investments contribute to Africa's long-term development. Formal intergovernmental regional initiatives should, therefore, be viewed as a complement to rather than a substitute for individual country-owned development strategies. To think otherwise is to repeat the mistakes of the past attempts at regional integration in Africa, in which rhetoric far outweighed actions at the national level. For example, countries like Angola and the Democratic Republic of Congo have lately managed to strike seemingly beneficial deals, with clauses safeguarding against capital flight and ensuring local employment (Vines and Campos, this volume; Vandaele 2009). National economic independence and regional integration and cooperation must be built brick by brick, and it will require actions at the national, subregional and continental levels.

Regional platforms for engaging China and India

In the preceding pages, we have argued that, as currently constituted, NEPAD will be a problematic prospect for engaging China and India from a position of strength. Many aspects of NEPAD have to be transformed to provide a stronger national and regionally coordinated basis for engaging China and India to enhance Africa's development. *What Africa needs at this critical juncture is a new or transformed NEPAD that will give the continent significant leverage to break free of the Western-led (or G8-dominated) neoliberal diktat.* Given the declining importance of the G8 in shaping global politics, part of the new NEPAD will have to deal with the transition from the G8–NEPAD dialogue (or what NEPAD calls partnership) to a more expanded dialogue with the G20, the future permanent members of an expanded UN Security Council (P14) (which might include Brazil, India, China, South Africa and Mexico) and a separate forum on BRIC–Africa dialogue, IBSA–Africa dialogue (India, Brazil and South Africa) and the next eleven (N-11) group of countries that form the second tier of emerging developing countries (Shaw et al. 2007 and Chapter 1, this volume; Cheru 2009; Bradford and Linn 2007). The economies of the BRIC countries, taken together, could be larger than those of the G7 by 2039. Thus, the BRICs have the potential to form a powerful economic bloc to the exclusion of the 'Group of Seven' (G7), of which Russia is a subordinate eighth member. The BRIC countries also play a critical role within the G20 coalition. Therefore, the new NEPAD needs to present a unified position vis-à-vis the G20, BRIC, IBSA and the N-11 countries.

Of course, the rise of the BRICs in itself does not guarantee the desired 'policy space' for African countries. National efforts in 'strategic integration', when complemented by strategic tactical alliance with the BRICs and other similar initiatives, can create the necessary space for African countries to manoeuvre and to chart their own path of development. It is our view that it is not too late to transform NEPAD into an entity capable of articulating an alternative African development agenda and a platform for engaging China and India from a position of strength. Among the key strategic platforms that a transformed NEPAD should put in place are the following:

A regional platform for harmonizing macroeconomic and investment policies
The legal framework and investment policies are crucial elements for creating a favourable climate for Chinese and Indian investment in Africa. At present,

however, macroeconomic, trade, investment and monetary and fiscal policies in Africa vary from country to country. To date, liberalization policies have been conceived as national programmes with national goals and using national financial policies and have thus lacked a regional dimension, and this has turned out to be a serious impediment to foreign direct investment (FDI). This policy disconnectness has been further exacerbated by the proliferation of bilateral trade and investment treaties over the past five years (Keet 2007, and Chapter 2, this volume). African governments must, therefore, take the lead to harmonize policies across the board and to improve conditions for a more active role by private agents across the frontiers of a subregion.

NEPAD so far has very weak and ineffective mechanisms for harmonizing national policies at a regional level; it lacks the legal authority to sanction countries that fail to do so. Its political status and authority remain poorly defined, and given its subordinate role to the African Union (AU), a final solution to the conflicting arrangement is unlikely to come soon. It is therefore imperative that NEPAD be transformed into an authority along the lines of the European Commission with full legal and administrative powers to coordinate and review the implementation of all policies and programmes. This would entail building a huge and competent bureaucracy, and an Africa-wide taxation system in order to cover NEPAD's operational costs. At present, the African Union and NEPAD jointly employ some 750 personnel compared to the 13,000 civil servants that the EU employs. Moreover, NEPAD ought to be able to ensure that regionally agreed policies and targets are integrated with national plans and budgets. In the absence of local budgetary contributions towards subregional programmes, it is very unlikely there will be a high degree of national ownership.

NEPAD should, therefore, have the authority to impose sanctions on member governments that fail to implement agreed-upon commitments. It should also have the authority to track the contributions of the various external partners, monitor compliance, track expenditures and evaluate the quality of output. Investment incentives must be complemented by ownership restrictions and performance requirements to protect national sovereignty and maximize benefits from FDI. Without a common regional framework, Chinese and Indian investors are likely to concentrate their investments in countries where the legal framework for a host of issues – from taxation to environmental and labour standards – is weak or non-existent.

A regional platform for coordinating strategic infrastructure development Transport costs are identified as the major impediment to doing business in Africa by private firms (World Bank 2009; Ndulu 2006; UNCTAD 2009: 37). Econometric estimates find that transport costs in Africa are 136 per cent higher than in other regions and that poor infrastructure accounts for only half of these costs (Limao and Venables 2001). Therefore, given Africa's infrastructural gap and its negative effect on regional integration, regional infrastructure projects are among the best candidates for regional FDI projects. China's involvement in infrastructure development is already filling this gap, but this growth is taking place without an agreed subregional framework. This is particularly important when it comes to infrastructures for corridor development, such as the Maputo, Benguela and Zambezi corridor projects.

The same applies to the development of subregional electricity grids, telecommunications and ports that are designed to serve several countries. When such ideas are agreed upon by governments in a particular subregion, NEPAD, in coordination with the respective regional economic community (REC), undertakes feasibility studies, prepares an assessment of the environmental impact of such projects, and puts out a call for tender, as well as taking action to mobilize the necessary financing for such projects, with each participating country as signatories to the project. In this regard, joint ventures and public–private partnerships with Indian and Chinese enterprises and SOEs could offer an investment model, given the complementarities of state and private sector actions combined with the enormity of the resources required to implement such projects (UNCTAD 2009: 99).

A regional framework for infrastructure development could also serve as a platform for mobilizing infrastructure finance, by attracting Chinese and Indian financial institutions into a co-financing arrangement with existing infrastructure finance mechanisms, such as the Africa Infrastructure Facility of the African Development Bank, the World Bank and the Development Bank of Southern Africa (DBSA). While the Industrial and Commercial Bank of China (ICBC) already owns a stake in the COMESA Trade and Development Bank, India's EXIM Bank has already opened up subregional offices in Addis Ababa, Dakar and Johannesburg.

A regional platform for investment and trade facilitation Good policies on their own do not drive investments. They must be complemented by good institutions and competent bureaucracies. One key dimension of investment promotion is the establishment of *effective national investment promotion agencies* (IPAs) and regular coordination among these at the regional level. Investment promotion must go beyond mere marketing of locations. Strong promotion services include 'one-stop' facilitation of administrative approvals; provision of specialized physical, customs-related and technical infrastructure; support for labour procurement and skills development; matchmaking between investors and local suppliers; and resolving administrative problems connected with various government bureaucracies (UNCTAD 2007a: 45). They could also include the provision of up-to-date and accurate information, and streamlining and simplifying approval procedures. Such measures are necessary prerequisites for attracting Chinese and Indian investments into Africa.

A subregional framework of investment promotion and trade facilitation developed in close consultation with national and subregional private sector associations (such as the chamber of commerce or manufacturers' associations) thus becomes the basis for directing Chinese and Indian private sector expansion into areas of national/subregional interest. Instituting a common regional framework reduces corruption and trade and investment diversion. It sets guidelines on technology and management skills transfers and on ways of ensuring backward and forward linkages in local economies. The end goal should be to promote domestic linkages. In some Asian countries, including China and India, governments have imposed joint-venture conditions to nurture domestic enterprises, and this experience should not be forgotten by NEPAD when developing a regional framework for investment promotion. There is no reason why NEPAD cannot replicate these successful experiments.

A strong regional financial sector Investment promotion and trade facilitation require the existence of a solid financial sector that can mobilize and lend resources to private agents. With few exceptions, capital market institutions to facilitate cross-border financial mobility are non-existent. In recent years, however, Nigerian banks in West Africa, and South African banks in southern Africa, have shown signs of vitality and are expanding their operations across their respective subregions. This is happening in spite of the absence of regional mechanisms to guide the development of a strong financial sector, with clear guidelines and incentives to help these banks link up with the largest financial institutions and sovereign funds, particularly institutions from China and India, through joint venture and asset acquisitions by African banks. The Industrial and Commercial Bank of China (ICBC), the Export-Import Bank of China, as well as the Export-Import Bank of India, are becoming major players in trade and investment financing in Africa. NEPAD could actively court and exert leverage on these banks to expand their lending facilities in Africa and to engage in co-financing of major regional infrastructure projects, as well as in national-specific projects in collaboration with national banks.

The South African banks are certainly the most powerful banks on the continent, and they want to expand their operations throughout the continent and beyond. For example, Standard Bank of South Africa sold 20 per cent of its share holdings to the Industrial and Commercial Bank of China (ICBC) for US$5.5 billion in 2008. Standard is now eyeing similar deals in India. South Africa's other two banks – Nedbank and Absa, majority owned by Old Mutual and Barclays of the UK – have similar ambitions. Nedbank has formed an alliance with Ecobank, a fast-growing institution that spans West Africa. FirstRand, the only South African bank without a substantial foreign shareholder, is also targeting India as an area of growth. It wants to dominate trade between India and Africa. Given the tremendous growth in trade between Asia and Africa, developing business in this area will require a bigger and more effective network of financial institutions in Africa (Burgis 2009: 2).

In West Africa, though not on the same scale as South African banks, Nigerian financial institutions are expanding their operations abroad, both inside and outside Africa, through mergers and acquisitions. According to UNCTAD (2009: 62), nine of the twenty largest banks in Africa are Nigerian. In 2008, Nigerian banks accounted for over 25 per cent of African bank capital and seven Nigerian banks are now part of the small number of African banks with capital of over US$1 billion. These emerging African financial institutions will affect intra-African investment significantly as they expand lending to domestic entrepreneurs, introduce new products, managerial and technological skills and financial networks across Africa, facilitating payment mechanisms between countries.

As more banks from South Africa, Nigeria and the Maghreb regions expand their operations, competition will intensify, and this will help reduce the cost of borrowing. NEPAD's role should be to facilitate links between African banks and their counterparts in China and India, and build institutional arrangements at the national and regional level for oversight and supervision of financial institutions, both African and foreign, so as not to repeat the mistake made in the Western world prior to the current bank-induced global financial crisis.

Regional rather than bilateral investment agreements We have indicated that the proliferation of bilateral trade and investment treaties with a multiplicity of trading partners is counterproductive and is likely to contribute to the fragmentation of the African continent. The Chinese government has already concluded such agreements with some twenty-four African governments, and the government of India is planning to do the same. In a recent report, UNCTAD (ibid.) recommended that African governments enter regional rather than bilateral investment agreements. UNCTAD suggested that the existing bilateral and investment treaties with a number of external partners need to be harmonized; ideally that African states renegotiate them as regional agreements under the umbrella of NEPAD. The preliminary discussion that took place in Kampala in late 2008 between COMESA, EAC and SADC about forming a Free Trade Area (FTA) among themselves so that they could negotiate an Economic Partnership Agreement (EPA) with the European Union as one regional bloc is very encouraging (Braude 2008). This was promoted after the member states of the East Africa Community (EAC) agreed to an interim EPA before the expiry of the Cotonou waiver at the end of 2007. While many critics see this move towards a regional EPA as contributing to the fragmentation of Africa and the end of African regional integration, a regional EPA is preferable to a bilateral arrangement.

A regional platform for coordinating research and human resource development Human resource development and strengthening research and analytical skills in many areas can be done on a regional basis – ranging from malaria eradication to trans-boundary issues such as environment and water resource management. There are still tremendous opportunities to scale up the quality of research in many sectors through strategic cooperation with China and India. The Chinese government currently offers training opportunities to up to ten thousand African students each year (FOCAC 2006). India is also expanding its training and technical assistance programme to African countries and currently provides 1,600 scholarships every year (Katti et al. 2009: 4). It is up to NEPAD to ensure that scholarships offered by Chinese and Indian authorities are in the critical skills areas identified by NEPAD and the member states. Chinese and Indian firms and universities may not necessarily possess the most advanced technology and expertise compared to Western firms and research institutions, but what they do possess may often be appropriate to the needs of many African countries.

Finally, knowledge of Africa on the part of the Chinese and Indians and African understanding of Chinese and Indian societies remain underdeveloped on both sides. From the African perspective, countering Chinese and Indian 'imperialism' requires significant investment by African governments on research and development on the politics, economics and foreign policies of these two emerging giants.

Conclusion

Clearly, policies and programmes to deal effectively with the economic imbalances between China, India and Africa have to be comprehensive, collectively created and implemented, and thus located within a very different paradigm. As it stands now, the entire NEPAD project is steeped in a neoliberal philosophy that relegates the state to playing a minimal role. It is focused on production, and less on distributive justice, leaving aside the rhetoric of poverty reduction. It recognizes the sovereignty of the market, but pays lip-service to the sovereignty of African nations and their citizens.

The high priests of neoliberalism, of which NEPAD is the stepchild, are wrong to suggest that dismantling trade barriers and removing government interference in the economy is a panacea for weak and poverty-stricken African countries. The recent global financial meltdown, and the unprecedented way in which Western governments intervened in the financial market, is a good reminder that an effective state is a prerequisite for a well-functioning market. The few instances of economic success in the developing world today have been countries that have marched to their own drummers and danced to their own music, and these are hardly poster children of neoliberalism. Such is the case of China, India and Vietnam – three important countries that have violated all the rules in the neoliberal guidebook, even while moving in a more market-oriented direction.

Moreover, these Asian countries also developed their domestic market adequately before they indiscriminately opened themselves up to external competition. They supported strategic industries, developed internal infrastructure, invested heavily in human capital and instituted radical land reform programmes, as well as social policies to address structural inequalities. They were able to succeed for the simple reason that the governments had the freedom to control basic economic policy. The NEPAD framework, unfortunately, does the opposite.

The alternative strategy of 'strategic integration' that we propose assigns the state a proactive role in providing strategic guidance on many fronts – from the way in which productive resources are organized to the mobilization of financial and human resources – in order to transform African economies, with the ultimate goal of eradicating poverty and creating the conditions for a just and democratic social order (Mkandawire 2001; Cheru 2002). Given the size of individual African markets and the nature of their economies, selective 'strategic engagement' with China, India and Africa's traditional Western trading partners through national and regional approaches is an economic and political imperative. Blind adherence to the much-discredited neoliberal globalization toolkit of the 'Washington Consensus' when dealing with China and India could only translate into what we would call *'neocolonialism by invitation'*.

It is not too late to transform NEPAD into a strong continental platform to negotiate effectively with Africa's external partners on an equal basis. For now, however, the challenge of harnessing China's and India's investment in Africa to support Africa's development agenda in a meaningful way rests at the national level. What individual African countries can do strategically, with regard to foreign direct investment flow, modalities of financing, profit reinvestment and repatriation, technology transfer and a host of other critical policy areas, can help determine to a considerable degree whether the outcome of this new engagement with the Asian giants is going to be beneficial to African countries or not. Although these capacities to engage external powers on the principle of equality are not always simple or easy to exercise, they have by no means completely disappeared from the national arena. As both China and India have developed their respective policy strategies towards Africa, there is no reason why African nations collectively cannot develop a policy on China and India that sets the ground rules for their engagements in the economic and political fields.

Notes

1 China, India and (South) Africa

1 The N-11, a notion introduced by Goldman Sachs in 2005, comprises: Bangladesh, Egypt, Indonesia, Iran, Korea, Mexico, Nigeria, Pakistan, Philippines, Turkey and Vietnam.

2 South–South strategic bases

1 Personal observation of a non-governmental African analyst invited on an official familiarization tour of China by the Chinese government.

2 This has already arisen in Zambia with trade union and community protests against Chinese company operations in the Mulungushi manganese mine on the Zambian copper belt.

3 Some analysts, however, such as Martin Khor of the Third World Network, argue that the USA needed to have the entire process stalemated over the SSMs (Special Safeguard Measures) and SP (Special Products) demands of the G33 in order to prevent the discussion of Washington's controversial subsidies to its cotton farmers.

3 India's African relations

1 Sanusha Naidu is research director of the China–Africa Project based with FAHAMU (www.fahamu.org) in South Africa.

2 In 2006 ONGC was the main contender for a deep-water oil block in Nigeria, but lost the contract to China National Offshore Oil Corporation (CNOOC), which acquired a 45 per cent stake in the offshore block after the Indian government obstructed the deal on the grounds that the investment was commercially unviable. Similarly in Angola, China eclipsed India's move to buy Shell's 50 per cent stake in Block 18 for approximately US\$620 million, by offering the Angolan government a US\$2 billion oil-backed concessional loan which outlined massive infrastructural projects in return for oil contracts.

3 *The Nation*, February 2007.

4 Some of the projects established under this initiative include US\$970,000 for the construction of the National Post Office in Burkina Faso, US\$30 million for rural electrification in Ghana, US\$4 million for a bicycle plant in Chad, US\$12 million for a tractor assembly plant in Mali and US\$15 million for potable water projects in Equatorial Guinea.

5 State Owned Telecommunications Consultants India Ltd (TCIL) will implement the network, which India will manage for five years before turning it over to the AU.

6 See meaindia.nic.in/interview/2006/01/25in01.htm.

4 China's development cooperation with Africa

1 *Long Live the Great Anti-Imperialist Unity of the Peoples of Asia and Africa* (a collection of Zhou Enlai's speeches, translated from the Chinese), Renmin, Beijing, 1964.

2 The Ministry of Foreign Affairs and the Party Literature Research Centre of the CPC Central Commitee (eds), *Selective Works of Zhou Enlai's Diplomacy*, Beijing Central Party Literature Publishing House, 1990, p. 406.

3 Interview with Xie Fei, official in charge of the Department of External Cultural Relations, Ministry of Culture, 8 January 2007.

4 See *People's Daily*, english.people daily.com.cn/dengxp/vol3/note/C0150. html.

5 ˌSee Ministry of Foreign Affairs, 'Premier Zhou Enlai's three tours of Asian and African countries', www.fmprc.gov.cn/eng/ziliao/3602/3604/t18001.htm.

6 www.focac.org/eng/wjjh/hywj/default.htm.

7 Working team of Sino-African educational exchanges and co-operations (eds), *Sino-African Educational Exchanges and Cooperations*, Beijing University Publishing House, 2005, pp. 44–54.

8 'The Symposium of Sino-African Sister Cities held in Beijing', Foreign Affairs Office of Wuhan Municipal Government website, www.whfao.gov.cn/data/2007/0531/article_1885.htm, accessed 23 May 2008.

9 *Programme of African with cultural fame in 2006*, China Culture website, www.chinaculture.org/cnstatic/doc/photo/sqzny.doc.

10 *Guide to apply for the African Culture Visitors Programme 2008*, China Culture website, www.chinaculture.org/gb/cn_news/2008-05/13/content_108575.htm; *Guide to apply for the African Culture Visitors Programme 2007,* www.chinaculture.org/gb/cn_news/2007-05/15/content_96307.html; *Programme of African with cultural fame in 2006*, www.chinaculture.org/cnstatic/doc/photo/sqzny.doc.

11 Angola, Equatorial Guinea, Eritrea, Cape Verde, Guinea Bissau, Ghana, Zimbabwe, Lesotho, Liberia, Rwanda, Malawi, Mozambique, Namibia, South Africa and Sierra Leone.

5 Engaging Africa

1 Prime Minister Manmohan Singh's speech at the India–Africa Forum Summit. The text of the speech is available on the website of the Ministry of External Affairs, Government of India, meaindia.nic.in/indiaafricasummit/africaframe.php?sec=ia,ss&act=1, accessed 13 December 2008.

2 The Ministry of External Affairs, Government of India, meaindia.nic.in/foreignrelations/sudan.pdf, accessed 13 December 2008.

3 See the prime minister's address at the Pravasi Bharatiya Divas, 7 January 2007, on the prime minister's official website, pmindia.nic.in/speech/content.asp?id=485, accessed 15 February 2009.

4 The figures are mainly from the CIA *World Factbook*; see www.cia.gov/library/publications/the-world-factbook/print/in.html, accessed 15 February 2009.

5 For details, check the ONGC website, www.ongcvidesh.com.

6 Prime minister's speech at the India–Africa Forum Summit, no. 2.

7 Dr Junbo, who is a lecturer at Fudan University in Shanghai, notes: 'Though China is not a colonialist, it is a successful capitalist in Africa … Of course, we cannot be blind to the possibility of China becoming a colonizing power some day. The day might come when African national economic systems have become so dependent on Chinese investments and export commodities that their domestic and foreign policies would in effect be decided by Beijing.'

8 The estimate is according to the CIA *World Factbook*, available on www.cia.gov/library/publications/the-world-factbook/geos/ch.html, accessed 21 April 2009.

9 'US helps Africa navies boost Gulf of Guinea security', Reuters India, 25 March 2009, available at in.reuters.com/article/oilRpt/dINL071018820090325, accessed 20 April 2009.

10 For India–Zimbabwe trade information, see the website of the Indian Ministry of Commerce at commerce.nic.in/trade/international_tpp_africa_13_zimbabwe.asp, accessed 13 February 2009.

6 Indian development cooperation with Africa

1 Evidenced by Indian Technical and Economic Cooperation (ITEC) and the Special Commonwealth African Assistance Programme (SCAAP).

2 pib.nic.in/archieve/lreleng/lyr2003/rjun2003/05062s_Final.pdf.

8 Chinese investment in African network industries

1 Ghemawat (2007: ch. 1) persuasively questions the utility of this notion, i.e.

'global' competitiveness, arguing that very few if any companies can truly attain it and that the search for it has led some major ones, such as Coca-Cola, astray.

2 The Chinese state offers a variety of inducements. Significant carrots include interest-subsidized loans to targeted resource investments; priority manufacturing and infrastructure products; development assistance packages to host-country governments with conditionalities linked to procurement from China; and risk assessment, control and investment assurance offered by the China Export Credit Insurance Corporation (OECD 2008: 85). In fairness such instruments are deployed by several countries. The Chinese government's use of the stick has diminished substantially in recent years, but it still requires a variety of approvals ranging from foreign exchange to various central and local government approval processes (ibid.: 84). Arguably these controls penalize the operations of Chinese MNCs, thus offsetting to some extent the positive inducements offered.

3 Underpinning this is overcapacity in a range of industrial sectors in China (OECD 2008: 80).

4 This discussion is an edited extract from Mthembu-Salter (forthcoming), based on his fieldwork in the DRC.

5 Based on various interviews with representatives of Sollateck, Solagen and Kenital Solar Power.

9 The role of India's private sector

1 The Confederation of Indian Industries (CII) is a non-profit non-governmental association that was established over a century ago and works closely with the government on policies affecting business and trade. It comprises India's foremost business associations with membership of over 7,500 business-related organizations in the private and public sector. The CII provides an interface between the international business community and Indian industry.

2 The EXIM Bank is a government-owned financial institution that was established in 1982 with the specific objective of 'financing, facilitating and promoting Indian foreign trade and thus globalizing Indian businesses' (EXIM Bank booklet, October 2008).

3 The term 'medical tourism' has gained currency and is used in common parlance with reference to the recent phenomenon whereby patients from countries with inadequate medical facilities seek healthcare beyond their state borders to obtain medical/surgical treatment at better-equipped hospitals and at comparatively cheaper rates than in their home countries.

10 Navigating Chinese textile networks

1 Until the early 1990s, it was indeed impossible for outsiders to participate in the highly protected market that the Nana-Benzes controlled. It was also nearly impossible to enter the textile market if the trader was not the offspring of an influential trading family – that is, if she lacked the necessary social and economic capital.

2 *Amina*, 453, February 2008, p. 66.

11 China and Africa

1 A typical example of what I term an 'indirect engagement' was the back-room role played by Chinese UN Ambassador Wang Guanyang in ensuring the initiation and sustainment of the Annan Plan for the deployment of peacekeeping forces in November 2006 in Addis Ababa, Ethiopia.

2 UNSC Resolution 1590 of 24 March 2005 established UNMIS to support the implementation of the Comprehensive Peace Agreement (CPA) signed by the government of Sudan and the Sudan People's Liberation Movement/Army on 9 June 2005; and to perform particular functions relating to humanitarian assistance and the protection and promotion of human rights. See www.un.org/Depts/dpko/missions/unmis.

3 *Forum on China–Africa Cooperation – Addis Ababa Action Plan (2004–2006)* and *China's African Policy*. See www.fmprc.

gov.cn/eng/zxxx/t230615.htm, accessed
10 September 2008.

4 See Davis (2007: 52–60).

5 For the French case, read D. Lecoutre
and A. Kambudzi Mupoki, 'Vers un divorce
entre Paris et le continent africain?', *Le
Monde diplomatique*, June 2006.

6 *The Africa–EU Strategic Partnership.
A Joint Africa–EU Strategy*, as adopted by
the Africa–EU Ministerial Troika Meeting
of 31 October 2007, Accra, Ghana.

12 The Darfur issue

1 CNN, 'Sudan faces threats of sanctions', 18 September 2004, available at www.
cnn.com/2004/WORLD/africa/09/18/sudan.
un.sanction, accessed 14 September 2005.

2 See 'Special feature: Darfur and the
politics of genocide', e-Africa, the electronic
journal of Africa, vol. 2, November 2004.

3 See Associated Press, 'Ad campaign
seeks to shame China into loosening ties
with Sudan', *International Herald Tribune*,
29 May 2007, available at www.iht.com/
articles/ap/2007/05/29/america/NA-GEN-
US-China-Sudan.php.

4 'Beijing boycott hot topic on
Capitol Hill', *USA Today*, available at www.
usatoday.com/sports/olympics/2007-06-
08-beijing-darfur-boycott_N.htm; see also
'Sudan: a hopeful wind of change', *The
Economist*, 10 May 2007.

5 'China–Sudan energy cooperation:
model of African foreign economic co-op',
21st Century Business Herald, 5 February
2007.

6 'CNPC in Sudan: model for south–
south cooperation', *China Daily*, special
supplement, 3 November 2006.

7 Ibid.

8 In Chapter I, Article 7 of the Charter
of the Untied Nations, the following article
was constituted: 'Nothing contained in
the present Charter shall authorize the
United Nations to intervene in matters
which are essentially within the domestic
jurisdiction of any state or shall require
the Members to submit such matters to
settlement under the present Charter.'

9 'Chinese envoy: sanctions wouldn't
help to resolve the Darfur issue'; see also

'Confrontation over Darfur "will lead us
nowhere"', *China Daily*, 27 July 2007.

10 'Sudan: a hopeful wind of change',
The Economist, 10 May 2007.

11 'General Martin Luther Agwai fears
Darfur force will fail', *The Times* (London),
26 October 2007.

13 China and Zambia

1 Personal communication from
Zhang Shudong, counsellor at the Chinese
embassy in Lusaka, 29 August 2007.

2 See 'Zambia: cold reception for
China's president', United Nations Office
for the Coordination of Humanitarian
Affairs – Integrated Regional Information
Networks (IRIN), 5 February 2007.

3 Personal communication from
Zhang Shudong, counsellor at the Chinese
embassy in Lusaka, 29 August 2007.

4 Personal communication from Ray-
ford Mbulu, president of the Mineworkers
Union of Zambia, 29 October 2007, in
Lusaka.

5 Personal communication from Syl-
vester Tembo, general secretary, Zambia
Congress of Trade Unions (ZCTU), Kitwe,
19 October 2007.

6 See www.chinamining.org (accessed
29 October 2007).

7 Ibid.

8 According to Rayford Mbulu, president of the Mineworkers Union of Zambia
(MUZ), 'Most Chinese-owned firms pay as
little as 200,000 kwacha, or 50 US dollars
per month.' Quoted in Isabel Chimangeni,
'TRADE-ZAMBIA: is China sneaking in
deals through the back door?', www.
ipsnews.net/news.asp?idnews=37107.

9 Personal communication from Rayford Mbulu at a workshop on 'The socio-
economic impact of Asian foreign direct
investment (FDI) in Zambia' organized by
the Friedrich Ebert Stiftung in conjunction with the Zambia Congress of Trade
Unions and held at Protea Hotel, Cairo
Road, Lusaka, 29/30 October 2007.

10 www.daily-mail.co.zm/media/news/
viewnews.cgi?category=1204793870.

11 Ibid.

12 Ibid.

14 African oil

1 SINOPEC is listed on the Shangai, New York and Hong Kong stock exchanges and was ranked 41st in the Forbes Global 2000 listing of international companies.

2 Brigadier-General (Retired) Arun Sahgal, Senior Fellow, United Service Institute, India.

3 This involved the sale of Shell's 50 per cent share of Oil Block 18 in 2004. While ONGC offered US$200 million for developing railways, CNPC offered US$2 billion for some projects, prompting Angola's state oil corporation, SONANGOL, to sell Shell's share of Oil Block 18 to the Chinese.

4 OMEL is an oil consortium made up of ONGC and Mittal Steel. The present status of this oil deal remains unclear.

5 An overseas investment arm of ONGC.

15 China and India in Angola

1 'Angolan leader addresses Opec summit in Saudi Arabia', Angola Press News Agency, 19 November 2007.

2 'PR defende cooperação constutiva com a China', *Jornal de Angola*, 21 June 2006.

3 'Aprovado acordo de crédito com Eximbank', *Jornal de Angola*, 29 November 2007.

4 Interview, Luanda, 3 October 2007.

5 'China's stock bubble can be traced to Angola', *Asia Times Online*, 27 March 2007.

6 'Hangxiao Steel Structure defends handling $4.4b Angola contracts', *Xinhua Online*, 27 March 2007.

7 'Governo nega mau uso dos créditos da China', Communication from the Ministry of Finance, *Jornal de Angola*, 18 October 2007.

8 Data provided by Banco Nacional de Angola (2007).

9 'Angola exporta 29.9 bilioes de dolares em petroleo', *Portugal News*, 8 August 2007.

10 'Angola em movimento', Agência para o Investimento e Comércio Externo de Portugal (AICEP), no. 35, August 2007.

11 'Milhares de empresarios chineses pretendem investir no pais', *Jornal de Angola*, 17 November 2007.

12 'Sinopec beats ONGC, gets Angola block', China Institute, University of Alberta, 14 July 2006.

13 'China buys more Angolan crude than Saudi', *International Herald Tribune*, 19 March 2006.

14 'Milhares de empresarios chineses pretendem investir no pais', *Jornal de Angola*, 17 November 2007.

15 José Eduardo dos Santos, OPEC summit, Riyadh, Saudi Arabia, 17 November 2007.

16 The price of 'openness'

1 Some of the BITs, however, have not yet been ratified. Information on BITs is available at www.unctad.org/Templates/Page.asp?intItemID=2344&lang=1.

Bibliography

Abbas, A. (2007) 'The United Nations, the African Union and the Darfur crisis: of apology and utopia', *Netherlands International Law Review*, pp. 415–40.

Abbas, H. (2007) 'African and Chinese CSOs discuss China in Africa', *Fahamu and Pambazuka News*, 306, 31 May, www.pambazuka.org.

Abramovici, P. (2004) 'United States: the new scramble for Africa', *Le Monde Diplomatique* (English edn), July, available at mondediplo.com/2004/07/07usinafrica, accessed 21 April 2009.

Accra Declaration (2002) 'Text of Accra Conference Declaration', adopted at the end of the joint CODESRIA–TWN–Africa conference on Africa's Development Challenges in the Millennium, Accra, 23–26 April, in Adesina et al. (2006).

Acharya, A. and A. I. Johnston (eds) (2007) *Crafting Cooperation: Regional international institutions in comparative perspectives*, New York: Cambridge University Press.

Adedeji, A. (2002) 'History and prospects for regional integration in Africa', Paper presented at the Third Meeting of the African Development Forum, Addis Ababa, 3–8 March.

Adejumobi, S. (2003) 'Globalization and Africa's development agenda: from the WTO to NEPAD', *Journal of Comparative Education and International Relations in Africa*, 5(1/2): 129–55.

Adejumobi, S. and A. Olukoshi (eds) (2009) *The African Union and New Strategies for Development in Africa*, Dakar: CODESRIA.

Adesina, O. J. (2002) *NEPAD and the Challenge of Africa's Development: Towards a political economy of a discourse*, Grahmastown: Rhodes University Press.

Adesina, O. J., Y. Graham and A. Olukoshi (2006) *Africa and Development: Challenges in the New Millennium, the NEPAD Debate*, Dakar, London and Pretoria: CODESRIA, Zed Books and UNISA Press.

AfDB/OECD (2008) *Senegal: Africa Economic Outlook*, 540, available at www.oecd.org/dataoecd/12/26/40578355.pdf.

Africa-Asia Confidential (2007) 'Strategic partnerships: India competes with China and the West in the rush for contracts, metals and energy', 1(2), available at www.africa-asia-confidential.com/article-preview/id/10/Strategic-partnerships, accessed 19 May 2009.

— (2009) 'Nigeria/Asia: from win-win to lose-lose', 2(6), available at www.africa-asia-confidential.com/article-preview/id/222/From-win-win-to-lose-lose, accessed 19 May 2009.

African Oil Journal (2007) 'Indian prime minister arrives in Nigeria to talk oil', 15 October, available at www.africanoiljournal.com, accessed 20 September 2008.

African Union (2000) *Constitutive Act of the African Union*, Adopted by the 36th Ordinary Session of the Assembly of Heads of State and Government, Lomé, Togo, 11 July.

— (2006a) Communiqué of the 66th Meeting of the Peace and Security Council PSC/AHG/Comm (LXVI) on the Situation in Darfur (the Sudan), 30 November 2006, Peace and Security Council, African Union, Addis Ababa.

— (2006b) 'Study on an African Union government: towards the United States of Africa', Addis Ababa.

— (2008) 'Chinese Foreign Minister Yang Jiechi signs MoU with Chairperson

Konare to strengthen technical and economic cooperation between China and the AU Commission', Press release no. 005/2008.

African Union Peace and Security Council (2006) Communiqué of the 66th Meeting of the Peace and Security Council PSCIAHG/Comm (LXVI) on the Situation in Darfur (Sudan), 30 November, African Union, Addis Ababa.

Agrawal, S. (2007) 'Emerging donors in international development assistance: the Indian case', Report prepared for IDRC, Partnership and Business Development Division, Ottawa: IDRC.

Agubuzu, L. (2004) 'Regional economic integration: a development paradigm for Africa', in B. Onimode (ed.), *African Development and Governance Strategies in the 21st Century: Looking back to move forward*, essays in honour of Adebayo Adedeji at seventy, London and Ijebu-Ode, Nigeria: Zed Books and ACDESS.

Ahmed, S. (2006) 'New economic opportunities beckon Indian industries', *Economic Times*, November.

Akopari, J. (2008) 'Dilemmas of regional integration and development in Africa', in J. Akokpari, A. Ndinga-Muvumba and T. Murithi (eds), *The Africa Union and Its Institutions*, South Africa: Centre for Conflict Resolution and Fanele Press, pp. 85–112.

Akyeampong, E. K. (2006) 'Race, identity and citizenship in Black Africa: the case of the Lebanese in Ghana', *Africa*, 76: 298–323.

Akyut, D. and A. Goldstein (2006) 'Developing country multinationals: South–South investment comes of age', Working Paper 257, OECD Development Centre, December.

Alden, C. (2005) 'China in Africa', *Survival*, 47(3), Autumn.

— (2007) *China in Africa*, London: Zed Books.

Alden, C. and A. Alves (2008) 'History and identity in the construction of China's Africa policy', *Review of African Political Economy*, 35(115): 43–58.

Alden, C. and M. Davies (2006) 'A profile of the operations of Chinese multinationals in Africa', *South African Journal of International Affairs*, 13(1): 83–96.

Alemayehu, G. (2002) *Finance and Trade in Africa: Macroeconomic response in the world economy context*, London: Palgrave Macmillan.

— (2006) 'The impact of China and India on African manufacturing, review of the relevant literature', Mimeo, Department of Economics and African Economic Research Consortium, Addis Ababa University, Nairobi.

Alemayehu, G. and H. Kibret (2002) 'Regional economic integration in Africa: a review of problems and prospects with a case study of COMESA', Draft report, Department of Economics, SOAS, University of London.

Alike, E. (2008) 'FG moves against oil firms over N2.5 trn investments', *Business Day*, 22 January, available at www.businessdayonline.com, accessed 20 September 2008.

Alves, P. (2007) 'India and South Africa: shifting priorities', *South African Journal of International Affairs*, 14(2): 95.

Amin, S. (1976) *Unequal Development*, Hassocks: Harvester Press.

Amnesty International (2006) *People's Republic of China: Sustaining conflict and human rights abuses*, London: Amnesty International.

Amosu, A. (2007) 'China in Africa: it's (still) the governance, stupid', *Foreign Policy in Focus*, Institute for Policy Studies, Washington, DC.

Ampiah, K. and S. Naidu (2008) *Crouching Tiger, Hidden Dragon? Africa and China*, Cape Town: Kwazulu Natal Press.

Ancharaz, V. (2009) 'David v. Goliath: Mauritius facing up to China', *European Jornal of Development Research*, 21(4): 622–43.

Anderson, J. E. (1979) 'A theoretical foundation for gravity equation', *American Economic Review*, 69(1): 106–16.

Anshan, L. (2007) 'China and Africa: policy and challenges', *China Security*, 3(3): 69ff.

Anyang' Nyong'o, P. (1990) *Regional Integration in Africa: Unfinished agenda*, Nairobi: Academy of Science.

Anyang' Nyong'o, P., A. Ghirmazion and L. Davinder (eds) (2002) *NEPAD: A new path?*, Nairobi: Heinrich Böll Foundation.

Apollo Hospital, Bangalore (2009) available at www.apollohospitalsbangalore.com/ News.htm, accessed 14 August 2009.

Apollo Hospitals, Indraprastha Apollo Hospitals, New Delhi (2009) available at www.indianhealthguru.com and www. apollohospdelhi.com/news, accessed 5 August 2009.

Arhin, K. (1979) *West African Traders in Ghana in the Nineteenth and Twentieth Centuries*, London: Longman.

Armijo, L. E. (ed.) (2007) 'The BRICs countries in the global system', *Asian Perspective*, 31(4): 1–224.

Aryeetey, E. (1994) 'Private investment under uncertainty in Ghana', *World Development*, 22(8): 1211–21.

Asante, S. K. B. (1997) *Regionalization and Africa's Development: Expectations, reality and challenges*, London: Macmillan.

Asian Times (2006) 'Curses, oil again!', 11 January, available at www.atimes. com/atimes/, accessed 11 July 2008.

Associated Press (2007a) 'China appoints special representative to focus on Darfur crisis', 10 May 2007.

— (2007b) 'China says strongly opposed to US House resolution on Darfur', *Sudan Tribune*, 30 May, available at www.sudantribune.com/ spip.php?page=imprimableandid_ article=22284.

Atnafu, Meskel G. (2007) 'The impact of China and India on African manufacturing exports on the third market', MSc thesis, Department of Economics, Addis Ababa University.

Ayee J. (2007) 'A decade of political leadership in Ghana', in K. Boafo-Arthur (ed.), *Ghana: One decade of the liberal state*, Dakar: Codresia.

Bajarachanya, R. (1999) In F. Flatters, 'Ghana's trade policies: tariff rate structure and revenues', available at qed.econ.queensu.ca/faculty/flatters/ writings/ff_ghana_tariffs.pdf, accessed 26 November 2008.

Bajpaee, C. (2008) 'The Indian elephant returns to Africa', *Asian Times* Online, 25 April, available at www.atimes.com/ atimes/South_Asia/JD25Df02.html, accessed 11 July 2008.

Baldauf, S. (2006) 'India steps up trade ties in Africa', *Christian Science Monitor*, 3 November, available at www.cs monitor.com/2006/1103/p04s01-wosc. html.

Bastholm, A. and P. Kragelund (2009) 'State-driven Chinese investments in Zambia: combining strategic interests and profits', in M. P. van Dijk (ed.), *The New Presence of China in Africa. The importance of increased Chinese trade, aid and investments for sub-Saharan Africa*, Amsterdam: Amsterdam University Press, pp. 117–41.

Baylies, C. and M. Szeftel (1992) 'The fall and rise of multi-party politics in Zambia', *Review of African Political Economy*, 19(54): 75–91.

Beeson, M. and S. Bell (2009) 'The G-20 and international economic governance: hegemony, collectivism or both?', *Global Governance*, 15(1): 67–86.

Beijing Review (2005) 'Cultural diplomacy', 48(48): 4.

Bellamy, A. J. (2005) 'Responsibility to protect or Trojan horse? The crisis in Darfur and humanitarian intervention after Iraq', *Ethics in International Affairs*, 19(2): 31–54.

Bennell, P. (1997) 'Foreign direct investment in Africa: rhetoric and reality', *SAIS Review*, 17(2): 127–39.

Berger, A. (2008) 'Sino-African bilateral investment treaties: implications for economic development', 12th EADI General Conference for Sustainable Development, Geneva.

Beri, R. (1999) 'India–South Africa defence cooperation: potential and prospects', *Strategic Analysis*, 23(10): 1681–1705.

— (2003) 'India's Africa policy in the post-cold war era: an assessment', *Strategic Analysis*, 27(2): 216–32.

— (2005) 'Africa's energy potential: prospects for India', *Strategic Analysis*, 29(3).

— (2007) 'China's rising profile in Africa', *China Report*, 43(3).

— (2008) 'India woos Africa', *IDSA Strategic Comments*, Institute for Defense Studies and Analysis, 19 March, www.idsa.in/publications/stratcomments/RuchitaBeri190308.htm, accessed 22 May 2009.

Bernal, L., R. Kaukab, S. Musungu and V. Yu (2004) 'South–South cooperation in the multilateral trading system: Cancun and beyond', Working Paper 21 (May), South Centre, Geneva.

Bernstein R. and R. H. Munro (1998) *The Coming Conflict with China*, New York: Vintage.

Besada, H., Y. Wang and J. Whalley (2008) 'China's growing economic activity in Africa', NBER Working Paper 14024.

Bing-Papoppoe, A. (2007) *Ghana and the APRM: A critical assessment*, Johannesburg: AfriMAP.

Birchall, J. (2006) 'Thousands die as world defines genocide', *Financial Times*, 6 July.

Black, D. (2008) 'Darfur's challenge to international society', Canadian International Council.

Blair, D. (2005) 'Oil-hungry China takes Sudan under its wings', *Daily Telegraph*, 23 April 23, available at www.telegraph.co.uk/news/main.jhtml?xml=/news/005/04/23/wsud23.xml.

Blakely, R. (2008) 'India takes on China over Africa's riches', *The Times*, 9 April, available at business.timesonline.co.uk, accessed 16 September 2008.

Boafo-Arthur, K. (2007) 'A decade of liberalism in perspective', in K. Boafo-Arthur (ed.), *Ghana: One decade of the liberal state*, Dakar: CODRESIA.

Bond, P. (ed.) (2002) *Fanon's Warning: A civil society reader on the New Partnership for Africa's Development*, Cape Town: Africa World Press.

Bonnett, D. (2005) 'India in Africa: an old partner, a new competitor', *Traders Journal*, 26, available at www.tradersafrica.com/PDF/traders_26_hires.pdf.

Boston Consulting Group (2006a) 'The new global challengers: how 100 top companies from rapidly developing economies are changing the world', May.

— (2006b) 'China's global challengers: strategic implications of China's outbound M&A', May.

Bradford, C. and J. Linn (2007) *Reforming Global Governance*, Washington, DC: Brookings Institution Press.

Braillard, P. and M.-R. Djalili (1986) *The Third World and International Relations*, Boulder, CO: Lynne Rienner.

Braude, W. (2008) 'SADC, COMESA, and the EAC: conflicting regional and trade agendas', IGD Occasional Paper no. 57, Midrand.

Brautigam, D. (1998) *Chinese Aid and African Development: Exporting green revolution*, London: Macmillan.

Brecher, M. (1959) *Nehru: A political biography*, Oxford: Oxford University Press.

Breslin, S. (2007) *China and the Global Political Economy*, London: Palgrave Macmillan.

Broadman, H. G. (2007) *Africa's Silk Road: China and India's new economic frontier*, Washington, DC: World Bank.

Brooks, P. and Ji Hye Shin (2006) 'China's influence in Africa: implications for the United States', *Backgrounder*, 1916, Heritage Foundation, Washington, DC, 22 February.

Buckley, P. J., L. J. Clegg, A. R. Cross, Xin Lui, H. Voss and Ping Zheng (2007) 'The determinants of Chinese outward foreign direct investment', *Journal of International Business Studies*, 38: 499–518.

Burdette, M. M. (1988) *Zambia. Between two worlds*, Boulder, CO: Westview Press.

Burgis, T. (2009) 'Tantalising chances in global strife', *Financial Times*, Special Report on South Africa, 17 July.

Burke, C., L. Corkin and N. Tay (2007) *China's Engagement of Africa: Preliminary scoping of African case studies. Angola, Ethiopia, Gabon, Uganda, South Africa, Zambia*, Centre for Chinese Studies, University of Stellenbosch.

Business Week (2007) 'China aims to clean up in solar power', 11 April.

CAADP (2001) 'Estimates of expenditures on the various components of the agricultural sector', NEPAD Framework Document, Midrand, South Africa.

— (2009) *CAADP: The Agriculture Unit and the food security declarations of the Africa Union: a progress report on key crops and initiatives*, CAADP, Midrand, available at www.caadp.net/library-reports.php, accessed 13 March 2009.

Cai, K. G. (2008) *The Political Economy of East Asia: Regional and national dimensions*, London: Palgrave Macmillan.

Campbell, H. (2008) 'China in Africa: challenging US global hegemony', *Third World Quarterly*, 29(1): 89–105.

Carey, K. et al. (2007) 'Sub-Saharan Africa: forging new trade links with Asia', Washington, DC: IMF, October.

Carlson, A. (2004) 'Helping to keep the peace (albeit reluctantly): China's recent stance on sovereignty and multilateral intervention', *Pacific Affairs*, 17(1): 9–27.

Centre for Chinese Studies (2007) 'China's engagement of Africa: preliminary scoping of Africa case studies', University of Stellenbosch.

Cera, V., R. Sandra and S. Sweta (2005) 'Crouching tiger, hidden dragon: what are the sequences of WTO entry for India's trade?', IMF Working Paper WP/05/101.

CFR (Council on Foreign Relations) (2007) *Africa–China–US Trilateral Dialogue*, Summary report.

Chan, C. (2007) 'China in Africa – spreading the wealth', *Canada–Asia Commentary*, March.

Chaturyedi, S. and S. K. Mohanty (2007) 'Trade and investment: trends and prospects', *South African Journal of International Affairs*, special issue: *India in Africa*, 14(2): 53–69.

Cheng, J. and Huangao Shi (2009) 'China's African policy in the post-cold war era', *Journal of Contemporary Asia*, 39(1): 87–115.

Cheru, F. (1989) *The Silent Revolution in Africa: Debt, Development and Democracy*, London: Zed Books.

— (2002) *African Renaissance: Roadmaps to the Challenge of Globalization*, London: Zed Books.

— (2009) 'Engaging the BRICs from a stronger platform: what prospects for "policy space" for African countries?', Paper presented at the Fifth International Conference on 'Hierarchy and power in the history of civilizations', Russian Academy of Sciences, Institute for African Studies and Russian State University, Moscow, 23–26 June.

Cheru, F. and C. Bradford (2005) *The Millennium Development Goals: Raising the resources to tackle world poverty*, London: Zed Books.

China Report (2007) 'White Paper on China's African policy', January 2006, *China Report*, 43(3).

CII (Confederation of Indian Industry) (2005) 'Ranbaxy Laboratories Limited', in *Success Models across Africa*, New Delhi, pp. 42–4.

CII-EXIM Bank (2009) *Trends in Indo-African Trade Relations*, Background paper on the 5th India–Africa Project Partnership Conclave, New Delhi, 22–24 March, pp. 10–13.

Clark, G. (1994) *Onions are My Husband: Survival and accumulation by West African market women*, Chicago, IL: University of Chicago Press.

Clinique Darne (2009) 'Fortis pledges to redefine healthcare in Mauritius', Press release, 25 March, available at www.cliniquedarne.com, accessed 1 August 2009.

Cockcroft, L. and R. C. Riddell (1991) *Foreign Direct Investment in Sub-Saharan Africa*, Washington, DC: International Economics Department, World Bank.

Cohen, H. (2008) 'In sub-Saharan Africa, security is overtaking development as Washington's top policy priority', *American Foreign Policy Interests*, 30: 2.

Confucius Institute Division (2007) *Global Distribution of Confucius Institutes*, 20 January, available at www.hanban.org-en-hanban/content.php.

Cooper, A. F. and A. Antkiewicz (eds) (2008) *Emerging Powers in Global Governance: Lessons from the Heiligendamm Dialogue Process*, Waterloo: WLU Press.

Cooper, A. F., A. Antkiewicz and T. M. Shaw (2007) 'Lessons from/for BRICSAM about South–North relations at the start of the 21st century: economic size trumps all else?', *International Studies Review*, 9(4): 673–89.

Cooper, F. (2002) *Africa since 1994: The past of the present*, Cambridge: Cambridge University Press.

Cooper, H. (2007) 'Darfur collides with Olympics, and China yields', *International Herald Tribune*, 12 April.

Coquery-Vidrovitch, C. (1997) *African Women: A modern history*, Boulder, CO: Westview Press.

Cordonnier, R. (1987) *Femmes africaines et commerce. Les revendeuses de tissu de la ville de Lomé (Togo)*, Paris: L'Harmattan.

Cornelissen, S., F. Cheru and T. M. Shaw (eds) (2010) *Africa and International Relations in the Twenty-first Century: Still challenging theory?*, London: Palgrave Macmillan.

Cornwell, R. (2005) 'Darfur killings not genocide, says UN group', *Independent*, 31 January.

Cullen, K. (2007) 'Genocide games', *Boston Globe*, 25 March.

Curtis, M. and C. Hickson (2005) 'Arming and alarming? Arms exports, peace and security', in L. Wild and D. Mephma, *The New Sinosphere*, p. 41.

Cutler, H., D. J. Berri and T. Ozawa (2003) 'Market recycling in labor-intensive goods, flying-geese style: an empirical analysis of East Asian exports to the US', *Journal of Asian Economics*, 14: 35–50.

Dalal, P. (2009), 'EXIM Bank's lines of credit: a shining example of South–South cooperation', *African Review*, Indo-African Chamber of Commerce and Industry (ASSOCHAM), May/June, pp. 60–64.

Dannreuther, R. (2003) 'Asian security and China's needs', *International Relations of the Asia Pacific*, 3.

Daojiong, Z. (2006) 'China's energy security: domestic and international issues', *Survival*, 48(1).

Darkwah, A. (2002) 'Going global: transnational female traders in an era of globalization', Unpublished thesis, University of Wisconsin-Madison.

Davies, M. (2008a) 'Beijing's friendship puts SA in key commercial spot', *Business Report*, 2(7), May.

— (2008b) 'China's developmental model comes to Africa', *Review of African Political Economy*, 35(1): 134–7.

Davis, P. (2007) 'China and the end of poverty in Africa: towards mutual benefit?', Joint report, Diakonia, Sweden, and the European Network on Debt and Development (Eurodad).

Dawar, N. and T. Frost (1999) 'Competing with giants', *Harvard Business Review*, March/April, pp. 119–29.

De Silva, L. (1983) 'The non-aligned movement: its economic organization and NIEO perspectives', in B. Palvic, R. Uranga, B. Cizelj and M. Svetlicic, *The Challenge of South–South Cooperation*, Boulder, CO: Westview Press.

De Waal, A. (2007) 'Darfur and the failure of the responsibility to protect', *International Affairs*, 83(6): 1039–54.

Denoon, D. B. H. (2007) *The Economic and Strategic Rise of China and India: Asian realignments after the 1997 financial crisis*, New York: Palgrave Macmillan.

DfID (2008) 'Managing aid effectively: lessons for China?', Workshop report, Beijing, 27/28 March, p. 2.

DfID/Centre for Chinese Studies (2006) 'China's interest in Africa's construction and infrastructure sectors', University of Stellenbosch.

Dikshit, S. (1989) *Nehru and Africa*, Nehru Centenary Volume, Oxford: Oxford University Press.

Dixon, R. (2006) 'Africans lash out at Chinese employees', *Los Angeles Times*, 6 October.

Dowling, M. and C. T. Cheang (2000) 'Shifting comparative advantage in Asia: new tests of the "flying geese" model', *Journal of Asian Economics*, 11: 443–63.

Downs, E. (2004) 'The Chinese energy security debate', *China Quarterly*, 177.

— (2007) 'The fact and fiction of Sino-African energy relations,' *China Security*, 3(3).

Draper, P. and P. Alves (2006) 'South Africa, China, and clothing conundrums', Evian Group Policy Brief, December.

Draper, P., M. Kalaba and P. Alves (2006) 'Deepening integration in SADC – South Africa's international trade diplomacy: implications for regional integration', in A. Bosl, W. Breytenbach, T. Hartzenberg, C. McCarthy and K. Schade, *Monitoring Regional Integration in Southern Africa Yearbook*, 6, Stellenbosch: tralac.

Duke, D., A. Jacobson and D. M. Kammen (2002) 'Photovoltaic module quality in the Kenyan solar home systems market', *Energy Policy*, 30: 477–99.

Dunn, K. C. and T. M. Shaw (eds) (2001) *Africa's Challenge to International Relations Theory*, London: Palgrave.

Dunning, J. H. (1973) 'The determinants of international production', *Oxford Economic Papers*, 25: 289–336.

— (2001) 'The Eclectic (OLI) paradigm of international production: past, present, and future', *International Journal of the Economics of Business*, 8(2): 173–90.

Dutta, S. (2007) 'Govt to set up energy security panel to counter China', *Times of India*, 7 March, available at www. timesofindia.com/Govt_to_set_up_ energy_security_panel_to_counter_ China/articleshow/1729102.com.

ECA (2006) *Assessing Regional Integration in Africa: Rationalizing regional economic communities*, Addis Ababa: Economic Commission for Africa.

ECLAC (1995) *Policies to Improve Linkages with the Global Economy*, Santiago: ECLAC.

Economic Times (2009) 'India set to sign pharma export deal with Nigeria', New Delhi, 3 August.

Economist (2007) *The World in 2008*.

— (2008a) 'The new colonialists: special report on China's thirst for resources', 15–21 March.

— (2008b) 'Africa: there is hope', 11–18 October, pp. 20, 33–6.

— (2008c) 'Dealing with sinophobia', 12 July.

— (2009) 'Buying farmland abroad: outsourcing's third wave', Special issue on India, 'Good news from India', 23 May.

Eichengreen, B., Y. Ree and Y. Tong (2004) 'The impact of China on the exports of other Asian countries', NBER Working Paper no. w1078, Cambridge, MA.

EIU (Economics Intelligence Unit) (2005) 'Sudan: country profile'.

— (2006) 'Sudan: country report', September.

Elbadawi, I. (1997) 'The impact of regional trade and monetary schemes on intra-sub-Saharan African trade', in A. Oyejide, I. Elbadawi and P. Collier (eds), *Regional Integration and Trade Liberalization in Sub-Saharan Africa*, vol. 1: *Framework, Issues and Methodological Perspectives*, London: Macmillan.

Embassy of India in Ethiopia (2006) *Market Survey on Bulk Drugs and Pharmaceutical Products*, HS no. 30, February, available at www.cii.in/ documents/ market_africa.pdf, accessed 23 July 2009.

— (2009) *List of Investments Approved by Indian Investors, July 1992–December 2008*, available at www.indianembassy. gov.et/FINAl_800by600/investment.xls, accessed 4 August 2009.

Enderwick, P. (2007) *Understanding Emerging Markets: China and India*, New York: Routledge.

Enfan, S. (ed.) (1997) *Memorabilia of Diplomacy of People's Republic of China*, vol. 1, Beijing: World Affairs Publishing House.

Engdahl, W. (2007) 'Darfur? It's the oil, stupid ...' *Financial Sense*, guest editorials, 21 May, available at www.financialsense.com/editorial/ engdahl/2007/0521.html.

Engineer, J. and A. Parimi (2008) 'Africa: great potential', in V. S. Sheth (ed.), *India–Africa Relations: Emerging policy and development perspective*, Delhi: Academic Excellence Press.

Ethiopian Embassy (2008) 'Ethiopia: Indian investment reaches US$1.8 billion – Tata International opens office in Addis', July, available at www.ethiopiaembassy.in/indian-investment-news.htm.

Evans, P. (1998) 'Transferable lessons? Re-examining the institutional prerequisites of East Asian economic policies', *Journal of Development Studies*, 34(6): 66–86.

EXIM Bank of India (2008) *Annual Report 2008–09: South–South cooperation and trade prospects*, New Delhi: EXIM Bank.

— (2009a) 'India to triple trade with Africa to US$100 billion in five years', *Indo-African Business*, Mumbai, November–January, pp. 5–10.

— (2009b) 'Bulk of EXIM Bank's LOCs goes to Africa, SME get preference', *Indo-African Business*, May–July, p. 34.

— (2009c) 'EXIM Bank's LOCs: expanding links in India–Africa Project partnership', *Indo-African Business*, February–April, p. 13.

— (2009d) *Impact of the Global Financial Crisis on sub-Saharan Africa*, 25 March, available at www.exim.gov/products/special/africa/pubs/impact_global_crisis_sub-saharan_africa_mar09.pdf, accessed 22 July 2009.

Eximius: Export Advantage (2008) Available at www.eximbankindia.com/exp-adv-mar09.pdf, accessed July 2008.

Falola, T. (1995) 'Gender, business, and space control: Yoruba market women and power', in B. House-Midamba and F. K. Ekechi (eds), *African Market Women and Economic Power: The role of women in African economic development*, Westport, CT: Greenwood.

Fandrych, S. (2007) 'China in Angola – sustainable reconstruction, calculated election campaign support or global interest politics?', Heft: Friedrich-Ebert-Stiftung.

FAO (2008) cited in *Factbox: Investing in Africa, Land and Agriculture*, Reuters, 7 October, available at farmlandgrab.org/2532, accessed 31 July 2009.

Farrow, M. and R. Farrow (2007) 'The Genocide Olympics', *Wall Street Journal*, 28 March.

Fenby, J. (2008) *The Penguin History of Modern China: The fall and rise of a great power 1850–2008*, London: Allen Lane.

Feus, T. (2008) Quoted in G. Mutume, 'Africa secures new southern partners', *Africa Renewal*, 22(3), available at un.org/ecosocdev/geninfo/afrec/vol22no3/223-africa-secures-new-partners.html.

FICCI (2007) Special Address by Honourable Minister Shri Murli Deora, 6/7 November, available at www.ficci.com, accessed 16 June 2008.

Financial Times (2007a) 'Solar power looks to brighter future', 14 September.

— (2007b) '"Wall of money" set to flow into Asian renewable energy', 29 October.

— (2008) 'The new scramble for Africa's resources', 28 January.

Finger, M. K. (n.d.) 'Evolving wave of competition in the international market: challenges for Africa through the rise of China and India', Mimeo, Economic Research and Statistics Division, WTO.

FOCAC (Forum on China–Africa Cooperation) (2003) 'Let us build on our past achievements and promote China–Africa friendly cooperation on all fronts', Speech by HE Mr Wen Jiabao, Premier of the State Council of the People's Republic of China, at the opening ceremony of the 2nd Ministerial Conference of the Forum on China–Africa Cooperation, Addis Ababa, 15 December, *Documents and Speeches*, pp. 29–46.

— (2006) 'Programme for China–Africa cooperation in economic and social development', Ministry of Foreign Affairs, People's Republic of China, Beijing, 6 October.

Fortune (2009) *Indian Company to Start Tendaho Sugar Factory*, Addis Ababa, 29 June, available at www.ethiopiaembassy.in/news/panel/frmNews.aspx, accessed 1 August 2009.

Frank, A. G. (1967) *Capitalism and Underdevelopment in Latin America*, New York: Monthly Review Press.

Frazer, A. and J. Lungu (2006) *For Whom the Windfalls?*, Lusaka: Civil Society Trade Network Zambia (CSTNZ).

French-Davies, R. (1988) 'An outline of a neo-structuralist approach', *CEPAL Review*, 34: 371.

Frynas, J. G. (2004) 'The oil boom in Equatorial Guinea', *African Affairs*, 103(413): 527.

Frynas, J. G. and M. Paulo (2007) 'A new scramble for African oil? Historical, political and business perspectives', *African Affairs*, 106(423): 229–51.

G77 and China (2003) *Ministerial Declaration of the Group of 77 and China on the Fifth WTO Ministerial Conference at Cancun, Mexico, 10–14 September 2003*, WT/L/536, 25 August.

Gadir, H. E. A. (2007) Paper presented at the international conference on 'China–Sudan Relations', Beijing, 26 July.

Ganguly, S. (ed.) (2003a) *India as an Emerging Power*, London: Frank Cass.

— (2003b) 'India's foreign policy grows up', *World Policy Journal*, 20(4): 41–7.

— (2007) *The ONGC: Charting a New Course?*, Report prepared in conjunction with an energy study sponsored by Japan Petroleum Energy Centre and the James A. Baker III Institute for Public Policy, Rice University, Houston, Texas, March.

— (2008) 'India 2007: a symposium on the year that was', Seminar no. 581, January.

Garlick, P. C. (1971) *African Traders and Economic Development in Ghana*, Oxford: Clarendon Press.

Gerlich, G. (2005) 'Wax prints im socio-kulturellen Kontext Ghanas', Working Paper no. 54, Institute für Ethnologie und Afrikastudien, Johannes Gutenberg-Universität, Mainz.

Gerth, H. H. and C. Wright Mills (1948) *From Max Weber: Essays in Sociology*, London: Routledge.

Ghemawat, P. (2007) *Redefining Global Strategy: Crossing borders in a world where differences still matter*, Harvard Business School Publishing.

Gibbon, P. (2002) 'Present-day capitalism, the New International Trade Regime and Africa', *Review of African Political Economy*, 29(91): 95–112.

Gill, B. and J. Reilly (2000) 'Sovereignty, intervention and peacekeeping: the view from Beijing', *Survival*, 42: 41–59.

Gill, B., Chin-hao Huang and J. S. Morrison (2006) *China's Expanding Role in Africa: Implications for the United States*, Washington, DC: Center for Strategic and International Affairs.

Global Insight (2007) *Indian and Chinese Companies Dominate Mini Licensing Round in Nigeria*, available at www.globalinsight.com/SDA/SDADetail5934.htm, accessed 16 June 2008.

Goldstein, A. (2007) *Multinational Companies from Emerging Economies*, London: Palgrave Macmillan.

Goldstein, A., N. Pinaud, H. Reisen and X. Chen (2006) 'The rise of China and India: what's in it for Africa?', Paris: OECD.

Goodman, P. S. (2004) 'China invests heavily in Sudan's oil industry', *Washington Post*, 23 December, available at www.washingtonpost.com/ac2/wp-dyn/A21143-2004Dec22.

Gopal, S. and U. Iyengar (eds) (2002) *The Essential Writings of Jawaharlal Nehru*, Oxford: Oxford University Press.

Gore, C. (2000) 'The rise and fall of the Washington Consensus as a paradigm for developing countries', *World Development*, 28(3): 789–804.

Government of India (1949) *Independence and After: A Collection of the More Important Speeches of Jawaharlal Nehru from September 1946 to May 1949*, Public Division, Delhi.

— (1993) 'Annual report', Ministry of External Affairs, New Delhi.

— (2001) *Report of the High Level Committee on the Indian Diaspora*, available at indiandiaspora.nic.in/diaspora.pdf./chapter7.pdf., accessed 13 December 2008.

Guest, R. (2004) *The Shackled Continent: Africa's past, present, and future*, Oxford: Macmillan.

Guijin, L. (2007) Speech by Ambassador

Liu Guijin, Special Representative of the Chinese Government for African Affairs, at the conference 'Partners in competition? EU, Africa and China', 28 June.

Gulfnews (2008) 'India's crude imports rise 9.1 per cent in 2007–08', 3 May, available at archive.gulfnews.com/articles/08/05/03, accessed 17 September 2008.

Haggard, S. (1990) *Pathways to the Periphery: The politics of growth in the newly industrialized countries*, Ithaca, NY: Cornell University Press.

— (1994) 'Politics and institutions in the World Bank's East Asia', in R. Wade et al. (eds), *Miracle or Design? Lessons from the East Asian experience*, Washington, DC: Overseas Development Council, pp. 81–104.

Hanson, S. (2008) 'China, Africa, and oil', Council on Foreign Relations, Washington, DC.

Hare, P. (2007) 'China and Zambia: the all-weather friendship hits stormy weather', China Brief 26-4-2007, Jamestown Foundation, Washington, DC.

Harsh, E. (2009) 'Senegal to fight hunger, modernize farming', *Africa Recovery*, 17(1): 14, available at www.un.org/ecosocdev/geninfo/afrec//vol 17no1/171food2.htm.

Hart, M. (2008) 'Soaring Asian trade benefits Africa', *Business Day*, 21 August, available at www.businessdayonline.com, accessed 17 September 2008.

Haselock, S. (2008) 'Pessimism hangs over Darfur', *New African*, August/September, p. 42.

Hate, V. (2008) 'India in Africa: moving beyond oil', *Africa Policy Forum*, 7 July, available at forums.csis.org/africa/?p=144, accessed 20 September 2008.

Heilbrunn, J. R. (1993) 'Social origins of national conferences in Benin and Togo', *Journal of Modern African Studies*, 31(2): 277–99.

Heine, J. (2006) 'On the manner of practising the new diplomacy', Working Paper no. 11, CIGI, Waterloo, October.

Herbst, J. (2005) 'Africa and the challenge of globalization', Presented at the Conference on Globalization and Economic Success: Policy Options for Africa, Singapore, 7/8 November.

Hilsum, L. (2005) 'We love China', *Granta, the View from Africa*, 92.

Hindu, The (2004) 'Apollo to assist Hygeia', 19 October.

Hindu Business Line (2008a) 'Karturi launches farm operations in Ethiopia', 24 October.

— (2008b) 'Technology, agriculture high on India–Africa meet agenda', 15 March.

Hodges, T. (2001) *Angola from Afro-Stalinism to Petro-diamond Capitalism*, Oxford: James Currey.

Holsag, J. (2007) 'China's diplomatic victory in Darfur', *BICCS Asia Paper*, 2(4), 15 August.

House-Midamba, B. and F. K. Ekechi (eds) (1995) *African Market Women and Economic Power: The role of women in African economic development*, Westport, CT: Greenwood.

Huang Meibo (2007) 'The mechanism of China's foreign aid: status and trend', *International Economic Cooperation*, 6: 4–11.

Hughes, C. (2006) *Chinese Nationalism in a Global Era*, London: Routledge.

Human Rights Watch (2003) *Sudan, Oil, and Human Rights*, New York: Human Rights Watch.

Humphrey, J. and D. Messner (2006) 'China and India as emerging governance actors: challenges for developing and developed countries', *IDS Bulletin*, 37(1): 107–14.

Hunter, A. (2006), *China: Soft power and cultural influence*, available at www.ipra2006.com/papers/CRPBC/ChinaSoftPowerAndCulturalInfluence.doc.

Hutchful, E. (2002) *Ghana's Adjustment Experience. The paradox of reform*, UNDRISD.

IFC (International Finance Corporation) (2009) *Agribusiness in Africa*, available at www.ifc.org/ifcext/africa.nsf/Content/Agribusiness, accessed 21 July 2009.

Ikome, F. (2007) *From the Lagos Plan of Action to the New Partnership for Africa's Development*, Midrand: Institute for Global Dialogue.

Imitira, J. (2008) Economic Regulation Department, Energy Regulatory Commission, personal interview, 12 August.

India–Africa Forum Summit (2008) *Delhi Declaration*, 8/9 April.

Indian National Congress (1976) *India and the African Liberation Struggle*, New Delhi.

Insoll, T. (2003) *The Archaeology of Islam in Sub-Saharan Africa*, Cambridge: Cambridge University Press.

International Crisis Group (2002) *God, Oil and Country: Changing the logic of war in the Sudan*, Brussels: International Crisis Group.

IPA (International Peace Academy) (2002) *NEPAD: African initiative, new partnership?*, IPA Workshop Report, New York.

IRIN News (2006) 'AFRICA: China's great leap into the continent', March, available at www.irinnews.org, accessed 30 May 2007.

Jacobson, A. and D. Kammen (2005) *The Value of Vigilance: Evaluating product quality in the Kenyan solar photovoltaic industry*, Berkeley: University of California.

Jakobson, L. and Z. Daojiong (2006) 'China and the worldwide search for oil security', *Asia-Pacific Review*, 13(2).

Jenkins, R. and C. Edwards (2005) 'The effect of China and India's growth and trade liberalization on poverty in Africa', Final report, African Economic Research Consortium, Nairobi.

Jobelius, M. (2007) 'New powers for global change? Challenges for the development cooperation: the case of India', *Dialogue on Globalization*, Briefing Paper, Friedrich Ebert Stiftung, Berlin, 5 March.

Johnson, C. (1995) 'Political institutions and economic performance: the government–business relationship in Japan, South Korea, and Taiwan', in F. Deyo (ed.), *The Political Economy of the New Asian Industrialization*, Ithaca, NY: Cornell University Press.

Johnson, H. (1976) 'The New International Economic Order', Selected Papers no. 49, Graduate School of Business, University of Chicago, available at www.chicagobooth.edu/factulty/selected papers/sp49.pdf, accessed 20 April 2009.

Junbo, J. (2007) 'China in Africa: from capitalism to colonialism', *Asia Times* (online), 5 January, available at www.atimes.com/atimes/China/IA05Ad01.html, accessed 13 February 2009.

Kajee, A. (2004) 'Nepad's APRM: a progress report, practical limitations and challenges', *South African Yearbook of International Affairs 2003/04*, SAIIA, Johannesburg.

Kanter, J. (2009) 'Bio fuels and "land grabs" in poor nations', Green Inc, reprinted *New York Times*, 13 August, available at greeninc.blogs.nytimes.com/2009/06/12/biofuels-and-land-grabs-in-poor-nations.

Kaplinsky, R. and D. Messner (eds) (2008) 'Special issue: the impact of Asian drivers on the developing world', *World Development*, 36(2): 197–340.

Kaplinsky, R., D. McCormic and M. Morris (2006) 'The impact of China on sub Saharan Africa', Asian Drivers Background Papers, Institute of Development Studies, Brighton.

Kasahara, S. (2004) 'The flying geese paradigm: a critical study of its application to East Asian regional development', United Nations Conference on Trade and Development, Geneva.

Katti, V., T. Chahoud and A. Kaushik (2009) 'India's development cooperation: opportunities and challenges for international development cooperation', Briefing Paper 3/2009, German Development Institute.

Kaunda, K. (1968) 'Zambia's economic reforms', *African Affairs*, 67(4): 295–304.

Kay, C. (1989) *Latin American Theories of Development and Underdevelopment*, London: Routledge.

Kay, G. (1975) *Development and Underde-*

velopment: A Marxist analysis, London: Macmillan.

KBL (Kirloskar Brothers Ltd) (2008) 'Kirloskar pumping solutions unleash green revolution in Senegal', Company leaflet.

— (n.d.) Kirolskar Pumps and Valves in Sugar Industry, available at web.kbl. co.in/kbl_internet/images/downloads/sectoralleaflets/Sugar.pdf, accessed 3 August 2009.

Keet, D. (2002) 'The New Partnership for Africa's Development: unity and integration within Africa? Or integration of Africa into the global economy?', IGD Occasional Paper no. 35, Midrand.

— (2006) 'South–South strategic challenges to the global economic system', Occasional Paper no. 53, Johannesburg: Institute for Global Dialogue.

— (2007) Economic Partnership Agreements (EPAs): Response to the EU offensive against ACP development regions, Amsterdam: Transnational Institute.

Kenya Ministry of Energy (2004) Sessional Paper no. 4 of 2004 on Energy, Nairobi: Government Printers.

Khor, M. (2001) Rethinking Globalization, London: Zed Books.

— (2009) Statement at the United Nations General Assembly Extraordinary Thematic Dialogue on the World Financial and Economic Crisis and Its Impact on Development, South Centre, New York, 25 March, available at www.south centre.org/index.php?option, accessed 10 April 2009.

King, K. (2006) 'China in Africa: A new lens on development cooperation, with a focus on human resources', Conference paper, Comparative Culture and Education in African and Asian Societies.

Kitissou, M. (ed.) (2007) Africa in China's Global Strategy, London: Adonis & Abbey.

Klare, M. and D. Volman (2006) 'America, China and the scramble for Africa's oil', Review of African Political Economy, 33(108): 297–309.

Kojima, K. (2000) 'The flying-geese model of Asian economic development: origin, theoretical extensions and regional policy implications', Journal of Asian Economics, 11: 375–401.

Konings, P. (2007) 'China and Africa in the era of neo-liberal globalisation', Codesria Bulletin, (1/2): 17–22.

Koyi, G. and A. Muneku (2007) 'The social and economic impact of Asian FDI in Zambia: a case of Chinese and Indian investments in Zambia, 1997–2007', Study commissioned by Friedrich Ebert Stiftung, Lusaka.

Kragelund, P. (2008) 'The return of non-DAC donors to Africa: new prospects for African development', Development Policy Review, 26(5): 555–84.

— (2009) 'Part of the disease or part of the cure? Chinese investments in the Zambian mining and construction sectors', European Journal of Development Research, 21(4): 644–61.

Kriger, C. E. (2006) Cloth in West African History, Lanham, MD: AltaMira Press.

Kristoff, N. D. (2006) 'China and Sudan, blood and oil', New York Times, 23 April.

Kumaraswamy, P. (2007) 'India's energy cooperation with China: the slippery side', China Report, 43(3).

Kurlantzick, J. (2007) Charm Offensive: How China's soft power is transforming the world, New Haven, CT: Yale University Press.

Kwami, A. (1995) 'Textile designs in Ghana: extracts from a report', in J. Picton (ed.), The Art of African Textiles: Technology, tradition, and lurex, London: Barbican Art Gallery in association with Lund Humphries.

Large, D. (2007) 'Arms, oil and Darfur: the evolution of relations between China and Sudan', Sudan Issue Brief, Small Arms Survey, 7, July.

— (2008a) 'China's role in the mediation and resolution of conflicts in Africa', Centre for Humanitarian Dialogue.

— (2008b) 'Beyond "Dragon in the Bush": the study of China–Africa relations', African Affairs, 107(426): 45–61.

— (2008c) 'China and the contradictions of "non-interference" in Sudan', Review of African Political Economy, 35(115).

Larmer, M. (2005) 'Reaction and resistance to neo-liberalism in Zambia', *Review of African Political Economy*, 32(103): 29–45.

Le Pere, G. (ed.) (2006) *China in Africa: Mercantilist predator or partner in development?*, Midrand: IGD.

Le Pere, G. and G. Shelton (eds) (2007) *China, Africa and South Africa: South–South cooperation in a global era*, Midrand: IGD.

Lee, M. (2003) *The Political Economy of Regionalism in Southern Africa*, Boulder, CO: Lynne Rienner.

Lee, M. C. et al. (eds) (2007) *China in Africa*, Current African Issues no. 33, Uppsala: Nordic Africa Institute, June.

Levkowitz, L., M. McLellan Ross and J. R. Warner (2009) 'The 88 Queensway Group: a case study in Chinese investors' operations in Angola and beyond', Washington, DC: US–China Economic & Security Review Commission.

Lewis, A. (1954) 'Economic development with unlimited supplies of labour', *The Manchester School*, 21: 139–91.

Li, A. (2007) 'China and Africa: policy and challenges', *China Security*, 3(3).

Li Yuliang (1999) 'China's foreign aid in the trend of international economic integration', *Journal of Beijing International Studies University*, 91(4): 91–5.

Liang, W. (2008) 'New Africa policy: China's quest for oil and influence', in G. Sujian and J.-M. F. Blanchard (eds), *Harmonious World and China's Foreign Policy*, Lexington, KY: Rowman & Littlefield, pp. 15–32.

Limao N. and A. J. Venables (2001) 'Infrastructure, geographical disadvantages and transport costs', *World Bank Economic Review*, 15(3): 451–79.

Liu, H. (2006) 'Status quo of Sino-African cultural relations', in *Confidential Report of Chinese Academy of Social Sciences*, Beijing: Chinese Academy of Social Sciences, pp. 63–71.

Longo, R. and K. Sekkat (2004) 'Economic obstacles to expanding intra-Africa trade', *World Development*, 32(8): 1309–21.

Luke-Boone, R. (2001) *African Fabrics*, Iola, WI: Krause Publications.

Lungu, J. (2008) 'Copper mining agreements in Zambia: renegotiation or law reform?', *Review of African Political Economy*, 35(3): 403–15.

Lungu, J. and C. Mulenga (2005) *Corporate Social Responsibility Practices in the Extractive Industry in Zambia*, Ndola: Catholic Commission for Justice Development and Peace (CCJDP), Development Education Project (DECOP) and Zambia Congress of Trade Unions (ZCTU).

Lutz, J. M. (1987) 'Shifting comparative advantage, the NICs and the developing countries', *International Trade Journal*, 1(4): 339–58.

Lv Xuejian (1989) 'Explore various ways of foreign aid to consolidate achievements', *International Economic Cooperation*, 2: 4–11.

Lyakurwa, W., A. McKay, N. Ng'eno and W. Kennes (1997) 'Regional integration in sub-Saharan Africa: a review of experiences and issues', in A. Oyejide, I. Elbadawi and P. Collier (eds), *Regional Integration and Trade Liberalization in Sub-Saharan Africa*, vol. 1: *Framework, Issues and Methodological Perspectives*, London: Macmillan.

Lyman, P. (2005) 'China's rising role in Africa', Presentation to the US–China Commission, 21 July, available at www.cfr.org/publications/8436, accessed 2 August 2006.

Madan, T. (2006) 'India', *Energy Security Series*, Brookings Foreign Policy Series, Brookings Institute, Washington, DC, November, available at www.brookings.edu/fp/research/energy/2006india.htm.

Mahmood, A. (2001) 'Shifting export specialization and the competitiveness of the Malaysian manufacturing: trends and analyses', *International Trade Journal*, XV(2): 187–219.

Mann, P. (2000) *India's Foreign Policy in the Post-Cold War Era*, New Delhi: Harman.

Martin, W. G. (2008) 'Africa's futures: from North–South to East–South?', *Third World Quarterly*, 29(2): 339–56.

Masters, L. (2008) 'The G8 and the Heiligendamm Dialogue Process: institutionalising the "Outreach 5"', no. 85, Midrand: IGD, November.

Mathews, K. (1997) 'A multifaceted relationship: a synoptic view', *Africa Quarterly*, 37(1/2): 1.

Matthews, J. (2006) *Strategizing, Disequilibrium and Profit*, Palo Alto, CA: Stanford University Press.

Matthews, S. (2004) 'Investigating NEPAD's development assumptions', *Review of African Political Economy*, 101: 497–511.

Mbachu, D. (2006) 'Nigerian resources: changing the playing field', *South African Journal of International Affairs*, 13(1), Summer/Autumn.

McCormick, D. (2008) 'China and India as Africa's new donors: the impact of aid on development', *Review of African Political Economy*, 35(115): 74–92.

McGreal, C. (2007) 'Thanks China, now go home: buy-up of Zambia revives old colonial fears', *Guardian*, 5 February.

McKeon, N. (2009) *Poverty Reduction in the Sahel: What do farmers have to say*, available at www.europafrica.info/file_download/128/poverty_final.pdf, accessed 3 August 2009.

Melber, H. (ed.) (2007) 'China in Africa', *Current Afrian Issues*, 35, Nordic Africa Institute, Uppsala.

Mepham, D. and L. Wild (eds) (2006) *The New Sinosphere: China in Africa*, London: IPPR.

Mills, G. (2008) 'The US and Africa: prisoners of a paradigm?', *Current History*, 107(709): 225–30.

Mills, G. and C. Thompson (2008) 'Partners or predators? China in Africa', *China Brief*, 8(2), January.

Ministry of External Affairs (various years) *Annual Report*, Prepared by the Policy Planning and Research Division, New Delhi.

— (2009) 'Civilian training programme: Indian Technical and Economic Cooperation (ITEC) and Special Commonwealth Assistance for Africa Programme (SCAAP), 2009–2010', Sponsored by the Ministry of External Affairs (New Delhi), available at itec.nic.in/t2009.pdf.

Ministry of Finance (2007) 'India Budget 2007–08', Budget speech by the minister of finance, P. Chidambaram, 28 February, available at indiabudget.nic.in/ub2007-08/bs/speecha.htm.

Miu Kaijin (2006) 'A study of China's cultural diplomacy', Graduate Faculty of the Party School of the Central Committee of the CCP.

Mkandawire, T. (2001) 'Thinking about developmental states in Africa', *Cambridge Journal of Economics*, 25: 289–314.

Mkandawire, T. and C. Soludo (1999) *Our Continent, Our Future: African perspectives on structural adjustment*, Dakar: CODESRIA.

Modi, R. (2009a) 'India and Africa: ideal and natural partners', *Pambazuka News*, 444, available at www.pambazuka.org/en/category/features/58068, accessed 1 August 2009.

— (2009b) 'Offshore health care management of Africans in India', cited in E. Mawdsley and G. McCaan (eds), *India and East Africa: Changing geographies of power and development*, Fahamu, forthcoming.

— (2009c) 'Pan-African e-Network: a model of South–South cooperation', *Africa Quarterly*, 49(1), Indian Council for Cultural Relations, New Delhi, February–April 2009, available at india africaconnect.in/africa%20quaterly/AQ-Feb-April09.pdf.

Mohammed, A. (2009) 'Towards an effective African Union: participation, institutions, and leadership', in S. Adejumboi and A. Olukoshi (eds), *The African Union and New Strategies for Development in Africa*, Dakar: CODESRIA, pp. 56–7.

Mohan, G. and M. Power (eds) (2008) 'The "new" face of China–African cooperation', *Review of African Political Economy*, 35(115): 2–166.

Mohiddin, A. (2009) 'The national process of the African Peer Review Mechanism: challenges and opportunities', in

S. Adejumobi and A. Olukoshi (eds), *The African Union and New Strategies for Development in Africa*, Dakar: CODESRIA, pp. 136–62.

Morphet, S. (2004) 'Multilateralism and the non-aligned movement: what is the global South doing and where is it going?', *Global Governance*, 10(4): 517–37.

Mosher, S. W. (2006) *China's Plan to Dominate Asia and the World*, San Francisco, CA: Encounter.

Mthembu-Salter, G. (forthcoming) 'Price power: China's role in the telecommunications sector of the Democratic Republic of Congo', SAIIA.

Muni, S. D. and G. C. Pant (2005) *India's Energy Security*, Delhi: Rupa & Co.

Munyao, J. (2008) Executive Director, Electrogen Technologies, personal interview, 12 August.

Murphy, D. (2007) 'Narrating Darfur: Darfur in the US press, March–September 2004', in A. de Waal (ed.), *War in Darfur and the Search for Peace*, Justice Africa/Global Equity Initiative, pp. 314–36.

Mwanawina, I. (2007) 'An assessment of Chinese development assistance in Africa: Zambia', Study commissioned by the Africa Forum and Network on Debt and Development (AFRODAD).

Naidu, S. (2007) 'The Forum on China–Africa Cooperation (FOCAC): what does the future hold?', *China Report*, 43(3).

Naidu, S. and L. Corkin (2006) 'Who was the real winner in China?', *China Monitor*, 13, Centre for Chinese Studies, University of Stellenbosch.

Naidu, S. and M. Davies (2006) 'China fuels its future with Africa's riches', *South African Journal of International Affairs*, 13(2).

Narlikar, A. (2006) 'Fairness in international trade negotiations: developing countries in the GATT and WTO', *World Economy*, 29(8): 10005–29.

Narlikar, A. and R. Wilkinson (2004) 'Collapse at the WTO: a Cancun post-mortem', *Third World Quarterly*, 25(3): 447–60.

National Intelligence Council (2004) 'Mapping the global future', Report of the National Intelligence Council's 2020 Project, NIC 2004-13, Washington, DC.

Natsios, A. S. (2008) 'Beyond Darfur: Sudan's slide toward civil war', *Foreign Affairs*, 87(3): 80.

Nayar, B. R. (2003) 'Globalization and India's national autonomy', *Journal of Commonwealth and Comparative Politics*, 41(2): 1–34.

Ndulu, B. (2006) 'Infrastructure, regional integration and growth in sub-Saharan Africa: dealing with the disadvantages of geography and sovereign fragmentation', *Journal of African Economics*, AERC Supplement 2, pp. 212–44.

Nelson, D. (2009) 'India joins the "neo-colonial rush" for Africa's land and labour', *The Telegraph*, New Delhi, 28 June, available at www.telegraph.co.uk/news/worldnews/asia/india/5673437/India-joins-neocolonial-rush-for-Africas-land-and-labour.html.

NEPAD (2001) 'The New Partnership for African Development (NEPAD)', Midrand NEPAD Secretariat, available at www.dfa.gov.za/events/nepad.pdf.

— (2002) *Underpinning Investments in African Agriculture and Trade-related Capacities for Improved Market Access: A continental vision*, CAADP, November, available at www.fao.org/docrep/005/y6831e/y6831e-02.htm, accessed 3 August 2009.

— (2003) *Objectives, Standards, Criteria and Indicators for the African Peer Review Mechanism*, 6th Summit of the NEPAD Heads of State and Government Implementation Committee (NEPAD/HSGIC-03-2003/APRM/Guidelines/OSCI), Abuja, 9 March.

Neumayer, E. and L. Spess (2005) 'Do bilateral investment treaties increase foreign direct investment to developing countries?', *World Development*, 33(10): 1567–85.

NIC (2008) *Global Trends 2025: A transformed world*, Washington, DC: US Government Printing Office.

Niquet, V. (2006) 'China's African strategy', *Politique étrangère*, 2.

Nkrumah, K. (1963) *Africa Must Unite*, London: Pall Mall Press.

Nkuhlu, W. L. (2005) *The Journey So Far*, Midrand: NEPAD Secretariat, available at www.nepad.org/2005/files/documents/journey.pdf, accessed 17 September 2008.

Nnadozie, E. (2009) 'NEPAD, APREM, and institutional change in Africa', in S. Adejumobi and A. Olukoshi (eds), *The African Union and New Strategies for Development in Africa*, Dakar: CODESRIA, pp. 136–62.

Nouve, K. and J. Staatz (2003) 'Has AGOA increased agricultural exports from sub-Saharan Africa to the United States?', Paper presented at the international conference 'Agricultural policy reform and the WTO: where are we heading?', Capri, 23–26 June.

Nwajiaku, K. (1994) 'The National Conference in Benin and Togo revisted', *Journal of Modern African Studies*, 32(3): 429–47.

OAU (1980) *Lagos Plan of Action for the Economic Development of Africa, 1980–2000*, Addis Ababa: Organization of African Unity.

Obi, C. (2008) 'Enter the dragon? Chinese oil companies and resistance in the Niger Delta', *Review of African Political Economy*, 35(3).

OECD (2003) 'Glossary of statistical terms: concessional loan', OECD statistical portal, available at stats.oecd.org/glosary/detail.asp?ID=5901.

— (2006) 'OECD policy dialogue with non-members on Aid for Trade: from policy to practice', Doha, Qatar, 6/7 November, available at www.oecd.org/ document/50/0,3343,en_2649_34665_37232754_1_1_1_1,00.html.

— (2008) *OECD Investment Policy Reviews: China – encouraging responsible business conduct*, Paris: OECD.

— (2009) 'Trade and agricultural directorate participation to the arrangement on officially supported export credits', TAD/PG/2009/21, OECD, Paris, available at www.olis.oecd.org/olis/2009doc. nsf/LinkTo/NT00004C12/$FILE/JT03268495.pdf.

OECD/WTO (2009) 'Aid for Trade at a glance: 2nd Global Review', available at www.wto.org/english/res_e/booksp_e/aid4trade09_e.pdf.

Ohmae, K. (2005) *Triad Power: The coming shape of global competition*, New York: Free Press.

O'Neill, J. (2003) 'Dreaming with BRICs: the path to 2050', Global Economics Paper no. 99, New York: Goldman Sachs.

— (2004) 'How solid are the BRICs?', Global Economics Paper no. 134, New York: Goldman Sachs.

Orr, T. (2006) 'Letter from China: FOCAC 2006', *China Monitor*, 13, Centre for Chinese Studies, University of Stellenbosch.

Owusu, G. and R. Lund (2004) 'Markets and women's trade: exploring their role in district development in Ghana', *Norsk Geografisk Tidsskrift*, 58: 113–24.

Oxfam (2002) *Rigged Rules and Double Standards: Trade globalization and the fight against poverty*, Oxford: Oxfam, available at www.markettradefair.com.

Ozawa, T. (2001) 'The hidden side of "flying-geese" catch-up model: Japan's *dirigiste* institutional set-up and deepening financial morass', *Journal of Asian Economics*, 12: 471–91.

Padmanabhan, M. (2003) 'Scope for more pharma exports, India–Africa health summit today', *Hindu Business Line*, 19 November.

Pan-African e-Network (2009) 'Pan-African e-Network project launched: a shining example of South–South cooperation', available at www.panafricanenetwork.com/Portal/AboutProject.jsp.

Pant, G. (2007) 'Making knowledge the focus of India–Africa relations', *Africa Currents*, 26(42): 16–32.

Patel, C. (2003) *ACP and African Union Role in Cancun – some reflections, lessons*, 19 September, available at twnside.org.sg/title/5423a.htm.

Payne, R. and C. Veney (2001) 'Taiwan and Africa: Taipei's continuing search for international recognition', *Journal of African and Asian Studies*, 36(4).

Pedersen, J. D. (2008) *Globalization, Development and the State: The performance of India and Brazil since 1990*, London: Palgrave Macmillan.

Peil, M. (1974) 'Ghana's aliens', *International Migration Review*, 8(3): 367–81.

People's Daily (2000) 'Exim Bank supports Congo', 14 December.

People's Republic of China (1990) *Selective Works of Zhou Enlai's Diplomacy*, Beijing: Ministry of Foreign Affairs and Party Literature Centre of the CPC Central Committee, Central Party Literature Publishing House.

— (2006) *China's Africa Policy*, Beijing.

Personal interview (2008a) Mobile phone operator officials, Kinshasa, April.

— (2008b) CCT official, Kinshasa, April.

— (2008c) Alcatel official, Kinshasa, April.

Pham, J. P. (2007) 'The Indian tiger's African safari', *Family Security Matters*, 19 July, available at www.familysecuritymatters.org/global.php?id=1162076.

Picton, J. (1995) *The Art of African Textiles: Technology, tradition, and lurex*, London: Barbican Art Gallery in association with Lund Humphries.

Ping, A. (1999) 'From proletarian internationalism to mutual development: China's cooperation with Tanzania, 1965–95', in G. Hyden and R. Mukandala (eds), *Agencies in Foreign Aid: Comparing China, Sweden and the United States in Tanzania*, Macmillan, p. 179.

Piot, C. (1999) *Remotely Global: Village modernity in West Africa*, Chicago, IL: University of Chicago Press.

— (2006) 'Jeux de frontière: la loterie des cartes vertes au Togo', *Politique africaine*, 101: 171–81.

Poddar, T. and E. Yi (2007) 'India's rising growth potential', Global Economics Paper no. 152, New York: Goldman Sachs, 22 January, available at www.usindiafriendship.net/viewpoint/India_Rising_Growth_Potential.pdf, accessed 30 January 2009.

Polgreen, L. (2009) 'As Chinese investments in Africa drop, hope sinks', *New York Times*, 26 March, available at www.nytimes.com/2009/03/26/world/

Africa/26chinaafrica.html, accessed 9 April 2009.

Pöyhönen, P. (1963) 'A tentative model for the volume of trade between countries', *Weltwirtschaftliches*, 90(1): 93–100.

Pradhan, J. P. (2008) 'Indian direct investment in developing countries', Paper presented at the Copenhagen Business School Conference on 'Emerging multinationals: outward FDI to developing countries', 9/10 October, Copenhagen Business School.

Quartey, P. (2006) 'The textiles and clothing industry in Ghana', in H. Jauch and R. Traub-Merz (eds), *The Future of the Textile and Clothing Industry*, Bonn: Friedrich Eberhart Stiftung.

Rabine, L. W. (2002) *The Global Circulation of African Fashion*, Oxford: Berg.

Rakner, L. (2003) *Political and Economic Liberalisation in Zambia 1991–2001*, Uppsala: Nordic Africa Institute.

Ramachandran, S. (2007a) 'India pushes people power in Africa', *Asia Times* (online), 7 July, available at www.atimes.com/atimes/South_Asia/IG13Df03.html, accessed 13 February 2009.

— (2007b) 'India turns its energies to Africa', *Asia Times*, 10 November, available at www.atimes.com, accessed 14 March 2008.

Ramo, J. C. (2004) 'The Beijing Consensus', London: Foreign Policy Centre.

Rana, P. B. (1990) 'Shifting comparative advantage in Asian and Pacific countries', *International Trade Journal*, I(3): 243–59.

Range, J. (2005) 'Zambia's miners pay price for copper boom', *Dow Jones Newswire*, 12 October.

Rao, S. R. (2006) 'EXIM Bank: partner in Africa's development', Presentation at the OECD, Paris, 16–17 March, available at commerce.nic.in/trade/international_tpp_africa_10.asp.

Rawnsley, G. (2000) *Taiwan's Informal Diplomacy and Propaganda*, Basingstoke: Macmillan.

Reeves, A. (2007) 'China in Sudan: underwriting genocide', Paper presented at US–China Economic and Security Review Commission conference 'China's role in the world: is China a responsible stakeholder?', Washington, DC, 3 April.

Reeves, E. (2007) 'China, Darfur, and the Olympics: tarnishing the torch?', available at www.dreamfordarfur.org.

Reisen, H. (2008) 'How to spend it: sovereign wealth funds and the wealth of nations', *Policy Insights*, 59, OECD Development Centre, February.

Reuters (2006) 'China pushes Sudan to let UN troops into Darfur', 14 September.

Robertson, C. (1976) 'Ga women and socioeconomic change in Accra, Ghana', in E. Bay and N. Hafkin (eds), *Women in Africa: Studies in social and economic change*, Stanford, CA: Stanford University Press.

— (1983) 'The death of Makola and other tragedies', *Canadian Journal of African Studies – Revue Canadienne des Etudes Africaines*, 17: 469–95.

— (1984) *Sharing the Same Bowl: A socio-economic history of women and class in Accra, Ghana*, Bloomington: Indiana University Press.

Rodrik, D. (1994a) 'Getting interventions right: how South Korea and Taiwan grew rich', NBER Working Paper no. 4964.

— (1994b) 'King Kong meets Godzilla: the World Bank and the East Asian miracle', in R. Wade et al. (eds), *Miracle or Design? Lessons from the East Asian experience*, Washington, DC: Overseas Development Council, pp. 13–47.

Rogerson, C. M. (2000) 'Successful SMEs in South Africa: the case of clothing producers in the Witwatersrand', *Development Southern Africa*, 17(5): 687–716.

Ronalsen, O. H. (2007) 'Sudan: the Janjawiid and government militias', in M. Boas and K. C. Dunn (eds), *African Guerrillas: Raging against the machine*, Boulder, CO: Lynne Rienner, pp. 151–70.

Ronge, E. (2000) 'Trade within the COMESA and between the East African Community and the European Union', Memo, Kenya Institute for Public Policy Research and Analysis (KIPPRA).

Rowlands, D. (2008) 'International Development Assistance Executive summary report: the Case of Brazil, China, India and South Africa', International Development Research Centre (IDRC), Partnership and Business Development Division, IDRC, Ottawa.

Rugman, A. and A. Verbeke (2004) 'A perspective on regional and global strategies of multinational enterprises', *Journal of International Business Studies*, 35: 3–18.

Rugman, A. and Jing Li (2007) 'Will China's multinationals succeed globally or regionally?', *European Management Journal*, 25(5): 333–43.

Rumley, D. and S. Chaturvedi (eds) (2005) *Energy Security and the Indian Ocean Region*, New Delhi: South Asia Publishers.

Russel, A. and W. Wallis (2007) 'China puts private pressure on Sudan', *Financial Times*, 19 June.

Saasa, O. S. (1987) *Zambia's Policies towards Foreign Investments. The case of mining and non-mining sectors*, Uppsala: Scandinavian Institute of African Studies.

Sachs, J. (2008) 'The rise of TNCs from emerging markets: the global context', in K. P. Sauvant (ed.) (forthcoming), *The Rise of Transnational Corporations from Emerging Markets: Threat or opportunity?*, Williston: Edward Elgar.

Said, D. (2009) 'Indian firm to build huge tractor plant', 15 July, available at allafrica.com/stories/200807151113. html; see also www.mahindratractor world.com/pdf/Vice%20President%20 of%20Tanzania%20visits%20Mahindra %E2%80%99s%20Tractor%20Plant.pdf.

Saint-Paul, M. A. (2004) 'China and Africa: between commitment and interest', *Géopolitique africaine*, available at www.african-geoolitics.org/show. aspx?Articled=3701.

Sata, M. (2007) 'Chinese investment in Africa and implications for international relations, consolidation of democracy and respect for human rights: the case of Zambia', Paper presented to the Harvard University Committee on Human Rights Studies

Events Series, 24 October, Harvard University, Cambridge, Boston, MA.

Sautman, B. V. (2006) 'Friends and interests: China's distinctive links with Africa', Working Paper no. 12, CCTR, HKUST, Hong Kong.

Sauvant, K. P. (2005) 'New sources of FDI: the BRICs – outward FDI from Brazil, Russia, India and China', *Journal of World Investment and Trade*, pp. 639–708.

— (2008) 'The rise of TNCs from emerging markets: the issues', in K. P. Sauvant (ed.) (forthcoming), *The Rise of Transnational Corporations from Emerging Markets: Threat or opportunity?*, Williston: Edward Elgar.

Schaffer, T. C. and P. Mitra (2005) 'India as a global power?', *Deutsche Bank Research*, 16, Frankfurt, December.

Schatz, J. (2007) 'Zambia's "all-weather friend." Analyzing China's growing role in Zambia and what it has provoked and what it may mean for other African governments', Master's thesis submitted to the Elliot School of International Affairs, George Washington University.

Schuller, M. and A. Turner (2005) 'Global ambitions: Chinese companies spread their wings', *CHINA Aktuell*, 4: 3–14.

Serpa, E. (1994) 'India and Africa', *Africa Insight*, 24(3): 187.

Sethuraman, D. (2005) 'Can oil unite the Elephant and the Dragon?', *Rediff News*, 21 May, available at www.rediff.com/money/2005/may/21guest.htm.

Sharma, A. (2008) Valedictory Address at the International Conference on 'Africa and energy security: global issues, local responses', organized by the Institute for Defence Studies and Analyses, New Delhi, 24 June.

Sharma, D. and D. Mahajan (2007) 'Energising ties: the politics of oil', *South African Journal of International Affairs*, special issue: *India in Africa*, 14(2): 37–52.

Shaw, T. M. (2008) *Commonwealth: Inter- and non-state contributions to global governance*, Global Institutions Series, London: Routledge.

Shaw, T. M., A. F. Cooper and A. Antkiewicz (2007) 'Global and/or regional development at the start of the 21st century: China, India and (South) Africa', *Third World Quarterly*, 28(7): 1255–70.

Shaw, T. M., A. F. Cooper and G. T. Chin (2008) 'Emerging powers in/around Africa: implications for/from global governance', *Politikon*.

Shaxson, N. (2007) *Poisoned Wells: The dirty politics of African oil*, New York: Palgrave Macmillan.

Shelton, G. (2007) 'China and Africa: advancing South–South Cooperation', in Le Pere (2006), pp. 99–122.

Sheth, V. S. (2008) *India–Africa Relations: Emerging policy and development perspectives*, Delhi: Academic Excellence Press.

Shi Lin (1989) *Foreign Economic Cooperation of Contemporary China*, Beijing: Chinese Social Sciences Publishing House.

Shoute, S. (2007) 'China, Zambia witness booming economic cooperation'. www.chinaview.cn, accessed 2 February 2007.

Shukla, S. (2008) 'The African oil rush', *India Today*, 4 April, available at indiatoday.intoday.in/index.php?issueid=&id=2039&option=com_content&task=view&sectionid=34, accessed 19 May 2009.

Sidiropolous, E. (ed.) (2006) 'China in Africa', *South African Journal of International Affairs*, 13(1): 7–138.

Sidiropolous, E. and A. Vines (eds) (2007) 'India in Africa', *South African Journal of International Affairs*, 14(2), Winter/Spring.

Singh, G. (2009) *India's Role in the Agriculture and Rural Development of Ethiopia*, 8 June, available at www.indianembassy.gov.et, accessed 1 August 2009.

Singh, S. K. (2007a) 'Peacekeeping in Africa: a global strategy', *South African Journal of International Affairs*, special issue: *India in Africa*, 14(2): 71–86.

— (2007b) 'India and West Africa: a burgeoning relationship', Briefing

Paper AFP BP 07/02, Chatham House, London, April, p. 10.

Söderbaum, F. and I. Taylor (eds) (2008) *Afro-Regions: The dynamics of cross-border micro-regionalism in Africa*, Uppsala: NAI.

Stevens, C. and J. Kennan (2006) 'Opening the package: the Asian drivers and poor-country trade', University of Sussex, Brighton, www.ids.org, accessed 28 November 2006.

Stocchetti, M. (2007) 'The development dimension or dillusion? The EU's development policy goals and the Economic Partnership Agreements', *Policy Notes*, 1, Uppsala: Nordic Africa Institute.

Sunkel, O. (1993) *Development from Within: Toward a neostructuralist approach for Latin America*, Boulder, CO: Lynne Rienner.

Sunmonu, H. (2004) 'Implementation of Africa's development paradigms: solutions to Africa's socio-economic problems', in B. Onimode (ed.), *African Development and Governance Strategies in the 21st Century*, London and Ijebu-Ode, Nigeria: Zed Books and ACDESS, pp. 63–71.

Suri, N. (2007) 'India and Africa: contemporary perspectives', in A. Sinha and M. Moharta (eds), *Indian Foreign Policy: Challenges and opportunities*, Foreign Service Institute, New Delhi: Academic Foundation Press, pp. 507–26.

Sylvanus, N. (2007) 'The fabric of africanity: tracing the global threads of authenticity', *Anthropological Theory*, 7: 201–16.

— (2008) 'Rethinking "free-trade" practices in contemporary Togo', in U. Schuerkens, *Globalization and Transformation of Local Socioeconomic Practices*, London: Routledge.

Tadesse, T. (2009) *Ethiopia Sets Aside Land for Foreign Investors*, Addis Ababa, 29 July, available at in.reuters. com/article/domesticNews/idINLT 58431220090729> 29 July 2009, accessed 5 August 2009.

Takana, Y. (1998) 'Effects of tribal strife in Darfur', in A. al-Zein Mohamed and I. Wedda (eds), *Perspectives on Tribal Conflicts in Sudan*, Institute of Afro-Asian Studies, University of Khartoum (in Arabic).

Tandon, Y. (2008) *Ending Aid Dependence*, London: Fahamu Books.

Tarling, N. (1992) *The Cambridge History of Southeast Asia: From early times to c. 1800*, Cambridge: Cambridge University Press.

Taylor, I. (1998) 'China's foreign policy towards Africa in the 1990s', *Journal of Modern African Studies*, 36(3): 443–60.

— (2002a) 'Taiwan's foreign policy in Africa: the limits of dollar diplomacy', *Journal of Contemporary China*, 11(30).

— (2002b) 'Towards the African century, or another false start?', *African Agenda*, 5: 2/3.

— (2006) *China and Africa: Engagement and compromise*, London: Routledge.

— (2007) 'China's oil diplomacy in Africa', *International Affairs*, 82(5).

— (2008) 'Sino-African relations and the problem of human rights', *African Affairs*, 107(426): 63–87.

Tettey, W., K. Puplampu and B. Berman (2003) *Critical Perspectives on Politics and Socio-economic Development in Ghana*, Leiden and Boston, MA: Brill.

Thaindian (2009) *Delhi Firm Wins US$100 Million Ethiopian Sugar Factory Contract*, 2 August, available at www. thaindian.com/newsportal/world-news/delhi-firm-wins-100-mn-ethiopian-sugar-factory-contract_100226495. html, accessed 3 August 2009.

Thakurta, P. (2008) 'India: taking on China in Africa', Inter Press Service News Agency (IPS), 16 September, available at ipsnews.net, accessed 16 September 2008.

Thompson, D. (2004) 'Darfur complications: disaccord on Sudan could poison China–US ties', *International Herald Tribune*, 18 November.

— (2005) 'China's emerging interests in Africa: opportunities and challenges for Africa and the United States', *African Renaissance*, 2(4), July/August.

Times of India (2003) 'India's makeover: from aid-taking to aid-giving', New Delhi, 2 June.

Tinbergen, J. (1962) 'Shaping the world economy: suggestions for an international economic policy', Twentieth Century Fund, New York.

Toman, M. (2002) *International Oil Security: Problems and policies*, Issue Brief no. 02-04, Washington, DC: Resources for the Future.

Toulabor, C. (1983) *Le Togo sous Eyadema*, Paris: Karthala.

Tsikata, K. (2007) 'Challenges of economic growth in a liberal economy', in K. Boafo-Arthur (ed.), *Ghana: One decade of the liberal state*, Dakar: CODRESIA.

Tull, D. M. (2006) 'China's engagement in Africa: scope, significance and consequences', *Journal of Modern African Studies*, 44(3): 459–79.

Udombana, N. J. (2005) 'When neutrality is a sin: the Darfur crisis and the crisis of humanitarian intervention in Sudan', *Human Rights Quarterly*, 27: 1149–90.

UNCTAD (United Nations Conference on Trade and Development) (2006) *World Investment Report 2006 – FDI from developing and transition economies: implications for development* (Executive Summary), New York: United Nations.

— (2007a) *Asian Foreign Direct Investment in Africa: Towards a new era of cooperation among developing countries*, New York: United Nations.

— (2007b) *Bilateral Investment Treaties 1995–2006: Trends in investment rulemaking*, New York and Geneva: UNCTAD.

— (2007c) *World Investment Report 2007. Transnational corporations, extractive industries and development*, New York and Geneva: UNCTAD.

— (2007d) *Development and Globalization: Facts and figures 2008*, Geneva: United Nations.

— (2007e) *Reclaiming Policy Space: Domestic resource mobilisation and developmental states*, Geneva/New York: United Nations.

— (2008) *Handbook of Statistics 2008*, New York/Geneva: United Nations.

— (2009) *Economic Development in Africa 2009: Strengthening regional economic integration for Africa's development*, Geneva: United Nations.

UNECA (2004) *Assessing Regional Integration in Africa*, ECA Policy Research Report, Addis Ababa: ECA.

— (2008) *Assessing Regional Integration in Africa III: Towards monetary and financial integration in Africa*, Addis Ababa: ECA.

United Nations (2006) 'Security Council expands mandate of UN Mission in Sudan to include Darfur, adopting Resolution 1706 by vote of 12 in favour, with 3 abstaining', UN Department of Public Information, New York, 31 August.

US Central Intelligence Agency (1978) *Communist Aid to Less Developed Countries of the Free World*, Washington, DC: CIA.

US Department of State (1976) *Communist States and Developing Countries: Aid and trade in 1974*, Washington, DC.

US National Intelligence Commission (2008) *Global Trends 2025: A transformed world*, Unclassified report, available at www.dni.gov/nic/PDF_2025/2025_Global_Trends_Final_Report.pdf, accessed 20 December 2008.

Van Agtmael, A. (2007) *The Emerging Markets Century: How a new breed of world class companies is overtaking the world*, New York: Free Press.

Vandaele, J. (2009) 'Development: China outdoes Europeans in Congo', Inter Press Service, available at ipsnews.net/news.asp?idnews=41125, accessed 13 May 2009.

Vines, A. (2006) 'The scramble for resources: African case studies', *South African Journal of International Affairs*, 13(1), Summer/Autumn.

— (2007) 'China in Africa: a mixed blessing?', *Current History*, May, pp. 213–19.

Vines, A. and I. Campos (2008) 'Angola and China: a pragmatic partnership',

CSIS Working Paper, Center for Strategic and International Affairs, Washington, DC.

Vines, A. and B. Orutimeka (2008) 'India's engagement with the African Indian Ocean Rim states', Briefing Paper AFP P1/08, Chatham House, London.

Vines, A. and E. Sidiropolous (2008) 'India and Africa', *World Today*, April, pp. 26–7.

Vines, A., L. Wong, M. Weimer and I. Campos (2009) *Thirst for African Oil: Asian national oil companies in Nigeria and Angola*, London: Chatham House.

VOA (2008) J. M. Kikwete, cited in *Africa Calls for Indian Investments throughout the Continent*, available at www.voanews.com/english/archive/2008-04/2008-04-11-voa.

Wade, R. H. (1990) *Governing the Market: Economic theory and the role of government in East Asian industrialization*, Princeton, NJ: Princeton University Press.

— (1994) 'Selective industrial policies in East Asia: is the East Asian miracle right?', in R. Wade et al. (eds), *Miracle or Design? Lessons from the East Asian experience*, Washington, DC: Overseas Development Council, pp. 55–79.

— (2003) 'What strategies are viable for developing countries today? The WTO and the shrinking of "development space"', *Review of International Political Economy*, 10(4): 621–44.

Wadke, R. (2007) 'Indian power flock to Africa, Middle East', *Hindu Business Line*, 20 February, available at www.blonnet.com/2007/02/20/stories/2007022002403000.htm.

Wang, M. Y. (2002) 'The motivations behind China's government-initiated industrial investments overseas', *Pacific Affairs*, 75(2): 187–206.

Wei Hong (1999) 'China's foreign aid reform: experiences and issues', *International Economic Cooperation*, 5: 4–8.

Wei Liang-Tsai (1982) *Peking versus Taipei in Africa 1960–1978*, Taipei: Asia and World Institute.

Wenping, H. (2007) 'The balancing act of China's Africa Policy', *China Security*, 3(3).

White House (2001) *Report of the National Energy Policy Development Group*, National Energy Policy, chaired by Vice-President Dick Cheney, chs 8, 11.

— (2002) 'National security strategy of the United States of America', Washington, DC.

Willetts, P. (1978) *The Non-aligned Movement: The origins of a Third World alliance*, London: Printer Publishers.

Wilson, G. (2006) 'Chinese investing in Zambia's Copperbelt', *Marketplace*, 31 July.

Wong, L. (2008) 'The impact of Asian oil companies in Nigeria', 12 December, www.ocnus.net/artman2/publish/Analyses_12/The_Impact_Of_Asian_National_Oil_Companies_In_Nigeria.shtml, accessed 1 April 2009.

World Bank (1989) *Sub-Saharan Africa: From crisis to sustainable growth*, Washington, DC: World Bank.

— (2000) *Can Africa Claim the 21st Century?*, Washington, DC: World Bank.

— (2006) *Republic of Senegal, Joint IDA–IMF Advisory Note of the Second Poverty Reduction Strategy Paper (PRSP)*, 20 December, available at www-wds.worldbank.org/external/default/WDSContentServer/WDSP/IB/2007/06/15/000112742_20070615155946/Rendered/PDF/381310FileoreplacementoIDA1SecM200710010.pdf.

— (2009) *Doing Business Database*, available at www.worldbank.org/.

World Economic Forum (2006) www.weforum.org/summitreport/africa2006, accessed 2 December 2006.

Wu, H. L. and C. H. Chen (2001) 'An assessment of outward foreign direct investment from China's transnational economy', *Europe-Asia Studies*, 53(8): 125–54.

Xie Yixian (1998) *The Diplomatic History of China (the period from 1949 to 1979)*, Kaifeng: People's Publishing House in Henan.

Xinhua News Agency (2006) 'Hu puts

forward proposals on Sino-African ties', 28 April, available at www.China.org.cn/english, accessed 16 October 2007.

— (2007) 'China, Africa build new partnership on old ties', 2 October, available at www.China.org.cn/english, accessed 5 October 2007.

— (2008) 'Oil output, consumption both hit record high in 2007', 31 January, www.chinadaily.com.cn/bizchina, accessed 17 September 2008.

Xu, Y.-C. (2008) 'China and the US in Africa: coming conflict or consensual coexistence?', Australian Journal of International Affairs, 62(1): 16–37.

Xu Jianping (1996) 'On how to combine foreign economic assistance and mutual-beneficial cooperation', International Economic Cooperation, 3: 14–16.

Yeats, A. (1999) 'What can be expected from African regional trade arrangements? Some empirical evidence', Policy Research Working Paper 204, Washington, DC: World Bank.

Yeates, N. (ed.) (2007) 'Special issue on the social policy dimension of world-regionalism', Global Social Policy, 7(3): 249–385.

Yergin, D. (2006) 'Ensuring energy security', Foreign Affairs, 85(2): 69–82.

Yu, G. T. (1988a) 'Dragon in the bush: Peking's presence in Africa', Asian Survey, 8(12): 1018–26.

— (1988b) 'Africa in Chinese foreign policy', Asian Survey, 28(8).

Yu, T. (1982) 'Learning dance in Africa', China and World Cultural Exchange, 2.

Yu, X. (2007) 'Harmonious world and China's path for peaceful development', Guoji Wenti Yanjiu [International Studies], 1: 7–12.

Yuan, J.-D. (1998) 'Multilateral intervention and state sovereignty: Chinese views on UN peacekeeping operations', Political Science, 49: 275–95.

Zhang Haibing (2007) 'China's aid to Africa: oil-oriented or not?', World Economic Research, 10: 76–88.

Zhang Hongming (2006) 'The evolution of China's aid policy towards Africa and its function in the bilateral relation', Asian and African Review, 4: 44–9.

Zhang Qingmin (2001) 'A common policy towards unalike countries: a preliminary analysis of China's policy towards developing countries', Contemporary China History Studies, 8(1): 36–46.

Zhao, S. (2008) 'China's global search for energy security: cooperation and competition in the Asia Pacific', Journal of Contemporary China, 17(55).

Zhongying, P. (2005) 'China's changing attitude to UN peacekeeping', International Peacekeeping, 12(1).

Zweig, D. and Bi Jianhai (2005) 'China's global hunt for energy', Foreign Affairs, 84(5), September/October.

About the contributors

Kwesi Aning Head of the Conflict Prevention Management and Resolution Department at the Kofi Annan International Peacekeeping Training Centre, Accra, Ghana.

Linn Axelsson PhD student at the Department of Human Geography, Stockholm University, Sweden.

Sanjukta Banerji Bhattacharya Professor at the Department of International Relations, Jadavpur University, Kolkata, India.

Gilberto Biacuana Researcher at the South African Institute of International Affairs.

Magnus Calais Research Assistant at the Nordic Africa Institute's Globalization Research Cluster.

Indira Campos Research Associate at Chatham House in London.

Tsidiso Disenyana Researcher at the South African Institute of International Affairs.

Peter Draper Head of the Development through Trade Programme at the South African Institute of International Affairs, Johannesburg, South Africa.

Alemayehu Geda Associate Professor at the Department of Economics, Addis Ababa University, Ethiopia.

He Wenping Director of the Division of African Studies at the Institute of West-Asian and African Studies, Chinese Academy of Social Sciences, Beijing, China.

Dot Keet Senior Fellow at the Centre for Southern African Studies at the University of the Western Cape, South Africa.

Peter Kragelund Assistant Professor at the Department of Society and Globalization at Roskilde University, Denmark.

Liu Haifang Researcher at the Institute of West Asian and African Studies, Chinese Academy of Social Sciences, Beijing, China.

Atnafu G. Meskel Lecturer at the Department of Economics, Addis Ababa University, Ethiopia.

Renu Modi Director of the Centre for African Studies at the University of Mumbai.

Fredrick Mutesa Professor of Development Studies at the University of Zambia.

Sanusha Naidu Research Director of the China–Africa Project based at FAHAMU, South Africa.

Timothy M. Shaw Professor and Director of the Institute of International Relations at the University of the West Indies, St Augustine, Trinidad & Tobago.

Pranay Kumar Sinha PhD student at the University of Manchester, UK.

Nina Sylvanus Visiting Assistant Professor of Anthropology at Reed College, Oregon, USA.

Alex Vines Research Director of Regional and Security Studies and Head of the Africa Programme at Chatham House, London, UK.

Index